Paul Blaisdell, Monster Maker

Paul Blaisdell, Monster Maker

A Biography of the B Movie Makeup and Special Effects Artist

by RANDY PALMER

with forewords by
FRED OLEN RAY *and* BOB BURNS

McFarland & Company, Inc., Publishers
Jefferson, North Carolina, and London

To the memory of my father, who took me to see
my first Paul Blaisdell movie, and
to my mother, who always knew that movies
don't make monsters out of little boys

For Jackie

Frontispiece: Blaisdell as the title monster takes a practice stalk up the
pier steps on location for *The She Creature.* (Courtesy of Fred Olen Ray.)

The present work is a reprint of the library bound edition of
Paul Blaisdell, Monster Maker: A Biography of the B
Movie Makeup and Special Effects Artist, *first published
in 1997 by McFarland.*

LIBRARY OF CONGRESS CATALOGUING-IN-PUBLICATION DATA

Palmer, Randy, 1953–
    Paul Blaisdell, monster maker : a biography of the B movie makeup
and special effects artist / by Randy Palmer with forewords by Fred
Olen Ray and Bob Burns.
        p.   cm.
    Filmography: p.
    Includes index.
    ISBN 978-0-7864-4099-3 (softcover : 50# alkaline paper) ∞
    1. Blaisdell, Paul, 1927–1983.   2. Cinematographers—United
States—Biography.   3. Cinematography—Special effects.   4. Film
makeup.   I. Title.
TR849.B575P36   2009
791.43'024'092—dc20
[B]   96-45718

British Library cataloguing data are available

On the cover: Poster art for the 1958 film *It! The Terror from Beyond
Space* (MGM/UA/Photofest)

Manufactured in the United States of America

McFarland & Company, Inc., Publishers
   Box 611, Jefferson, North Carolina 28640
   www.mcfarlandpub.com

Contents

Foreword
by Fred Olen Ray

If you had never heard of Paul Blaisdell before picking up this book, you will soon see how damned lucky you are to have stumbled onto him. Like Roger Corman and Bert I. Gordon, you too will discover the rich imagination and ingenious talents of one of Hollywood's most creative fringe dwellers.

That it took the world so long to catch on to one of filmdom's best-kept secrets is a true shame. That, as for many others who toiled in the empty grocery stores that passed as movie studios, his contributions were only realized after such recognition could have yielded any benefit to the creator is a crime.

I think what attracted the admiring fans to his work over the years was not only the images he conjured up into physical being, but the method with which he undertook the task. Obviously, the monsters in *Day the World Ended*, *The She-Creature*, and *It Conquered the World* were astonishingly original in design, but it is also the fact that Blaisdell created them in his garage out of literally nothing more than carpet-laying foam and paint that instills his fans with that certain sense of awe.

What first attracted me to the creations of Paul Blaisdell, at least in the sense that I noticed who was actually creating these monsters, were the "how to" articles in Paul's magazine, *Fantastic Monsters of the Films*. In these articles Paul would provide details to knowledge-hungry kids, explaining how they could recreate the Beast with a Million Eyes or construct their own alien suit just like the one in *It! the Terror from Beyond Space*. Wanting nothing more than to be a monster maker, I read these articles over and over again, never tiring or ceasing to be amazed at what this man could do with so little money and such common household items.

But the monsters themselves were the real treat. Regardless of how quickly or cheaply they were constructed, Blaisdell's creations were always "way cool" looking. One need search no further than *Invasion of the Star Creatures* or *Killers from Space* to see what a low-budget movie without Paul Blaisdell was like. The guy had style—flat out. In his mind's eye, he knew what a great-looking monster was. His designs were different and lasting and had a flair all their own that exceeded his budget and schedule.

It is often remarked that Roger Corman could take a no-budget concept and elevate it into something memorable because Roger had that special "something"—a combination of intelligence and awareness that superseded just "getting the job done." The same could and should be said about Mr. Paul Blaisdell. He did so much more than just "getting the job done."

That Paul insisted on playing his creatures, even though he was far too small in stature to pull it off, also contributes to his legendary position in the die-hard Monster Hall of Fame. People like Corman and Sam Arkoff still delight in recounting how Paul's *Day the World Ended* suit soaked up a large quantity of water, causing its weight to increase drastically and sending both monster and starlet tumbling to the ground. Similar stories abound around his other creations—Ray Corrigan was too fat, *It Conquered the World*'s beastie was too short, and on and on—these are just good Hollywood yarns that beg repeating. And that's what Paul Blaisdell's life was—a good Hollywood yarn. It had everything the big-time moguls look for in a story—ups and downs, comedy and tragedy, creation, destruction, and ultimately a downbeat finale. Hollywood had Paul Blaisdell in its grasp, but somehow it foolishly let him slip away.

Fortunately for us he left a little something of himself behind.

Foreword
by Bob Burns

When Randy Palmer asked me to write a preface for this book, I felt very honored. Paul Blaisdell was not only my mentor, he was my very good friend. In the mid-fifties, my wife, Kathy, and I used to hang out with Paul and his wife, Jackie, at their Topanga Canyon (California) home. We had more fun than people should be allowed to have.

I don't think that most people knew that Paul had a great sense of humor. We shot many gag photos and 16mm movies of our antics. I still have the films today. What wonderful memories they bring back.

Paul was one of the most multitalented guys I've ever known. He could do it all. He was an artist (he did covers for magazines). He was a sculptor, model builder, wood worker (the flying saucer from *Invasion of the Saucer Men* was made of white pine). He was a master of just about any other talent or craft that you could come up with.

Paul was a pioneer. He had an art background but no formal training in making monsters. There was no "Monster Academy" or books on how to make a movie monster in those days. He did everything by the seat of his pants and from his imagination.

I used to marvel at the way he came up with ideas to make his creations. For instance, the antennae on the She-Creature's head were carved out of candles. He painted on layers of liquid latex, let them cure, then slit them up the back and peeled off the rubber. He put a wire in the tubes and stuffed them with cotton. Next he painted them, and there you have it—She-Creature antennae!

Jackie was very talented too. She helped Paul with everything. Together they made a perfect team. I had the extreme pleasure of helping Paul on some of his movies that have since become "cult classics." I learned a lot from my friend, and I miss him very much.

I'm so pleased that Randy took the time to write this book because you now have the chance to learn all about this wonderful, talented man. When you've finished reading, you'll know something I was lucky enough to learn years ago: Paul Blaisdell was one of a kind.

Preface

The late Paul Blaisdell can be described as neither long-lived nor especially prolific. As a self-taught makeup and effects artist working in low-budget movies made during the 1950s, Blaisdell competed with established professionals like Bud and Wally Westmore, Bill Tuttle, and Jack Kevan, the creator of *The Creature from the Black Lagoon*. Without the resources that were so readily available to those makeup experts, Blaisdell was by necessity forced to rely on his own ingenuity to design and build B-budget beasts for pictures like *The Day the World Ended* and *It! the Terror from Beyond Space*.

In his own lifetime Blaisdell received little fame. The fantasy film press for the most part ignored his work for producers like Roger Corman and film companies like American International. Year after year the seminal *Famous Monsters of Filmland* magazine published retrospectives of pictures like *The She-Creature* and *Invasion of the Saucer Men* but never mentioned the name Paul Blaisdell.*

Although *Fantastic Monsters of the Films* magazine (1962-63) provided occasional coverage of Blaisdell's movie work (Blaisdell was in fact the magazine's editorial director), it wasn't until the late 1970s, 20 years after the "B" movie monster's horror heyday, that the monster maker's creations finally began to be appreciated by fantasy film fans. *Fangoria* magazine was the first to offer substantial coverage, running a two-part article on the makeup artist in 1979, and the short-lived *Monster Times* also printed a feature on his work.

Finally, in 1990, *Cinéfantastique* published an in-depth look at the career of this innovative effects man, with 16 color pages devoted to Blaisdell and his creations. At the same time, a series of limited-edition model kits of Blaisdell monsters began to be produced in Japan, and these were eventually distributed domestically by Billiken USA. Shortly thereafter, videocassette

---

Actually, the very first issue of Famous Monsters *carried a short article about Blaisdell's work on* Invasion of the Saucer Men, *but a falling-out between Blaisdell, editor Forry Ackerman, and publisher James Warren led to an internal promulgation at Warren Publishing that banned Blaisdell's name from the contents of any future company publication. The Saucer Men piece was the only article in* FM #1 *that was never reprinted in any subsequent issue of the magazine.*

releases of some of Roger Corman's earliest pictures sparked further interest in Blaisdell. RCA/Columbia issued a series of "Drive-In Classics" that included *Voodoo Woman, Invasion of the Saucer Men, Day the World Ended, The Amazing Colossal Man, How to Make a Monster, The Spider,* and others. There is still much that has not been released, however.

Paul Blaisdell died in 1983 after a long and arduous struggle with cancer, unaware that a legion of devoted film fans would soon emerge to applaud his contributions to film fantasy. I am grateful for the assistance of Blaisdell's wife Jackie, who helped him on many film assignments during the 1950s. She now lives in seclusion in Topanga Canyon, California, the site of the couple's home during their active Hollywood years. Fortunately, Paul's close friend and fellow makeup artist, Bob Burns, continues to champion the work of the visionary Blaisdell, who for the most part remains "Hollywood's Forgotten Monster Maker." Thanks are due Burns for his devotion to this project and the many hours of personal time he gave up to supply facts, figures, anecdotes, and other tales of wonderment from Hollyweird concerning Paul Blaisdell's all-too-brief film career. And thanks to Forrest J Ackerman, Dennis Druktenis, Alex Gordon, Fred Olen Ray, and Tony Timpone for their time, assistance, enlightenment, and encouragement.

—RANDY PALMER
Greensboro, N.C.
Summer 1996

A Note Concerning the Text

Unless otherwise specified, the quotations from Paul Blaisdell that appear in this book are from personal correspondence with the author. The majority of Blaisdell's comments are from the years 1971–1982, although a very few date back to 1966. In a few instances where Blaisdell's remarks conflict with comments provided by others (as in discussions about the making of *It Conquered the World*), I have elected to give Blaisdell's remarks precedence.

Conversations between Paul Blaisdell and other individuals have been recreated from descriptions of events provided by Blaisdell in personal correspondence with the author. In all such cases, quoted conversations are condensed recitations of remarks from involved parties as recalled by Blaisdell. In those few instances in which Blaisdell was unable to recall specifics, reconstruction of conversations or events was not possible. In these instances, in the interest of accuracy I have elected to sum up Blaisdell's personal feelings, rather than to rely on faulty memories or guesswork.

Quotations from Jackie Blaisdell and Bob Burns are from personal correspondence with the author conducted during the periods 1982–1989 (Blaisdell) and 1989–1995 (Burns).

1

Turning Hollywood
into Horrorwood

Old monsters never die, no matter how long ago they were shot.
—*Paul Blaisdell*

Hollywood has always had its own peculiar way of doing things. During the 1930s and 1940s, actors were signed to long-term, studio-exclusive contracts, and producers were the ones who called the shots—unless you were a Hitchcock or a Welles. Even then you were lucky to escape interference from the "suits" if they thought your picture was a bit too pretentious, too arty, or—horror of horrors—"uncommercial." Back then, a "B" film wasn't synonymous with the term *exploitation*. But as the 1940s drew to a close and the dawn of the nuclear decade approached, Hollywood was about to undergo some tumultuous changes, perhaps not all of them for the better.

More than anything else, television became the catalyst for a whole new approach to moviemaking. The "idiot box" had the effect of keeping scores of potential ticket-buyers at home, where, except for the periodic intrusion of commercial messages and station identification breaks, Mom and Pop and the kids were enjoying entertainment that was essentially free and, for all intents and purposes, very, very movielike.

To woo patrons back to the cinemas, Hollywood embarked on a systematic search for something television couldn't duplicate. CinemaScope, Panavision, VistaVision, Todd A-O, Cinerama, 3-D Stereo-Vision, and other specialized photographic processes were conceptualized, refined, and released amid reams of promotional fanfare and kaleidoscopic hoopla. The strategy worked. Ticket sales perked up, and all of Hollywood breathed a collective sigh of relief.

Along with 3-D and CinemaScope came something else: a new film genre, born out of the fear of Armageddon and America's new preoccupation with nuclear superweapons, the atomic bomb and, later, the hydrogen bomb. In previous decades the term *horror film* had meant Frankenstein, Dracula, haunted houses, and, as often as not, Boris Karloff and Bela Lugosi. The horror films of the 1950s, however, featured new types of terrors—radioactive mutations, prehistoric monsters reborn in an atomic haze, overgrown ogres split from the atom. Horror experienced a kind of metamorphosis, eventually becoming "science-fiction-horror." For a while there were no more Frankenstein monsters, at least not until Britain's Hammer Films revitalized the gothic horror genre with their color remakes of Universal's chillers from the 1930s and 1940s. There were only giant bugs, blobs, brains, fiends, and monsters, monsters, monsters—from outer space, from beneath the sea, from green hell, from Yucca Flats, from the ocean floor, from the year 5000. So many new*fang*led freaks that *Life* turned to death for a special issue on the monster craze, and Forrest J Ackerman and James Warren were prompted to unleash the world's first pulse-pounding periodical, *Famous Monsters of Filmland*, which cataloged the new creature-features almost as quickly as Hollywood created them.

But it wasn't the old guard that created the monster movie craze of the 1950s; it was the new boys on the block—independents like American International Pictures, which came into existence just as Hollywood was catching its breath from the blow of public television. As AIP's top brass well knew, it wasn't the easiest time to establish a new independent production company, but company president James H. Nicholson and vice president Samuel Z. Arkoff saw the turmoil of the times as a way to "buy in." Whether they were dilettantes or not (and they weren't) didn't matter. Arkoff was a lawyer and figured he would make a decent, hard-line movie mogul. Nicholson, who actually had some previous film business experience working with Realart Pictures, liked good movies but didn't care if he made any or not. What he cared about was making money. Motion pictures, Nicholson knew, didn't necessarily have to be made well to make money; they just needed to be sold well.

And AIP did make money. In time, they made lots of it. The way they did that was by hiring young people, many new to the industry, who had little or no professional motion picture experience but possessed a seemingly inexhaustible supply of energy and dedication to making the most entertaining and respectable products possible under trying, sometimes difficult, and occasionally nearly impossible circumstances.

Like many persons who went to work for Nicholson and Arkoff, Paul Blaisdell could not boast any previous professional motion picture experience. Born on July 21, 1927, in Newport, Rhode Island, Blaisdell grew up in Quincy, Massachusetts—a long way from the glamour, glitter, and schmooze of Hollywood. As a child he was bright and imaginative and possessed a superb sense of visualization that helped him design homemade kites, puppets, marionettes, and similar playthings. He often spent Saturday afternoons at the local cinema, enjoying the latest "spooky movies" at special matinee showings. His father, an aviation buff, took Paul to see just about every aviation picture that came along. As Paul explained it, "I couldn't lose. I liked both kinds of movies, especially if they had square heads and more than one wing. Whoopee!"

Like most children, Paul exercised his imagination regularly, but it sometimes landed him in hot water. There were occasions in grade school when, instead of studying whatever subject had been assigned, he would begin daydreaming and doodling, making sketches of whatever happened to be on his mind at the time. On especially choice days, when the teacher was feeling good, Paul would be hauled up in front of the class and told to share his private work with the other students. Sometimes his classmates laughed, but just as often they didn't, especially if he had been sketching something the kids found interesting. If it was the instructor's intention to embarrass or ridicule the prideful Blaisdell, the ploy failed; his artwork was invariably better than what the other students could manage.

As the years passed, Paul graduated from using only pencils and pens to working with charcoal, water colors, acrylics, and oils. As a teenager his interest in putting together model aircrafts escalated, and he began blueprinting and building his own designs from scratch. When he grew older and started to discover the opposite sex, Paul devoted less time to his usual pursuits, but his interest in imagining and inventing never waned. It was this interest, coupled with his innate talent for building three-dimensional objects from scratch, that would eventually lead to work in motion pictures as a makeup and special effects artist.

After graduating from high school, Blaisdell repaired typewriters and other types of mechanical equipment and worked for a while at a local drugstore as a retail clerk. "They stocked these green Frankenstein monster masks that sold for a few dollars," he recalled. " I sold quite a few of them myself. It was exactly the same mask that turned up on the cover of the first issue of a particular monster film magazine that came out in 1958."*

Blaisdell was eventually inducted into the military. A European stint in the army may not have conjured up many pleasant memories for the 20 year old, but the GI Bill at least provided opportunities for veterans to acquire specialized education. After his discharge from the army in 1947, Paul found that jobs in the Northeast were scarce, so he took advantage of Uncle Sam's invitation to further his education and enrolled in the New England School of Art and Design, a commercial art school where he studied techniques for creating logos, letterheads, trademarks, and the like. At times it could be rather tedious work, but since it was part and parcel of the artist's spectrum, why complain? Besides, a degree held forth the promise of future employment in a faltering economy.

---

*Paul is referring to the first issue of Famous Monsters of Filmland. It was the magazine's publisher, James Warren, who appeared on the cover wearing a Frankenstein Monster mask.

This page and opposite: Futuristic pen-and-ink illustrations created for various science-fiction pulp titles of the 1950s. Note the design of the disc-shaped spacecraft in the top two drawings, reminiscent of the starship designed by Blaisdell for Edward L. Cahn's *Invasion of the Saucer Men* (1957); the abbreviated pseudonym in one of the fallen banners on opposite page. (Courtesy of Bob Burns.)

Paul spent three years at the school honing his artistic talents, and it was there that he met Jackie, the girl who was destined to become his wife and lifelong companion.

After graduation Paul and Jackie got married and relocated to California, where Paul enrolled in another school that specialized in engineering and drafting design. This eventually led to employment with the Douglas Aircraft Company as a technical illustrator. It was not very rewarding work from an artistic standpoint, but at least Paul was making enough money to sustain himself and his young bride in a discreet new home in the secluded Topanga Canyon area of Southern California. Whenever he could, he would grab a spare typewriter and spend his lunch break working on ideas for short stories. One particular story took three lunch periods to complete. Years later it ended up in *Fantastic Monsters* magazine.

Each night after work Paul relaxed by sketching and painting, further honing his talents in a wide variety of media. Before long his efforts bore real fruit when he sold a painting to *Spaceway*, a science-fiction pulp magazine owned and edited by Bill Crawford, who ran the Fantasy Publishing

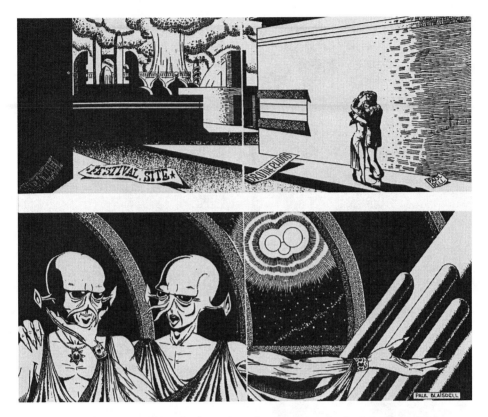

Company. Over time Crawford purchased a number of paintings from Blaisdell, and he eventually hired him to be the magazine's art editor. Blaisdell later recalled, "I wasn't too proud of some of [the magazine covers], but I did the best I could in the time I was given."

Crawford was also buying articles about new and upcoming science-fiction and horror movies written by a fellow named Forrest J Ackerman. Ackerman, a sci-fi fan and collector who had grown up in Los Angeles and hung out with Ray Harryhausen and Ray Bradbury when the two Rays were just starting out in their respective fields, gained fame by coining the term *sci-fi*. He eventually became a celebrity in his own right when he began editing *Famous Monsters of Filmland* magazine in 1958. He got interested in the artwork Blaisdell was doing for *Spaceway* and asked Crawford to put him in touch with the young artist.

Soon Blaisdell received a startling phone call. The voice on the end of the line belonged to Forrest Ackerman, and although Paul recognized Ackerman's name from the bylines on the film articles that had been appearing in Crawford's magazine, he was totally unaware that Ackerman was also a literary agent, representing both new and established genre authors like A. E.

Above: A Blaisdell cover for *Rocket Comics* from the early 1950s. The organic flying saucers anticipate the biomechanical designs of Swiss surrealistic H. R. Giger (creator of the *Alien*) by several decades. (Courtesy of Bob Burns.)

Opposite page: A variety of science-fiction scenes which appeared in *Hapna* and other genre publications of the 1950s. The leftmost two illustrations were rendered in full color.

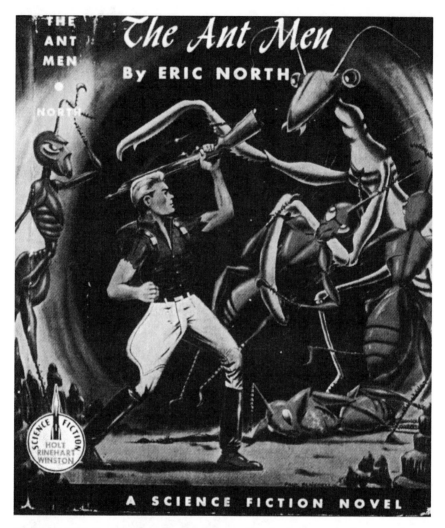

Blaisdell's full-color artwork appeared on the covers of several paperback science-fiction novels published in the early 1950s. Interestingly, the human hero has elected to defend himself with the butt of his rifle instead of going for all-out melee action with guns a-blazing. Respect for alien life forms was rare in low-brow sci-fi novels of the era. (Courtesy of Bob Burns.)

Van Vogt and Ib Melchior. Ackerman explained that he could help popular-ize Blaisdell's work by marketing his talents more aggressively in the United States as well as overseas. In return Ackerman expected a ten-percent cut of Paul's earnings, the standard fee charged by most agents at the time. The thought of having someone else doing the legwork when it came to selling his work professionally sounded like a pretty good idea to Blaisdell.

Jackie was excited by the prospect and urged Paul to accept Ackerman's offer. He did, and before long his material was being purchased for publication in *Other Worlds* and *The Magazine of Fantasy and Science Fiction*, as well as in foreign markets like the Swedish science-fiction magazine *Hapna*. For a time Paul also wrote and drew a serial sci-fi comic strip for *Famous Funnies*.

Paul later recalled: "I'd been trying to draw or make up new ideas from my imagination ever since I was six years old. Needless to say, in the beginning I wasn't very good at it, but I kept trying. I never gave up." His feel for the fantastic was becoming sharper than ever as he began selling more and more art pieces to the sci-fi markets of the day. It wouldn't be much longer before his artistic ingenuity would be put to the test in a special assignment that would end up taking him permanently in a rather unexpected direction.

2

The Eyes Have It

I think [Roger Corman] got exactly what he wanted.
—Paul Blaisdell

While Forrest J Ackerman was busy marketing Blaisdell's colorful canvasses to a clutch of science-fiction magazines, Jim Nicholson and Sam Arkoff were working hard on getting their new film company, the American Releasing Corporation (ARC), off the ground. ARC's films—many of them older pictures with snazzy new titles dreamed up by Nicholson—were pure fodder for the exploitation market; cheap black-and-white programmers destined for quick playoffs on the drive-in and grind-house circuits.

Being the new kid on the block wasn't easy. Established movie merchants were sweating bullets while the industry scrambled to find ways to combat television, which was doing a bang-up job keeping families at home, away from the nation's theaters. Fox, Paramount, Universal, Warner Bros., and MGM all suffered fiscal losses in the early years of the 1950s, while the studios tried every gimmick they could think of to lure patrons back to the boxoffice. Widescreen images, the multiprojector Cinerama experience, 3-D "Stereo Vision" with polarized glasses (that gave some viewers headaches as well as depth-perception), more color, bigger budgets, all-star extravaganzas, "casts of thousands." How could the fledgling ARC hope to hold its own against all this?

Some said it took guts; others intimated that Arkoff and Nicholson were being downright foolhardy. But the pair had a working plan: to market films aimed specifically at America's youth. Teenagers were the one segment of the motion picture market that didn't want to sit at home and watch television—especially on Friday and Saturday nights.

The risk paid off. Soon ARC would cease repackaging and rereleasing previously seen pictures and begin producing their own features. The films would be low-budget affairs to start, but the stories would be as exciting and original as they could make them.

Coincidentally, there was another newcomer to the City of Angels who wanted to make movies and who also didn't have much money. But he did have a great deal of chutzpa and a persuasive ability to interest film investors in the unlikeliest of projects. His name was Roger Corman.

On his own, Corman managed to raise $12,000—just barely enough money to produce an ultracheap science-fiction picture called *It Stalked the Ocean Floor*, later retitled *The Monster from the Ocean Floor*. Wyott Ordung, a struggling actor who wrote and directed the film for Corman, introduced him to Arkoff and Nicholson. Each had something the other wanted, and several distribution deals were discussed. There was a bottom line from which ARC was unwilling to budge, however: the company could not offer Corman any money up front for *Monster from the Ocean Floor*. Nicholson suggested they release the picture on a regional basis, which meant there would be a long wait before Corman would see any substantial return on his OPM (*Other People's Money*) investment.

Roger didn't want to wait, so he sold the film outright to Lippert Pictures. That deal made him enough money to reimburse his investors and reap a decent profit besides. The profits helped fuel his second project, a race-car drama called *The Fast and the Furious*, which would eventually become ARC's premiere release. Corman could boast that his new picture cost four times as much as *Monster from the Ocean Floor*, but that didn't change the fact that it was still an extremely low-budget affair. He cut a deal with ARC which called for Arkoff and Nicholson to do all the legwork involved in getting up-front money for the film from regional exhibitors. This allowed Corman to reinvest in more features without having to wait for cash returns as *The Fast and the Furious* slowly made its way across the country.

Recognizing that he could cut production costs further by directing as well as producing films himself, Corman began developing several more projects, including two Westerns, *Five Guns West* and *Apache Woman,* and a science-fiction picture.

The production of *Five Guns West* was excruciatingly nerve-wracking for Corman, and not only because this was the film that marked his directorial debut. Location shooting was hampered by rain storms from the very first day, and the picture ended up running over budget—one of Corman's worst nightmares. Because the deal with ARC stipulated that any budget overruns would have to come out of the producer's pocket, the only way Roger could cover the cost of finishing *Five Guns West* was to slash the budget of one of his other pictures. Thus, what was a little picture to begin with became a very little picture with a very big title: *The Beast with a Million Eyes. Beast* was one of Jim Nicholson's most outrageous film titles, and it ended up saddled with a budget of less than $30,000. (Some say the picture was made for a mere $23,000.) By this time Corman had joined the Director's Guild and couldn't work on the film directly—that would make it a union picture, and there wasn't enough money left in the budget to pay union scale wages. So Corman decided to turn the script over to his production assistant, David

Kramarsky, who took a producer-director credit for his work on the picture, even though most of the film actually ended up being directed by Lou Place. (Place later had his name removed from the credits, letting Kramarsky take all the credit—or blame—for the finished product.)

The Beast with a Million Eyes was scripted by Tom Filer under the title *The Unseen.* For a relatively early entry in the mushrooming sci-fi screen sweepstakes of the 1950s, it was a surprisingly highbrow concept. Instead of making his monster a gargantuan insect, radioactive blob, or space-helmeted horror, Filer made it a "nonentity"—a metaphysical force invisible to the human eye that preyed upon the minds of terrestrial life-forms. (A similar idea would be used to outstanding effect ten years later in a little-seen British sci-fi film of 1964, *Unearthly Stranger.*)

Roger Corman was all smiles after he read Filer's screenplay because it meant he could make a monster movie without having to bother showing a monster. The upshot, of course, was an even lower production budget than had first been planned. Perhaps Corman was unaware that audiences would feel cheated when no million-eyed monstrosities showed up during the film's scant 78-minute running time. Although it was a common practice for '50s monster movies to "beef up" their namesakes in publicity and advertising materials such as one-sheet posters and newspaper advertisements, no producer had as yet dared make a movie with a title like *The Beast with a Million Eyes* and neglect showing at least some kind of monster.

Jim Nicholson had designed a splendid promotional package for *Beast* before the first frame of film was ever exposed. In fact, almost all the early ARC pictures were designed in this fashion, with Nicholson first dreaming up a title and hiring an artist to design the poster and pressbook ads. Only after the advertising campaign was finalized would a script be written, based on either the poster art or the film title; it would then be turned into a movie. In the case of *The Beast with a Million Eyes*, the promotional posters featured a ferocious, multieyed, tentacled visage with needlelike fangs menacing a young couple on the beach. The monster was apparently so enormous that only part of its head could fit into the picture. A prominent blurb declared the picture was "filmed for wide-screen in terror-scope." It was a textbook example of what would eventually be recognized as typical ARC/AIP overkill. Nicholson sent copies of the poster design to his regional film exhibitors to drum up interest in the picture while Corman, David Kramarsky, and Lou Place began rounding up a cast and crew.

The cast for the film was small. Paul Birch, who would work with Corman on two other Blaisdell monster pictures, *Day the World Ended* and *Not of This Earth*, took the lead role of Allan Kelly. Lorna Thayer was his bitchy wife, Carol. Dona Cole was cast as their daughter Sandy, and there were smaller roles for Chester Conklin and Leonard Tarver, who played a mute farmhand nicknamed "Him." ("He can't talk, and nobody knows his name,

American Releasing Corporation (the predecessor of American-International Pictures) distributed its very first science-fiction movie in 1955. Most of the posters and ad mats designed for *The Beast with a Million Eyes* featured a tentacled, multiorbed monstrosity that never showed up in the actual film.

so we just call him 'Him,'" explains Sandy.) Dick Sargeant, a decade away from taking over Dick York's role as Darrin on CBS-TV's "Bewitched" sitcom, turned in an embarrassingly lame performance as Larry, a deputy sheriff who falls in love with the teenaged Sandy.

The opening of the film, with its eerie panning shots of a desert wasteland and Paul Birch's moody voice-over, is appropriately haunting, but the film betrays a fundamental impoverishment moments later and never recovers. An early scene with Allan and Carol serves to establish the reason behind their tumultuous relationship (Carol abhors the desolation that surrounds the ranch and feels compelled to vent her frustrations against the family) and introduces the virginal Sandy and her affectionate dog, a German Shepherd called Duke. There is also the mute farmhand, "Him," who serves mainly as a red herring and early victim of the alien invader.

When Allan leaves the house to irrigate his farmland, Sandy takes Duke for a walk, leaving Carol alone in the house. A shrill, ear-piercing whine bites through the air, shattering Carol's favorite chinaware and drinking glasses. She phones the sheriff's office to complain about "low-flying jet planes" and is reassured that Deputy Larry will check everything out. Larry is unable to confirm the existence of any jets flying over such a remote region of California, but Carol is adamant—she knows a jet when she hears one.

Of course it's no jet, but an interstellar craft from another solar system with not just one but two alien life-forms aboard. And it has landed in the desert not very far from the Kelly ranch. Before long, flocks of birds and roving animals begin acting strangely, purposefully—as if they have acquired a kind of superintelligence. Allan is the first to be attacked when a flock of blackbirds descends on his station wagon in a nightmarish fury of beating wings and stabbing beaks. But the attack subsides as quickly as it began, and the WW2 vet dismisses the weird occurrence as just a freakish quirk of nature.

Later the same day Duke wanders into the desert, where he becomes attracted to an immense, funnel-like crater that periodically emits flashing beacons of light. At the center of the pit is a strange metallic object, apparently several stories high, topped with an anomalous propeller whipping the air furiously. Duke emerges from the crater a maddened, salivating thing. Back at the ranch, he goes after Carol in a frenzy, his fangs dripping like a python's. Carol grabs the closest available weapon—an axe—and destroys Duke before the dog can hurt her.

Sandy accuses her mother of killing Duke unjustly, but her words are blunted barbs, born mostly out of the frustration that has arisen between her and her mother. Both feel trapped by a nihilistic existence in a brutal environment. Only Allan seems to believe wholeheartedly in the family unit, which he strives to keep together as events around him spiral out of control.

Ironically, it takes the arrival of a hostile alien force to goose Carol into shifting gears and beginning to take the first positive steps she has taken in years. Carol describes in no uncertain terms her feeling that the desert has become a refuge for a malevolent, inhuman intelligence which has arrived on Earth and taken control of its wildlife. Her theory is strengthened when Allan discovers that a neighbor has been gored to death by one of his own cows. When the animal shows up at the Kelly ranch and attacks the women, Allan is forced to kill it with a shotgun.

The weird attacks increase. Carol suffers a skirmish with the farm chickens, and there is a second scuffle with a mass of blackbirds. "Him" is drawn to the desert crater and becomes possessed by the alien mind occupying the spaceship. Allan discovers that "Him" is missing and senses that the alien presence is closing in on them all. He sends Carol and Sandy into town to fetch the sheriff and returns to the ranch in case "Him" should show up. The blackbirds attack again, but Allan eventually reaches the ranch only to discover that Carol and Sandy were forced to turn their truck around and return home when massive flocks of blackbirds drove them off the road.

Newly invigorated with a sense of purpose, Carol realizes that the animal attacks are precipitated by human isolation. The strength of love and the family unity seem to operate as deterrents to the alien's influence. While she and Allan strive to work out some kind of defense plan, Sandy, in a move of astonishing stupidity, climbs out her bedroom window to search for the missing Deputy Larry. Hiding nearby, "Him"—his mind now completely controlled by the alien brain—abducts Sandy and carries her toward the glowing crater.

Larry, who was delayed en route by an encounter with "Him," finally arrives at the ranch only to discover Sandy missing. Allan orders Carol to bolt the door while he and Larry make their way to the precipice of the crater, where they see "Him" carrying Sandy toward the ship. Allan calls out to "Him," who somehow defies the alien's controlling influence and returns Sandy to her father's outstretched arms. Enraged, the alien kills "Him" by frying what is left of his brain.

Out of range of the crater, Allan meets up with Carol, who fled the ranch when it was invaded by a mass of attacking blackbirds. Convinced that together they are stronger than the alien, they return to the rim of the crater. A telepathic voice tells them that life on the alien's planet is dying out. Its race seeks a new world rich with "food"—brains—on which this race of formless energy can feed. Emissaries have been sent to many solar systems to locate a planet with suitable life-forms which could be easily assimilated. Earth would be next, if not for this unusual force the alien senses—the strength of human love and companionship.

A porthole opens in the side of the craft, exposing the slave of the Beast with a Million Eyes. With chains and manacles dangling loosely from its wrists, the creature approaches the ship's airlock and gazes down hypnotically at the diminutive figures on the desert floor. The thing's face wears a triumphant sneer as a ghostly cyclopean eyeball appears before it—a representation of the "real" Beast—and a (very brief) battle of wills commences. Overpowered by the collective passion of its human adversaries, the alien consciousness flees its corporeal host and escapes—to where? Allan thinks it may have entered the body of a mouse or eagle which seem to have appeared literally out of nowhere—but there is no real way of telling. Abruptly, the spaceship, apparently predetermined to lift off at a specific time, shudders to life and rushes up into the night sky, rocketing away from the Earth forever.

With proper care and funding, Tom Filer's uneven screenplay might have been developed into an entertaining little picture. But the severe constraints of the film's miniscule budget, the sloppy staging of the story's events, and the rather undistinguished direction by Lou Place (with possible input from Kramarsky or Corman) all combine to sabotage whatever sense of mood and mystery *The Beast with a Million Eyes* might have had to begin with. Except for Paul Birch, who tended to overact at the drop of a hat (he is even worse in *Day the World Ended*), the cast members meander through their roles in the most forgettable fashion. Richard Sargeant is especially bad in an extended desert fight sequence which was shot without synchronous sound with an undercranked camera. The unfortunate result is that the actor's motions mimic the most exaggerated silent film antics.

Until Roger Corman began making use of him in early pictures like *Apache Woman* and *Five Guns West*, Paul Birch's film roles had been limited to smallish parts in *Assignment—Paris!* (his 1952 screen debut), *Ride Clear of Diablo*, and George Pal's memorable *The War of the Worlds* (both 1953). Prior to 1952 his acting experience extended only to Broadway, which is probably where his tendency to overact originated. (Stage actors invariably overplay roles in order to project characterization into the cheap seats at the back of the theater.) In *The Beast with a Million Eyes* Birch tries hard as the henpecked rancher who never seems to run short of bad luck, but the film's technical deficiencies are simply too overwhelming to allow him a chance to pull off any kind of acting coup. In actuality Birch never learned to corral his exaggerated methods, which is probably why he landed his meatiest roles in the undiscriminating '50s, even though he continued acting through the sixties. He died in 1969.

Throughout *The Beast with a Million Eyes*, numerous scenes were photographed without the benefit of synchronous sound, adding to the film's bare-bones look and feel. The minimalist interior sets were starkly and unimaginatively lit, and much of the location photography turned out dark and murky. In fact, only during the picture's severely abbreviated climax is any measure of imagination evidenced by the filmmakers, mainly in the juxtaposition of elements leading up to the cast's descent into the crater and Paul Birch's face-off with the alien monster. Everett Baker, who was a professor at UCLA's cinema department, is cited during the credit crawl as director of photography, although the uncredited Floyd Crosby provided important footage at Roger Corman's direction. (Crosby was employed on a number of Corman projects, from the director's picayunish debut in 1955 well into the 1960s.) Nine days into production, Corman stepped in to direct some scenes when the film fell behind schedule.

The frenetic musical score by John Bickford is unusual but anachronistic, sounding almost as if it were composed for a thriller from the 1940s instead of a sci-fi film of the 1950s. Much of the time it is too mechanically melodramatic to be anything other than just plain obtrusive. Bickford's blend of swooning strings, staccato horns, and hammering drums mainly recalls elements from Hans J. Salter's scores for Universal but anticipates the then-emerging style of Hammer Films' James Bernard, whose scores for *The Creeping Unknown* (British title: *The Quatermass Experiment*) and *Enemy from Space* (*Quatermass 2*) helped define that studio's orchestral calling card.

Even though ARC's advertising campaign claimed the picture was filmed "for wide-screen in terror-scope," *The Beast with a Million Eyes* was projected in standard 1:1.66 ratio. This probably served as the first tip-off to exhibitors that they might not be getting exactly what Arkoff and Nicholson had promised. The clincher, of course, was that the film ended without showing any physical manifestation of the Beast at all. Not surprisingly, this infuriated most of the exhibitors, who had been primed by ARC's promotional artwork to expect something extraordinary. All they got, after suffering through 78 numbing minutes of monsterless, nearly plotless footage, was a dark, bullet-shaped object buried in the sand with an incongruous spinning propeller that looked about as unearthly as a miniature ceiling fan.

A lame attempt to rationalize the title was made when ARC tacked on a precredits prologue picturing the Earth revolving in space with voice-over oratory by the invisible Beast, who crows about all the millions of terrestrial eyes it will use to spy on mankind—rather like a galactic peeping tom. This bit (which was later excised from television prints) may have explained away the title to the satisfaction of the producers, but there was still no monster, and after all, this was supposed to be a monster movie.

According to some reports (including one from Sam Arkoff), when the exhibitors started raising a stink about the substandard quality of the picture, Jim Nicholson snuck the last reel of film into another room and carefully scratched lines into the film emulsion so that when it was projected it looked as if some kind of dangerous rays were being emitted by the bullet-shaped spacecraft. It's extremely doubtful that Nicholson actually did this, but if he did the footage must have been deep-sixed because as the film stands there are no "rays" flashing from the spaceship in any scene in the film, except the final shot of the craft as it is propelled skyward, leaving a trailing "ray" of exhaust behind. Alex Gordon, producer of numerous early ARC and AIP films, claimed that the spaceship was nothing more than a customized teakettle. (Arkoff said it was a coffee percolator.) Other reports claimed that the exhibitors offered Nicholson and Arkoff $100,000 to burn the movie and start over from scratch. This is very hard to swallow because Nicholson and Arkoff probably would have taken the hundred G's, offered Corman enough money to remake the film, and used the remainder to make another picture.

Whatever the actual circumstances, it is true that Roger Corman eventually recognized the need for a climactic on-camera confrontation between Man and Beast, whether the Beast had a million eyes or not. He got in touch with Forrest J Ackerman, who had numerous contacts in the film industry, to see who might be able to save his picture. Ackerman recommended his good friend Ray Harryhausen, the stop-motion "Dynamation" expert who had breathed life into *Mighty Joe Young, The Beast from 20,000 Fathoms, It Came from Beneath the Sea,* and many other monster films. But Harryhausen didn't work cheaply—especially not as cheaply as Corman had in mind. Ackerman subsequently recommended Jacques Fresco, who had designed the special effects for a 1953 film called *Project Moonbase*, which boasted a script cowritten by Jack Seaman and Robert A. Heinlein. But Fresco wanted a thousand dollars for the job, and Corman thought that was too expensive. Ackerman cut to the chase by asking how much Corman actually intended to spend on his film's special effects. Corman said he was willing to go as high as $200 for a reasonably well-made million-eyed monster.

Ackerman knew the offer was patently ridiculous, but he went along with the gag. For $200 Corman couldn't expect much; obviously no established Hollywood effects specialist was going to nibble at such miserable bait.

Eventually it occurred to Ackerman that Paul Blaisdell might be interested in the gig. Blaisdell had recently signed up with Ackerman's literary agency and was selling cover paintings to some of the science-fiction periodicals of the day on a semiregular basis. Ackerman knew very well that Blaisdell had no experience as a monster-maker, but recalled that Blaisdell had mentioned building his own model airplanes from scratch and working with soap carvings and homemade puppets when he was growing up in the '30s. He gave Paul a call and explained what Corman wanted.

Blaisdell said he might be willing to give it a try, but he wanted to see a copy of the film script before he committed himself. Corman sent him one. After Paul and Jackie looked it over, they got in touch with Corman to discuss the details. The producer assured them that the only thing the picture required at this point was a miniature monster to come on screen for a few seconds, point a ray gun at its (offscreen) human adversaries, and topple over gracefully when it died. That was all there was to it.

Paul asked for another $200. (He was figuring $200 for materials, $200 for labor.)

Corman agreed. (He had to agree. At this point there was no one else around who could help out.)

And so a beast was born.

Blaisdell later described the relationship between the Beast he created and the Beast of the movie's title:

> For the 3,451st time, I must explain that the Beast that appeared in the film was the slave of the Beast with a Million eyes. The "real" Beast had no material concept in reality. The title comes from the supposed fact that this was a creature that was a malevolent entity, possibly made up of a molecular cohesion, that can look through the eyes of all the creatures of whatever planet it lands on, whether they're human, dogs, cats, rats, or you-name-it. But it had no physical being, so it used a creature from another star system to pilot its ship, and that creature was its slave. If you can get a glimpse of all of the creature that opens the airlock door, you might notice he has on manacles and chains that have been released so he can do the Beast's bidding.
>
> Why they superimposed that awful eyeball over Little Herky is something I'll never understand, because it just made the whole scene look ludicrous. The Beast is supposed to be controlling the slave from the inside, like a kind of parasite, not floating above him like a disembodied orb. Of course, how the real Beast was able to pilot the ship away after Paul Birch shot it with a .30-30 Winchester rifle is something even I can't explain. That's one reason why I'd like to get hold of the scriptwriter someday!

The miniature monster Paul and Jackie built for the film was a lifesaver as far as Roger Corman was concerned. The exhibitors who had raised such a fuss about the sand-covered bullet, or teakettle, or coffee percolator, or whatever it was, could finally stop bitching. The film might be a cheapie, but at least the producers were going to have an honest to God monster in their monster picture.

There was one other little hitch: according to the script that Blaisdell read, the monster didn't have a million eyes. In fact, it didn't have any eyes. It was a mind with no substance, a being composed of pure energy. Since there was no way Blaisdell could create a dimensional mockup of a cumulous molecular force, he decided the monster would actually be the slave of the Beast with a Million Eyes. It made sense. After all, how could an invisible force pilot a rocket ship from one solar system to another? It couldn't, unless it was controlling some other life-form that already possessed the lineaments necessary to twist dials and push buttons and grab hold of an interplanetary steering wheel.

Once Blaisdell accepted the assignment the pressure was on to get things moving as quickly as possible. Working under the gun was something that Blaisdell would become very much accustomed to as the 1950s progressed and Roger Corman and other budget film producers began turning to him not only for their movie monsters, but for props, scenery, and special stunt effects as well. For *The Beast with a Million Eyes*, Corman promised that the monster only had to perform three actions: open the spaceship's airlock, point a ray gun at its offscreen adversary, and drop dead. How tough could the job be?

The "slave" of the Beast with a Million Eyes was an 18-inch hand puppet nicknamed Little Hercules. The batlike wings, clearly visible here, were obscured in the film by a hypnotic spiral and floating eyeball superimposed over the action.

From the outset of his involvement with the project, Blaisdell realized he would be working with miniature effects. No life-size props were required because this movie monster would not be conducting any direct action with the cast. The only time it would be seen was at the climax of the picture, when it appeared in the doorway of its spaceship some 20 feet above the desert floor. The creature itself was supposed to be between seven and eight feet tall, so Paul decided to build it one-quarter life-size. That meant it would measure about 18 inches in height, on the same scale as the most famous stop-motion movie monster ever created, Willis O'Brien's King Kong.

Corman allowed Blaisdell free reign when it came to dreaming up the look of the creature. Since Tom Filer's script never specified where the alien came from, there was no need to worry about whether its appearance would reasonably match its geographical background, and Blaisdell let his imagination run free. (Not that anyone else involved with the film might care. Blaisdell typically thought through the most meticulous exegeses to extrapolate visual plans for his creations, most of the time merely for his own amusement. Undoubtedly, if Filer had specified that the Beast came from the planet Neptune, Blaisdell would have designed something that could withstand extreme cold, perhaps a being with a thick hide or bushy hair.) Since the thing inside the spaceship was going to be the slave of the real Beast, Blaisdell decided to add some elements to the design which would help convey the idea that it was a life form that had been captured and imprisoned against its will. Although most of these design details were obscured in the finished film, they did show up in some of the promotional photos released by ARC.

Blaisdell began work on the project by first developing pen-and-ink sketches to schematize the overall shape of the monster. The basic design incorporated humanoid as well as reptilian and mammalian features—an interesting combination that would recur frequently in some of the artist's later work. The finished sketches served as a blueprint for the three-dimensional model. Since there would be no stop-motion animation used in the film, there was no need to make an expensive and problematic ball-and-socket armature. Water-based modeling clay served Paul's purposes very well. It was comfortable to work with, mistakes could be corrected with relative ease, and its plasticity offered the widest possible margin for sculptile trial and error.

Blaisdell experimented with different approaches to the design of his extraterrestrial interloper, eventually settling for a humanoid outline with an oversized, exposed brain that would represent the creature's advanced intellect. Once the pen-and-ink preliminaries had been completed, Paul went to work with his modeling clay, building up the Beast's abdominal structure in successive quarter-inch layers. The elongated head was shaped almost like an upside-down teardrop, the cerebral striations and eye sockets delicately gouged out of the clay with an artist's knife. When all sculpturing work was completed, the figurine was allowed to stand overnight to give the clay time to harden. It was then coated with liquid latex, a substance which slowly congeals into rubber when exposed to the air. Later, the dried latex rubber was slit up the back and carefully removed from the sculpture. This then became the "positive mold" which would be hand-painted and outfitted with various latex appendages to be brought to life as the slave of the title monster of *The Beast with a Million Eyes.*

Blaisdell dubbed the finished figure "Little Hercules." A pair of eyes were made from small plastic spheres obtained from the Frye Plastics Company, one of the largest suppliers of plastic goods in Southern California during the 1950s. Reptilianlike irises were painted directly onto the plastic, which was bound to the latex skin with a strong contact-bond cement. Above each eyeball was added a drooping antennae. Although for later projects Blaisdell would use materials such as candles to create this sort of fleshy protuberance, in this instance he utilized the tails of rubber lizards which were sold in many magic shops as joke items. The lizard tails proved to be just the right size for Little Hercules and were as flexible as anything that might have been fashioned by hand. Paul glued them directly to the latex and allowed the "antennae" to dangle freely.

Also added were a pair of lobsterlike pincers on either side of the mouth and a pair of curved horns attached to the Beast's elbows, all of which were fashioned out of rubber latex painted over positive clay molds. Flexible bat-like wings were made by bending ordinary wire hangers into the desired shape and coating them with numerous layers of liquid latex. When dry, the wings were bonded into place on the back of the model's shoulders. The wings could be bent into various positions, as long as care was taken not to rupture the latex skin or snap the metal joints. These, along with the creature's elongated head, exposed brain, pointed ears, (plastic) fangs, and antennae foreshadowed future Blaisdell creations such as the She-Creature and the "little green men" from *Invasion of the Saucer Men*.

Paul added a black vinyl spacesuit to the figure to cover the torso, arms, and knobby, five-fingered hands. (The hands, incidentally, were sculpted by Jackie Blaisdell.) A metal band encircled its waist. Since the Beast would only be seen from the waist up, there was no reason to design any of the lower extremities. A shield made of vinyl surrounded its neck and covered most of the chest. Glitter was glued to the vinyl so it would shimmer under the harsh movie lights. Blaisdell even designed an ornamental, otherworldly jewel for his brainy buddy to wear. This eight-pointed star was made from tiny pieces of colored plastic that were glued to the center of the shield and highlighted with silver modeling paint. Lastly, manacles and chains were added to the creature's wrists—a detail intended to convey its servile status—and a metallic-looking ray gun (a customized dime-store toy) was placed in its right hand.

In addition to the Beast, Blaisdell was asked to design the spaceship's "automatic" airlock door. Built to the same scale as Little Hercules, it consisted of a single sliding panel made out of corrugated cardboard. When the film began rolling, a hidden assistant pushed the cardboard panel up by hand while Jackie Blaisdell, also hidden from view behind the cardboard "airlock," furiously shook a couple of hand-held movie lights to create a weird strobo-scopic effect. Paul was sandwiched in between the two, operating Little Hercules as best he could under the rather congested circumstances. A floating eyeball and hypnotic spiral were later superimposed over the footage of the Beast, obscuring it further.

Blaisdell was also asked to design the rocketship briefly seen in the picture's conclusion. Actually, Paul had to build two ships because someone on the film crew neglected to do their homework. ARC had given Blaisdell carte blanche to design the miniature spacecraft however he chose. "Whatever you want to do is fine with us, just so long as it looks as if it's from outer space." Meanwhile, the second-unit crew made their own life-size version of the alien ship and carried it into the desert to shoot inserts for the picture. Nobody ever thought to touch base with Blaisdell to find out what he was doing.

Not surprisingly, Paul's finished model didn't match the full-scale mockup in the slightest. According to Blaisdell, the full-size ship was a hodge-podge of materials pieced together from a junkyard in Indio, California: an airplane fuselage and nose, some Model-T Ford mufflers, garbage cans, and a bunch of iron rods and plastic teacups. Someone decided it would be eas-ier for Paul to rebuild his miniature than it would be for the crew to try and build a brand-new matching mockup, so Paul set aside his meticulously designed egg-shaped starship and started work on a second model, undoubt-edly grumbling under his breath the whole time.

As an adjunct to his spaceship, Paul built a realistic-looking miniature landscape of the California desert, complete with its own impact crater. Scores of tiny rocks and bits of shrubbery were glued to the sand-coated surface, and the entire set was constructed on a wooden platform with a false bottom which allowed the model ship to rise up out of the crater on cue. The space-ship scenes were shot at the studio owned by Lou Place, who helped Paul rig the wires used to maneuver the miniature ship. According to some sources, the first time they set up the shot, Place's assistant, John Milani, strolled into the room and casually tripped over the wires, sending the ship into orbit well ahead of schedule. It was painstakingly repositioned and rewired the follow-ing day, and the shot was finally captured on film without Milani's unex-pected intervention.

Blaisdell's attention to detail was mostly lost on audiences who saw the finished feature in theaters in 1955 or caught it on television years later. Because Roger Corman wanted to get *The Beast with a Million Eyes* in the can as quickly as possible, none of Little Hercules's inbuilt talents were uti-lized on camera. Paul Blaisdell recalled that the crew was pretty impressed with the Beast—so much so that everyone wanted to be on hand during the shooting and try to get their fingers into the pie. By the time the cameras were ready to roll, Blaisdell was surrounded by so many people he barely had room to turn around. Consequently, Little Hercules's debut was severely restricted. Although the flexibility of the model could at least allow for var-ied arm movements, the director was in too much of a hurry to let Paul exper-iment with obtaining the best possible effects. The end result was a flatly lit, unimaginatively staged shot of the opening airlock and a quick cut to the Beast positioning his ray gun, along with one or two close-ups of the monster's snarling face before it inexplicably falls over dead. According to Blaisdell:

> When the film was shot everybody was climbing all over the mock-up of the spaceship and trying to light the Beast, and everybody wanted to get in on the act. And that's just what they did, until the Beast was so choked up he could hardly move. Unfortunately, that shows on the film, along with the wrong camera angle—after all, Paul Birch was supposed to be looking up at the spaceship, not at it. Those scenes were all shot within the space of about ten minutes, and unfortunately, it shows.

A model shot of the extraterrestrial spacecraft seen in *The Beast with a Million Eyes*. For this photo, human figures have been added to show the craft's relative size. The impact crater constructed by Paul and Jackie can be seen briefly in the film's conclusion as the starship departs Earth for destinations unknown (courtesy of Bob Burns).

When he saw the finished monster footage, Paul was horrified to discover that not only had the cameraman filmed the Beast at a totally inappropriate angle but a ghostly floating eyeball and hypnotic spiral had been superimposed over the scene, which made it look even worse. The scene played so quickly and was shot so poorly that the Beast's devil-bat-wings, the chains and manacles, and even the ray gun could barely be discerned at all. A unique closeup of the Beast with smoke pouring out of its nostrils was totally obscured by the ill-advised superimposition of the eyeball and spiral, but the effect can clearly be seen in some extant color footage of the scene currently in the hands of private collectors. (Blaisdell achieved the smoking nostrils effect by inserting a tube into the back of the model and blowing cigarette smoke through it. The smoke slowly seeped out of the only openings facing the camera—the creature's upturned nostrils.)

The scenes which followed, showing the liftoff of the alien craft and its flight through space, came off a bit better, though by today's standards the presentation can only appear somewhat archaic. But curiously enough, the sheer unearthliness of the craft, coupled with the harried and hurried nature of the photography, infuse the scene with a delicious sense of surreality.

Corman and Place spliced the new monster footage into the climax of the film and turned the project over to Sam Arkoff and Jim Nicholson, who were able to convince their regional exhibitors that *The Beast with a Million Eyes* had been "rescued." The monster didn't look anything like what the advertising campaign promised, of course—but at least now the picture had a monster. And that made enough of a difference to get the film out the studio door and into the nation's theaters.

Most adult viewers considered *The Beast with a Million Eyes* a lackluster Hollywood dud. In its review of the film, the trade paper *Variety* labeled it a "tedious science-fictioneer for less discriminating program spots." (Was that a kind way of saying that the picture would be laughed off the screen in regions like New York and Los Angeles?) *Variety* warned its readership that the film's premise became "lost in a maze of drawn-out situations and tiresome dialogue which leads to a confusing windup not likely to be readily understood by general audiences." In fact, the conclusion of the film remains somewhat open to interpretation.

According to Paul Blaisdell, the Beast was a "malevolent molecular cohesion," a form of energy that could not be killed. If the host was destroyed, however, the Beast had to burrow into another body immediately or it would be doomed to drift forever through the cosmos, a consciousness without form or substance. When Paul Birch confronted the alien creature in the spaceship airlock and shot it with a 30-30 Winchester rifle, he merely destroyed the alien's current physical home. (Recall that the monster in the ship is a creature from another star system which has been enslaved by the real Beast.) The real Beast escaped into the body of the closest living creature—a rat scurrying across the desert floor.

That's the story according to Blaisdell. But what seems to happen in the climax of the film is that the combined mental efforts of Allan, Carol, Sandy, and Larry overcome the creature in the ship. Although Allan is carrying a rifle, we never see him point it at his extraterrestrial adversary. When the Beast leaves its host, the alien slave falls over dead. There is the suggestion that the Beast has invaded the body of the nearby rat, but when Carol points at an eagle soaring through the sky we realize that the alien intelligence could just as easily have "climbed aboard" the eagle. (Why didn't it take over the mind of one of the human characters? That's something only scriptwriter Tom Filer knows for sure.) To add even more confusion to the mix, there are several lines of dialogue spoken between Paul Birch and Lorna Thayer that seem to suggest that the Beast was destroyed by the intervention of God.

The pictures Paul Blaisdell worked on during the 1950s, which were panned by many critics during their original theatrical run, began to be reevaluated by fans in the 1980s, who learned to look at them in an affectionate and nostalgic light. *The Beast with a Million Eyes* was no exception. Phil Hardy, in his monumental *Encyclopedia of Science Fiction Films* (1984, Woodbury Press), writes that the film was "clearly intended as an allegory about a malevolent God. The film remains interesting, for all its flaws, if only for its unusual central idea." As Hardy implies, circumstances surrounding the production were so bizarre that the overall mood of the finished film bordered on the surrealistic. Scenes depicting hypnotic flashing lights emanating from the alien craft and Blaisdell's "whirligig-bullet" spaceship rising into the desert sky like a refugee from George Melies's 1902 silent fantasy, *A Trip to the Moon*, only add to the dreamlike quality of the film.

No matter what anyone else may have thought of the picture, Paul Blaisdell was proud of his contribution to *The Beast with a Million Eyes*. Although the rushed nature of the film schedule severely restricted his ability to utilize his monster to full advantage, Roger Corman knew what Little Hercules was capable of. Recognizing the good return he got on a measly $400 investment, Corman promised to give Blaisdell a call whenever he started work on another science-fiction picture.

To Paul's surprise, the phone call came through just a few weeks later. (Corman worked really fast in those days.) It seemed the world was coming to an end, and Roger wanted Paul Blaisdell to create the ultimate doomsday monster.

3

The Mutant of Topanga Canyon

In *Day the World Ended,* I was supposed to be a mute mutant, able to use only hand gestures to try to explain to Lori [Nelson] that I had no intention of harming her and that I'd just come back to find her.

—*Paul Blaisdell*

Jim Nicholson and Sam Arkoff made money with *The Beast with a Million Eyes,* but not nearly as much as they would have liked. One problem was that the picture was booked as a second feature in double-bill situations. In those days the top half of a double-feature package always got the lion's share of ticket sales. All Nicholson and Arkoff could hope for was a standard flat weekly rental rate of $100, $200, or, if they were really lucky, perhaps as much as $300. To get better payoffs than that, ARC would have to supply their own tailor-made double features.

Jim Nicholson had recently come up with another sure-fire hit film title—*Day the World Ended.* Although he hadn't yet worked out the details, Nicholson knew the story should deal with nuclear weapons and the threat of atomic annihilation, which would play on the public's preoccupation with the cold war. In the 1950s the spectre of Communism reared its totalitarian head nearly every day as Americans read one report after another in their newspapers about nuclear weapons tests conducted by the USSR and the U.S. Fearing that another world war was imminent, many families started building backyard bomb shelters. School children practiced "duck and cover" safety routines in their classrooms during biweekly air raid drills. The possibility of atomic destruction was on everyone's mind, and *Day the World Ended* was one of the earliest exploitation films to tap into the terror of the nuclear threat.

Nicholson described his concept of the film to Lou Rusoff, a brother-in-law of Sam Arkoff, who was destined to write numerous scripts for ARC/AIP during the 1950s and 1960s. To keep production costs to a minimum, Nicholson decided the aftereffects of a nuclear world war would not be shown. Instead, a narrator would simply explain that the world had been disastrously blown up. Rusoff's script would concentrate on the aftermath of "TD-Day"—Total Destruction Day—and its impact on a handful of American survivors. The picture's single special effect would be a monster created by radioactive fallout.

Like *The Beast with a Million Eyes* before it, *Day the World Ended* proved to be an inspired appellation. Who could resist a title like that? And this time ARC's promotional campaign would feature an imaginative (rather than imaginary) title monster. Given the opportunity to pen the screenplay, Lou Rusoff concocted a fantasy formula that would serve as a kind of blueprint for later entries in the low-budget "atomic monster" sweepstakes. The action was straightforward, the plotline moved steadfastly from point A to point B without meandering aimlessly about, and the story even had a moral for warmongers of the 1950s. For its time, the film offered a chilling message that must have seemed well within the realm of near-future possibilities or probabilities. There were even a few crisply delineated characterizations, hackneyed though they might be. (But at least the film had characterizations, unlike *The Beast with a Million Eyes*, whose cast had seemed to be sleepwalking through the shallowest conceptualizations of Man, Woman, Girl, and Boy.)

Day the World Ended was produced by Alex Gordon, a young movie fan who ran the Gene Autry British Fan Club while working in the publicity department of Renown Pictures in Great Britain.* Gordon moved to New York in November 1947 to work as an assistant booker for the Walter Reade chain of theaters and eventually became involved in the production end of a picture called *The Lawless Rider*. That film ran so far over budget Gordon required legal help to extricate himself from the monetary mess that threatened to squelch his newfound career as a feature film producer. His search for a lawyer who specialized in the entertainment field led him to Sam Arkoff's doorstep. With Arkoff's help, Gordon managed to get *The Lawless Rider* released through United Artists, eventually making enough money to pay off the film's investors and resolve his legal differences.

Coincidentally, Gordon met Arkoff's future film production partner, Jim Nicholson, when he tried to interest Realart Pictures in a script called *The Atomic Monster* written by the infamous Edward D. Wood, Jr.† Someone at Realart appropriated Wood's title and slapped it on a rerelease of the 1941 Lon Chaney Jr. film, *Man Made Monster*. When Gordon found out about it, he threatened to sue the company, which led to a meeting with Arkoff and

---

*Autry was a radio star before he graduated to motion pictures. He became known as the "Singing Cowboy" during the 1930s when he made a series of popular Western-musicals.

†Wood's script was credited to him and Alex Gordon, but it was really a solo effort by Wood. It was eventually filmed as Bride of the Monster, *starring a down-and-out Bela Lugosi. Wood and Gordon were sharing an apartment in Hollywood at the time.*

Nicholson (who was still working for Realart at this time). Presumably all legal differences were resolved because Gordon was subsequently invited into the newly created ARC fold, which is how he got involved with *Day the World Ended*.

Day would make use of a budget several times larger than that of ARC's first science-fiction release, but it was still a low-budget picture. According to Alex Gordon, Rusoff received a little over $3,000 for his screenplay—a pittance even in 1956. The cast received a combined total of $15,402.63, a figure almost matched by the crew's salary, $12,952.21. Set construction, dressing, and general operations came to less than $10,000. By far the costliest ingredient of the film was Sam Arkoff's $25,000 salary, which was paid on a deferred basis (after the film was actually out the door and making money).

Given that there is no dollar figure cited for "special effects" or "makeup," payments to Paul Blaisdell for his construction of the Atomic Mutant might have come from the $1,472.78 allotted to some mysterious "special equipment." Presumably Blaisdell would have also received a portion of the monies claimed by the cast because he also played the role of the Mutant. ("I've often wondered why the guy who plays the monster in a monster movie is invariably listed last in the credits," Blaisdell would gripe jokingly to fans.)

The remainder of the production costs balanced out as follows:

Bits & Extras	$ 5,048.48
Wardrobe	1,983.35
Production Office	959.06
Lighting	1,972.50
Camera	3,937.29
Sound	4,982.99
Music	3,478.75
Transportation	2,149.79
Location	1,993.40
Studio Rental	6,000.00
Editing	6,449.34
Film Stock	1,490.52
Laboratory	5,192.31
S. S. Benefits	4,026.14
Titles, etc.	1,021.06
Insurance	755.63
Miscellaneous	1,288.89
Alex Gordon (executive producer)	2,500.00 (deferred)
Sam Arkoff	25,000.00 (deferred)
TOTAL	$96,234.49

Arkoff's and Gordon's deferred fees would be paid later, once the film has been released and was accruing revenue.

Rather than being called in at the last minute to help rescue a picture from impending disaster, Paul Blaisdell was involved with *Day the World Ended* from its inception. During the film's preproduction stages, he got together with Lou Rusoff to help smooth out some of the script's rough edges. The story was to take place in far-flung 1970, after World War III has char-broiled the earth into one vast wasteland. Remote pockets of civilization still exist, but radioactive fallout threatens to eradicate even these last vestiges of humanity. Blaisdell's contributions to the story included an important ratio-nale for the surivival of the seven people who make up the cast of the film. He describing to Rusoff how a deep valley might offer a refuge from radia-tion. Protected by its sloping hills, the people in this valley could remain hid-den from the devastating effects of nuclear radioactivity. This would also help explain why one of the characters begins a slow metamorphosis into a degen-erative life-form as he wanders across the hills. The closer he goes to the top of the ridge, where a kind of "nuclear vapor" cuts off the valley from the rest of the world, the more he begins to mutate.

Blaisdell also discussed with Rusoff how the film's monster, the Atomic Mutant, would evolve, given the conditions of the story line. Paul based his concept on two interconnected ideas: one, that a human being poisoned by radiation from a nuclear blast would experience a radical physical change at the molecular level, precipitating a rapid mutation into something quite different; and two, in a world blanketed by atomic fallout such an individual would generate a thick, metallic hide as a kind of "protective armor" against further exposure to harmful elements. In essence, Blaisdell's Atomic Mutant was "the man of the future," in a future where the air and the food are radioac-tive and the purity of the Earth is a thing lost irrevocably to the past.

Executive Producer Alex Gordon, who earlier worked with Roger Cor-man on *Apache Woman*, lined up some of his favorite actors for *Day the World Ended.* Raymond Hatton and Adele Jergens were cast in secondary roles. Gor-don loved to talk to the old-time stars about their experiences working for the major studios, and in between takes he would often pull up a chair and shoot the breeze. Younger faces included Richard Denning and Lori Nelson, who had both recently worked for Universal, and Paul Dubov, a Corman dis-covery. Paul Birch portrayed a retired sea captain who seemed like a second cousin to his character in *The Beast with a Million Eyes*, and Mike Connors, who would gain a respectable degree of popularity with his "Mannix" televi-sion series twenty years hence, was billed as "Touch" Connors in his role as two-bit gangster Tony Lamont.

Day the World Ended begins with stock footage of an actual atom bomb explosion. Over a blooming mushroom cloud, the disembodied voice of a nar-rator intones, "This is TD-Day: Total Destruction by nuclear weapons. And from this hour forward, the world as we know it no longer exists. And over all the lands and waters of the Earth hangs the atomic haze of death. Man has done his best to destroy himself. But there is a force more powerful than Man, and in His infinite wisdom, He has spared a few."

A man who has been exposed to a high dose of radiation, Radek (Paul Dubov), tumbles down an incline gasping for breath. His face is ravaged by radiation burns; his black and lumpy skin is streaked with poisonous decay. Rick (Richard Denning), a geologist, comes across Radek's prone form and carries him to a secluded house nearby.

The house belongs to Jim Maddison (Paul Birch), a retired sea captain who knows much more about the capabilities of nuclear weapons and residual effects of atomic radiation than anyone might expect. Maddison once tugged target boats for the navy during a series of nuclear tests, and will never forget what he *saw* during those unnerving times. In his tiny refuge, a cabin nestled in the bottom of a deep valley, hidden from the irradiated wastes of New Earth, he monitors the entire range of short-wave radio frequencies, desperate to capture some other sign of life. But there is only static. Maddison's daughter Louise (Lori Nelson) tests the interior of the house with a Geiger counter. Some radioactivity has leaked inside, but not enough to kill them yet.

A succession of doomsday survivors come upon the Maddison house: Radek and Rick, Tony Lamont ("Touch" [Mike] Connors) and his striptease girlfriend Ruby (Adele Jergens), and an elderly gold prospector named Pete (Raymond Hatton), who arrives with his constant companion, Diablo (a burro). Jim doesn't want to let them in—there aren't enough supplies to go around—but Louise insists that as good Christians they are obliged to provide refuge to these lost souls from the poisoned world outside. Jim acquiesces and advises his unwelcome visitors to bathe and change into clean clothes as a safeguard against any radiation they may have absorbed. (Maddison apparently stocked up on clothing as well as food and fuel when he anticipated the coming of the Big Blast. There's no shortage of clean-pressed duds for everyone.)

Jim explains that although the outside world has been virtually destroyed, the people in his house have survived because the surrounding hills are full of lead-bearing ore, which acts as a barrier against radioactivity. A strong, steady wind blows through the gorges with enough velocity to keep the contamination away—but who knows how long the winds may last? And should it rain, the whole valley will be soaked with fallout from the heavens. There is also another potential threat to their well-being: mysterious "other forces," which Jim declines to describe at the moment.

Rick carries the debilitated Radek into one of the bedrooms. Although Radek seems to be close to death, he tells the geologist, "I thought I was going to die, but I'm not." Nodding, Rick assures him, "You'll be all right." He is ready to shrug off Radek's mutterings as those of a fevered, radiation-weakened brain, but Radek is already beginning to adapt to a strange, new kind of life. "I must have red meat, nearly raw. I don't know why, but it'll do me good." Rick doesn't know it yet, but Radek's metabolism is undergoing a radical metamorphosis; he is becoming the man of the future.

Jim seems to draw strength from Rick, who is young and determined to survive against all odds, even on a planet leveled by atomic despoliation. They become friends, and one evening Jim cautiously mentions his navy training and a group of test animals he once saw that had survived exposure to an H-bomb blast. The animals underwent a rapid metamorphosis, but Jim doesn't offer Rick any further details just now. In the distance is heard the baying of a coyote. "There's lots of game here now," muses Jim. "But it's contaminated. They started coming in a week ago, like this valley was Noah's Ark." This is the second allusion to a biblical legend (the first occurs during the opening narration).

Over the next two months, Tony develops a crush on Louise, who happens to have fallen in love with Rick. Jim realizes that the people in his house may represent the beginning of a new race. He urges Rick and Tony to consider marrying Louise and Ruby. The only problem is, Tony wants Louise, not Ruby. Old Pete, meanwhile, is interested only in continuing to prospect for his ever-elusive gold.

Each night Radek slips out of the house to hunt down wild game. One evening he traps a rabbit, but before he can eat it, a dark, massive shape lumbers into view, scaring him away. A metallic, triple-taloned claw reaches down to grab the carcass for itself.

The following day Rick and Jim discover the remains of the rabbit and test it for radioactivity. It tips the Geiger counter at 49 roentgen—enough to kill a normal human being. Rick thinks Radek ate the poisoned meat, but Jim isn't so sure. Rick surmises that if a man were somehow able to survive complete radioactive saturation, a thousand generation changes could take place in a matter of days. What would such a man look like?

Back at the house Jim tells Rick the rest of the story about the navy test animals. He shows Rick a series of drawings he made of the animals that survived the H-bomb blast. Each animal lived for three days in its altered state. What had been a chipmunk grew enormous fangs, scales, and horns; a dog also grew elongated fangs and horns. The third animal, a monkey, developed a third eye as well as a pair of rudimentary arms and hands depending from each shoulder, effectively making it a four-armed creature. Like the others, it was covered with metallic scales.* "That was Nature's answer to complete nuclear radiation," Jim explains, "a million years of evolution with one bomb."

When Rick and Jim make a check on the radiation density near the edge of the valley, they encounter a mutated man (Jonathan Haze) who bears an

*Paul Blaisdell drew the sketches seen in the film.

unnerving resemblance to Radek. Like Maddison's unwanted house guest, this man's bone structure is starting to change, and there are black, metallic scales growing up the sides of his neck. As he dies, he warns them that there are others, stronger than him, out beyond the valley walls. Later that night Radek mysteriously tells Rick, "There are wonderful things happening up there [beyond the ridge]." Rick discovers the skeleton of the mutated man the following morning. The flesh has been stripped off and eaten.

Louise complains to her father that she has been hearing voices, as if something has been calling to her telepathically. Later Jim discovers a trail of three-taloned footprints encircling the house. He and Rick decide to take turns keeping a watch on the house.

Late that night after everyone is asleep, Radek unties Diablo and leads the burro into the woods, intending to make a meal of him, but he is killed by the roaming mutant. When Rick and Jim find Radek's body, they notice deep puncture wounds in the throat. Jim believes that whatever it is they are fighting may have once been human.

Back at the house, Pete discovers that Diablo is missing. He goes mad and makes for the top of the ridge. Pete dies in the choking, radioactive vapors, knocking Jim, who has pursued him, unconscious with a blow from his walking stick. Jim remains on the perimeter of the valley, soaking up dangerous amounts of radiation, until Rick rescues him. During all the commotion, Tony grabs a kitchen knife and forces Louise outside, apparently intending to rape her. When Ruby sees what's happening, she intervenes, giving Louise an opportunity to escape. Enraged, Tony stabs Ruby and throws her body off a cliff. With Ruby out of the way, all he needs to do is get rid of Rick and Jim, and he can have Louise for his own.

In bed that night, Louise is roused by the mutant's telepathic call. She places a photograph of her boyfriend, Tommy (Roger Corman), next to her bed and then, as if in a trance, opens the bedroom window and climbs outside. As she is walking through the woods the mutant scoops her into his armor-plated arms.

Jim, now confined to a sickbed, asks Rick to check on Louise. He discovers her missing and sets out on a search, armed with a rifle from Jim's storeroom. Outside, he calls to Louise and the sound of his voice causes her to regain consciousness, still trapped in the mutant's arms. As they approach a miniature waterfall, the creature sets her down and moves nervously away, seemingly afraid of the fresh lake water. Instinctively, Louise backs into the lake and calls to Rick, who follows the sound of her voice. Seeing the creature hovering over Louise in the lake, Rick unloads several rounds of ammo into its hide, but the bullets just bounce off its armor-plating. He throws down the rifle and dives into the lake beside Louise.

At the house Jim hears a voice on the radio and realizes they aren't the only ones who have managed to survive the nuclear devestation. A clap of thunder

Marty the Mutant (Blaisdell) gazes longingly at Louise (Lori Nelson) during a lull in the action of *Day the World Ended* **(1956).**

heralds the coming of a rainstorm, and when the downpour begins, Jim tests a cupful of the rainwater and miraculously finds it free of contamination.

At the lake the mutant's skin begins to smoke as torrents of pure rainwater cascade off its radioactive flesh. The creature seeks shelter under a tree, but the storm is too great, and it perishes in the cleansing liquid. Rick and Louise climb out of the lake and head back to the house.

But Tony is planning to kill Rick and aims a revolver out the open window as he and Louise approach the house. With his last reserves of strength, Jim pulls out a gun from beneath his pillow and shoots Tony dead. Jim tells the young lovers about the voice on the radio, of the possibility of starting a new life over. "If that thing couldn't live, then neither could others of its kind," Rick theorizes. Any other nonhuman threats will soon perish as well.

Jim, his body weakened by radioactivity, expires. The following day Rick and Louise pack supplies in preparation for their new journey. Before leaving her family home forever, Louise turns the photograph of Tommy facedown beside her bed, perhaps never to realize it was his monstrously mutated form that had been calling to her telepathically and had then carried her off before being liquefied by the rainstorm.

Although it may not be obvious at first that the unseen boyfriend (who is named only once, in the opening scene when Paul Birch refers to him as "Tommy") is the three-eyed mutant seen in the film's climax, clues do exist in Lou Rusoff's script. Unfortunately, the rushed nature of low-budget filmmaking obscures what should be more apparent. What is not explained is how Tommy became trapped on the far side of the valley, where radioactivity is mutating all life-forms. The early reference to a plan to save three people—Jim Maddison, Louise, and Tommy—would seem to suggest that the boyfriend was thought to be close enough to the valley to be saved. Perhaps he even lived with the Maddisons.

Since the only time Tommy's human form is shown is when Louise looks at the framed photograph in her bedroom, budget-conscious Roger Corman eliminated the need of hiring a professional model or actor to pose as the boyfriend by taking a photograph of Lori Nelson and himself for the picture. It might have made more sense to photograph Paul Blaisdell standing next to Nelson, since Blaisdell in fact played the mutated Tommy. But who knows? Maybe Corman was feeling rather Hitchcockian that day.

Paul Blaisdell's monster outfit, which he nicknamed "Marty the Mutant," was the first in a long line of full-body costumes he manufactured during the 1950s that accentuated innovation rather than realism. For Corman's doomsday tale, Blaisdell was freed from the kind of pressures that had so constrained his contribution to *The Beast with a Million Eyes*, and consequently he was able to design a much more versatile movie monster. Instead of a miniature puppet or automaton thrust awkwardly at the camera lens during a harried and hurried climax, Blaisdell's three-eyed Atomic Mutant was a full-body suit manufactured to his own build. Although his creations for other science-fiction pictures would be even more impressive, Blaisdell's first life-size film monster gave 1955 audiences enough of a rise to generate invaluable word-of-mouth promotion for the film.

Long before the first frame of film was ever exposed, Blaisdell began working on a series of sketches of the mutant for executive producer Alex Gordon. Brainstorming sessions with scriptwriter Lou Rusoff opened up an entire line of thought on the creature's appearance and habits. According to Rusoff's story, the Mutant was originally a human being; therefore the monster had to be roughly humanoid in shape. (Those who argue that Blaisdell took the easy way out by making his creatures humanoid in appearance sometimes forget that when a script called for something truly different—as in the case of *It Conquered the World*, made several months later, or *Not of This Earth*, which followed in 1957—Blaisdell designed something remarkably different.)

In the details as they were worked out by Rusoff and Blaisdell, the Mutant's appearance was dictated by two important considerations: (1) radioactivity, which had to be the catalyst for changing a human being into a monster, and (2) environment, which determined the extent of those changes.

The more contaminated the air, food and water, the more severe the changes would be. Blaisdell later recalled: "I designed the three-eyed mutant on the basis of how such a creature might evolve as the result of atomic explosions, along with how the people in the house could avoid becoming mutants by maintaining themselves in a valley hidden from atomic radiation. Lou Rusoff managed to incorporate that idea into his story." For the "first-stage mutant" design—the degenerating human, Radek—Paul came up with a weblike makeup used to suggest a kind of spreading disease. Although he didn't actually apply the makeup materials, Blaisdell advised the production's makeup artist, Steven Clensos, how it could be done using a special liquid adhesive (the kind used to glue down false eyelashes) and ordinary dime-store glitter. The triple-orbed Atomic Mutant, of course, required quite a bit more work.

Blaisdell postulated that a man undergoing rapid mutation would develop a protective hide against the elements. Since radiation permeates flesh so easily, Paul decided to give his creature a scaly, almost reptilian "skin"—what the characters in the film refer to as armor plating. In addition to the tough outer hide, Paul thought that a person who was undergoing a profound physical change all the way down to the molecular level would change on the inside as well. "If someone were to actually survive the kind of effects described in the story, the entire body would have to change, not merely the skin and flesh," Blaisdell reflected. "Some parts of the body might be deformed, some other parts might be entirely new, specifically developed to deal with their new, radioactive world." Blaisdell envisioned a bulked-up body with the outer "skin" made of metallic scales which would protect the flesh and inner metabolism from further radiation-induced change.

To reflect the severity of bone deformation, Paul gave his mutant an elongated, bullet-shaped head and added cavernous ears, which like the head itself, stretched upward and tapered to a point. Because the mutant also developed extrasensory powers, strange projections from the cranium would be used to send and receive telepathic messages.

Besides the alterations and malformations generated by radiation, Blaisdell figured the body would also suffer some general deformations such as rotted teeth and the collapse of the nose bone. The gums would probably recede; eyes might be blasted from their sockets and replaced by new, larger orbs—possibly even an extra eye that would let the creature see in a kind of ultra 3-D. This supervision would be used to deal with all the new and unknown potential threats that would exist in this poisoned, irradiated world.

But the metamorphosis had to stop somewhere, and to suggest this idea Blaisdell envisioned a useless second set of arms growing from the shoulders. (In the earliest design sketches the monster sported tentaclelike outgrowths on the shoulders, waist, and kneecaps. The concept was dropped when it was determined there was no way to realistically manipulate the tentacles on camera.) These diminutive appendages would suffer a kind of arrested development because the body's bombardment by nuclear energy abruptly ceased after the last bomb was detonated. Thus the arms would stop growing before they were fully developed. (It also would have been much more difficult to play a four-limbed Mutant on camera.)

After the sketches were submitted to Alex Gordon, ARC initiated its long and sometimes circuitous approval process. According to Blaisdell, it probably took two or three weeks of consultations with Gordon, Lou Rusoff, Roger Corman, Jim Nicholson, and Sam Arkoff before the monster design satisfied everyone. When it was finally approved, the actual construction process began.

It took Paul and Jackie a little over four weeks to build the suit. (By contrast, it would take almost eight weeks to construct the more elaborate costume for *The She-Creature*.) Most of the monsters coming out of rival studios, such as Universal's "Gill Man" in the *Creature from the Black Lagoon* series, were crafted in spacious, well-stocked makeup and effects laboratories with solid monetary backing by the studio. Conditions were much different for Paul and Jackie Blaisdell. Their effects "lab" was their Topanga Canyon home. Supplies were purchased on an as-needed basis, and as often as not they had to make do with materials and methods that the Hollywood "big boys" probably would have scoffed at. When costumes were being made for young, low-budget outfits such as ARC, there were no assistants, no supply requisitions, no invoices to be turned over to a bookkeeping department. These things could make for rough going at times, but it was the kind of working environment that would beget a unique prosperity of its own, with dividends paid in pure imagination.

The process by which Paul Blaisdell created Marty the Mutant may seem bizarre in comparison to the way things are done today in even the lowest low-budget movie. But when Blaisdell first began making film monsters, there was no right or wrong way of creating the illusions for these pictures. Whatever worked was just fine. Blaisdell had no formal training in the art of molding and casting but relied on his own intuition and artistic sensibilities. The bottom line was all that mattered, and for Blaisdell the bottom line was that his techniques worked.

Keeping all this in mind, it may not sound so strange that Blaisdell built his first life-size monster suit over an ordinary pair of long johns. Paul occasionally utilized the most mundane materials to finish the task at hand, like the rubber lizards' tails that ended up masquerading as antennae on his Beast with a Million Eyes. For *Day the World Ended*, the snugness and flexibility of a pair of long johns meant that the material would assure a good fit and that the finished costume would be articulated in all the right spots. And as a bonus, it would allow for ready ventilation.

Work began on the costume with Paul and Jackie cutting pieces of block foam rubber into small, half-moon shapes. Once painted and fitted into place, these would become the "armor plates" of the Mutant's scaly hide. The foam rubber chunks were glued directly onto the long johns using contact bond cement, which sealed the materials together as well as any kind of modern household "super glue." The plates were arranged in rows to emulate a lizard's skin and were colored varying shades of brown. The chest and shoulder areas were built up with larger pieces of block foam. Deep ridges were gouged out of the material to give the monster's hide a rough, pock-marked appearance.

Blaisdell kept a quantity of different size scissors on hand to cut and trim the block foam to whatever shape or size he needed. Although this was the first time he had worked with such a large quantity of foam rubber, it wouldn't be the last: this material formed the basis of almost every one of his creations, from Marty the Mutant to the Ghost of Dragstrip Hollow. Eventually, Blaisdell became so adept at working with block foam he was able to cut the material into virtually any shape and thickness he desired with minimal effort. He got so good at creating rounded edges and curves that later creations like the She-Creature took on a surprisingly naturalistic look. (It looked less like a costume and more like a sculpted form.)

Marty's claws were actually a customized pair of commercially available monster claws purchased at the same magic supply shop where Blaisdell had discovered the rubber lizards. By covering the gloves with chunks of block foam which had been cut and painted to match the look of Marty's torso, Blaisdell was able to disguise the origin of the claws. He carved fingernails out of soft white pine, painted them bone-white, and cemented them into place over the painted nails on the gloves. He did the same thing with the lower extremities, using a pair of "monster feet" manufactured by the same company, which were customized in the same way.

To suggest an interrupted mutation of the creature's biological system, Blaisdell attached a pair of diminutive arms, also carved from block foam, to each shoulder. These were painted with an airbrush and highlighted with streaks of light and dark shading. Long white fingernails were added to each of the tiny hands.

The tentacles on the shoulders, waist and knees of the original mutant design were eliminated, and a bony horn was instead added to each kneecap—a design element that would reappear in *The She-Creature* a year later. The headpiece was almost identical to the original blueprint with its elongated, bullet-shaped skull, pointed ears, and upthrust horns. Blaisdell began the mask-making process by painting a rubber latex skin over a bust of his face which Jackie had sculpted some years before. Once enough layers of latex had been applied to form a thick base, it was carefully peeled away to become what Blaisdell referred to as a blank—the starting point for the actual monster mask. As a precautionary measure, the headpiece was constructed over an army helmet liner, which allowed Blaisdell to secure the mask under his chin during filming so it would not slip out of alignment with the enormous dimensions of the body suit.

Using individual pieces of block foam rubber cut to shape, Blaisdell slowly built up the facial features of the mutant. The cheekbones and brow were heavily exaggerated, and the sides of the head were given a full, rounded look. Foam rubber was also used to build up the cranium. Once all the foam pieces had been applied, Blaisdell painted a second latex skin over the entire head. Holes were cut out to allow for breathing and for the insertion of plastic eyes and teeth. Serving as the three large eyes were plastic spheres obtained from the same company that supplied materials to Paul during the making of *The Beast with a Million Eyes*. As he had done when designing Little Hercules, Blaisdell painted the pupils directly onto the plastic. To offset the brown color scheme of the body Blaisdell gave the mutant bright green irises.* Each eyeball was then slotted into the mask just beneath the brow. (Although it wasn't in Marty the Mutant's repertoire of tricks, blinking eyes were a fairly early innovation in Blaisdell's movie monster career. The effect was originated for *The She-Creature*, but was not used on camera until 1959, when the effect was finally seen in *The Ghost of Dragstrip Hollow*.)

Teeth were an even simpler matter. By using several sets of commercially available fangs (the plastic kind sold in many stores at Halloween), Blaisdell was able to piece together a formidable set of choppers. The long canines were removed from each set with an X-Acto knife, and the remainder of the teeth were cemented into place inside the mutant's mouth. It took three sets of fangs to produce the single row of pointed teeth seen in the finished costume.

Blaisdell added thin, elflike ears to either side of the head. Like the other facial features, the ears were first modeled in clay and the resultant positive mold served as the basis for separate foam rubber and latex pieces. The latex was painted dark brown and highlighted with streaks of black to provide a sense of depth. To make the telepathic horns which jutted out from the monster's forehead, Blaisdell used candles which were slowly heated and bent into the desired shape. After the candles cooled and rehardened, they were coated with multiple layers of latex and allowed to dry. When the latex was peeled off, Blaisdell had two hollow rubber tubes which he stuffed with cotton to prevent their collapsing. A thin wire was pushed through the cotton to further fortify their shape, and they were glued into place on the mask and airbrushed to match the main color scheme.

Blaisdell also fashioned a neckpiece for the creature costume. Not seen in the finished film, the neckpiece served as a kind of flap, fitting under the

---

*Although these films were made in black and white, Blaisdell gave each of his creations a unique color scheme to make them more lifelike. "It was also good for morale," Blaisdell said, though he neglected to mention whose morale he had in mind—the film crew's or his own.

neck opening of the body suit and helping conceal portions of Blaisdell's anatomy not already hidden by the suit's prodigious shoulder extensions. Although the film's monster scenes were kept to a minimum until the very end of the picture, Paul wanted the full-body suit to appear as realistic as possible under the studious eye of Jock Feindel's camera, which is why he went to such lengths to insure the integrity of the costume.

Paul was not a big individual. He stood between 5'7" and 5'8" and therefore needed to construct all his monsters in such a way as to make them seem much taller. To achieve this effect with Marty the Mutant, he made the mask much larger than normal, which allowed him to look out of the open mouth, instead of the eyes. This padded the creature's height by as much as eight inches, bringing the final measurement of the full costume to over six feet. Although the suit could get unbearably hot under the photo floodlamps, the extra-wide dimensions of the head provided Blaisdell with plenty of breathing room and helped conceal his face with shadows. He also wore sunglasses during the filming to make certain the camera would not pick up a pair of human eyes staring out of the creature's mouth.

ARC co-chief Sam Arkoff worried that Blaisdell was taking too long getting the costume ready. In his book *Flying Through Hollywood by the Seat of My Pants* (1992, Birch Lane Press), Arkoff claims that Blaisdell actually fell behind schedule and failed to deliver the suit on time. As Arkoff also tells the story that the monster in *The Beast with a Million Eyes* was nothing more than "an $8 teakettle," it's a bit difficult to take him at his word—especially since Paul Blaisdell has said repeatedly that all his movie props were invariably delivered on time and within the agreed-upon budget. Blaisdell's pal Bob Burns supports that claim, and since no one else has ever indicated otherwise, it may be that Arkoff's memory has grown a bit hazy 40 years after the fact.

Arkoff also claimed that ARC originally hired a seven foot tall actor to play the part of the mutant, but that Blaisdell intentionally designed the costume to fit only his own build. While it is true that Blaisdell built his monster costumes to match his own dimensions, he did this knowing well beforehand that he would be playing the monster. (The single exception was *It! the Terror from Beyond Space*, which was made for United Artists, not ARC/AIP.) In his book, Arkoff almost makes it sound as if Blaisdell conspired to force ARC to give him the role of the mutant at the expense of the other (unnamed) actor in some kind of devious, underhanded fashion. It's perhaps significant that no one else has been able to confirm Arkoff's version of events in this instance. In any event Blaisdell continued to play the on-screen role of the monsters he created for American-International in every future film he made for the company.

Day the World Ended was filmed on a ten-day schedule, which included seven days of interiors and three days of location shooting. Roger Corman was interested in playing up the psychological suspense elements of the story created by throwing together a diverse collection of characters under trying and unusual circumstances. Imprisoned in a small house by events over which they had no control, these people would be driven to rape, murder, madness, and even suicide. Since the mutant didn't really figure in the action until late in the picture, Corman had ample opportunity to explore all the relationships he wanted. Unfortunately, Rusoff's script was heavily burdened by stereotypes, and none of the characters had much room (or time) to develop beyond their immediate purpose in the story.

Another inhibiting factor was the film's length. At 78 minutes there was barely enough time to tell the story in the most straightforward fashion possible, let alone trying to tackle lofty characterizations and suspense dramatics. Corman did shoot bits of footage that seemed to be deliberate attempts at poignancy (Ruby's striptease act, Rick's monologue about a brother who died after studying for the priesthood, for instance), but they are rather clumsily staged and too obvious. The dialogue also tells us how ironic the characters' situations are instead of letting viewers formulate that opinion on their own. Although these efforts demonstrate that Corman was willing to add a little spice to his science-fiction salad, he hadn't sufficiently developed as a director to pull it off just yet. (By the time of his next science-fiction picture, made less than a year later, his talents had improved tremendously.)

Day the World Ended maintains an appropriately claustrophobic feel, which is heightened by the film's cramped staging and flat lighting and Corman's extended use of medium shots and close-ups. Even when Jock Feindel's camera is roaming outdoors, the film exudes a choking, oppressive atmosphere. Part of this overbearing sense of stagnation and wretchedness is a result of the constrained location shoot, which involved filming under rather inauspicious conditions at the Sportman's Lodge Restaurant on Ventura Boulevard in the San Fernando Valley. Behind the restaurant was a small, lagoonlike pond kept well-stocked with fish which were served fresh to customers who ordered dinner entrees from the seafood menu. This pond stood in for the uncontaminated lake of Rusoff's story.

The problem was that Corman and his crew were only allowed to film there when the restaurant wasn't serving its clientele. Since Sportsman's Lodge did not have a lunch menu, Corman was allowed to use the location for most of the day, as long as the crew cleared out well before the dinner hour. A single morning and afternoon of filming had to suffice for shooting not only the girls' waterfall bath and Rick's wooing of Louise while she senses the mutant nearby, but most of the climax of the picture as well, including scenes of Paul Blaisdell in his monster outfit. There was little time to plan particulars; it was basically a "point the camera and shoot" situation. This resulted in a lot of medium close-ups and tight framing shots, which actually help underscore the sense of claustrophobia viewers share with the characters in the story as their world is reduced to a meager shadow of its former glory.

Corman shot another two days of locations at Griffith Park and Bronson Canyon, a favorite location of filmmakers shooting low-budget science-fiction and horror films during the 1950s. It was here that Blaisdell, on camera in full monster regalia, absconded with Lori Nelson and almost broke his ankle when he lost his balance while carrying her. According to the script, Louise would be abducted while wandering in a trancelike state outside the Maddison house. The mutant was to carry her toward the irradiated ridge (perhaps he intends to expose her to the radioactivity so she will mutate into the same kind of creature he has become). Because Paul had built the costume nearly a head taller than he was himself, he would have to lift Lori up almost to his chin just to make it look like the mutant was carrying her at normal chest height. To make sure things would go as smoothly as possible, Paul and Lori discussed the scene beforehand and worked out exactly how to perform the actions required in order to get the scene done in one take. They decided that Lori would take a swing at Paul and lock her arm around the neck of the costume in the process. That would give Blaisdell enough leverage to lift her easily.

When it was time for the cameras to roll, Blaisdell sauntered up to the actress and waited for her to do her thing, but she never did. Maybe she forgot. While a puzzled Roger Corman looked on, Paul struggled with the cumbersome monster suit, doing his darnedest to lift the 105-lb. actress up to his chin without toppling over backward in the process. He silently congratulated himself when he managed to get her off the ground and realized he was still standing up.

Blaisdell didn't stand up for long, however. He started joking with Lori, growling about how no one understood monsters and just generally tickling her funny bone. She started giggling, so he kept it up. "You know, underneath this costume I'm actually completely naked." She laughed again, harder, and every time she laughed after that she bounced against the monster's foam rubber chest, knocking Paul off balance. About to lose his already precarious grip, he warned her they might have to take a tumble. It was possible he would even fall on her. For some reason that seemed even funnier, and Lori let out one big guffaw. She rocked against Blaisdell's foam rubber chest, pushing him backwards. One of the mutant feet popped off, taking Paul's sneaker with it. That felt really peculiar, and he started hobbling around, trying to regain his balance, but it was too late. Down they went, with Lori falling on top of him. Neither of them was hurt, but as Lori continued to giggle, she kept bouncing up and down on the monster's rubber hide. Paul was afraid the material was going to rip (which is one reason why Jackie always kept a supply of contact cement handy during film shoots).

Corman caught enough of the action on film to be able to piece the scene together during editing, so the crew assembled for the next shot. Roger had decided he wanted to include a shot of the monster swatting away bullets that the hero is firing at it from point-blank range. He called Richard Denning and Blaisdell aside and explained just what it was he wanted. Blaisdell thought the idea was ridiculous and said so. "It's going to look like he's swatting at flies," he warned. "Well, I'm the director," Corman reminded Blaisdell. They ended up shooting the scene exactly as Corman had wanted. Sure enough, it looked like the mutant was swatting at flies. Corman kept the shot in the film anyway.

After the monster releases his human quarry at the lake, a rainstorm kicks into high gear, sounding the monster's death knell. Although the encounter with Rick and Louise was filmed at the Sportsman's Lodge Restaurant, Blaisdell's death scene was shot at Griffith Park. The crew hooked up a set of water sprinklers which were used to simulate falling rain. Corman instructed Blaisdell, "Okay, Paul, you go stagger around that tree and then, after getting nice and wet, fall over and die." It sounded simple enough, and once the camera was rolling Blaisdell performed the required action without a hitch.

At the last minute Corman decided to add a disintegration effect. While Paul remained prone on the water-soaked ground, the crew ran a hose up the leg of his costume and hooked the other end to a portable fog machine. When Corman called "Action!" they began pumping fog into the suit. Corman thought the effect looked pretty nifty as the smoke slowly leaked out of the suit, but inside, Paul was beginning to get claustrophobic. The crew was pumping him so full of fog he couldn't see out the mouthpiece. Not only that, but water from the sprinkler system had gotten into the suit and was combining with the special effects fog, making it difficult to breathe.

After a few minutes, Blaisdell realized he was in trouble. By now there was so much water in the suit he could barely move. Every time he tried to sit up, the weight of the water-logged rubber held him back. That, coupled with not being able to see because of the special effects fog, caused him to panic, which made things even worse. He began waving his claws around wildly—the only part of his anatomy he could still lift. Every time his arm hit the ground the suit belched out another poof of smoke. Corman thought that looked good. "Keep it up, Paul!"

Sensing that something was not quite right, Jackie, who was watching all this from the sidelines, said, "I think something's wrong with my husband." Finally somebody realized that Blaisdell might really be in trouble. Members of the crew scurried over to help him to his feet. As they pulled him to an upright position, the accumulated water in the suit rushed to the bottom and gushed out the legs. *This probably looks pretty damned indecent,* Blaisdell thought, but at that point he didn't much care. When they finally got his mask off, a huge cloud of fog billowed out around his head, creating a kind of halo effect. He wasn't feeling very angelic, however. Smoke was still coming out of his hair 20 minutes later.

Alex Gordon remembered the *Day the World Ended* shoot as a particularly uneventful one. "We only had a few problems," he said. "It was a little difficult for Paul to see at times because he was a fairly short man and he had made the monster suit so big, and occasionally one of the hands would drop off; but other than that everything worked out fine. Paul was invaluable to us. He always gave a hundred percent. He made all of AIP's best monsters."

After the film was finished, ARC's still photographer, Bill Clarey, took some special promotional photos of Blaisdell in his Atomic Mutant getup. Paul grabbed Lori Nelson, and together they did a "soft shoe" dance routine which Clarey captured on 35mm film. That photograph became a favorite memento of Paul's Hollywood days, and he treasured it for many years afterward.

To drum up publicity for the film, Arkoff and Nicholson thought it would be a neat idea to send Marty the Mutant out on a press tour. Theaters that were running ARC's first double feature were shipped the costume for display. (*Day the World Ended's* cofeature, *The Phantom from 10,000 Leagues*, was a Woolner Bros. production from a Lou Rusoff script about a radioactive undersea monster. Woolner Bros. had approached Blaisdell to build its Phantom, but he turned down the offer.)

Most theater managers set up Marty in their lobby, where curious ticket-buyers reached out to wiggle the antennae and tug at the scales, dislodging them by the fistful. The scales became souvenirs for greedy moviegoers who thought the purchase price of a ticket entitled them to a genuine Hollywood monster movie artifact. When it was returned to Blaisdell weeks later, the costume was in tatters. He later recalled: "'Marty' was shipped all over the U.S. to publicize *Day the World Ended* in theater marquees. He would get damaged and they'd ship him back to me and I'd repair him, repack him, and reship him. The last time he was shipped back to me from Chicago, I did the repairs and reshipped him. After that he went to Hong Kong, and after that nobody could ever figure out where he finally ended up. For all I know, he's in a Buddist temple somewhere in Mongolia." It was the first and last time Blaisdell allowed one of his creations to be so mishandled by movie promoters.

Although the ARC double bill opened in January 1956 to mostly lukewarm reviews, both pictures ended up making a respectable profit. *Variety* noted that *Day the World Ended* "packs enough novelty in its plot theme to carry off its horror chores satisfactorily, even though imagination runs away with the subject at times and the dialogue is inclined to be static and the direction slow-paced." But sci-fi fans of the days had few complaints, lining up for blocks during the early months of 1956 to see the world come to a rather nasty conclusion. Super-alert fans might have spotted the Atomic Mutant again several years later in Roger Corman's *Teenage Caveman*. (No new footage

Marty the Mutant does a soft-shoe routine with costar Lori Nelson during a break in the filming of *Day the World Ended.* **This photograph was one of Paul Blaisdell's favorites (courtesy of Bob Burns).**

of Marty the Mutant was shot, however; Roger merely spliced in a clip of the monster from *Day the World Ended.*)

Once the film rental profits started pouring in, Alex Gordon became interested in continuing *Day*'s storyline and signed Richard Denning to appear in a follow-up. But the sequel never materialized, and Gordon and Denning eventually moved on to other projects. "Touch" Connors, who received a total of $400 for his role in the picture, continued to work for Alex Gordon and Roger Corman and eventually returned to oppose Paul Blaisdell in *Voodoo Woman*.

Before that could happen, however, Corman had set his sights on another global threat. Only this time, instead of world obliteration via nuclear weapons, there would be world domination via a grandiose Venusian vegetable.

4

Venusian Vegetable

I told them, I pleaded with them not to have It chase anyone. The script said It was supposed to stay on a rock shelf in a cave. The actors were supposed to come to It.

— *Paul Blaisdell*

In November 1955, James Nicholson and Sam Arkoff opened up new ARC offices on Sunset Boulevard in Los Angeles. By now the company had arranged lucrative deals with exhibitors across the country, as well as in Montreal and England. As profits continued to climb, Nicholson, feeling bullish, announced a slate of new film titles scheduled for release throughout 1956 and 1957. At last ARC was beginning to think in terms of years instead of months.

One of the company's newest double bills was *The Female Jungle* and *Oklahoma Woman*. The former was an actionless whodunit helmed by Bruno VeSota, who also appears in a minor role in the cofeature. VeSota, a pedestrian director hampered by budgets that were invariably tighter than Corman's, often took on acting assignments during the 1950s and was a better actor than he was a director. He is most recognizable as Dave the shopkeeper, married to a scheming Yvette Vickers in Bernard L. Kowalski's *Attack of the Giant Leeches* (1959). *The Female Jungle* was a "pick-up" for ARC. It had been financed by Burt Keiser, who tried to sell it to Paramount and Allied Artists — neither of whom wanted it — and eventually ended up offering it to Nicholson and Arkoff. The film is most notable for featuring Jayne Mansfield in a leading role.

Peggie Castle played the title role in *Oklahoma Woman*, Roger Corman's third Western following *Five Guns West* and *Apache Woman*. Lou Rusoff, who was by this time becoming something of a permanent fixture around the ARC offices, scripted the film, which featured *Day the World Ended* alumni Richard Denning, "Touch" Connors, Jonathan Haze, and Paul Blaisdell. Instead of creating a costume or rigging up special effects, Blaisdell appeared in a minor role in *Oklahoma Woman* as one of Peggie Castle's henchmen. It was one of his very few straight acting roles. He had no lines.

Soon after the release of ARC's Western double feature Nicholson and Arkoff decided to change the name of the company. After all, they weren't just releasing motion pictures any more, they were making them. So early in 1956, the American Releasing Corporation became American International Pictures (AIP). One of the first films to come out under the new AIP banner was a science-fiction-monster movie.

Like many other films produced by ARC/AIP, the title of the new picture was conceived by American International president Jim Nicholson. Nicholson was a science-fiction fan from way back—he had worked with *Famous Monsters'* editor Forry Ackerman on a sci-fi fanzine when the two were in high school—and he enjoyed getting involved in the nuts and bolts of AIP's monster movies. Nicholson got in touch with Paul Blaisdell to discuss the creature that Paul would be building for AIP's new movie.

Although the general design of the monster would be left to Blaisdell, Nicholson said he wanted "something that no one had ever seen before, something that was really different." Blaisdell wanted just a couple of particulars before he started work on the new creature: what was the monster required to do in the movie and where did it come from? Nicholson replied that according to the script Lou Rusoff was working on, it came from the planet Venus. And as for what it did, that was evident from the movie's title, *It Conquered the World.*

Like many other youngsters who grew up in the 1930s, 1940s and 1950s, Blaisdell had seen lots of science-fiction movie serials and had read lots of Buck Rogers and Flash Gordon stories in the pulps, which paved the way for his interest in astronomy. As he got older, he began checking out books on the subject from his local library and spent quite a bit of time reading up on the cosmos. Paul told Jim Nicholson that the current thinking about the planet Venus was that it was hot, humid, and probably quite misty—the kind of environment that was not all that conducive to animal life. If something were actually to grow there, it would probably be along the lines of vegetation or plant life. Using that idea as his jumping-off point, he promised Nicholson he would develop something "truly unique" for AIP's new science-fiction picture.

At home Blaisdell worked out a theoretical plan for the development of a superintelligent Venusian mushroom. The belief about the physiognomy of Venus at that time led him to envision a creature that would develop slowly over many eons in the darkness and dampness of an alien world. In lieu of animal life, a mushroom or fungus might develop a kind of rudimentary intelligence that would grow exponentially until it eventually achieved self-awareness. Once that happened, it would realize that its physical limitations severely restricted its ability to conduct direct action. It would move (when it moved at all) like a perambulating plant. Because it could not go very far or fast, Nature would provide such a creature with the ability to produce

Paul Blaisdell's miniature sculpture of the perambulating mushroom from *It Conquered the World*. The original design was more rounded and squat, but still significantly larger than a human being (courtesy of Bob Burns).

offspring that could move quickly and conduct direct action for its parent whenever it needed.

Following this outline, Blaisdell's superintelligent mushroom became an asexual creature that could give birth to small, flying, batlike creatures which Blaisdell dubbed "Flying Fingers." He built a ten-inch model of the monster mushroom and showed it to Jim Nicholson. Nicholson loved it. "You've done it again, Paul," the AIP prexy exclaimed. "There's never been anything like this!" Although the model actually looked a little different from the final design (the model was more squat), Nicholson thought it was going to make a terrific film monster. Unfortunately, by the time Roger Corman got through with it, "It" would generate more titters than terror.

Lou Rusoff developed the screenplay for *It Conquered the World* around ideas already hammered out during a meeting between Blaisdell, Nicholson, and himself. It was a pretty straightforward invasion-from-space story, one of the two science-fiction plots Hollywood seemed stuck on using at the time. (The other was the monster-created-by-radiation shtick.) Compared to the characters Rusoff created for *Day the World Ended*, those of *It Conquered the World* were more realistically drawn, the dialogue was much less hackneyed, and the action was tight and as logical as it could be within the confines of a science-fiction script.

To be fair, however, Rusoff didn't do it alone. Although he was given sole credit for the screenplay in the film's credit crawl, according to American International's own pressbook, Charles B. Griffith coauthored *It Conquered the World*. Some sources claim that the script was more Griffith's work than it was Rusoff's. Griffith had come to Hollywood shortly after graduating from military school. He began writing television scripts, but none of his scripts ever got produced. His pal Jonathan Haze, who was already working for Roger Corman, showed several of Griffith's scripts to the producer-director, who was impressed enough to hire Griffith to write a Western, *Gunslinger*. He eventually became one of Corman's favorite scriptwriters.

When Corman read Rusoff's script for *It Conquered the World* he found it disjointed and confusing, and he sent it to Griffith with a message asking for a rewrite. According to Griffith, Rusoff's brother was dying in Canada at the time he composed the screenplay and that undoubtedly impacted on his work. Griffith rewrote the script from scratch in three days.

The story begins with a mystery: why are U.S.-launched satellites exploding in their own orbits? According to crackpot physicist Tom Anderson (Lee Van Cleef), there is an alien intelligence sequestered in the blackness of outer space that monitors our terrestrial activities constantly. They want to make certain we puny humans don't screw up the cosmos as we have our own little planet; ergo, they are destroying our every attempt at extraterrestrial exploration. In a meeting with Secretary of Defense Platt (Marshall Bradford) and General Tomlinson (David McMann), Anderson tries his best to convince the government to shut down its space program, but he's too late. The newest satellite is being readied for liftoff as they speak.

Despite Anderson's warnings, everything seems to go well with the launch and the satellite remains in orbit for three months. Anderson's friend and colleague Dr. Paul Nelson (Peter Graves) and his wife, Joan (Sally Fraser), join Tom and his wife, Claire (Beverly Garland), for dinner one evening. While Nelson crows about the success of the U. S. space program (he's in charge of the satellite installation), Anderson begins dropping hints about something much more important that he is in charge of, right here in his own home. Against Claire's wishes (she thinks her husband is dangerously close to going off the deep-end), Tom unveils a radio-telescope setup he has built which allows him to listen to signals from the planet Venus. Nelson is unimpressed. "We've bounced signals off the moon, why not Venus?" he snorts. But Anderson explains that beyond the static is a voice, a voice from the stars.

The phone rings; it's the space installation with a message for Nelson: the satellite has vanished from its radars. As he and Joan prepare to leave, Nelson tells Anderson, "I don't like what you're thinking." In their car outside Joan comments, "I always knew Tom was a little 'off,' but tonight he went too far." (But Joan was in the kitchen with Claire when Tom was talking to Paul about the Venusian voice. Did director Roger Corman forget something here?)

General Pattick (Russ Bender) arrives at the installation to confer with Nelson's team of scientists, Pete Shelton (uncredited screenplay coauthor Charles B. Griffith), Ellen Peters (Karen Kadler), and Floyd Mason (Paul Harbor). None of them can offer a reasonable explanation why the satellite disappeared from the radar trackers, but by the time Nelson arrives it has reappeared and reestablished its usual orbit. Nelson believes the equipment might be faulty, but to be absolutely certain, they will have to bring the satellite down and recheck the instrumentation.

Meanwhile, Anderson is conversing with his Venusian "friend," who responds to questions with unintelligible beeps and blips. (Are we to believe that Anderson can decipher this gibberish on the spot? Has he memorized a decoding key?) He excitedly tells Claire, "He drew the satellite to his world, and now he's back, within an hour!" (This is some all-powerful alien.) Claire, who obviously thinks her husband has become totally delusional, pleads with him to come to bed. "You'll feel better in the morning," she promises. For someone as brilliant as Anderson is supposed to be (Paul Nelson refers to him as "a genius" in an early scene), Tom is blithely unaware of Claire's opinion that he's in need of psychiatric help. He elects to sleep by his radio wave equipment in case there are any incoming messages during the night.

The following day the satellite crew attempts to guide the craft back to Earth safely, but it begins behaving erratically. General Pattick warns, "Don't experiment with it! Send it back up!" But it's too late: the satellite explodes before control can be regained. Moments later Anderson receives a communication on his own equipment. The alien has survived the crash and is less than ten miles south of the town of Beechwood. Anderson is ecstatic, but Claire chides him, "You're a sick man, Tom." He ignores her. "The whole world's sick, darling, but that's all over now." Tom believes the alien has made the journey to Earth to "rescue Mankind from itself."

Lumbering through the brush at the crash site, the alien uses its antennae to send out invisible waves which disrupt all forms of energy. All at once clocks run down, telephone and telegraph lines lapse into silence, engines die (there's an amusing shot of a forklift lapsing into inactivity as the operator none too subtly lets go of his control stick), and TV and radio stations go off the air.

Like everyone else, Paul and Joan find themselves stranded when their car dies en route to the installation. A horrendous whining from above rivets their attention on the sky, and they watch helplessly as a small airplane crashes into a ravine, killing the pilot. "We may be needed as witnesses," says Paul. They decide to hike to Tom's house to report the incident.

At home, Anderson provides the alien with the identities of the key citizens of Beechwood: Mayor Townsend, Chief of Police N. J. Schallert (Taggart Casey), General Pattick, and Paul Nelson. Along with their wives, this makes a total of eight persons the alien intends to put under mental lock and key. It begins producing batlike offspring which implant control devices in their victims' necks. But like a bee, once they've stung their target, they die. Furthermore, there is the implication (conveyed by several lines of dialogue, though never explicitly stated) that the control bats are programmed, in a fashion, to target a specific individual and can't be used on anyone else.

A creeping terror is slowly spreading through the town of Beechwood. Claire narrowly avoids getting caught up in mob violence. She finds Tom being accosted by a fellow who blames him for the sudden eruption of martial law mentality that the city's leaders are using to control the populace. Tom dodges his assailant's attack and jumps into his car—the town's only functioning automobile—to head for home. On the way he explains to Claire that Beechwood has been selectively "de-energized." With a shudder Claire realizes Tom has been telling the truth all along and that he has the potential to become a dangerous and powerful ally of the Venusian invader.

General Pattick leaves the satellite installation on foot. Moments later he is attacked by one of the Flying Fingers and becomes a slave to the will of the alien. When he returns to the installation, Pattick tells the staff that they have been caught in the midst of a Communist uprising. He orders Sgt. Neil (Dick Miller) to assemble his men and set up camp to the east, where they are to observe any unusual activity. Little does Sgt. Neil know that Pattick is sending the troops on a wild goose chase to keep them out of the way while the alien does its dirty work.

When Paul and Joan arrive at Anderson's home, Tom assures them there is a method to the alien's madness. This creature, he insists, has come to Earth to help mankind, not harm it. Paul isn't sure he believes everything Tom is telling him about this thing he keeps calling a "benefactor"; his natural inclination is one of caution. Tom admits to a feeling of triumph—after all, he has been predicting these very events for years. Paul resents Tom's blind devotion to the invader; he feels that his friend is being misled, but Tom refuses to discuss the matter.

Paul asks for a ride to the satellite installation, but Tom tells him that, like everything else in Beechwood, the lab has become totally inoperative. Instead, he offers the Nelsons a ride home. While Joan and Paul walk outside to the car, Tom relays a message to the alien: "Trace the energy from the car. It will lead you to Nelson's home. He's difficult, but his mind is of the utmost value." In spite of its strange requests and demands, Tom honestly believes the alien is a benevolent creature and friend of mankind.

From their living room window, Joan and Paul watch fearfully as panic creeps through the streets of Beechwood. Paul tells Joan to keep the doors and windows locked while he ventures outside to see what he can learn, but as soon as he grabs a bicycle and leaves the house, Joan is stung by one of the Venusian's Flying Fingers.

On his way to the installation, Paul watches Chief of Police Shallert (who has been controlled) gun down Edgar Haskell, owner of the local newspaper, for refusing to follow evacuation procedures. When Paul demands an explanation, Shallert cryptically refers to orders and tries to place Nelson under protective custody. Paul fights his way free and makes his way to the installation, which he finds locked and apparently abandoned. General Pattick suddenly appears and offers Nelson a ride back to Beechwood—a tip-off that Pattick has been controlled. (The audience already knows this but Nelson does not.) When Paul notices a metallic wire attached to the back of Pattick's neck, he realizes that everything Tom Anderson has been telling him is true. He knocks Pattick unconscious and commandeers the jeep, then drives to Tom's house to try and reason with him.

But Tom isn't ready to give up his dream. He explains to Paul how he paved the way for the alien to come to Earth. The creature is one of only nine surviving members of a race of beings that was "born too soon" amid the eruptions and gases of the primordial planet Venus. What is readily apparent to Paul—that the alien is an opportunistic creature using its intellect to woo Tom into helping it escape a dying world—is anathema to Tom, who rationalizes the orchestration of recent events (such as the herding of the townsfolk into the desert and the controlling of minds by the Flying Fingers) as unfortunate temporary byproducts of a new world order that will ultimately benefit mankind. A disgusted Paul Nelson leaves Tom's house determined to find a way to thwart the alien's plans on his own.

But things worsen rapidly. The invader cuts the power to the jeep, forcing Paul to return home on the bicycle. By then, Joan has become possessed. In one of the film's best sequences, Joan greets her husband and offers him a present—one of the Flying Fingers, which flutters away from her outstretched hands as she chillingly comments, "I'm going for a walk. When I get back you'll feel much better." In her absence Paul manages to kill the little creature and almost immediately the telephone rings: it's Tom, who claims he wants to apologize and invites Paul back to his house to talk things over. "Joan's car will run," he offers—a hideous reminder that Paul's wife has shed her humanity forever. Paul accepts the invitation, but before he can leave there is something he must do. He must kill Joan.

The alien has actually ordered Tom to murder his best friend. As Tom explains to Claire, Paul is one of four persons on the list of key people who were not placed under mind control. The others—General Tomlinson, the mayor, and the mayor's wife—were all killed in the crush of the evacuation. Rather than see Paul die at the hands of his best friend, Claire suggests using one of the remaining attack bats to infect him, but Tom explains that they have in fact already been used on the members of Paul's own scientific staff.

The alien is unable to manufacture any more control devices for at least another week—too long a time to allow Paul to live. Outraged by the alien's command to her husband to kill his own best friend, Claire switches on Tom's transmitting equipment and tells the creature she is going to find and kill it.

When Paul arrives, Claire slips out a side door and drives Tom's car to the cave where the alien is hiding. Oblivious to his wife's absence, Tom admits to Paul for the first time that certain doubts are clouding his mind. Grabbing at this unexpected opportunity, Paul launches into a tirade, steamrolling over Tom's objections in the process with his observation that this creature from a dying planet is nothing more than an alien conquistador, an emotionless being who has preyed on Tom's emotions and desire to help his own race simply to further its own nefarious ends.

Meanwhile, armed with her husband's rifle, Claire explores the convoluted passageways of the cave, determined to destroy the creature that has ruined her marriage and her life. When she sees the huge, conical shape of the beast shuddering to life out of the dank shadows of the cave, she falters momentarily, then cocks the rifle and fires.

But the bullets are ineffective. With arced, razor-edged pincers, "It" reaches out to Claire's neck and drags her down, as she screams hideously.

Claire's screams reach Tom through the transmitting equipment which Claire has inadvertently left on. Here at last is incontrovertible proof that the alien is not what it says it is. When Tom hears the creature mauling his wife, he finally admits the reality of the situation. With Paul's help, he plots to take out the humans serving the alien and then crush the creature itself.

Tom drops Paul off at the satellite installation. Inside, General Pattick, Pete Shelton, and Floyd Mason—who have murdered fellow scientist Ellen Peters—are plotting the overthrow of the American government. Paul opens fire with his pistol, killing Shelton and Mason but only wounding Pattick, who manages to escape in one of the installation's jeeps.

Meanwhile, Tom almost runs straight into Chief of Police Schallert, who has parked his cruiser in the road to block the only entrance to Elephant Hot Springs, where the alien is hiding. Ducking his gunfire, Tom circles through the woods and sneaks up behind Schallert, setting him afire with a blowtorch. As his body burns silently in the grass, Tom jumps into the cruiser and heads up the road to the cave.

The jeep driven by Paul comes to an abrupt stop, its power cut by the alien. As he begins a slow trek up the winding road to Elephant Hot Springs, Paul hears in the distance the unmistakable sound of another car engine. Hiding in the brush on the side of the road, Paul ambushes and kills the driver of the approaching vehicle—Gen. Pattick—and then heads in the direction of the cave.

Meanwhile Sgt. Neil's troops, having heard screams from inside the cave, cautiously advance into the darkness. There they find the alien entity hovering over the body of Claire Anderson. Neil orders his men to fall back as the thing crushes one of them in its enormous pincers.

The creature pursues the troops outside. Riflemen unload dozens of rounds of ammunition, but the bullets bounce harmlessly off the creature's tough hide. Even bazooka shells seem to do little damage. Neil hears the sound of a car and shouts at the driver to back off, but it is Tom Anderson, who convinces Neil to call off his troops. Tom uses his blowtorch to burn through the only penetrable part of the thing's exterior—its eyes. But getting this close to the creature means certain death in its razor-sharp pincers. As its brain is cooked into mush, an impossibly long arm reaches out, grabbing Anderson by the throat.

By the time Nelson arrives, Anderson lies broken and bloodied alongside the carcass of the thing that almost conquered the world.

It Conquered the World proved to be a significant improvement over *Day the World Ended*. The script was tightly structured, and the dialogue was more realistic and delivered by actors of a higher calibre. The chemistry between Lee Van Cleef and Peter Graves was fervent and dynamic. Both actors met their roles with enthusiasm and commitment. Nowhere was there a hint of embarrassment at finding themselves in a low-budget monster movie. Graves had already appeared in *Red Planet Mars* and *Killers from Space*, and would go on to star in several other genre offerings, and Van Cleef had previously appeared in *The Beast from 20,000 Fathoms*. Graves especially shined in his penetrating exchanges with Van Cleef and the encounter with Sally Fraser as his alien-possessed wife. Regrettably, Fraser was probably the weakest link in a chain of otherwise strong performers, including the ever-dependable Beverly Garland (who proves in this film that she's a much better actress than she is a screamer). In secondary roles, Dick Miller and Jonathan Haze provided unobtrusive comic relief, and up-and-coming Corman scriptwriter Chuck Griffith wasn't bad as Pete Shelton, one of the scientists who relinquishes control to the alien.

On the technical side, the film offered serviceable, if unremarkable, cinematography by Frederick West. Continuity suffered somewhat from a short shooting schedule, notably in scenes with the military jeep, which sometimes displayed a "No Riders" sign and sometimes did not, and in the climax which involved the driving and abandonment of various vehicles. The music score by Ronald Stein (who soon became AIP's in-house film composer) is not his best; at times it is severely melodramatic and not very memorable. Still, it doesn't damage the film all that much.

What did damage the movie were some of the changes Roger Corman made to the picture's climax. According to the script, the monster never left the confines of the cave in which it was situated. It had no need to move from place to place because it used its batlike offspring to infect human beings, who could then carry out its nefarious commands and desires. There was to have been only one scene where the creature moved at all, and that was when it left the satellite and was briefly shown moving through the bushes, wiggling its antennae.

There are several versions of what really happened on April 10, 1956, the date the scene was shot. Roger Corman has been quoted as saying that since he paid for the monster, he was going to show it, whether or not the film suffered as a result. Corman himself has often told the story that the monster had to be rebuilt after Beverly Garland laughed at it during rehearsals; his version of events appeared most recently in his book *How I Made a Hundred Movies in Hollywood and Never Lost a Dime.* The claim that "by that afternoon our monster was rebuilt ten feet high" is not only implausible, it's untrue. Blaisdell's Venusian stood six feet high from day one. It was never rebuilt. It was never modified. The fact of the matter is that Corman would never have stood for the amount of time and money it would have taken to rebuild the costume at that late date.

There is another story that when Beverly Garland first saw "It" she snickered, "So you're going to conquer the world, eh?" and kicked it over. Bob Burns, who often visited the set of many Blaisdell film projects, knows that this never happened. "The very construction of the costume wouldn't allow for someone kicking it over," he said. "In fact, it took three off-camera people to tip the thing over when 'It' died at the film's conclusion."

All things considered, the most likely scenario seems to be one offered by Paul Blaisdell himself: someone on the crew forgot to bring the generator which was needed to power the lighting equipment or the generators failed (it was difficult to recall with precision so many years after the fact). Consequently, Corman was forced to bring "It" out of the cave so the film could be finished using natural light.

Instead of filming on a soundstage, Corman and crew had set up camp near Bronson Quarry in Griffith Park, a favorite location for many 1950s sci-fi and monster films. Blaisdell protested the decision to shoot the climax of the film outside the cave. He had constructed "It" as a stationary being—the monster had no walking appendages—which would merely sit on a rock shelf in a niche inside the cave. To try and force it to move or make it look even somewhat ambulatory would probably prove disastrous. Blaisdell felt certain audiences would laugh once they saw "It" in direct sunlight. But Corman was adamant: the film could not run over schedule or over budget. There wasn't time to get the generators up and running. So the castors that Paul had built on the underside of the costume (used to roll it from the workshop to the movie set) became the monster's walking gear.

The only way to get the creature to move on film was to have Paul "duck-walk" inside the suit, inching it along bit by bit. Sure enough, once viewers saw the monster in broad daylight, theaters filled with catcalls and laughter.

Blaisdell was at the premiere, watching the audience's reactions in dismay. He got up and walked out before the picture finished playing.

Months before, when Blaisdell began working on the full-size creature (which he affectionately dubbed "Beulah"), expectations were running high that "It" would raise hackles, not hoots from viewers. Everyone from AIP prez Jim Nicholson to director Roger Corman felt that this would turn out to be one of Paul's most awe-inspiring creations. The three of them agreed that a creature that came from the planet Venus, with its low gravity, should naturally be built rather low to the ground. Blaisdell envisioned it as a kind of "miscalculated mushroom," but the finished costume was often referred to as "the cucumber creature" by the press.

Blaisdell later recalled how he had developed his conception of the monster:

> The writer wanted some kind of a creature that was pretty invulnerable and came from the planet Venus. At that time the belief about the physiognomy of Venus was that it was hot, humid, conducive to plant life but not too well suited to animal life. If anybody would care to think it out, there is a kind of vegetation we have right here on Earth that you wouldn't particularly feel like fooling around with. Not a carrot or an ear of corn, but something that grows in the darkness and the dampness, something that might grow on the planet Venus. Something that might, in lieu of animal life, develop an intelligence of its own. Wouldn't you be inclined to pick a toadstool or a mushroom or fungus of that particular species? It would move like a perambulating plant, but it would not move very far. When it wanted to conduct direct action, it would send out small creatures which it would give birth to, and they would do its dirty work.

The design of "It" was so radically different from the standard bipedal movie monsters of the 1950s that Blaisdell was forced to completely rethink his working methods. There was no way the design concept could be realized using the standard man-in-a-suit approach. After discussing the problem with Jackie, Paul decided to construct the monster mushroom out of wood and foam rubber. It would be bulky and maybe a bit clunky, but since its only moving parts would be the arms, that didn't really matter. Or so he thought.

Blaisdell made a wood "skeleton" to establish the creature's overall shape. Using quarter- and eighth-inch plywood, he assembled a kind of lattice-work that resembled an airplane fuselage, or teepee, fitted to a circular swivel-base which was capable of swinging right or left through a 90-degree arc. Over this skeleton were fitted large panels of foam rubber, each measuring about two inches thick. The panels were glued to each other and attached to the frame with generous amounts of contact bond cement. Holes were cut into the material to allow for the insertion of the arms, antennae, and facial features. A smaller hole drilled between the eye sockets provided a viewport for Beulah's human operator.

Midway through the construction process Paul suddenly realized that the dimensions of the framework would prevent the finished costume from fitting through his workshop door. (The frame stood 6 feet tall and measured nearly 12½ feet in circumference at the base.) Try as they might, there was no way he and Jackie could get it outside. So out came the screws and bolts; down came the plywood frame. Paul took his materials to a makeshift workshop near the film studio and began the process all over again.

Although Beulah had no lower extremities, she did sport an enormous arm on either side of her conical body. Measuring almost six feet in length, the arms were built in the same fashion as the body, using a wood interior and thick foam rubber exterior. Blaisdell sculpted huge crablike pincers out of white pine, which served as a positive mold for the liquid latex used to finish the claws. To enable the pincers to open and close, Blaisdell outfitted each arm with a flexible interior cable which operated much like a bicycle's hand brake. By squeezing an attached grip control, the cable line tugged on a pin embedded in one of the pincers, pulling it toward the other. When combined with a variety of arm movements which Blaisdell controlled from within, the effect was uncannily lifelike. The arms, though cumbersome, were capable of 180-degree arcs of movement.

Creating the hornlike antennae which "It" used to de-energize the town of Beechwood involved the use of large-size candles which were heated until they were flexible and were then bent into the desired shape. These were covered with multiple layers of liquid latex and allowed to dry, then peeled away and stuffed with cotton and wire to maintain their shape. They were painted with an airbrush and attached to the apex of the creature costume with contact bond cement.

The creature's perpetual scowling visage was capable of a little bit of movement. By using layers of block foam, Blaisdell formed a jutting brow and mouth and added pock-marked detailing around the nose and eyes. White pine, carved to shape, was used to make the famous stalactite teeth. The tongue was latex. Blaisdell attached a single wire, about the thickness of a coat hanger, to the back of the lower lip inside the costume, which he could use to give the mouth some up and down movement. For eyes Paul once again turned to the Frye Plastic Company, painting irises onto plastic orbs about 3.5 inches in diameter. He drilled holes into the back of the finished eyeballs and secured each one to an ordinary pocket flashlight. Inside the costume Blaisdell used the flashlights as "handles" to twist and turn the eyeballs in whatever direction he wished. In addition, the flashlights' beams made the plastic eyes glow eerily during low-light location filming inside the Bronson Quarry cave.

When all the various parts of the costume were locked in place, Beulah was coated with bright red lacquer paint and highlighted with streaks of black. On film the bright red color would register as a kind of medium-gray, allowing the highlights to stand out. As a final touch, Blaisdell used a ball-peen hammer to pound texture into the monster's foam rubber skin. This also gave the costume better flexibility and erased any reflective tendencies of the paint, making "It" appear more realistic.

Paul invited Jim Nicholson in to take a look at the life-size version of the model he had presented to AIP's president weeks earlier. While Nicholson stood silently by, Blaisdell crawled inside the costume and began working the controls that operated the claws. To Nicholson's surprise, one of Beulah's arms snaked upward, opened a crablike pincer, and swiped the handkerchief right out of his breast pocket. It was a stunt Paul had been practicing for a couple of days with Jackie, and it came off without a hitch. Nicholson was suitably impressed. "Paul, you've done it again," he exclaimed. "I never thought you'd come up with something this far-out!"

For the film, Blaisdell also built four attack bats nicknamed Manny, Moe, Mack, and Sleepy. Blaisdell called these the Flying Fingers and originally their design was quite different; they looked nothing like bats, but were globular creatures that had the ability to float through the air. About the size of a ten-pin bowling ball, they sported two stubby horns above a singular cyclopean eye with a slitted, catlike iris. A gibbous, slanting brow helped give the eye a bit of menacing character. Blaisdell created a three-dimensional model of this early design from clay, but that was as far as he got. Ultimately, he decided that the look "just wasn't right," so the model was scrapped and the Flying Fingers were redesigned from the ground up.

The new version proved to be more aerodynamic. Whereas a spherical organism would have to float from place to place, the redesigned model with its angular wingspan could actually fly (with the help of an invisible wire). It also looked a lot more like a bat. A weird bat, but a bat nonetheless.

Blaisdell's clay model became the positive mold for the creation of an army of Flying Fingers. Liquid latex, built to about a quarter-inch thickness, became the flesh of the bat creatures, which were later customized with strips of foam rubber and additional layers of latex. The eyes, once again, were tiny plastic balls obtained from the Frye Company. Blaisdell added an eerie effect to the flock of Fingers by coating the backs of the eyes with a highly reflective copper paint, giving them a weird kind of glint. Lastly, fingernails were added to each model. For these Paul used the commercially available "Glo-Fangs," a Halloween party staple, which he painted a bright red and glued down with contact bond cement.

All except one of the bats were rigged to fly on monofilament wires attached to the rubber latex body. Blaisdell used two different flying techniques: overhead and zooming. For the overhead method, he manipulated a gadget called a fishpole, so named because the long arm that depended from its tripodlike base looked almost exactly like one. By gently shaking the fishpole, he could make the attached rubber wings jiggle up and down, creating the illusion that they were flapping. Blaisdell likened the operation to working with a string marionette. He practiced with the Flying Fingers at

Paul Blaisdell's original design for the Flying Fingers from *It Conquered the World* consisted of a globular, cyclopean shell that possessed the power of levitation and controlled its human victims by clamping onto the back of their necks with its viselike mouth. The design was radically altered after Paul decided that the creatures would look more realistic if they were batlike in appearance and used a standard wing-flapping kind of locomotion. The globular design is slightly obscured by two of the final models, resting above and below the original (courtesy of Bob Burns).

home for several days prior to filming and got so good at working the fishpole rig he could make the bats loop, dive, arc, and just generally "go crazy."

When an actor shared the stage with one of the Flying Fingers, timing was difficult and critical. The actor in the scene had to avoid hitting the wires while swatting at the creature in as forcefully realistic a fashion as possible. Blaisdell often remarked on Peter Graves's ability to smash just about every prop in sight without getting tangled up in the wires during the filming of the scene in which his character kills his "control device."

Less frequently employed was a hands-off zooming technique. For this effect, a length piece of piano wire was stretched across the set, which created the trajectory of the bat's flight path. Loosely fitting one of the latex models to the wire would allow it to glide down or through the film frame. For proper balance the trajectory line was threaded through two tiny metal loops attached to the front and rear of the bat. The obvious drawback to the zooming technique was that the wings could not be made to flap. For that reason this effect was used as little as possible, only in those scenes requiring a bat to hit a specific target such as an actor's neck.

One of the models was a stationary prop used for a single scene in the film where it appears to be resting in a bush. (This was the one Paul nicknamed Sleepy.) It was the only prop from *It Conquered the World* that managed to survive in Blaisdell's personal collection; the others were given to Bob Burns, Jim Nicholson, and Forrest Ackerman after the picture finished filming. Big Beulah herself was destroyed in the major 1969 flood that ravaged much of Southern California.

To make it appear as if Sleepy was a living, breathing entity, Paul devised an early bladder effect by hooking a CO_2 tank and O_2 valve (similar to that used in an artist's airbrush) to a liplike opening on the back of the latex body. By alternately inflating and deflating the latex rubber, Blaisdell could make it appear as if the creature were actually breathing. The effect was startlingly realistic. (Many years later a similar effect was used for David Cronenberg's science-fiction-horror film *Scanners*, which popularized the so-called bladder effect.)

To play the role of the Venusian mushroom, Blaisdell had to enter the oversized costume from the bottom. (It was built very much like a teepee, with an opening in the bottom.) By tipping the costume up at an angle, Paul could crawl in underneath. Once situated inside, he was able to manipulate the swivel base as well as the individual controls for the antennae, eyes, mouth, arms, and claws. Although it was a tight fit, there was room enough to accommodate a battery-powered light and a copy of the script. In fact, Jackie once got inside the costume with Paul so that they could operate all the controls simultaneously.

Unfortunately, disaster struck the very first time the costume was wheeled to the set. With members of the crew scurrying about to set up the camera and lights, Paul left Beulah by herself in a stationary position, with the arms resting on the ground. Before he knew it, one of Corman's crew dragged a grip cart over the outstretched arms. The weight of the cart, piled high with film equipment, snapped the inner cables inside that worked the claw-pincers. When he checked, Blaisdell found he could still raise and lower the arms, but the pincers would never again be able to pluck a handkerchief out of a breast pocket unless they were rebuilt and rewired, and there clearly wasn't time for that. Too late, Paul realized he should have tied the arms above Beulah's pointy head.

When it was time to film some of the monster footage, Paul wheeled his monstrous mushroom into place inside the cave and took his place inside. Corman wanted to film some shots of the monster's glowing eyes using a 45-degree angle with the camera aimed down at the creature from above. Paul operated the controls that moved the oversized mouth, which allowed for some pretty neat fang-gnashing, and switched on the flashlights to make the eyes glow. With suitably eerie lighting these quick-cut scenes turned out to be Beulah's finest moments.

This was then followed by one of her worst screen moments. When Pvt. Ortiz (Jonathan Haze) rushes the monster and tries to kill it with a bayonet, "It" crushes him to death with its enormous piledriver arms. Because the cables controlling the claws had been severed, Blaisdell was unable to operate the pincers, which flapped uselessly on camera as Paul worked the arms around his attacker. Despite the ludicrousness of the scene, Corman kept it in the final cut.

But there were more problems behind the cameras. While the cast and crew were gearing up to film this scene, Blaisdell was fiddling with the damaged pincer controls to see if he could get them to work. Jonathan Haze was practicing with his prop bayonet while Roger Corman was blocking out the shot. Jackie Blaisdell started to get a "funny feeling" about the activity. It was almost like a precognition; there was too much adrenaline in the air. At the last minute, she asked Paul to wear one of the prop army helmets for protection. Paul borrowed a helmet from Danny Knight, an actor who was playing one of the other soldiers who didn't appear in the scene.

Sure enough, when Corman called for "Action!" Jonathan Haze bounded headlong toward Beulah, ramming the bayonet into the costume as Corman had instructed. Inside the costume Paul heard a loud clink as the bayonet bounced off his helmet. After he heard the director call "Cut!" Blaisdell climbed out from the costume and thanked Jackie for saving his life. Then he called Haze aside. "Next time, aim a bit higher," he growled.

More problems cropped up when it came time to film Beverly Garland's death scene. According to the script, Garland's character uses a Winchester rifle to fill the monster full of lead in between lines of dialogue, but ends up perishing in its lethal grasp. To help Blaisdell play the scene, Corman stationed two prop men below the camera lens who would help maneuver the costume's monstrous arms into the frame. The first take was ruined when one of them misjudged the target and smacked Garland square in the chest with those oversized pincers. Scrap take one.

Everything went according to plan in take two—to a point, as Blaisdell later recalled:

> There was enough light in the cave during the fading of the afternoon for Beverly Garland to try and kill me with a Winchester rifle. Beverly has a wonderful sense of barracks language when she gets mad. She's my kind of gal. There was a lot of cussing on both our parts when the rifle jammed on the first shot and I only got one bullet through my head. I ended up grabbing everything in the cave except her neck, as scheduled.

A puzzled Corman refrained from yelling "Cut" until Garland finally ditched the rifle and slid to the floor with Beulah's rubber claws wrapped around her neck. Precise editing allowed the scene to be pieced together in postproduction.

After the squabble over the climax of the film, when Roger Corman decided the hitherto immobile mushroom monster would suddenly acquire the power of locomotion, the crew began setting up for Beulah's big death scene. Although the setting had changed (from a niche inside the cave to outside the mouth of the cave), the details of the script had not. The monster would be riddled with bullets and bazooka fire and cooked by a blowtorch to boot. Blaisdell had incorporated into the costume all the appropriate responses his creation would need.

For the scene in which the monster is riddled with bullets, Beulah was outfitted with explosive squibbs to simulate gunshots. For reasons of safety Blaisdell remained outside the costume, watching from the sidelines as the soldiers let loose with a barrage of rifle fire. On cue the squibbs detonated, leaving trails of smoke drifting in the air. When he thought he had enough footage, Corman yelled "Cut!" He failed to notice that Beulah's interior had become saturated with smoke, which started leaking out of every orifice on the creature's conical body.

Dick Miller, who had badly twisted his ankle in an earlier scene but remained on the set because Corman had drafted him into the crew, countermanded the director's order: "Don't cut!"

"I said cut!" Corman screamed.

"Keep filming!" Fingers were pointing at something behind Corman.

Corman turned around and saw his movie monster smoking like a cherry bomb. He ran over to his cameraman, Fred West. "Did you get that?" Corman asked.

"No, you said to cut," West replied.

"Shit."

Corman may have missed out on the fireworks display, but he managed to get a dynamite closing shot for the monster's demise, thanks to Paul and Jackie Blaisdell. After the costume was fumigated and returned to Topanga Canyon, Blaisdell set the stage for a neat bleeding effect. (This insert shot was filmed on Blaisdell's own property with a second-unit crew. Corman was not there.) Paul decided to use Hershey-brand chocolate syrup to simulate blood because its rich brown color registered well on film. With the camera running, Blaisdell opened up prefabricated wounds in the monster's hide, letting a small quantity of "blood" gush out.

Many of the cast found it difficult to keep a straight face playing against such an odd-looking monster, and it was no different for Lee Van Cleef, who was required to destroy the invader by blowtorching it to death. As he was trying to psych himself up for the picture's finale, members of the crew were shouting, "Do it, Lee! Kill that fucking overgrown ice cream cone!" Instead of laughing, Van Cleef got angry. "Get off my back!" he yelled. When Corman called for "Action," Van Cleef delivered his lines faithfully. Then he leaned down to burn out the creature's eye, at which point the editor inserted another shot that had actually been filmed at Topanga Canyon.

For the close-up of the dissolving eyeball, Jackie Blaisdell loaded an ordinary grease gun with Hershey's chocolate syrup. After a close-up of Paul's hand holding the fiery blowtorch (he was standing in for Lee Van Cleef), there was a quick cut to the monster's face. Inside the costume Jackie wiggled the eyeball around and then pulled the trigger of the grease gun. Nothing came out. She squeezed again. Still nothing. The syrup had congealed in the tip of the gun.

"Squirt harder!" Paul yelled.

Jackie began pumping the trigger as hard as she could. Big globs of chocolate syrup suddenly shot out of the creature's eye socket, splattering Paul and several members of the second-unit crew. The syrup also squirted out the other end of the grease gun as well, hitting Jackie full in the face. By the time she climbed out of the costume, she looked as if she had been in a mud fight.

Over the strenuous objections of Blaisdell, Corman had decided that Beulah had to fall over when she died. "But it couldn't fall over, Roger," Paul had told him. "It's not made that way."

"I don't care, the monster has to fall over," Corman decreed. "How else is the audience going to know that it's dead?"

When Paul realized he wasn't going to win this fight either, he whipped up a couple of rubber latex eyelids to insert into Beulah's eye cavities. Technically there should only have been a single eyelid because Lee Van Cleef had torched one of the eyeballs into mush, but the monster ended up with two closed lids. If members of the audience could believe it would fall over, they could believe it still had two eyelids.

Not many film critics liked *It Conquered the World*. For one thing, it was just too easy to laugh at the monster, and critics found it difficult to resist making cracks in their reviews. As Blaisdell had predicted, many viewers giggled at the sight of such a creature chasing a group of soldiers out of the Bronson Quarry cave. What made it even worse was Roger Corman's insistence that the monster had to fall over dead at the end of the picture. (It took three people to tip the costume over during the filming.)

To its credit, however, the trade paper *Variety* pointed out that *It Conquered the World* was "a definite cut above normal." The reviewer, "Kove," took matters seriously enough to mention that the film "poses some remarkably adult questions amidst the derring-do." *Variety* also liked Lee Van Cleef's performance, citing it as "an impressive character-acting chore," as well as that of Peter Graves, who "makes a properly dashing anti-Venusian resistance hero a man of some intellectual position as well." The reviewer went on to comment favorably on the performances of Beverly Garland and Sally Fraser. In fact, the only sour note of the entire review came at the end, when Kove remarked that "Corman would have been wiser to merely suggest the creature, rather than construct the awesome-looking [but] mechanically clumsy rubberized horror."

AIP got a little surprise when it shipped a print of *It Conquered the World* to the film review board in the United Kingdom prior to its British release. Then, as now, many horror films were rated "X", which meant juveniles could not get in to see the picture. (All of Britain's Hammer Film productions got "X" ratings.) AIP expected its latest monster extravaganza would be passed, but as the weeks went by with no message from the board, Sam Arkoff began to get worried. Even intercontinental phone calls to the review board failed to get a positive response. Since the film was booked for distribution through the ABC chain of theaters in Britain in advance, Arkoff decided to fly directly to England to meet with John Travelian, the chief of the review board, to see what the problem was.

"It's the blowtorch, Sam," said Travelian. "You have the monster getting destroyed by a blowtorch."

Arkoff was flabbergasted. "So what if it's killed with a blowtorch? What difference does that make?"

It turned out the British film review board couldn't decide if the Venusian invader was human or animal. Travelian thought it looked like an animal, and he didn't want to upset any English animal lovers.

Arkoff told him it definitely wasn't an animal. "Actually, it's human," Arkoff said with a straight face. "That's what humans from the planet Venus look like." With that assurance, Travelian gave the film his blessing, just in time for its British debut.

Like some other low-budget pictures made in the 1950s, *It Conquered the World* seemed to improve with age. At the very least, it is clearly more fondly appreciated today than when it was first released, almost as if it were waiting for the wide-eyed youngsters of 1956 to grow into adults who would be able to read between the lines and see something special about it at last.

5

Blaisdell in Drag

> The making of *The She-Creature* caused a great deal of excitement in the offices of the producers, and they all had their own pet ideas. "Give her a face like a cat." "Make her swim out of the water like an amphibian." "Make her a prehistoric creature." "Give her an enormous tail." In fact the She-Creature did end up being the most durable, the longest-lasting, and the most imaginative of any creature that was ever created for American International Pictures, in spite of all the superfluous demands that were placed upon her by people who could not even begin to see or imagine it in their minds, and who forgot what they said the day after they said it. I decided, "Okay, if you guys can't conceive of the problems in doing this for your movie—which, being producers, you're supposed to do—then you're just going to have to leave it up to me and my imagination. It's going to have a little bit of what each of you wants, but in the end it's going to be the best one I've ever done."
>
> *—Paul Blaisdell*

In the mid-1950s the public imagination was captivated by the story of Bridey Murphy. Who was Bridey Murphy? In his best-selling book *The Search for Bridey Murphy*, author Morey Bernstein described how he worked with a woman named Ruth Simmons who claimed to be the modern-day reincarnation of someone called Bridey Murphy. Under hypnosis, Simmons would recount the details of her previous life in the late 1700s. Whether or not the story had any basis in fact is irrelevant; what matters is that for month after month after month, the Bridey Murphy story was on everyone's lips. AIP president Jim Nicholson thought his company should make a picture incorporating elements from Bernstein's book, such as reincarnation and age regression, while the Bridey Murphy case was still "hot." He asked Lou Rusoff to start thinking about a story.

Meanwhile, Nicholson went with Alex Gordon to a Christmas party at the house of Newton "Red" Jacobs, an AIP subdistributor who would eventually become the president of Crown International Pictures. Shortly after they arrived, Jacobs sauntered up to Nicholson and Gordon and said, "I have a great title for a movie, but I don't have a story to go with it."

"What's the title?" asked Gordon.

"*The She-Creature*," came the reply.

Nicholson and Gordon agreed it was a neat-sounding title. The following day Nicholson got in touch with Rusoff to make sure the script he was working on would have a female protagonist. When Rusoff assured him that it already did, Nicholson hung up and began pondering the details of an advertising campaign that would help tie AIP's new monster movie to the Bridey Murphy case without naming specific names (and having to pay any associated fees). In the end, AIP settled for including a line of copy on the posters and print ads that proclaimed, "It can and did happen! Based on authentic FACTS you've been reading about!"

It was important to get *The She-Creature* into production as quickly as possible in order to capitalize on the reincarnation craze while it could still be called a craze. A budget was set at $104,000 for a nine-day shoot. After Rusoff delivered his script to American International, Alex Gordon started pulling strings to see if he could get a few of his favorite performers into the film. Unfortunately, when it came to casting, everything that could have possibly gone wrong did go wrong. Alex wanted to get Edward Arnold and Peter Lorre for the roles of Timothy Chappel and Carlo Lombardi—the business tycoon and the hypnotist, respectively—because he liked the way the two actors played off each other in the 1935 production *Crime and Punishment*. He also thought they would be great marquee names for an American International movie. Gordon made a deal through the Jaffe Agency to acquire Lorre for the picture, and once the paperwork was signed, he turned his attention to securing the services of Arnold.

But Lorre hadn't a clue as to what *The She-Creature* was all about. When his agent finally gave the rotund actor a copy of Rusoff's script, Lorre quickly scanned the pages and determined, "This is a load of crap!" He refused to do the film and even fired his agent for committing him to the picture without consultation.

Next Gordon tried to get John Carradine interested in the script, but Carradine didn't want anything more to do with horror movies. He had just worked with Cecil B. DeMille on *The Ten Commandments*, and he was pumped up. He was only going to do Shakespeare and similar "legitimate" roles in classy productions from here on out. (Within a year Carradine would appear in *The Black Sleep* as well as *The Unearthly*, a film that makes *The She-Creature* look like an "A" production by comparison.)

The She-Creature was scheduled to be directed by Edward L. Cahn, an old hand at movie-making whose credentials went back many years and included the 1932 Western *Law and Order*, featuring Walter Huston as Wyatt Earp. Gordon prevailed upon Cahn to try and get Edward Arnold signed, figuring that since Cahn had worked with Arnold on the 1944 film *Main Street After Dark* at MGM, it might be fairly easy for him to get the actor interested. As a matter of fact, Cahn did get Arnold's commitment to be in the film for a flat $3,000 fee.

But two days before *The She-Creature* was to go into production, Arnold died. Gordon panicked. It was too late to reschedule the film's shoot; the studio had already been booked. He called Chester Morris, who was in New York at the time, to see if Morris would take over Arnold's part in the picture. Morris agreed to fly out to L.A. for a week to be in the picture, but by the time he arrived Gordon had switched his role from the business tycoon to the evil hypnotist. That was okay with Morris; he was a successful amateur magician as well as a respected actor and actually looked forward to taking over the lead role of Dr. Lombardi. Also scheduled to appear in the film was Tom Conway, who was going to play the police detective. When Conway arrived from England, he found out he was no longer the detective, he was now the business tycoon.

That left the part of the detective still open. Gordon got hold of Ron Randell, who had just finished a film in L.A. and was about to leave for Australia, and offered him $750 to play the part of Lt. James. Randell said okay, even though he'd never seen the script.

Once the dust had settled from the shuffling of the main cast members, Gordon began filling up secondary roles with some of his old-time favorites, including El Brendel, Jack Mulhall, and Luana Walters, who had once worked with Gordon fave Bela Lugosi. With old pro Eddie Cahn at the helm of his new picture, Alex felt he could relax at last.

The She-Creature was refreshingly original. Nowhere in Lou Rusoff's script was there the slightest hint of radioactivity, dictatorial monsters from outer space or overgrown nuclear nightmares. Using the Bridey Murphy affair as a jumping-off point, Rusoff managed to fortify his screenplay with qualities that were absent in many other monster movies of the time. As low-budget and quickly made as it was, *The She-Creature* turned out to be one of the most memorable of the "drive-in classics."

Following the credits (and a haunting opening theme by Ronald Stein), we are introduced to Dr. Carlo Lombardi (Chester Morris), a hypnotist of extraordinary talent. Stuck in a nickel-and-dime amusement park sideshow where indiscriminating customers seeking cheap thrills are the only ones who ever see him perform, Lombardi harbors a strange and terrifying secret: he alone among men can call forth from the depths of time and space the primordial life-form of a person living today. For years he has kept a carnival follower named Andrea (Marla English) under his Svengali-like mental spell.

But Lombardi has another secret as well: he is a social misfit, a megalomaniacal miscreant who harbors a bitter hatred for the human race. By predicting a series of gruesome murders and using Andrea's prehistoric alter ego as the mechanism to fulfill his prophecies, Lombardi figures to gain recognition as a master manipulator of the human mind. Late one night Lombardi sneaks into the beachside home of the Jefferson family to survey his creature's latest handiwork. The place is a wreck: furniture overturned, lamps shattered, and in the middle of all the debris, the cold, stiff bodies of the young Jefferson couple.

Not far away, in the elegant home of business tycoon Timothy Chappel (Tom Conway), a party is going strong. One of the guests, Dr. Ted Erickson (Lance Fuller), is repelled by the meandering socialites' never-ending preoccupation with money and status. He finds the subject tiresome and feels severely out of place. "I don't belong in all that," he tells his date, Dorothy (Cathy Downs), Chappel's daughter. They slip out for a romantic oceanside stroll, but the mood is interrupted when they happen to spot Dr. Lombardi leaving the Jefferson beachhouse. Ted takes a quick look at the butchered bodies inside and tells Dorothy to call the police.

Lt. Ed James (Ron Randell) and his sergeant (Frank Jenks) investigate the scene and discover traces of seaweed stuck to an enormous, obviously inhuman footprint. Jenks believes Lombardi's tales of a murdering "She-Creature," but Lt. James is skeptical. He believes Lombardi killed the youngsters himself and staged the scene just to drum up business for his failing sideshow act.

On the way back to his boardwalk showplace, Lombardi encounters Johnny (Paul Dubov), a nosy carnival barker who operates the wheel of fortune. Johnny mentions a scream he heard coming from Lombardi's place earlier that evening. Thinking Andrea could be in trouble, he rushed over to check on her; but there was nothing amiss, and Andrea seemed unhurt, merely sleeping. Apparently Johnny is nurturing a crush on Lombardi's young assistant. "I knew her long before you did, Doc," he reminds the hypnotist. "I knew her when she was a carnival follower." Johnny's reference to Andrea's somewhat shady past is followed by Lombardi's comment, "I've asked you to forget that." It's an acrimonious exchange that suggests Andrea may have been doing a lot more than just "following" carnivals.

Shrugging off Lombardi's concerns, Johnny persists: "What's it all about, doc? Why do you keep her under like that?" For the first time, Lombardi allows the hint of a smile to cross his face. "I have an idea you'll find out soon," he suggests menacingly.

Inside the theater Lombardi wakes Andrea from her hypnotic trance. "You've had me in a deep hypnosis for more than an hour," she says weakly. "I've asked you not to do that." Lombardi smirks. "Well, you were tired. You needed the rest." She gets dressed while Lombardi remains in the room. Although she's standing behind a blinder, the scene plays as if the two know each other intimately. The idea of a weak-willed woman held in some kind of sexual bondage by an older, domineering (and possibly homicidal) mate is further strengthened by Andrea's line: "I hate this place. I hate the sound of the ocean. I hate you."

A knock at the door defuses one situation and ignites another, as Lombardi is confronted by Lt. James and Dr. Erickson. Lt. James takes Lombardi in for questioning regarding the Jefferson case, leaving Andrea to join Erickson for a cup of coffee. But when they step outside, Andrea stops dead in her tracks. "I can't go with you," she whispers, as the force of Lombardi's mental powers (now operating at a distance) suddenly overwhelms her.

The following morning Erickson joins his tycoon friend Chappel for breakfast. Chappel sees big money in Lombardi's act and encourages Erickson to join the publicity bandwagon if he wants to make some easy money. Erickson refuses, so Chappel goes to see Lombardi himself. Having been questioned by the police but not held, the mentalist has returned to his run-down showplace, where he has been awaiting Chappel's expected visit. Chappel offers to help promote Lombardi's hypnotism/age-regression/soul transmigration act for a 50-50 cut of the proceeds. Lombardi agrees but reminds Chappel that what he does is no "act." To prove his point, he predicts another beachside murder.

That night, after Lombardi regresses Andrea back in time, the She-Creature emerges from the bubbling depths of the ocean and climbs up the pier. In his room, Johnny can hear sloshing footfalls outside the walls. Suddenly the door explodes open as the monster smashes its way inward and slaughters him.

The next day Lt. James arrests Lombardi for the latest murder, but since there is no evidence linking him to the crime Chappel's lawyer springs him. That evening, during a special performance for a group of influential guests invited by the wealthy entrepreneur, Lombardi age-regresses Andrea back to her former life as Elizabeth Ann Wetherby, a royal subject of the British crown. At the end of the show, Lombardi warns his audience that Elizabeth says the She-Creature is in the ocean preparing to come out. The guests scatter in terror.

Outside, Erickson is standing alone when the creature lumbers up behind him, its claws raised threateningly. But Andrea, waking suddenly from her hypnotic trance, breaks the connection between her soul and her first terrestrial body and the creature fades into the ancient mists of time.

Erickson wants Lombardi to stage a demonstration of age-regression under clinical conditions. When the hypnotist agrees, Lt. James joins the group and tape records everything that happens. Unable to learn anything from watching Lombardi and listening to his presentation, the lieutenant begins to shadow him. That night, as he watches Lombardi walk along the beach, he hears a nearby scream. The She-Creature, materialized once again, pushes a car over a cliff, killing the two young lovers inside. "I was walking

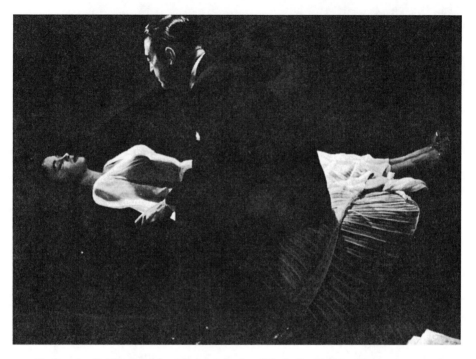

Dr. Lombardi (Chester Morris) places Andrea (Marla English) in a hypnotic trance in *The She-Creature*. The backdrop behind the actors contains surrealistic designs which presumably are there to telegraph Lombardi's occult powers.

with Lombardi when I heard the scream," James tells Erickson, "but I know he did it. He's a murderer, yet I can't touch him."

Soon Lombardi hits the big time with syndicated newspaper columns, live auditorium performances, and a best-selling book, *The True Story of Elizabeth Wetherby*. Chappel, who has slowly grown to dislike Lombardi, asks the hypnotist to vacate his premises. When Lombardi refuses, Chappel insults him. "You're very foolish to say those things to me," Lombardi warns him.

The following evening, following a failed attempt to kill Erickson by mentally controlling Chappel's dog, Lombardi puts on another demonstration for the house guests. Once again he regresses Andrea to her primordial state, and once again the She-Creature walks. Lt. James, stationed on the beach, sees the scaly monstrosity materialize right in front of him. Before he can escape, the creature slays him with one of its hooked, razor-edged claws, then makes its way to Chappel's office, where it kills him as well. Under Lombardi's command, it returns to Andrea's side, where it finds Erickson waiting. Gloating in triumph, Lombardi orders the creature to kill Erickson. The lethal claws are raised high in the air, but at the last moment the creature hesitates, then turns and strikes Lombardi instead. During a surreal moment,

Dr. Erickson (Lance Fuller) futilely attempts to rouse Andrea (Marla English) from the hypnotic trance in which Lombardi has placed her in *The She-Creature*. Marla English was thought by many to resemble Elizabeth Taylor, which undoutedly delighted Sam Arkoff and Jim Nicholson.

the She-Creature gazes down at its future body, then leaves to return to the ocean and the past.

With his last breath, Lombardi releases Andrea from her mental prison. "You couldn't kill the man you loved," he acknowledges in defeat, falling lifelessly at her side. With the monster lost forever to the past, Andrea wakes one final time and leaves to take up a new life with Erickson.

Rusoff's script for *The She-Creature* included several scenes calling upon its title monster to perform actions that no AIP monster had ever performed before. Although its actual screen time would be minimal, the actions required by the script meant that the creature costume was going to have to be pretty durable.

With that in mind, Paul Blaisdell began working on ideas for the physical appearance of the She-Creature. It was important to keep the preliminary sketches of the beast feminine in appearance—or at least as feminine as possible within the context of something that was totally inhuman. To that end, Blaisdell designed the look of the creature using as few straight lines

The She-Creature lumbers away after clawing to death its latest victim in a scene cut from the final print. Look closely and you'll notice several strands of the monster's "hair" (actually plastic tubing) that have unravelled and are hanging down the front of the suit. The prone figure on the beach is Ron Randell (courtesy of Fred Olen Ray).

and as many curves as possible, which helped to magnify the suggestion of femininity. Some of his earliest sketches included tentaclelike arms (which actually showed up in a preliminary AIP poster design), but Blaisdell abandoned that approach when he realized such an effect would be too difficult to pull off realistically. In the end, over 100 sketches of the creature's anatomy were made before everyone was completely satisfied with the design.

As he had with Marty the Mutant, Blaisdell began the monster-making process with an ordinary pair of long johns. Since this monster came from the depths of the ocean as well as the beginning of time, Blaisdell wanted to give its flesh the look of a dried seabed. He and Jackie began sectioning blocks of foam rubber that would be arranged in a jigsawlike design. No two pieces had exactly the same shape. Each of these "scales" measured between one and

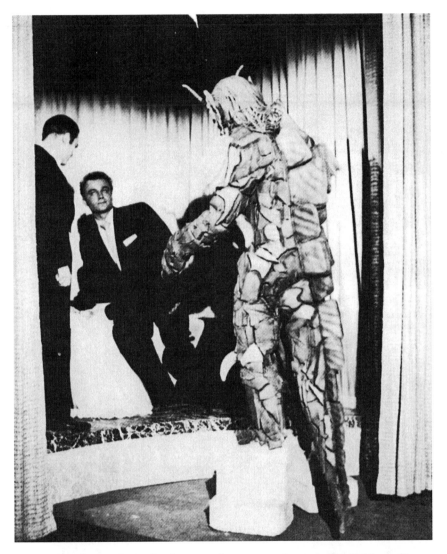

During the climax of *The She-Creature*, the monster threatens Dr. Erickson (Lance Fuller) as Lombardi (Chester Morris) looks on approvingly. Since this scene was filmed from chest-height, Blaisdell wore the cumbersome lifters which added over 12 inches to his height.

three inches thick and was bonded to the long johns using contact bond cement.

In the center of the abdomen, Blaisdell constructed what he called the She-Creature's "lunch hooks." These outsized claws or teeth were carved from soft pine, coated with layers of liquid latex and allowed to dry. The latex was

then slit up the back, stuffed with cotton, and bonded to the costume directly. Although there was nothing in the script about them, Blaisdell thought the lunch hooks broke up the monotony of the jigsaw design and made his monster look even more formidable. By simply exercising his stomach muscles in the tight-fitting costume, Blaisdell could make the lunch hooks close and open up again—the idea being that this monster could disembowel its victims if it wanted.

On the back of the costume, Blaisdell arranged twin columns of "armored plates" made of foam rubber. Since entry into the costume was effected by an industrial-size zipper that ran the length of the spine, the plates were not merely decorative, but also served to hide the zipper. Each plate was fashioned separately and coated with latex rubber which was colored by hand. Highlights were airbrushed onto each plate to give them a ribbed appearance, suggestive of waves breaking against the seashore. Once Paul was zipped into the costume, the dual columns of plates were pushed together and fastened in place with small metal snaps.

A long "prehistoric tail" was added to the costume at the suggestion of the film's director, Eddie Cahn. The tail, which continued the jigsaw design of the creature, was assembled from chunks of foam rubber trimmed to shape. Its complete flexibility allowed it to be rigged on the film set, if desired, so that it could slap wildly back and forth. Unfortunately, in the finished film the tail simply drags along behind the monster because Cahn was in too much of a hurry to bother setting up the effect.

For the She-Creature's claws, Blaisdell used a pair of thick welder's gloves which were first painted black and then covered with foam rubber pieces that followed the jigsaw pattern of the body. Once all the pieces were in place, the black paint between each piece helped to highlight the pattern and give the claws a sense of depth. A long, curved hook was added to the tip of each glove to suggest a razor-sharp claw. The hook was carved from white pine, attached to the material with contact bond cement, coated with latex, and

Opposite: Contact sheet from *The She-Creature*. Left column, top to bottom: (1) Marla English and Lance Fuller seem oblivious to the unidentified crew member inspecting part of the rock outcropping behind them. (2) Dr. Carlo Lombardi (Chester Morris) and "King," the canine he can hypnotically control. (3) Director Eddie Cahn (with pipe) consults with another crew member during location filming at Paradise Cove. (4) Marla English awaiting the acting call during a break in the filming.

Middle column, top to bottom: (5) (6) and (7) which are printed in reverse order. The monster (Blaisdell) approaches Lt. James (Ron Randell) and strikes him dead. (8) Chester Morris in character as Dr. Lombardi.

Right column, top to bottom: (9) The creature materializes in the waters of the Pacific. (10) The monster buddies up to an unidentified friend during the location shoot. (11) and (12) The monster lumbers off after killing Lt. James. Photo (11) plainly shows loose strands of She-Creature "hair" (plastic tubing) which are swinging outward as Paul Blaisdell makes his way across the beach.

Blaisdell's most popular creation, the She-Creature (1956), was built up from over 70 lbs. of foam rubber and latex. The bony protuberances on her elbows, claws, knees, and heels were carved out of white pine. The "lunch hooks" in the creature's abdomen were also made from pine. Using his stomach muscles, Blaisdell could make the lunch hooks open and close, but director Edward L. Cahn never utilized the effect in the movie.

This location photograph from *The She-Creature* nicely captures details barely seen in the finished film, including the bony hooks on the back of the heels, the double row of dorsal fins, and the tail that could have (and should have) "slammed and slapped to and fro," if only director Eddie Cahn had taken time to rig the effect.

painted. Because the script required the monster to break through a wooden doorway, Blaisdell screwed small plywood panels directly into the pine talons to give the monster gauntlets the necessary stability to perform the scene. To avoid embarrassing and potentially dangerous accidents, the plywood panels were removed for scenes with live actors.

To create the huge, double-toed, feet Paul used the kind of "swim-fins" normally worn by deep-sea divers. Individual pieces of block foam, covered with latex and painted, were bonded to the fins in the jigsaw pattern, and a pine-sculpted hook on the back of the heel completed the effect. The finished swim-fin feet were able to completely hide a pair of low-cut sneakers that Blaisdell wore during the filming.

To make his monster appear bigger on-screen, Blaisdell added extra foam padding to the shoulder areas. Breasts, also made from pieces of block foam, were glued to the front of the suit. (When the director saw them, he said they weren't big enough, so Blaisdell returned to his workshop and gave the She-Creature Dolly Parton–size boobs.) In addition, rudimentary wings were attached to the back of the shoulders. The wings were made from a wire frame and several coatings of liquid latex. Six-inch "claws" made by the pine/latex method were added to the elbows and kneecaps to help conceal the foam's tendency to crease when the suit was being worn.

Work on the She-Creature headpiece began with one of Blaisdell's "blanks," created by painting numerous layers of latex over the bust previously made by Jackie. Using small pieces of block foam, Blaisdell gave the head its catlike shape and feline features. He used larger strips of foam to add depth and some slight protrusions around the cheekbone area. When the features were exactly the way he wanted them, Blaisdell covered the entire head with more layers of liquid latex. He bought several yards of plastic tubing to use for the creature's hair. The tubing was bonded to the top of the headpiece and allowed to hang loose at the neck. By tangling up the loose ends, Blaisdell was able to make it stay in place. (Most of the time. Once in a while during the filming a few of the tubes would come loose. There are several stills in existence showing one or two long strands of "hair" hanging down the front of the costume.)

The She-Creature's ears ran from the jowl line to the top of the head. Paul sculpted each ear in clay, then coated the resultant positive mold with multiple layers of liquid latex. After carefully removing the dried latex from the mold, the ears were spray-painted and bonded into place on the headpiece. The monster's four antennae, designed to suggest a cat's whiskers, were made from twelve-inch long candles. Blaisdell would first heat a candle until it became soft and pliable, then bend it to the desired shape. A kind of notched design was pressed into the wax, which was set aside and allowed to harden. Several layers of liquid latex were later painted over the candles. When the latex dried, it was carefully removed and stuffed with cotton and wire so the antennae would maintain its shape. These were later airbrushed and bonded to the headpiece with contact cement.

Blaisdell obtained black plastic from the Frye Plastics Company to create the She-Creature's unusual eyes. Vertical slits were cut into the plastic to enable him to see. The pupils were hand-painted, and a thin line of sequins was added around each iris so that the eyes would glitter in the sunlight during location photography.

The fangs came, once again, from a local novelty store. In this instance Blaisdell used two sets of "vampire fangs," cut in half and glued together backwards to make one long row of teeth with a single long canine on either end. Once the teeth were glued in place and all the other features were exactly as he wanted them, Blaisdell texturized the latex skin and added pores to the cheekbones using a tiny metal hammer he had purchased especially for that purpose.

The final accoutrement to the costume was a circular finlike projection that attached to the headpiece just below the chin. It was made from latex rubber over a wire frame and helped conceal the place where the headpiece fit onto the body suit.

Although the She-Creature has been erroneously described as a crustacean, it was really supposed to be a deep-sea mammal. The source of the confusion is a promotional lobbycard from the film which depicts a lobster-red creature costume, but this is nothing more than a colorized black-and-white photograph. (Most lobbycards from 1950s films were colorized.) In fact, Paul gave the costume a green/green-blue color scheme with black and white trim. The armor plating along the back was light green with dark highlights. The "lunch hooks" were white trim on black, and each of the claws was ivory with a hint of brown trim. The lips were given pale pink highlights. Blaisdell christened his lady-fiend "Cuddles." The completed costume weighed in at a cumbersome 72 pounds.

There was not enough money in the budget to create a watertight costume which could be submerged for underwater photography as in Universal's *Creature from the Black Lagoon*, so Cuddles was neither watertight nor waterproof. She was, as Paul explained, water-resilient. "In other words, she's able to cope with it," he said. For the one shot in the film where the monster would be seen emerging from the ocean, this would be good enough, or so he thought.

Blaisdell took pride in his work on the She-Creature costume. He believed it was not only his best-looking creation, but the most durable and the most functional. It had taken nearly eight weeks to complete, twice as long as *Day the World Ended*'s three-eyed mutant and two weeks longer than *It Conquered the World*'s mushroom monster. In fact, the costume was made well enough to survive the rigors of making not only *The She-Creature*, but three other American-International films in which it appeared, as well as a 1956 television special. As Blaisdell later noted:

> The way I designed *The She-Creature*, she could do anything the script said she would have to do, and more. She could eat, she could sleep, she could drink, she could smoke. She could borrow a cigarette from you, inhale it and blow smoke out of her nose. She could eat a ham sandwich, she could drink a bottle of Coke or sip a cup of coffee. And in spite of how clumsy her claws appear to be, she could pick a handkerchief out of your pocket. It was probably the most comfortable suit you could wear and stay in for a couple of hours. These were things I built into her to make her more lifelike.

Several years before *The She-Creature* was made, Paul and Jackie had met Bob Burns and his wife Kathy at a science-fiction convention in Los Angeles. Both couples attended the convention mainly to hear Ray Bradbury talk about his work on *Moby Dick* and a brand new film called *The Beast from 20,000 Fathoms*. During a break in the festivities, the Blaisdells and Burnses began talking, and Paul mentioned that he was working on a low-budget movie called *The Beast with a Million Eyes*. He invited Bob and Kathy up to his Topanga Canyon workshop, and before long the Burnses were making regular pilgrimages every weekend. They became fast friends, and during Paul's stint on *The She-Creature*, Bob Burns made himself available to help out in whatever way he could.

The night Blaisdell finished the She-Creature and first tried the costume on, Burns was there. He took a series of slides, some in 3-D, that showed off the costume's best attributes. They shot a roll of 35mm film on and around Paul's property, then walked to the nearest street that snaked through lonely Topanga Canyon.

Blaisdell felt like having a little prankish fun. "Listen, Bob, I've got an idea," he whispered from inside the creature costume. "You hide behind these bushes, and I'll hide over there, and when we hear a car coming up the canyon, I'll jump out and give the driver a little scare."

The road was not very heavily traveled, and it took a few minutes before they heard the sound of an approaching auto. "Get ready," Burns said from his hiding place. "I can see the headlights coming up over the hill." Blaisdell waited for just the right moment to be sure the driver would see him; then he sprang across the road in full She-Creature regalia as the car's headlights reflected off the costume. He leaped behind a bush and waited, listening breathlessly. Sure enough, the sound of squealing brakes sliced through the chilly night air. The car skidded to a stop about 20 feet up the road. After a moment, it began backing up. Then it stopped.

From his hidden vantage point, Burns watched to see if anybody would get out of the car. It was too dark to see inside, but he had the feeling the driver was alone. And probably by this time pretty freaked out.

Blaisdell refused to come out of the bushes. He couldn't see what was going on, but by listening to the car's engine he could pretty well guess that the driver had backed up to see what kind of hideous apparition was lying in the road. After a moment of silence, with no further reaction from his victim, Blaisdell decided to peek over the top of the brush.

The car was stopped right in front of him, and somebody was staring out the driver's side window.

Burns couldn't see his pal peering over the foliage, but he figured that Paul must have come out of hiding because suddenly the car's tires began burning rubber as the driver hit the gas to high-tail it out of there. As Burns said later, "Whoever it was probably had a pretty good tale to tell at the local bar, if he made it that far. I just hope we didn't give him a heart attack."

Blaisdell didn't normally terrorize the neighborhood populace with his Hollywood monsters, but he did have a tremendous sense of humor and enjoyed playing around at home with the costumes and props he made for American International and other film companies. Jackie often posed for gag shots with Paul while he was decked out in his monster regalia. Bob Burns would take photos of their antics with his 35mm camera and use the negatives to produce greeting cards which Paul and Jackie sent to their friends at Christmas and on other holidays.

Blaisdell's pranks sometimes even extended to the film set. When Eddie Cahn got a good look at Paul's first female film monster, he decreed that the creature wasn't top-heavy enough. "She's gotta have bigger boobs," Cahn decided. Paul transported the costume back to the workshop for an evening of alterations. When he returned to the set the following day, Cahn took one look at Cuddles' new set of double-D knockers and exclaimed, "Holy Christ! Well, at least now you can tell it's definitely a woman." Grinning from ear to ear, he glanced down at the creature's waist. "Wait a minute. What's that?" he asked, pointing at the abdomen.

"I call them 'lunch hooks,'" Blaisdell explained, and he demonstrated how they clinched together.

"Forget it, Paul," Cahn said. "They're too scary. We can't use them."

"Why not? I thought this was supposed to be a horror movie."

"Yeah, but they're too horrible," Cahn replied.

The She-Creature shoot went smoothly. The atmosphere on the set was user-friendly, because by now most of the crew had worked together before on other AIP productions. Eddie Cahn's many years of film experience enabled the crew to get through as many as 40 setups in a single day. Blaisdell explained: "Eddie liked to show off how fast he could be. We would hardly be finished with one scene when he'd get up from his director's chair and point to some other spot on the ground and say 'there.' That meant that was where he wanted the camera to go. So then the crew would scurry over and begin setting up for the next shot."

The only problem anyone ever had with Eddie Cahn concerned his heavy English accent. He always had a pipe clenched in the center of his mouth, and when he barked out instructions, it usually came out sounding like "Grmlislkft fkdlmrp stdflbnd." Invariably someone would say, "What'd you say, Eddie?" Then he would remove the pipe and repeat whatever it was he had just said in plain English.

Unlike Roger Corman, Cahn never changed things in the script. He always filmed exactly what was written, which is why his cast and crew felt they could count on him. "Eddie never would have decided to have the mushroom monster chase the actors out of the cave in *It Conquered the World*," confided Blaisdell. "Corman would change just about anything if he thought it would be cheaper, or faster, or almost as good."

Although there are only two major and two minor monster sequences in *The She-Creature*, Blaisdell was on call for five of the film's seven shooting days. One of the earliest shots he filmed was for the opening of the picture, when the monster's ghostly form swims through the ocean while Chester Morris intones some eerie voice-over narration. All that was required for the shot was a simple superimposition, so Blaisdell was photographed in the studio lying face-down on a black-draped mattress, mimicking the motions of a swimmer. The image was later combined with a long shot of the ocean, but the two viewpoints were improperly lined up, with the result that the creature seemed to be drifting above the water rather than swimming in it.

Another superimposition was utilized for the scene in which the She-Creature materializes in the seawater beneath the amusement pier. In this instance Blaisdell crouched down against a black studio floor covering while the camera was rigged about eight or nine feet overhead. On Eddie Cahn's cue, Blaisdell stood up and flailed his arms. The shot was superimposed over footage of bubbling seawater filmed at Paradise Cove. The bubbling effect was created with an underwater agitator.

For the scene in which the creature smashes into Johnny's (Paul Dubov) apartment, the crew had prepared a specially scored door made of balsa wood that would come apart easily in sections. The only problem was that it was so delicately fitted together that if anyone brushed up against it the whole thing came tumbling down. Since there was just the one door (there was never enough money in the budget to do these kinds of things twice), someone had the foresight to protect the breakaway prop by reinforcing it with plywood from the opposite side.

When it was time for Blaisdell to knock the hell out of the door, no one remembered that it had been reinforced. Eddie Cahn had two cameras running (a rarity on such an early AIP film) so the action could be caught from both a front angle (Johnny's viewpoint) and a rear angle (from behind the creature). When Cahn called "Action," Blaisdell raised a creature claw and smashed at the door, but the rubber-coated pine costume just bounced off.

Blaisdell hit the door with such force he was knocked backward and fell on the creature's tail. There was so much latex and foam in the tail it almost bounced Paul back up.

Finally someone remembered that the breakaway door had been reinforced with plywood. Down came the plywood for take 2. When the cameras started rolling again, Blaisdell smashed through the doorway easily, but tripped on a piece of splintered wood. This time he fell forward. Because the painted, prescored balsa door had splintered so nicely, Cahn decided just to trim off the end of the sequence, in which the She-Creature sprawled face-down on the floor.

For the next scene, in which the creature overturns the cot on which Paul Dubov is lying, a special lifting prop was used. This time Paul made it across the room without falling over, and then, resting one of his creature claws against the frame, he yanked the cot upward. Actually, it moved pretty slowly, but Cahn was undercranking the camera so that the action would appear speeded-up during projection.

Jackie Blaisdell always had a supply of contact cement on hand for any emergencies that might crop up during filming. If one of the creature's antennae accidentally came loose, for instance, it could quickly be patched back together using the contact cement, and the film crew would lose no real production time. At the end of the day, Blaisdell could redo the repair more thoroughly in his home workshop. Fortunately, the construction of the She-Creature was so solid that it could withstand plenty of physical wear and tear. In fact, Blaisdell was so self-assured about the quality of the She-Creature costume that he told Sam Arkoff it could withstand the firing of .22-calibre blank ammunition. According to Arkoff in his book *Flying Through Hollywood by the Seat of My Pants*, Blaisdell encouraged him: "Go ahead, try shooting .22-calibre blank ammunition at it at close range. It's not going to penetrate the material." Arkoff decided to take Paul's word for it.

The climactic appearance of the monster was filmed on location at Paradise Cove near Los Angeles. This was the only time in the film the monster would actually be seen emerging from the waves, and Eddie Cahn wanted it to look impressive.

"Get out in the water, Paul," Cahn told Blaisdell. "Way out."

Blaisdell walked into the surf and turned around.

"Farther!" Cahn yelled.

Blaisdell backed up a few paces.

"No, no! Get really far out! Farther! Get out up to your waist!"

By the time Paul reached the point where Cahn was happy with what he saw, Blaisdell had become a mere dot in the camera lens. Cahn had set everything up as a wide-angle long-shot, but Blaisdell didn't know that. Besides, he had other things to worry about. The costume was acting just like a big sponge. The foam rubber was saturated with so much sea water he could barely move.

When Cahn finally called "Action!" Blaisdell pressed forward. The water-logged suit of foam rubber felt like it weighed a ton. Every time Paul pushed forward the outgoing ocean current pushed him back. So he started lunging through the water. It was the only way he could make any progress.

"That looks good! Keep it up!" Cahn yelled from the beach. He had no idea Blaisdell was wading through the water the only way he could. After a moment, Cahn yelled, "Move faster, Paul, move faster!"

"Oh sure, Eddie, I'll be right with you," Blaisdell shouted back some-what angrily.

Getting from the ocean to the beach proved to be a pretty difficult feat, but Blaisdell gave it all he had. As many viewers of the finished film would recall, the She-Creature didn't walk, it lumbered. Even the crew didn't real-ize until later that that was the only way Blaisdell could walk in the water-drenched costume. As it turned out, Blaisdell suffered through the oceanic acrobatics all for naught. The image of the monster lumbering out of the ocean had been shot from so far away that nobody could tell what it was, and most of the footage ended up on the cutting-room floor. In the final print, only the creature's feet seem to be in the surf.

Ron Randell, who was standing by waiting to play his death scene, thought the whole thing was ludicrous. He happened to look down and see that sand was getting into his shoes. "Damn, Eddie, look! I'm getting sand in my shoes!" he complained. While everyone else was busy shooting the scene with Blaisdell, Randell was picking sand off his socks.

In later years, Blaisdell recalled this difficult scene:

> Having an outgoing tide did not exactly help to solve the problem of getting the She-Creature to come out of the ocean. The costume weighed in at 72 pounds. Add to this another 50 pounds of cold seawater, and add to that the weight of the guy that's trying to carry this load, and you'll know why she comes out of the ocean so slowly. At least I got a little bit lighter as I got closer to the shore. Between takes I could hear Ron Randell complaining to Eddie about the sand that was getting in his shoes. Meanwhile, Jackie was trying to squeeze all the salt water out of the tail, which weighed a helluva lot more than any sand Ron Randell could get in his shoes.

When the stage was finally set for the She-Creature to clobber Randell sense-less, Blaisdell lumbered across the beach menacingly. Knowing the sound would be rerecorded in postproduction, Blaisdell said, "Listen, Ron, one more laugh out of you and you can forget about any sand in your shoes because you're going to get hit with the She-Creature's arm and end up taking all the salt water that's in this suit back to the prop department with you."

Tom Conway, who was also scheduled to die at the claws of the She-Creature, seemed to be enjoying himself on the set. According to Blaisdell and Bob Burns, he thought the film was "a kick." Blaisdell's scenes with Conway all took place on dry land, and because Conway was the taller of the two,

Paul had built special lifters for the costume so it would appear taller on screen. To make the lifters, Blaisdell glued a pair of sneakers to large styrofoam blocks, which increased his height by another twelve inches. But the lifters proved enormously difficult to walk in, and Blaisdell had to practice for days beforehand just to be able to shuffle from one side of the set to the other. The styrofoam was so light it could easily throw him off balance. One misstep and he would fall flat on his face again.

In the end only three scenes required use of the lifters. The shots of the monster coming at Conway through the bushes were filmed normally, but for a side view of the creature gesturing menacingly at Conway, who also appears in the frame, Paul wore the lifters. Even with practice, walking in them was a problem, so Blaisdell had to "shuffle" forward during the scene. (Alert viewers will spot the white tops of the sneakers and styrofoam blocks at the very bottom of the film frame in this scene.) The lifters were also used when the creature lunges at Conway, who is trying to reach a revolver in his office desk.

Blaisdell's impression of Conway changed as they worked together:

> Before I got to work with Tom Conway, I used to wonder if the man ever smiled. When we worked together on *The She-Creature* he still had that stiff British upper lip. As I recall, he did eventually give in and crack a smile, and smiles grew to kidding around, and that grew to outright laughs. But this is understandable, considering the way I used to look most of the time.

During the film's actual climax, Blaisdell used the lifters one last time to augment the creature's height as it approached Chester Morris (Lombardi) and Lance Fuller (Erickson). Blaisdell towered so high over Fuller that he had to lean into the frame when he took a swipe at the actor with one of the oversized creature claws.

For the final shot, in which the She-Creature gazes longingly at its future body, Blaisdell took off the lifters and replaced them with the normal monster feet. But because Marla English is lying down in the scene, there is no real way for the casual viewer to know that the creature's height has changed in the slightest.

Blaisdell, always at the ready with a cute quip, started teasing Marla before the camera began rolling. By the time Eddie Cahn was ready to shoot the scene, Blaisdell had been joking with Marla so much she couldn't think of him as a monster any longer. When Cahn fired up the .35mm Mitchell camera and the She-Creature's face loomed over her, she started laughing.

"Cut!" yelled Cahn. "What the hell's so funny?"

Marla just giggled, pointing at Blaisdell.

"That's not funny, that's a She-Creature," said Cahn in his heavy British accent, making Marla laugh all the harder.

Blaisdell described the final scene in this way: "The She-Creature didn't die. She was exorcised, not executed. The script called for machine guns and fire to destroy her, but I didn't get hit with any artificial fire and as far as machine guns went, there weren't any. I don't recall anybody putting out the money for the blanks. There were some revolver shots. I probably got shot at with some police positives. It's a lot cheaper."

They eventually got the scene wrapped, but it took a while. It was one of the few times when an AIP picture required more than a single take.

The She-Creature would eventually become a fan favorite, but it didn't win many accolades when it was first released in September of 1956. Some reviewers labeled it "pedestrian," and *Variety*, the industry Bible, called it a "tossed green salad of the Bridey Murphy theme, mixed with [a] helping of monster-from-the-past, and served up with a dash of Svengali." Although *Variety* cited Chester Morris's "capable performance," as well as turns by Marla English, Tom Conway, and Ron Randell, the magazine thought the plotline was "disjointed" and "haphazard" and said "the monster becomes ridiculous when viewed in the strong light of the kliegs." Even so, the reviewer seemed to like something about the film, remarking, "Director Edward L. Cahn manages to mix in a good quota of chills, especially for impressionable small fry."

There was definitely a limit to the horror, however, as Blaisdell later noted:

> When you're making a monster movie, the one that is most fearful of the monster is the producer, not the audience, because the producer sometimes doesn't quite know what to do with it. Isn't it funny that today we can have movies where a zombie gets its head chopped off because it walks too close to the rotoblades of a helicopter and his head bursts apart into the screen like a ruptured watermelon [a reference to George A. Romero's *Dawn of the Dead*]. But when pictures like *The She-Creature* were first produced, we weren't allowed to show anything too horrible.

American International sent *The She-Creature* out as part of a double feature with Roger Corman's *It Conquered the World*. To really get ticket sales booming, AIP wanted Blaisdell to appear on a Los Angeles television show—not in a special "behind the scenes" story, but in full character as the She-Creature herself.

Blaisdell dreaded going on television. "Jackie and I had just got finished working on the film, and you couldn't have got me back inside that suit at that particular time if you'd squeezed me through a cake decorator," Blaisdell insisted. "I'd had enough of that suit to last me at least a week, or until I got caught up on my sleep." But AIP wanted him immediately; they couldn't wait a week. Since Paul didn't want to let Jim Nicholson down, he turned to his pal Bob Burns and asked him if he would be interested in becoming the She-Creature for a day.

"Are you kidding, or what?" Burns said. Of course he would do the TV show. What could be more fun?

Actually, the She-Creature was scheduled for appearances on two Los Angeles shows—*Quinn's Corner* and *Campus Club*. The former was an afternoon talk show hosted by Louis Quinn, who would go on to appear as "Roscoe" in TV's fondly remembered *77 Sunset Strip*. Since Burns was about the same size as Blaisdell, the She-Creature costume fit him remarkably well. With the help of Bob's friend Lionel Comport, who remained on hand to zip Burns in and out of the costume, the She-Creature was soon destined for television stardom.

Things went smoothly for Burns on *Quinn's Corner*, but the *Campus Club* stint nearly turned into a riot as the show's college-age live audience stampeded the stage to get an up-close and personal look at a "real live monster" in the flesh. In retrospect it was a wildly successful publicity stunt, but there was a moment or two when Burns wasn't so sure this had been a good idea. It looked as if the students were going to mow him down in their enthusiastic rush onto the stage. He could imagine Paul's costume being ripped to shreds as dozens of students grabbed for a piece of movie monster to take home as a souvenir.

In *Fantastic Monsters of the Films*, vol. 1, no. 2, Bob Burns described that television appearance:

The Day the She-Creature Invaded TV

While sitting out the 40 minute wait before the [Louis] Quinn interview [on "Quinn's Corner"], Lionel took off my She-Creature head for me, then put it back, suggesting he needed a drink, even if I didn't.

There was a Coke machine in the basement of the TV station, so we got into the elevator and started down. When the doors rolled back to reveal the basement, it also showed us two attractive young secretaries—and they saw us.

Their screams and footsteps faded into the distance like an old "Hi-Yo Silver Away ..."

Finally, at the machine, I found it difficult to hold a pop bottle between my two claws, so I slipped off my huge monster gauntlets and drank the Coke through a straw stuck in the mouthpiece of The She-Creature mask.

Just then, another cute secretary strolled by. Even the sight of my human hands could not soothe her, and she ran screaming off to convince her two friends she had just seen a monster walking around, one with a tongue that hung out, big as a Coke bottle.

As Lionel and I walked back towards the elevator, two other girls sitting at snack tables didn't even look up from the book they were discussing, *The Man Who Made Maniacs*.

It was now time for the TV-appearance of The She-Creature.

On Quinn's Corner, Louis and I gagged it up for a good (I hope) ten minutes, playing it strictly for laughs. Since it was three in the afternoon, the station didn't want any irate mothers saying we scared their kids so bad they weren't able to enjoy the murders on "Martin Kane, Private Eye."

We had opened with Quinn sitting at his desk, giving everybody a big smile of welcome, when I came in through the window behind him, and reached over to tap the cheerful Louis on the shoulder with a scaly claw.

Undaunted, Quinn had gone on to talk casually with me on the fine points of monster film-making, and even sympathized with me about how the poor monster never wins in horror movies.

The bit with Gene Norman was going to be different.

For one thing, on "Campus Club," Norman had a live audience of school kids, and he was going to surprise them with The She-Creature.

They were surprised, all right. The next moment turned into a time of terror.

I was scared stiff that I might get trampled in the mad rush they made up onto the stage, practically driving me through the backdrop, scales and all.

Finally, Norman restored order, and it was time for fun and games.

After we talked about the picture for a while, Norman asked "Cuddles" to join in the marshmallow-eating contest. Admittedly, marshmallow eating is fairly simple—but it does get a little harder when the marshmallow is on a one foot string, and you have to drag it up to your mouth by eating the string. Pure string, I found, tastes nothing like string beans.

Finally, I made it and got my prize—two tickets to see *The She-Creature* at my local theater.

Growling, I gave them to the runner-up.

Then, at the end of a perfect day, Lionel and I headed for the vault—for films—that I had used as a dressing room. As the elevator opened on the 2nd floor, one of the same secretaries we had met in the basement was standing there, her mouth open.

I decided to say something to quiet her. "Don't worry, honey," I said, "I'm not a She-Creature. I'm a man."

But, alas, she just ran off screaming again.

Lionel Comport helped me out of the horror suit, after I had been in there for some four hours. And by that time I was drenched in sweat, just as if I had been in a steam cabinet. I lost three pounds doing the TV spots, but the movie studio figured that it was better I lose pounds than they lose dollars.

Burns enjoyed his TV time with the She-Creature so much that he asked Blaisdell if he could borrow the costume for a few days.

"Sure, no problem," Paul told him, knowing his friend would take good care of it.

Burns had a neighbor who wanted to see the costume up close, so Bob agreed to bring it over that evening. But Burns didn't just bring it, he wore the costume over. It was about 9:30 P.M. on a warm summer night as he made his way through the neighborhood. A little girl no more than seven years old was running and playing by herself. She was so caught up in what she was doing, she never bothered to watch where she was going. Naturally, she ran straight into Burns. Before he could say anything, the girl let out a banshee-like howl and took off running in the direction she'd just come from. The girl was so terrified she accidentally tripped over the curb and chipped her two front teeth on a concrete sidewalk. Burns's first thought was *Oh, my God, lawsuit city*.

He jerked the She-Creature mask off and helped the girl home. When her parents opened the door and saw Burns in the monster costume, they didn't bat an eye. ("They knew I had some pretty weird friends in the movie business," said Burns.) He apologized and explained what had happened as the father walked his daughter upstairs.

"Oh, don't worry about it," the mother said. "Linda has been sneaking out of her room every night for a while now, just to defy us. We told her if she kept it up, one day she was going to run into the Devil."

No lawsuits were forthcoming, but Burns has never forgotten that night. He thinks Linda probably never forgot either. "She was scared so bad, she's probably still in that house," Burns laughed.

The She-Creature came and went during the summer of 1956, and Blaisdell hung the costume out to dry. Little did he dream that he would end up inside that unforgettable "72-pound suit of armor" not once but twice more for two different films and would loan the headpiece to AIP for yet a third production. Not only that, but clips of the lumbering monster (lifted from the sequence where it was stalking Ron Randell) were incorporated into Roger Corman's 1958 production of *Teenage Caveman*, so the costume was seen in a total of five different AIP movies.

The She-Creature barely had time for a summer vacation, and her retirement was a long way off.

6

Voodoo and Venom

The producers wanted to do a quickie at the old Charlie Chaplin studios, so they dreamed up this story literally on a couple of weekend afternoons. Russ Bender wrote the script, and he had never written a script in his life—he was an actor—and he had no idea what to do with a creature called a "zombie." In fact, I don't think anyone connected with *Voodoo Woman* had ever read a pulp magazine when they were kids to find out what a zombie was.

—Paul Blaisdell

Alex Gordon liked *The She-Creature* so much he decided to make a second picture about a female fiend for AIP. He didn't much care what the story was about, so long as its protagonist was a woman. Since screenwriters Lou Rusoff and Chuck Griffith were busy working on other pictures, Gordon turned over the scriptwriting chores to Russ Bender, the actor who had played General Pattick in *It Conquered the World*.

Bender hadn't written a screenplay before, but as an actor he'd read numerous scripts and was well aware of the mechanics of putting them together. With advice from Sam Arkoff and Lou Rusoff, and the help of a cowriter named V. I. Voss, Bender figured he could pull off a decent script. As it turned out, Bender knew how to put together a script; he just didn't know how to tell a good story.

Bender turned in his finished screenplay, entitled *Black Voodoo*, to Alex Gordon and thereby ended his scriptwriting career. (He continued acting in films for Roger Corman and AIP throughout the 1960s. One of the last pictures he did for Nicholson and Arkoff was *Devil's Angels*. He died in 1969.) Gordon now owned a fairly uninventive and uneventful script about a she-monster conjured into being by a cross-breeding of voodoo and modern medicine. It wasn't very impressive, and it definitely was not as memorable as Rusoff's script for *The She-Creature*, but it would have to do. Alex began lining up a cast and crew and asked Paul Blaisdell to take a look at the script and begin working out some ideas for the film's title monster.

Meanwhile, Roger Corman was also working on a movie that had a female protagonist. Known during preproduction as *The Trance of Diana Love,* the title of the script by Chuck Griffith, it was eventually released as *The Undead*. It was mainly a fantasy with horrific overtones. Griffith had originally written his script entirely in iambic pentameter, which Corman thought was a neat idea. Later on, of course, Roger had second thoughts and asked Griffith to rewrite the script without any poetic touches.

Like *The She-Creature*, *The Undead* tried to exploit interest in the Bridey Murphy story. A streetwalker is regressed through hypnosis to an earlier life (seen in extended flashback sequences) as a fairytale princess accused of witchcraft. The real witch (Allison Hayes) and her familiar are shape-shifters who can change into cats or bats.

Corman wanted Blaisdell to do some work for *The Undead*. Since his new picture would rely mainly on opticals (and poor ones at that) for its effects, there would be no need for a full-figured monster, so Paul agreed to design and build the flying bats. But later, when it became apparent that *The Undead* would interfere with his commitment to Alex Gordon's film, Blaisdell got Corman's approval to repaint and reoutfit two of the Flying Fingers he had originally designed for *It Conquered the World*. In the end, the bats were flown through the mythic sets of *The Undead* using the same fishpole device Paul had used on the earlier film. Although they didn't really look all that much like the fairy-tale bats Corman had in mind, they sufficed, and no one ever complained.

Blaisdell also had a cameo in *The Undead* as a staring-eyed corpse. (The makeup was handled by the film's regular makeup artist, not by Blaisdell himself.) During his brief bit, Paul came face to face with Pamela Duncan, who played the double role of Princess Helene and Diana Love. While Helene is trying to escape the notice of a band of witch-hunters, she climbs into a coffin occupied by a corpse (Blaisdell). Paul had fond memories of his stint on *The Undead*: "Frankly, I thought I made a pretty good corpse," he opined. "I mean, how many times do you get a chance to be a corpse and have a very attractive girl using you for a mattress?" There was a downside to the role, however. "It was a bit difficult, though, because I was supposed to be a staring-eyed corpse, and insulation from the ceiling was constantly floating down and getting into my eyes."

As *Black Voodoo*—now retitled *Voodoo Woman*—neared its start-up date, producer Alex Gordon began rounding up his cast. Some familiar faces from *The She-Creature* showed up in the new film, including Marla English, Tom Conway, Lance Fuller, and Paul Dubov, who were under contract to AIP. With Blaisdell playing the part of the monster, that made a total of five cast members from the earlier film returning to engage unearthly forces in the new production.

The She-Creature had cost American International over $100,000 to make, and it wasn't interested in sinking that much money into *Voodoo Woman*. As quickly and cheaply made as most of AIP's movies were to begin with,

Voodoo Woman was even cheaper and quicker. The film was budgeted in the neighborhood of $60,000. When Gordon figured out the logistics, he realized there wasn't enough money in the budget to make the picture he had in mind. Corners had to be cut somewhere.

Most of the cuts ended up coming out of the makeup and effects budget. That meant Paul Blaisdell had even less money to work with than usual. No matter how the numbers were juggled, there was simply no way AIP could finance an entirely new movie monster this time around.

Blaisdell had been doing a series of pencil sketches of the title monster when Alex Gordon broke the bad news. Blaisdell's pivotal idea for the "zombie woman" survived up to the final sketch—the one he would use to sell the idea for the design to AIP and the one which he would use as a starting point for his full-size costume. But that was as far as he got in designing an entirely new creature. Bob Burns, one of the few persons outside of Paul and Jackie, Alex Gordon, and Jim Nicholson to ever see the sketch (which unfortunately has not survived over the years), said it had the appearance of "a sickly, shrunken head," although it was normal-sized on a normal-sized woman's body. Blaisdell himself said the monster "would give you the dry heaves if she served you a cup of tea." But AIP wasn't having any of it—potential for dry heaves at drive-ins across the country or not. Arkoff told Blaisdell what they had decided. "We'll just dust off your She-Creature costume, Paul. You can make a couple of changes here and there, give her something new, make her look a little different. By the way, you don't have much time. We've got to have this thing ready in about a week because the studio has already been booked."

At that point Blaisdell lost whatever enthusiasm he may have had for the picture. He agreed to redesign the She-Creature's body only if AIP would find someone else to design a new headpiece. "We can't use the same face," Paul argued. Reluctantly, AIP agreed. They'd find somebody else to create the new headpiece.

At their home workshop, Paul and Jackie began the task of revamping the She-Creature costume to make way for "Voodoo," which is what Blaisdell called the new monster. Off came the rudimentary wings, the dorsal fins, the tail and three pairs of horns from the elbows, knees, and feet. The lunch hooks were removed and newly cut pieces of block foam were cemented into all the gaps and colored with an airbrush to match the greenish-blue hue of the rest of the costume. A large piece of burlap was wrapped around the body to further disguise it.

Meanwhile, AIP had awarded the job of designing the monster mask to Harry Thomas, a makeup artist whose credits included *Frankenstein's Daughter* and *The Neanderthal Man*. Thomas was "between assignments," as they say. He promised to have the headpiece ready by the time Blaisdell finished revamping the She-Creature costume.

When Thomas eventually turned in his finished mask, everyone at AIP was horrified all right—but for all the wrong reasons. The head looked cheap. It looked phony. It looked like he had purchased it from a novelty shop.

In fact, that's exactly what Thomas had done. According to a source at AIP, Thomas had gotten hold of an ordinary "over the top" latex skull-mask—the kind anyone could buy at Halloween for $5 or so—and glued a cheap blonde wig to the top of it. "My God, we can't use this," Alex Gordon told Sam Arkoff the first time he saw it. Sam got on the phone to Blaisdell and told him what had happened. "Can you do anything to save this thing?" he asked.

Paul was not happy. He hadn't wanted to reuse the She-Creature costume in the first place. It didn't look anything like a zombie, but no one seemed much concerned about that. Now they wanted him to fix this travesty of a headpiece, which is what he had hoped to avoid all along.

"Oh, all right," Blaisdell grumbled. "Drop it off at my workshop."

AIP sent the mask to Topanga Canyon. When Paul opened the shipping carton he couldn't believe his eyes. He was looking at a dime-store Halloween mask. Did AIP actually pay Thomas for such a monstrous miscarriage?

For years Blaisdell never told the media the complete truth about poor old Voodoo. Never one to speak badly of a colleague, he merely said that Harry Thomas's headpiece "required a little bit of cutting and trimming" to make the mask fit his own measurements. "It didn't turn out too badly," he lied.

But Bob Burns told the truth. "That mask looked just awful," Burns revealed. "Thomas had poked two holes in the latex eye sockets so Paul could see out of it—or maybe it was that way when he bought it—but there were no eyeballs, no teeth, nothing. Paul had to rebuild that mask almost from scratch, and he only had three days to do it. That's all the time AIP gave him."

Rescuing the headpiece involved a laborious building up process. Blaisdell covered the mask with sections of foam rubber and latex in order to bring out the monster's cheekbones and chin. The eye sockets were accentuated as well and colored black. A skeletal nose cavity—one of the mask's few attributes that Blaisdell retained—was rendered three-dimensionally by building it up with nose putty and latex, then "pinching out" the nostrils, with the result that the face took on a semblance of Lon Chaney's Phantom of the Opera.

Blaisdell added fangs and eyeballs with huge pupils, which gave the mask a uniquely eerie appearance. He glued a tongue depressor to the inside of the mouth so he could give the face a bit of life on camera by wiggling it between his teeth. After painting it to match the hue of the She-Creature bodysuit, he lacquered it to give the foam-rubber "flesh" a reflective sheen.

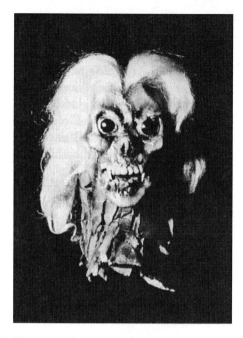

The zombified Voodoo Woman was a composite of the She-Creature bodysuit and a brand new headpiece provided by makeup man Harry (*Frankenstein's Daughter*) Thomas. Unfortunately, Thomas's work was so inferior that AIP had to ask Paul Blaisdell to rescue the film's title monster. Blaisdell ended up having to rebuild the mask almost from scratch (courtesy of Bob Burns).

When photographed, Voodoo looked right at home in a steaming jungle set, her monstrous visage seemingly drenched in sweat.

Blaisdell also changed the costume's hands and feet, removing the oversized monster gauntlets and swim-fin feet originally designed for the She-Creature. Out of time and money, he purchased fresh pairs of commercial monster claws and monster feet and outfitted them with pine-carved toenails and fingernails, which were customized with foam rubber and painted with an airbrush to simulate the jigsaw pattern of the body suit.

Although the headpiece had started out as a disaster, it ended up looking a lot more frightening than anyone ever expected it could. Although she was never shown very clearly in the finished film, Voodoo nevertheless made a memorable addition to Blaisdell's creature canon.

The film opens in the savage jungles beyond French Bantalaya. Dr. Roland Gerard (Tom Conway) has infiltrated a voodoo tribe whose high priest, Chaka (Martin Wilkins), stands in awe of "white man's magic." Through a combination of modern medical science and ancient sorcery, Gerard is able to alter the physical constitution of the human body. He has been experimenting on a young beauty from a neighboring village named Sirandah (Jean Davis), but so far the results have been mixed. Gerard's Hitleresque dream is to create an entire new race of beings—half-man, half-beast—that can carry out telepathic commands. With an army of such hybrids at his disposal, a man would be a king.

In a Bantalayan pub, Marilyn Blanchard (Marla English), a conniving beauty from the slums of Pittsburgh, and her boyfriend Rick (Lance Fuller) are keeping a watchful eye on Harry West (Norman Willis), an opportunist who possesses a jungle map that shows the route to a native village rich in gold artifacts. Money-hungry Marilyn asks her barkeeping friend Marcel

(Paul Dubov) to create a diversion so that she and Rick can sneak into West's room and purloin the map. Marcel sends the resident barroom singer (Giselle D'Arc) to West's table to keep him occupied while Marilyn and Rick take a powder. (Sharp-eyed viewers will spot Paul Blaisdell, in one of his few non-monster roles, sitting at a table in the pub.)

West surprises the couple during their search but is killed by a bullet from Marilyn's pistol. Marcel agrees to arrange a burial that won't raise any questions—for a fee. Marilyn promises to pay him when she returns from the jungle with her gold.

The next day Ted Bronson (Mike "Touch" Connors), a part-time guide West had hired by mail, arrives at the pub. Since Bronson never met the real West, Rick poses as the fortune hunter and outlines Marilyn's plan. Bronson warns them that stealing from a voodoo cult can only result in death by retribution, but Marilyn thinks she can outsmart any native tribes that dare interfere with her plans and make it back to civilization alive.

Back at the village, Dr. Gerard continues his experiments on Sirandah. He leads her to an underground laboratory and injects her with a drug that changes her flesh into a stony substance capable of withstanding the impact of a bullet as well as scorching fire and burning acid. Gerard's wife Susan (Mary Ellen Kaye) is a reluctant witness to her husband's twisted experiments. She believes he is insane and lives in mortal terror of him. Guarded round the clock by Gerard's manservant Bobo (Otis Greene) and Chaka's guard Gandor (Emmett E. Smith), she is a virtual prisoner in her own home.

Gerard changes Sirandah into a hulking monstrosity and leads her to a neighboring village, where the natives flee in panic. He commands her to destroy one of the native huts, and with her newfound strength she is able to pull it down with one bony claw. But when Gerard orders her to kill a young village couple, the spell is broken and Sirandah reverts to her human form. "You must kill in order to survive," Gerard warns her, but Sirandah has a good heart and is unable to take a human life.

Chaka explains that Sirandah disobeyed Gerard's instructions because there is no evil within her soul. But Gerard remains convinced he can train Sirandah to murder at his command and continues the experiments. He changes her once more into a she-monster and demonstrates her invulnerability to his captive wife. Fearful of her husband's escalating madness and what he might have in store for her, Susan enlists Bobo's aid to help her escape, but Gandor kills Bobo with a spear before he can get outside the village perimeter.

Gerard finally admits that Chaka was right about Sirandah and sends the girl back to her own village. Meanwhile, Marilyn and her entourage are making their way through the jungle. Scouting ahead of the rest of the troup, Rick runs into Sirandah and recognizes a trinket she is wearing as a gold artifact from the legendary voodoo village. He murders her and takes her necklace to Marilyn. "The gold's right in our backyard," he tells her.

Dr. Gerard (Tom Conway) shows off the indestructible Voodoo Woman (Paul Blaisdell) to his wife Susan (Mary Ellen Kaye).

Guards from Chaka's tribe discover Sirandah's corpse and move in to surround Marilyn's camp. Dr. Gerard accompanies them and explains that the tribe demands a death to recompense the murder of Sirandah. To make matters worse, the victim must be killed by a white man. As soon as she hears that, Marilyn pulls out her pistol and kills Rick instantly. Gerard realizes he has found the perfect woman for his experiments.

Ted is imprisoned in Gerard's house while the doctor and Chaka initiate Marilyn into the tribe's voodoo rites. Gerard explains that once she has been made a tribal priestess she can have anything the tribe has, including its gold. In actuality he wants her to submit to the voodoo ritual as the first part of the chemical process that will turn her into one of his monstrous superbeings. After he leads her to his lab and injects her with a special serum, Marilyn changes into the she-beast.

Ted makes a break for freedom, killing Gandor in the process. Susan tries to escape next but runs right into Gerard and his she-creature. Gerard decides to give Susan to Chaka's tribe, which is demanding another sacrifice. He orders the creature to carry Susan to the tribe's sacrificial altar.

When Ted returns to find out what happened to Susan, he is captured by two guards and tied up next to her at the sacrificial stake. Chaka surprises Gerard by telling him that the tribe demands his life as well. Gerard silently wills the she-beast to come to his aid. When Chaka's men see the approaching

The Voodoo Woman (Paul Blaisdell) abducts Susan Gerard (Mary Ellen Kaye) at the direction of her megalomaniac husband Roland (Tom Conway).

apparition, they scatter in terror. The vengeance-minded Gerard then tells his creation, "Chaka must die, too." The monster throws the voodoo priest into a pool of poisonous vapors.

During the confusion Ted manages to break free of his bonds, and he and Susan escape. Now alone with his indestructible superbeing, Gerard watches as it examines the tribe's ritual artifacts. "Clay—that's all they are," Gerard reveals. "There was only one gold idol, and Chaka took that with him into the pit." Outraged by Gerard's deception, the creature pins him against a tree, crushing his neck. With Gerard's death, the spell is broken, and Marilyn reverts to her true form. She remembers Gerard's words about Chaka's gold idol and sees it wedged between the edge of the pit and its poisonous surface. As she kneels at the edge of the pit, she loses her footing and tumbles straight into the poisonous vapors.

When Ted and Susan arrive at the pub in Bantalaya, Marcel asks them about Marilyn and Rick. "They're both dead," Ted tells him. Marcel shakes his head knowingly. "Her friend, maybe. But Marilyn? I have a feeling that one still lives."

Sure enough, in the film's closing shot the indestructible she-beast climbs out of the sacrificial pit, a familiar gold idol clutched in one scaly claw.

The Pit of Death from *Voodoo Woman*. Voodoo shaman Chaka (Martin Wilkins) pre-
pares to sacrifice Susan Gerard (Mary Ellen Kaye) to the dark gods. Sitting atop the
wooden post at left is the film's "MacGuffin"—the native idol pursued by Marilyn Blanchard (Marla English, not shown).

Marla English, who played the character of Marilyn, particularly
impressed Paul Blaisdell:

> Marla English was such a wonderful lady to work with. She was a beauty
> by any contemporary standard of beauty—very tall and statuesque, she could
> make your heart melt. But she was also a very down-to-earth and a very
> conscientious person. She was just an all-around terrific person to know.
> And Marla worked hard on her scripts. She studied them and rehearsed her
> scenes over and over like a beaver trying to build a dam. She really did a lot
> more than she should have been required or expected to do. But Marla was
> that conscientious and that studious, and everyone on the set really tried to
> help her when it appeared that things might be getting too strenuous for
> her. We all tried to joke around with her and get her to relax. She was a real
> trooper.

In addition to the revamped She-Creature outfit, Blaisdell designed and
built the voodoo idol that registered dollar signs in the eyes of Marla's character, Marilyn Blanchard. The sculpture was modeled in clay, using a papier-
mâché Halloween pumpkin decoration as a base to give it bulk and was then
painted gold so it would resemble an actual artifact, even though the film was

"Ugga," the mysterious idol that causes all the hubbub in *Voodoo Woman*, was so named because, according to Paul Blaisdell, "you'd take one look at it and go 'ugga-*ugga*!'" Ugga's girfriend is one of the Puppet People created by Blaisdell for Bert I. Gordon's *Attack of the Puppet People* (courtesy of Bob Burns).

made in black and white. "I nicknamed the idol 'Ugga,' because you'd take one look at it and go 'ugga-*ugga*,'" joked Blaisdell.

Blaisdell has often referred to *Voodoo Woman* as "a hard-luck picture" because, among other things, many of the cast and crew came down with colds and viruses, including himself. The picture was made during the winter of

1956–57 and the studio sets were often permeated by an uncharacteristic Southern California chill.

AIP gave the project to Eddie Cahn to direct because he could work faster than even Roger Corman. Cahn was in no mood to hear about aches and pains and the flu season. He was under the gun to get *Voodoo Woman* finished in record time, and he expected his crew to be ready and available on time each morning in order not to fall behind schedule. This made working conditions even more strenuous, and tempers sometimes flared.

Marla English was one of those who caught the flu bug. Oddly enough, the disabling fever that she began to run eventually helped cool off most of the tempers Cahn had been stoking with his vociferous attitude during the production's unrelenting physical pace. Marla was trying hard not to let the bug get the best of her. When the crew saw how she was struggling to cope, everyone pulled together to help her out. That defused a potentially volatile situation which, left unchecked, might have threatened to shut down the entire production.

Tempers and temperatures weren't the only problems that surfaced during the making of *Voodoo Woman*. The rush-rush nature of this AIP quickie was partially responsible for an inadvertent relaxation of standard safety precautions, and Paul Blaisdell ended up on the wrong end of a potentially gruesome incident that should never have occurred in the first place.

The mishap took place during the shooting of a scene in which Dr. Gerard (Tom Conway) demonstrates the indestructibility of his zombie creation to his hysterical wife (Mary Ellen Kaye). The script called for Conway to pour "acid" on the creature's exposed leg. The "acid" would smoke and bubble, but the creature's skin would remain unaffected.

Blaisdell was outfitted in his Voodoo garb and climbed into position on the table that served as Gerard's experimental platform. While Tom Conway and Mary Ellen Kaye stood patiently by, a prop man appeared with the vial of "acid" and showed Conway how to pour it so that Fred West's camera could catch the best angle. Blaisdell took one look at the container and tapped a scaly Voodoo finger on the fellow's shoulder. "That's not the kind of chemical smoke made from ammonia and hydrochloric acid, is it?" Blaisdell asked suspiciously.

"Oh, no! This is something new. It's called 'Brett Smoke,'" the fellow assured him. "It's completely harmless."

"Well, okay."

After Conway and Kaye took up their positions on the set, the camera began rolling. Conway poured the liquid onto the leg of Paul's costume. Although he couldn't see how it looked from his vantage point inside Voodoo's headpiece, Blaisdell figured the stuff must have given out a pretty good blossom of smoke because Eddie Cahn was letting the camera roll.

But a moment later Blaisdell felt the telltale signs of a real acid burn collecting on his leg inside the costume. Within seconds his skin felt as if it was on fire. Cahn finally yelled "Cut," and that's when Blaisdell started yelling—for help. Despite all the assurances, the "Brett Smoke" proved far from harmless and left a scar on Blaisdell's leg that stayed there for the rest of his life. Blaisdell never forgot that day:

> The kind of chemical smoke we used to make in chemistry class will give out a beautiful cloud of smoke … as long as you don't pour it on living tissue. I was assured that "Brett Smoke" contained a new type of chemical that caused no harm whatsoever. The only mistake Tom Conway and I made was in taking the prop man's word for it. After the scene was over, I told Eddie, "Look, I'm going to have to go to the dispensary and get this wrapped up if we're going to finish this picture," and he said okay. Fortunately, the studio had a good dispensary. They also had a nurse named Peggy that had been versed in theatrics for a long, long time, and she had treated injuries of this nature. I ended up down in the dispensary with Marla [English], who was really having a tough time with the flu. We ended up with our cots smacking head to head and exchanged commiserations with each other. Peggy the nurse was a really wonderful gal. She patched my leg up, and she got Marla up on her feet again so she could finish doing *Voodoo Woman*. Like I said, it was a real hard-luck picture. Everybody on that film ended up recovering from something.

Eddie Cahn wanted Voodoo to look larger than life, so Blaisdell brought along the special lifters he had made for the She-Creature. Cahn got the effect he wanted in those scenes where the village natives take one look at the monster and run for the hills. With the camera positioned directly behind Blaisdell for an over-the-shoulder shot, the natives appeared puny while the monster seemed enormous.

Blaisdell plodded along in the lifters for several scenes, and in one shot very nearly lost his balance, which could have resulted in a serious injury—not only to himself, but to Mary Ellen Kaye. For the scene in which Dr. Gerard commands the she-monster to abduct his wife, Cahn wanted Blaisdell to carry Mary Ellen under one arm so the audience could see how strong this female fiend was. Blaisdell was a small-framed individual, but he was muscular and a lot stronger than he appeared. He sized up the situation and decided he could do it.

"Yah, good," Cahn said. "Now, go put on the lifters."

Of course, Paul hadn't counted on that. Picking up Mary Ellen Kaye in one arm was one thing, but doing it in those foot-tall lifters was something else. He started to argue, but Cahn was adamant. He had to wear the lifters. Tom Conway was in the scene as well, and Voodoo had to look big.

In the end Blaisdell pulled off the stunt, but not without a bit of a strain. In the finished film, after the monster grabs Kaye she goes shuffling off through the jungle. And she goes shuffling off slowly. "I had to walk as carefully as possible during that scene," Blaisdell said. "One misstep and Mary

Ellen and I would've ended up horizontal instead of vertical, possibly with a broken limb, or broken teeth, or who knows what? And I had no desire to visit the dispensary again, and neither did she."

Blaisdell wasn't the only one who wore special lifters to appear taller on screen. Costars Mike Connors and Lance Fuller were enjoying a friendly sort of rivalry, and each wanted to look taller than the other. Every time the actors reported to the set, one of them had somehow gained an extra half-inch or so of height. The crew wondered what the hell was going on because every day someone different was taller. Finally Connors admitted he and Fuller had been putting lifts in their shoes, wondering when somebody was going to catch on. No one ever told Eddie Cahn that over half of his movie had been shot with costars whose heights changed literally from scene to scene.

While Cahn was directing *Voodoo Woman*, Roger Corman was finishing up *The Undead* and AIP was designing ad campaigns for both pictures. In most situations the films were booked together as a double feature. Invariably, Corman's feature scored higher marks from audiences, who seemed to warm to *The Undead*'s skewered storybook peculiarities, while *Voodoo Woman*, for the most part, was dismissed as "dull and hackneyed." *Variety* called the story "routinized" and pointed out, "There's little worry to make things credible."

After he finished *The Undead*, Corman went to work for Allied Artists, directing *Attack of the Crab Monsters* from a script by Chuck Griffith. Corman invited Blaisdell to design the title creatures—gigantic crabs born of (what else?) atomic radiation—but Paul declined after looking at the script. While it was obvious there would be only one full-size monster required for the film, he thought the budget appropriation for special effects was just too skimpy. Paul just didn't see how he could do it justice. (Although there was supposed to be a whole "invasion" of crab creatures, Griffith's script, written to Corman's formula, ensured that there was never more than a single monster on camera at one time.)

Blaisdell did accept Corman's offer to work on the cofeature, however. It was another science-fiction entry, this time based on a script coauthored by Griffith and Mark Hanna entitled *Not of This Earth*. Blaisdell found the assignment appealing because there were no oversized monsters to build and no full-bodied costumes to wear. Instead, he would be designing a few key props and a single alien entity that would be shown on-screen for less than sixty seconds. It was an opportunity to take a break from all the headaches that had become part and parcel of the latest AIP projects.

Although *Not of This Earth* was made by a different motion picture outfit, it was still a rushed production. After all, anything Roger Corman was involved with always turned into a rush job. The distributor, Allied Artists, never put much money into its films in the first place. Allied Artists had begun life as Monogram Pictures, the source of some of the worst movies ever to come out of Hollywood during the 1940s. Revitalized in the 1950s and rechristened Allied Artists, the company was still making bottom-line films. Some of them were just lousy, and others—the ones made by Corman, for example—ranged from forgettable to forgivable.

Not of This Earth turned out to be one of Corman's better 1950s features. It was made with the same brevity as most of his other productions, but the Griffith/Hanna screenplay contained enough off-the-wall elements to make it seem fresh and exciting. The story begins with the murder of a young girl on her way home from a late-night date. A strange man in dark glasses blasts her brain out of existence with one look from his solid-white eyeballs. Death is instantaneous. Leaning over her still body, the killer opens a metal briefcase and unsheathes a needle-tipped tube. A moment later the victim's blood begins spilling into one of the glass containers inside the briefcase.

Paul Johnson (Paul Birch), the stranger with the dark glasses, visits the offices of Dr. Frederick Rochelle (William Roerick) to request a blood transfusion. Johnson claims to be dying from a rare blood disorder, but refuses to submit to a routine blood test. He hypnotizes Dr. Rochelle and explains that he is from a planet called Davanna. On this world, humans are dying from a disease that grew out of severe adventitious effects generated by a prolonged nuclear war. The blood in their bodies is literally turning to dust. Johnson has been sent to Earth to determine whether human blood is compatible with his own. If it is, the entire human race will be put through a pasteurization process to supply the millions of gallons of plasma that will be needed to sustain the lives of the Davannians.

Rochelle's nurse, Nadine Storey (Beverly Garland), begins Johnson's treatments by functioning as a live-in nurse on loan from Rochelle's office. Johnson's manservant, an ex-con named Jeremy (Jonathan Haze), has the hots for Nadine, but she's dating a cop named Harry Sherbourne (Morgan Jones), who is suspicious of Johnson and Jeremy as well. Nadine thinks Harry is overreacting, but the longer she stays in Johnson's house the more she begins to wonder—what is Johnson really up to?

In his personal quarters, Johnson uses a remote control device to open a concealed door that houses an interplanetary matter transmitter. Through this device he is able to communicate with his home planet and receive instructions from the Controller (also Paul Birch), who outlines a six-part plan to subjugate the human race.

Periodically Johnson fries the brains of unfortunates who happen to cross his path (including Dick Miller in a cameo role as Joe Piper, a door-to-door vacuum cleaner salesman) and transfuses their blood into glass containers which he then refrigerates in his cellar. A Chinaman (Harold Fong) is the first live specimen sent through the matter transmitter for Davannian research, but the body is compressed by the teleportation process and arrives on Davanna crushed beyond recognition. Johnson learns this from a Davann-ian female (Anne Carroll) who uses the teleportation device to escape her dying world. In need of an immediate transfusion, she and Johnson break into Rochelle's office to obtain the required plasma, but Johnson unwittingly trans-fuses blood from a rabid dog into the girl's body. She later expires in a hos-pital. When her body is examined, the telltale dark glasses and white eye-balls give Harry further reason to suspect Johnson's motives.

Johnson surprises Nadine and Jeremy while they are examining the mat-ter transmitter. Johnson fries Jeremy's brain, then pursues the fleeing Nadine through the woods. Not used to driving an automobile (Jeremy had always chauffered him), Johnson comes perilously close to death. Harry gives pur-suit in his police cruiser and turns on the siren, which breaks Johnson's con-centration. The alien's hearing is so acute that the sound shatters his senses, and his car plummets over a cliff, killing him on impact.

Later, at the gravesite ("Here lies a man who was not of this earth"), another Davannian, a double for Johnson, appears in the distance.

Corman asked Blaisdell to supply a variety of props for *Not of This Earth*, including the blood suitcase, remote control box, teleportation machine, an alien "embryo," and the "flying umbrella monster." As always, there was barely enough time to design one decent effect, let alone several, but Blaisdell man-aged to do the impossible once again. Everything Corman asked for was delivered on time and within budget.

The blood suitcase was an easy prop to make. Blaisdell customized an aluminum Hallibuton suitcase, adding glass containers and plastic tubing to the interior and securing everything in place with metal bands. The "tele-portation portal" took a bit more time to prepare. Beginning with a balsa wood framework, Blaisdell set up horizontal rows of flashing lights across the bottom panel and wired everything from the back. A double lever made from plastic globes attached to a wooden frame was added to the right side of the device to represent a master "on-switch." Lastly, a combination of rods and orbs was hung directly overhead. Altogether, the finished device stood nearly seven feet tall and about two and a half feet wide.

A simple "remote control" was carved out of pine and outfitted with sev-eral black knobs, six tear-drop stationary lights, a telescoping antennae made from plastic tubing, and a glowing dial that was illuminated with AC power using a cord that ran up Paul Birch's coat sleeve, down his back, and off the set to a wall socket. There was also a two-inch plastic figure inside the box that was supposed to be an image of the Controller of Davanna. In reality it was a "Marskman," a commercially sold tie-in figure from the old "Space Patrol" television series.

The embryonic version of the jellyfish creature measured about seven inches long and was made from liquid latex poured over a positive clay mold. The embryo was wrapped in colored tissue paper and placed in a plastic

Paul Blaisdell not only designed movie monsters, he also built props like this "interplanetary teleportation controller," a favorite device of the uncanny Mr. Johnson (Paul Birch), a man who was most definitely *Not of This Earth* (courtesy of Bob Burns).

cylinder inside the blood suitcase. This version of the creature was on-screen for less than 15 seconds. A simple photographic dissolve suggested the embryo's growth into the full-size adult alien.

Working from a single preapproved pencil sketch, Blaisdell created the jellyfish monster with latex, foam rubber, and wire coat hangers. The hangers served as a framework for the monster's umbrella-shaped body. Blocks of foam rubber were used to pad out the central portion of the body. Liquid latex was painted over the assembled wire frame and foam rubber in successive layers. After it had dried, the latex was given a purplish sheen and highlights were added with an airbrush.

Hooks or nails carved out of pine and coated with latex were cemented to the creature's bell-shaped posterior, and a face of sorts was added to the top. The face was actually a rubber prop that was obtained from a magician's supply shop and customized with pieces of block foam and latex. Paul also bought a handful of the famous rubber lizards that had served the Beast with a Million Eyes so well, cut off their tails, and used them to further augment the appearance of the monster's head. The finished alien prop was attached to the fishpole flying rig Blaisdell used on *It Conquered the World*. He didn't

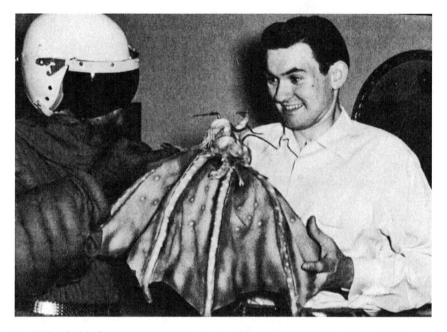

Paul Blaisdell (left, in "Major Mars" getup) and Bob Burns examine the umbrella creature from Roger Corman's *Not of This Earth*. There is no truth to the rumor that Paul based the monster's design on Hedda Hopper's outrageous frippery (courtesy of Bob Burns).

have much time to practice flying the umbrella monster, so in the finished film it merely glides through the air as if it were levitating.

The monster's only purpose in *Not of This Earth* is to kill the good Dr. Rochelle (William Roerick). After Paul had flown his creature into the doctor's office, he carefully maneuvered it across the room, letting it hover slightly before eventually lowering it so that the creature appeared to land directly on top of Roerick's head. The actor then took over, grabbing the alien by its rubber-coated wire frame and struggling on camera while slowly pulling the wire frame closed around his neck to simulate a horrendously slow strangulation. Spirits were running high as Roerick agreed to "bleed" on camera for Corman, who wanted to punch up the scene with a little 1950s-style grue. In a black-and-white film, just about any liquid can be used to simulate blood if it's dark enough and opaque. In *Not of This Earth*, Roerick bled pure grape juice. By letting it slowly leak out of his mouth onto the desktop after the alien has squeezed his head like a ripe boil, Roerick gave the film that extra touch of the grisly which was probably responsible for generating quite a few Technicolor nightmares.

Blaisdell not only made the necessary props, he was always on hand to see that they worked properly, as he later explained:

Back in the days when we made these pictures, the unions were not as strict as they later became, so I would hang around the set almost all the time just to make sure all the effects worked properly and that there were no slip-ups. Nowadays that wouldn't be possible. I doubt I'd be on the set at all. But back then, you had to be there if you wanted things to work out right. Building something like the jellyfish monster for *Not of This Earth* and then handing it over to some prop man to try and make it fly ... uh-uh, no way. I was there to make sure Roger Corman got what he was paying for. He might not have been paying much, you understand, but he *was* paying, and he was entitled to the best effect he could get at the price we had agreed on.

Although Corman had no problems with the props Paul made for the film, he did encounter some difficulties with his star, Paul Birch. In fact, Corman managed to so upset Birch that the actor ended up walking off the picture. It all had to do with a special set of oversized contact lenses Birch was required to wear for scenes in which his eyes were to appear totally white. The lenses proved quite uncomfortable to wear for long periods of time. (Christopher Lee would experience similar problems with the contact lenses Hammer asked him to wear for its series of Dracula films.) Naturally, Birch wanted to keep the lenses in as little as possible. Corman, on the other hand, wanted Birch to wear them around the clock, even when he was not on camera. Not that the director was being purposefully sadistic; he merely wanted Birch to be "ready to go" whenever Corman decided to shoot more alien footage. Birch thought that was ridiculous and told Corman so. Roger simply replied, "Wear the lenses, Paul."

Birch finally got so upset he challenged Corman, and the two nearly got into a fistfight. According to Chuck Griffith, "They pushed and shoved each other, but it was really just a farce that came to nothing." Nevertheless, Birch was angry enough to walk off the set, disrupting the film schedule. Fortunately for Corman, most of the actor's scenes were already in the can. Since Birch wore dark glasses and a hat slouched over his brow for most of the film, it was relatively easy to substitute a stand-in for the few scenes that remained to be filmed.

The substitution was successful: neither reviewers nor audiences of the time detected the subterfuge.

7

Here Comes Mr. Gordon

Although I was a member of the Screen Actors Guild, I was stepping over the line every once in a while as far as intruding on other union territories. When AIP was just getting started, the unions tended to be more lenient. I was kind of stepping over the line by doing the creature costumes and the props while acting the parts of the monsters as well. Then again sometimes I would appear basically as myself in a nonspeaking "bit" role, like when I played one of Peggie Castle's heavies in *Oklahoma Woman*, so I guess I was intruding on all the union territories at one time or another. There were so many—the Screen Actors Guild, the Screen Extras Guild, the Directors Guild, the Prop Builder and Model Makers Union, the scenery makers union, the makeup artists union. But back in those days the whole team of us—the actors, grips, the prop masters, the director, the cameraman—we all kind of tried to help each other out whenever the need arose. "Hey, I want to go get a cup of coffee, how about taking over for me for a minute, Paul?" Sure, pal. But as time went on, the union rules got stricter and stricter. You really had to toe the line after a while, because they seemed to have spies everywhere—maybe even more than Moscow headquarters. That's one of the reasons why AIP and some of the other film producers started making pictures in Europe and doing coproductions with Japan.

—*Paul Blaisdell*

An eventful year for celluloid sci-fi and horror came in 1957. Month after month, from January through December, one new genre production after another bowed at theaters and drive-ins across the country. *Voodoo Woman, Not of This Earth, The Deadly Mantis,* and *Attack of the Crab Monsters* all opened within the first quarter of 1957, and the summer season was to prove even more bountiful with bad ol' boogies like *Kronos, The Monster that Challenged the World, The Cyclops, X the Unknown, The Unknown Terror, The Black Scorpion,* and *The Monolith Monsters* all battling one another for the almighty consumer dollar. Then there was *The 27th Day, Twenty Million Miles to Earth, The Land Unknown, Beginning of the End, The Unearthly,* and *Enemy From Space,* as well as producer-director Bert I. Gordon's budget-minded inversion

118

of Jack Arnold's *The Incredible Shrinking Man* that he called *The Amazing Colossal Man*.

The Incredible Shrinking Man sounded like one of Jim Nicholson's titular namesakes for an American-International product, but it actually originated with Universal. Universal had purchased the rights to Richard Matheson's best-selling novel *The Shrinking Man* and wedged the "incredible" adjective into the title in a misguided effort to reach AIP's drive-in clientele. (The picture deserved better.) Jack Arnold, who seemed to be directing as many sci-fi and horror films for Universal as Roger Corman and Eddie Cahn were for AIP and Allied Artists, was working from Matheson's own screenplay, which telescoped the action of the novel into an 87-minute, A-class production boasting state-of-the-art special effects. In Matheson's novel, Scott Carey (Grant Williams) is exposed to a double dose of pesticide and radiation, the combined effect of which is to make him shrink, inch by inch, day by day, until he virtually disappears from the face of the earth. *The Incredible Shrinking Man* was previewed by Universal on January 23, 1957, and released shortly thereafter. By September of the same year, AIP would have its own outrageous answer to Matheson's minuscule marvel unspooling at drive-ins across the nation.

Bert I. Gordon, who was destined to become another low-budget monster movie monarch during the 1950s, had migrated to the Los Angeles area from Kenosha, Wisconsin. Shortly after arriving in L.A., he got involved in early television series like *Cowboy G-Men* and *Rocket Squad*, on which he served as production assistant. Before long he began challenging AIP's turf by producing and directing a number of low-budget science-fiction movies.

Gordon must have been fascinated by the concept of gigantism. Virtually every one of his pictures explores the theme, from *King Dinosaur* (1955) to *Village of the Giants* (a 1965 adaptation of H. G. Wells's *Food of the Gods*), *Food of the Gods* (a 1979 attempt at adapting the same tale), and *Food of the Gods 2* (1989). Unfortunately, Gordon—like Roger Corman, Edward L. Cahn, Bernard Kowalski, and other directors of low-budget movies of the 1950s— never had the kind of funds at his disposal to do justice to the pictures he wanted to make. While Corman et al. produced films which required a minimum of photographic effects and specialized props to tell their story, Gordon's complicated properties, with their gargantuan gargoyles and attendant logistical headaches, necessitated the use of expensive and problematic optical effects. It would obviously have been easier and cheaper to make a series of less grandiose fantasy films, but that was not Gordon's vision.

Optical effects didn't come cheap, so Gordon tried creating his own. Unfortunately, his poverty-induced ineptitude resulted in pictures marred by blatant matte shadows (as in *The Amazing Colossal Man*) or bizarrely mismatched matte lines (as in *Earth Versus the Spider*, when the tarantula's legs repeatedly disappear into the ground). Even relatively simple superimpositions suffered from his undernourished film budgets; in *The Cyclops* (1957), for example, background elements could plainly be seen through the foreground image of the title monster.

Apparently the desire to make the kind of movie that interested him most overrode any considerations Gordon might have had about what types of effects he could reasonably expect to achieve on a limited budget. Having heard that monster specialist Paul Blaisdell seemed to be able to consistently pull rabbits out of hats on low-budget projects, Gordon put out feelers to see if Paul and Jackie would be interested in working on his picture *The Amazing Nth Man*. The title originated with Jim Nicholson, who recalled a short story he had read some years earlier called "The Nth Man," about a man who grows two miles tall. Frequent Roger Corman conspirator Chuck Griffith began a treatment based on Nicholson's retelling of the tale, but the finished version (written with actor Dick Miller in mind as the title character) was way out in left field. Griffith agreed to rework the scenario, but walked out of the project after spending a single day with Gordon, who was closely supervising everything he did. "He could never stop looking over my shoulder," Griffith complained. "I just couldn't work like that."

The script, newly retitled *The Amazing Colossal Man* to avoid any possible legal conflicts with the author of "The Nth Man," was rewritten by Gordon with Mark Hanna, who had worked on *Not of This Earth* and *The Undead* for Roger Corman. Blaisdell thought the story line was pretty hackneyed, but agreed to join the payroll because the film seemed to offer "interesting possibilities" as far as prop-making went. Since there were no foam rubber monsters to be devised (the film's "title monster" would be rendered via photographic effects during postproduction), Blaisdell thought the assignment would be an interesting change of pace.

The Amazing Colossal Man begins with an effectively orchestrated low-key sequence that generates a surprising amount of suspense. The U.S. Army is conducting an experimental bomb test in the Nevada desert. The first-ever plutonium bomb is about to be exploded, and no one is sure just how big the blast might be—least of all Col. Glenn Manning (Glen Langan), one of the army's team of hand-picked observers. Tensions mount during the countdown to detonation, but when the timer reaches zero nothing happens; there is no explosion, just a foreboding silence punctuated by a metronomic beeping as the activated bomb ticks away the seconds.

In the distance the moan of a low-flying airplane can be heard. Through his field glasses, Manning can see that the pilot is in trouble. The small craft makes an emergency landing, but crashes right in the center of the test site. Manning instinctively rushes to the pilot's aid, despite orders from his superiors to return to the safety of the observation trench. Suddenly the

This promotional still from the British release of *The Amazing Colossal Man* **ably illustrates the style of AIP's campaign writers.**

incessant beeping of the unexploded plutonium bomb stops. A heavy silence fills the air.

And then the bomb explodes.

Manning's body is suffused with radiation from the explosion. His protective clothing is blasted away, every particle of hair is evaporated in an instant, every inch of skin is blackened and blistered by the bombardment of irradiated atomic nuclei. But somehow, by some cruel twist of fate, Manning survives. He is transported to an army hospital where he remains in a coma; the doctors are amazed to find him still alive. Treatment is initiated for the third-degree burns that cover 98% of his body, but the outlook is not good.

The next day, however, the surgical team is astonished to discover that Manning's body has begun its own accelerated regenerative process. Dr. Paul Lindstrom (William Hudson) meets with army spokesperson Richard Kingman (Russ Bender) to discuss the recondite phenomenon. Kingman believes the newly developed plutonium bomb to be merely one more in a long line of wartime destructive devices, but Dr. Lindstrom suggests the possibility that plutonium inherently possesses some sort of restorative properties—how else can one explain Manning's miraculous recovery?

Manning's fiancée, Carol Forrest (Cathy Downs), learns of the accident and rushes to the hospital to be by his side. But when she arrives, an army spokesperson tells her that Manning has been moved to a different location for "security reasons." Repeated questions only result in typical army stonewalling, so Carol tracks down the surgeon in charge of the case. Under pressure to reveal the truth about Manning's condition, Dr. Lindstrom finally admits that radiation from the explosion has caused Manning to mutate into a giant. In effect, Manning has developed a bizarre form of cancer: his cells have started reproducing exponentially and his body is manufacturing new tissue even while the old cells refuse to die. The result is that Manning is growing proportionately at the rate of several feet per day. While Lindstrom's team of medical experts feverishly search for a way to halt the process, they learn one unexplainable fact: Glenn's heart is growing at only half the rate of the rest of his tissues. It will eventually collapse from the strain of supporting an ever-expanding body, and Manning will die.

Manning at last regains consciousness. At first he is unable to understand why everything around him appears disproportionately tiny. When he picks up the receiver of a diminutive telephone and hears the operator's voice on the line, Manning abruptly realizes that the telephone and everything else around him are not miniature replicas, but normal size objects. As the terrible truth dawns on him, Manning begins screaming in abject terror at his surroundings.

Carol tries her best to offer her fiancé hope for the future, but the giant is rapidly succumbing to a madness induced by latent effects of radiation poisoning. Housed in a circus tent like some kind of grotesque sideshow freak, Manning eventually escapes and ravages the countryside. While Dr. Lindstrom organizes a search party, his assistant, Dr. Coulter (Larry Thor), announces his discovery of an antidote that should be able to reverse Manning's condition. By injecting a sulfur-hydrogen compound directly into the giant's bone marrow, one can short-circuit the growth process. A return to normal dimensions could later be effected by high-frequency stimulation of the brain's pituitary gland, but in order for the treatment to be successful it would have to be administered without delay.

Coulter begins making the necessary rescue mission preparations, which include supervising the construction of an oversized hypodermic syringe which will be used to inject the growth antidote, while a helicopter reconnaissance team begins a systematic search for Manning over the Nevada desert. Now standing nearly 60 feet tall, and with his mind deteriorating almost by the minute, Manning begins destroying Las Vegas landmarks. Finally he is distracted by the buzz of the approaching choppers, which lure him into the Nevada desert.

The Amazing Colossal Man (Glenn Langan) may well wonder who did the redecorating during his enforced hospitalization. Most of the miniature knick knacks were manufactured by Paul and Jackie Blaisdell.

Dr. Lindstrom tries to reason with Manning as Major Carter (Scott Peters) readies the enormous hypodermic syringe which will be used to inject the sulfur-hydrogen solution into the ankle bone. Balancing the huge device between themselves, Lindstrom and Carter rush toward Manning and jam the needle home. Manning rages at the pain. He plucks the stinging syringe from his ankle and strikes back, throwing it like a spear at his tormentors. Carter is killed instantly when the needle pierces his heart. A moment later Manning reaches down and scoops up Carol into his palm, carrying her in the direction of Boulder Dam.

Dr. Lindstrom radios word to the ground troops, who station themselves strategically around the dam. As soon as Manning puts Carol safely down, the army sharpshooters open fire, mortally wounding the giant, who topples into the churning waters of Boulder Dam and is quickly lost from sight forever.

"Forever" isn't quite the right word to use, because AIP brought the Colossal Man back in a 1958 sequel, *War of the Colossal Beast*, also directed by Bert I. Gordon. This time around Dean Parkin took over the role of Col. Manning, who escapes apparent death in the waters of Boulder Dam and turns

up across the border in Mexico, looking rather bruised and battered and a helluva lot more pissed off than before. Although Paul Blaisdell did not contribute
to *War of the Colossal Beast* during production, a few of the props he designed
for *The Amazing Colossal Man* turned up in the sequel's flashback sequences.

Designing and manufacturing serviceable miniature props, Blaisdell discovered, could result in just as many headaches as the construction of a typical movie monster costume. According to *The Amazing Colossal Man* script,
only a handful of props would be required because Bert I. Gordon was planning on executing the majority of special effects himself in postproduction.
As he was reading through the script, however, Blaisdell suddenly realized
how much of a headache designing the props from scratch was going to be.
Because the story's hook was that the Colossal Man suffered from rapid,
unending growth, the relative sizes of the miniatures would constantly be
changing. That meant making not just one version of each prop, but two,
three, four or more. Once again it seemed AIP was reaching for more than
what might be possible, given the tight budget and schedule.

As it turned out, there was really no need to design different configurations of each and every prop. The economy-minded Gordon thought it would
be effective enough to simply tell the viewer, via secondary character dialogue,
how much bigger the Colossal Man was growing each day. This meant that
Blaisdell would only be required to produce a single version of each prop. Still,
it took nearly six weeks for him and Jackie to finish everything the assignment required.

Blaisdell had been a model airplane enthusiast for years and owned quite
an extensive collection of World War I and WWII replicas. His ability to
piece together the miniature frameworks that were the basis for such high-
end model kits would come in handy while working on Gordon's film. Since
so much of the picture consisted of dialogue, there were really only two major
sequences which called for the use of miniatures. The first sequence would
begin with Manning discovering his colossal predicament and escaping from
the army base; the second sequence would come near the conclusion of the
film, with the giant stalking the streets of Las Vegas.

For the first sequence, Blaisdell designed a number of miniature replicas of everyday items such as a newspaper, telephone, pillow, sheets, chest of
drawers, water pitcher, barrel, and "big top" circus tent. The tent was merely
a piece of tarpaulin cut to size and shape and used as a background for the
actor to play against. Most of the other props were made either from plastic,
balsa wood, or pine. Paul especially enjoyed working with pine because of its
softness and its natural tendency to yield easily to his sculpting tools. The
miniature chest of drawers and barrel were both fashioned from pine, as well
as the desktop telephone, which was painted flat black and shellacked to give
the appearance of plastic.

Existing miniaturized versions of the Bible and a water pitcher were located at local novelty shops, but Blaisdell did make the diminutive newspaper which carries the banner headline, "Man Lives Through Plutonium Blast!" The typeface was produced by using press-on letters—the kind available at many art supply shops—which were affixed to tiny sheets of real newsprint paper.

The bed on which Manning slept was actually a cot mattress, but Jackie supplied pillows made from standard cloth material stitched over pieces of foam rubber which had been trimmed to the appropriate size and shape.

For the Colossal Man's rampage through the streets of downtown Vegas, Paul and Jackie built miniature versions of famous casino landmarks which the actor could destroy on cue. Renditions of the revolving high-heeled Silver Slipper, the Royal Nevada King's Crown, the Sands Motel sign, and the Frontier Cowboy were all designed to be appropriately manhandled by Glenn Langan during the picture's climax. The Silver Slipper and Royal Nevada crown were, like many of the props that came out of the Blaisdell workshop, fashioned out of pine, coated with latex rubber, and given a paint job to match the real thing as closely as possible. The crown contained reflective bits of colored plastic which were added to suggest jewels.

The construction of the Sands sign involved significantly more work. Using pine wood, each letter was painstakingly carved to shape and buffed to remove sharp edges. They were then coated with a special reflective paint that mimicked the color and intensity of a neon light display. The letters stood between two and three feet tall and were screwed onto vertical support beams arranged in a latticework and painted gray to simulate cement struts. The whole thing was prescored so that when Langan took a swipe at it, the display would collapse. An added sense of realism was achieved by scoring only the top portions of the letters so that when the sign was destroyed, portions of the lettering would remain standing. (Incidentally, the cream-colored convertible which the Colossal Man tosses through the air like a metallic frisbee actually came out of a commercial kit. Blaisdell only customized the model car for the film; he did not create it from scratch.)

The Frontier Cowboy proved easier to build than the Sands Hotel sign because the entire display could be carved from a single piece of balsa. By painting the image directly onto the wood, the actual Vegas landmark could be convincingly realized. Like the Sands miniature, the Frontier Cowboy was prescored so that it could easily be torn apart by Langan.

For the scene where Manning unearths a palm tree and throws it at a crowd of onlookers, Blaisdell created a miniature that stood more than five feet tall. This remarkably realistic-looking prop was developed around a balsa-and-pine base that was covered with foam rubber painted to resemble tree bark. Leaves were fashioned out of pure latex because the consistency of the rubber made a convincingly "leafy" illusion. (Blaisdell's recipe for fashioning

Director Bert I. Gordon is responsible for this composite shot of the Amazing Colossal Man (Glenn Langan) and a seven-person "crowd" cringing in terror outside the Sands Hotel in Las Vegas, Nevada.

tree bark from a simple concoction of foam and latex would be put to good use in an Allied Artists horror picture also made in 1957.)

The single most impressive prop Blaisdell designed for *The Amazing Colossal Man* was the oversized hypodermic syringe used to inject Col. Manning with the chemical antidote near the film's finale. Blaisdell later recalled:

> I designed it in such a way that the needle would slip back into the barrel when it impacted against anything solid. When Bert Gordon said it was time to shoot that scene, I shut my eyes and hoped the darned thing would work the way it was supposed to.

As described in the script, the super-syringe stood nearly as tall as an average-sized man and measured about 20 inches in diameter. Blaisdell did even better: his finished prop was over 6 feet in length and measured 25 inches in diameter. The entire mechanism, consisting of an outer shell and sliding interior plunger, was constructed from Lucite plastic and plastic tubing which Blaisdell obtained through his usual contacts at the Frye Plastic Co. Together, both pieces barely weighed over three pounds.

Blaisdell scored the outside of the syringe and added hand-painted calibrations which counted off units of measure—a typical Blaisdell detail that can't clearly be seen in the finished feature. The two-foot-long needle was made from a hollow aluminum rod that telescoped into the barrel on contact with a solid surface.

The giant hypodermic actually worked. According to Bob Burns, it could hold 5 quarts of liquid and was able to shoot a stream of water 25 feet. Although the effect was not used in the film, Blaisdell went the extra mile to make the hypo operable because, if nothing else, it gave him personal satisfaction. He, Jackie, Bob Burns, and Burns's wife, Kathy, took turns using the the Amazing Colossal Syringe as a kind of super water pistol, hosing each other down back at the Blaisdell home after the filming was over. Paul eventually made a present of it to Bert I. Gordon, who maintained a collection of props from his pictures.

Unfortunately, no matter how realistic or detailed Blaisdell designed his props to be, they—along with the majority of the film's photographic effects— suffered from budgetary constraints and Gordon's insistence on cutting corners when it came time to do the all-important in-camera effects. According to Mark McGee, author of *Fast and Furious: the Story of American International Pictures*, Gordon created the Colossal Man's rampage through the streets of Las Vegas by interweaving three separate elements: slide photographs, live actors, and superimpositions. Because there was not enough money in the budget to rope off sections of downtown Vegas for the purpose of setting up special shots for the film, Gordon simply had photographs taken of those Vegas streets that looked the emptiest during early morning hours. The slides were then enlarged through a photographic process and rear-projected onto a special screen. A small crowd of extras was hired to stand in front of the screen and react in mock terror to the figure of the Colossal Man, which was superimposed into the frame as a separate element. This method of sandwiching the Colossal Man between a crowd of extras and back-projected stock shots resulted in a final photographic montage that, although lacking in quality, at least managed to get the point across. It is one of the oldest photographic tricks in the book. (Gordon also cut corners by using only one traveling matte for scenes combining the giant Col. Manning with normal-size live actors. This resulted in a semitransparent image of the Colossal Man whenever he was placed against a dark background. The same problem plagued Gordon's follow-up, *War of the Colossal Beast*, as well as *The Cyclops*, a film he directed for Allied Artists which beat *The Amazing Colossal Man* into theaters by a month.)

The Amazing Colossal Man had strong box-office "legs." It was destined to become one of American-International's biggest money-makers when it was released in September 1957, just in time to take advantage of the new school season. Teenagers wanted a nice, cozy place to take their dates on Saturday nights—preferably someplace where they could do a little making out without being noticed. What better place than the local drive-in which happened to be showing the latest AIP double feature?

Colossal Man's cofeature was a little something called *Cat Girl*, one of AIP's early coproductions with Great Britain. Lou Rusoff envisioned it as a low-budget spinoff of the famous 1944 Val Lewton production starring Simone Simon, *Cat People*. The picture probably would never have been made if AIP hadn't had an eye on the growing foreign film market. Sam Arkoff had determined that by loaning out a scriptwriter or director and perhaps one or two actors to make a film overseas and agreeing to finance a portion of the budget, AIP would be able to claim 50 percent ownership of the finished feature, giving the company distribution rights throughout most of the Western Hemisphere. This translated into a minimal monetary risk for AIP and promised eventual returns that far outweighed the original investment. This method of coproducing new feature films would eventually result in some of the genre's most highly regarded foreign-made features, notably Mario Bava's *Black Sunday* and *Black Sabbath*. (It would also result in an avalanche of seedy sword-and-sandal schlock imported from Italy during the early years of the 1960s.)

As part of their first coproduction deal, AIP sent Rusoff and his *Cat Girl* script to a British production company run by Nat Cohen called Anglo-Amalgamated. A budget was approved and the film was made with British actress Barbara Shelley in the lead role and Alfred Shaughnessy directing. AIP's expenditure was about $25,000.

Rusoff's original script was an out-and-out thriller about a woman who takes on the form of a leopard when provoked, and AIP was expecting the finished film to pretty much resemble their typical mid–1950s output. According to Barbara Shelley, Shaughnessy decided to rewrite the script, however, turning the lead character from a "were-cat" into a run-of-the-mill psychopath who only thought she could change into a fanged, feline fiend. Shelley thought that Shaughnessy's changes improved Rusoff's script immeasurably. Her character became a great deal more complex, and the story itself gained a certain respectability it had been lacking, at least in the director's opinion. (No doubt it also made Shelley feel as if she was working on a more important film. *Cat Girl* was her first English feature. Previously she had worked only in Italy.)

By changing the focus of Rusoff's screenplay and dispensing with many of the horrific elements, Shaughnessy made the story into nothing more than a psychological nightmare. His revision of the script wreaked havoc with AIP's plans to get the picture released in a hurry, though it's doubtful he knew or cared what AIP thought. In the rewritten version, Leonora Brandt (Barbara Shelley) believes herself to be the victim of an ancient family curse that extends back through time 700 years. When her uncle dies, the terrible legacy is activated, and Leonora sees herself taking on the characteristics of a leopard. She learns that her husband has been unfaithful and mentally wills his death at the claws of a great cat. The following day his mutilated body is discovered by police.

Dr. Brian Marlowe (Robert Aryes) tries to convince Leonora that the family curse she fears is so much hogwash. "This is all in your mind," he admonishes. But when an escaped leopard is killed by an automobile in the film's climax, Leonora perishes simultaneously. Was she the victim of a hallucination or an actual curse?

Shaughnessy's *Cat Girl* is appropriately moody but too low-key and slow moving for its own good. When Arkoff and Nicholson saw a print of the finished film, chaos erupted. Arkoff had been expecting to see a standard monster melodrama, but there were only shadowy psychological shudders instead of the good old-fashioned "creature" comforts to which he was accustomed. No one was interested in subtlety from Shaughnessy, and Arkoff told him so. "We can't even release this picture, it's so awful," Arkoff complained. "Where's the monster?" (Arkoff's insistence that every horror movie produced by AIP ought to have a monster in it somewhere prevailed at least through 1960, when Roger Corman directed his first Edgar Allan Poe adaptation. *House of Usher* featured Vincent Price, cobwebs, fog, and lots of foreboding atmosphere, but—"Where's the monster?" Arkoff wanted to know. Corman added a line to the script to appease his boss: "The house *lives!*" Price whispers at one point in the film, thus making the house itself the story's "monster.")

To add some visual pizzazz to *Cat Girl*, Jim Nicholson phoned Paul Blaisdell and asked if he could help bail them out. "This picture is in terrible shape, Paul; there's nothing scary in it at all," Nicholson told him. He wanted Blaisdell to give *Cat Girl* its requisite title monster. If AIP could film a quick insert shot of some kind of "cat-woman," Nicholson thought the film would be salvageable.

"How much time do I have to do this?" Blaisdell asked.

"Two days," Nicholson replied.

There was a pregnant pause, then; "You're kidding, aren't you, Nick?"

No, he wasn't. *The Amazing Colossal Man* was finished and ready to go. All it needed was a cofeature, and that was supposed to be *Cat Girl*.

Nicholson called Blaisdell with the *Cat Girl* assignment on a Friday. The finished product had to be ready to go before the cameras early Monday morning. Considering the circumstances, what Blaisdell managed to dream up over the weekend turned out to be pretty remarkable. He later reminisced about the assignment: "The part where the girl woke up in the insane asylum, took a look in the mirror and thought she was changing into some kind of a leopard—that was the makeup AIP wanted me to do for the movie. It involved the head and the paws and of course the rest of me had to be wearing pajamas because, frankly, when I take my shirt off, I don't look too much like a girl."

As was his custom, Paul began work on the mask using one of his "blanks" as the base. With his standard makeup materials—foam rubber, liquid latex, pine, contact bond cement, and cutting and coloring tools—Blaisdell created a "were-cat" headpiece and a pair of furry, taloned claws. The face of the cat creature was sculpted out of block foam cemented directly to the latex blank and coated with numerous layers of latex. When cured, the rubber latex was spray-painted dark brown and covered with tufts of crepe hair, a synthetic available from theatrical supply shops. Elongated ears made from cut sections of block foam were covered with latex and crepe hair on the outside but left smooth on the inside. Color highlighting made the interior of the ears appear realistically fleshy. Lastly, thin pieces of wire were inserted into the mask on either side of the nose to simulate a cat's whiskers.

Claws were made over a pair of normal winter gloves, as opposed to the heavy-duty gloves Blaisdell usually used for monsters such as the She-Creature, so that the finished product would appear thinner and more feline. Latex rubber was applied to each glove and allowed to dry; then the latex was spray-painted and covered with crepe hair, which was bonded to the latex with an adhesive called "spirit gum." Talons fashioned from pine were glued to the tips of the fingers with contact bond cement.

As he had promised, Blaisdell had everything ready early the following Monday. When he arrived at AIP, he was ushered into an empty room and told to don the cat-girl mask and claws, as well as a pair of pajamas. A camera was rolled in and set up for a couple of quick insert shots. In the first, Paul was photographed clenching and unclenching the beastly claws; in the other he held a claw to his throat as if gasping in terror at seeing "his" alter ego in the mirror.

Both inserts were filmed so quickly that apparently no one bothered to pull focus. Although the shot of the clenching claws—seen not once but twice in the finished film—turned out reasonably well, the full-length shot of Blaisdell in his cat-mask was photographed completely out of focus. AIP used the shot anyway; there simply wasn't any time available for reshoots.

A second monster makeup had been designed for the film, but this seems not to have survived over the years. According to Blaisdell, there was another scene in the film to which AIP wanted additions made. "When Leonora partially changes into a cat-woman," Blaisdell explained, "I utilized a couple of photos of Lilly Christine, the famous 'cat-girl' dancer who performed at Las Vegas. I did have to look up some original shots of a gal who performed like a cat-gal because I'm afraid I'm not quite that much of a gal." Whatever scenes or makeup Paul was referring to will probably remain a mystery.

(Incidentally, the few seconds of cat-creature screen time afforded Blaisdell in the original theatrical release of *Cat Girl* were later excised for TV showings when American International sold the picture to television in the early 1960s as part of its "Chiller Theatre" movie package. The footage was restored by Columbia/Tri-Star when the videotape version was released in 1994.)

Blaisdell attended the Los Angeles premiere of *Cat Girl* with his wife and close friends Bob and Kathy Burns. He cringed as soon as he saw himself on screen. The cat-creature was such an obvious splice-in (at least to his trained eyes) it seemed jarringly out of place. And not only was it out of place, it was out of focus.

"Look at that, will you," a disgruntled Blaisdell whispered to his companions. "It looks awful."

"Well, maybe it's supposed to be that way. Maybe they wanted it to be an arty, soft-focus kind of thing," Bob suggested.

"Oh, bullshit," Blaisdell countered. "That's just sloppy filmmaking, pure and simple."

As poorly lighted and photographed as the cat-creature was, at least it legitimized the film in the eyes of its executive producers. AIP was satisfied, even if Paul wasn't.

A lot more footage of the cat mask had been shot than was ever used in the movie, and Blaisdell was surprised at the brevity of his "cameo." He suffered through another few minutes of the slow-moving, muddled melodrama before quipping, "I think we should get out of here before one of us falls into a coma." They left a good twenty minutes before the end of the picture.

Blaisdell had been so disappointed with the minimal amount of cat-monster footage AIP incorporated into the finished feature that he decided to put the cat-mask to further use in a homemade 16mm featurette shot with Bob Burns's brand new Bolex movie camera. Paul donned the cat-creature makeup and chased Bob and Lionel Comport all around his Topanga Canyon home, finally "killing" Comport with his lethal cat-talons. The youthful filmmakers attempted a couple of professional effects, including an in-camera "dissolve" that was supposed to show Blaisdell changing from a human to an animal without resorting to a cutaway. But the film had to be backwound to a predetermined point perfectly to achieve the effect, and they were never able to get it to work properly.

Burns has fond memories of making the 16mm short, entitled *The Cat Man*. He said, "It was the kind of thing that Paul loved to do, just fooling around and acting kind of nutty, using some of the props he had worked on for AIP." According to Burns, Blaisdell was at his happiest during such times. Even Jackie joined in the fun.

When they gathered together to watch the processed film footage a few days later, Paul noticed that the cat-creature mask looked a lot more realistic than it had in the AIP feature. He was so impressed, in fact, that he suggested they try out a brand new makeup technique right then and there. Lionel Comport would be the actor in the makeup chair, and Bob would be the

AIP thought they could pump up the fear factor in the monsterless British film, *Cat Girl*, by splicing in a shot of Blaisdell wearing a cat-monster mask. Blaisdell was given just three days to create the mask and a matching set of claws. The result wasn't half bad, but AIP's blurry photography obscured the effect they wanted. Paul later wore the mask in a homemade horror movie, *The Cat-Man* (from which this frame blowup was taken). The mask was accidentally destroyed in the fiery finale of Herman Cohen's 1958 production, *How to Make a Monster* (courtesy of Bob Burns).

cameraman. Lionel was the son of Lionel Comport, Sr., who owned the Comport Movie Ranch that supplied animals for use in motion pictures. He was a pretty big fellow, so Paul wouldn't be able to use one of his ready-made "blanks" to create a monster makeup; they'd have to make a life cast of Lionel's face first.

"You know, I think I know a way to create a life mask really quickly," Blaisdell said. "Instead of using plaster and making a negative mold first, I'm going to use my airbrush to apply latex directly to Lionel's skin. That'll get the job done a lot faster. And when we peel it off, we'll have an 'instant' life mask."

Burns thought that sounded like a good idea. He really got Paul's enthusiasm pumping when he suggested that Blaisdell might be on the cutting edge of a new type of makeup process. "Just think, Paul, you'll be able to market it and everything."

Paul got out a jar of liquid latex, the same rubber-based compound he used to create his professional masks and monster outfits, and poured it into his airbrush equipment. "Okay now, Lionel, you sit in this chair," Blaisdell directed. Comport eagerly followed his pal's instructions, excited to be a part of this makeup breakthrough.

"Keep your eyes closed and just relax," Paul advised as he began spraying the latex on Lionel's face. Within minutes every inch of skin was coated with multiple layers of the quick-drying rubber. Suddenly Lionel began gesticulating wildly.

"Uh, Paul, did we make little holes for Lionel to breathe?" Burns wondered.

Blaisdell's eyes grew big. "Oh, shit!" He ducked down to take a look at Comport's nose. It was completely plugged up with hardening latex. "We're killing him!"

Blaisdell and Burns both started tearing frantically at the latex, but it was stuck to every single hair growing out of Lionel's skin. "Jesus, Lionel, why didn't you shave this morning?" Paul grumbled.

"Phmmmphh," came the reply.

They finally made enough progress to expose one cheek, a nostril, and part of Lionel's mouth, but the eyes remained completely covered. "I wonder why it won't come off?" said Burns.

"Come to think of it, we didn't cover his eyes with cotton or anything, did we?" Paul mused.

Burns shook his head solemnly. The latex had solidified completely around each one of Lionel's eyelashes.

"I don't know how we'll ever get this off," admitted Blaisdell. They finally managed to uncover most of Comport's face (which had gone pale and blotchy as the result of either a weird skin reaction from the application of the latex or a panic attack, they could never figure out which). At last he could breathe a bit easier. "Fellas, I can't go home like this," Lionel complained. "What are we going to do?"

Blaisdell conferred with Burns and finally decided the only thing to do was to cut off Lionel's eyelashes. There was some objection on the part of the subject, but once Lionel realized the latex was not going to come off any other way, he relented. When he got home that night, he looked pretty odd. (The lashes grew back in about two weeks.)

Later, Blaisdell confided to Burns, "I have to admit that was not one of my better ideas." He did like to experiment, however:

> There were many times that Jackie and I tried using different types of makeup compounds, but for the kind of work I was doing at the time, latex and foam rubber offered more possibilities than just about anything else because they are so easy to work with. You were only limited by your imagination. Well, that and the budget.
>
> I have to admit, I enjoyed working on a lot of these films and trying to come up with new and different ways of giving the audience a little jolt. But I'll tell you something I learned a long time ago, that most of the producers in Hollywood never seemed able to understand. Under the right conditions, the "monster" that can really scare you the most is the one that looks and acts almost human and almost familiar. A friend? A relative? A pet dog? A makeup artist, maybe?

8

Cosmic Creeps

Jim Nicholson and I grew up about the same time during the '30s and '40s. He read the same science-fiction pulps that I did, the ones that always pictured Martians as these little guys with scrawny bodies and great, enormous heads and brains. Jim started his career as a theater usher, and he used to stand inside the door and watch the films as they played each week, and he saw all the Buck Rogers and Flash Gordon types of pictures, as well as whatever science-fiction pictures came out at the Saturday afternoon matinees. No matter how good or bad or indifferent these pictures were, one thing Jim noticed was that not one of them ever had an alien creature that looked like that sort of thing we used to see in the pulps.

One afternoon when Jim and I were talking he said, "I'd just love to do a picture with one of those classic Martians—you know, the kind with the enormous head and little tiny body, and he doesn't worry about a thing; you just look like you're going to hurt him and he points a finger at you and goes *B-z-z-z-z-z-t!* And you've had it!" I'd never thought about it, but Jim was right: there had never been a motion picture using this kind of a Martian.

I don't know why that turned out to be the "classic" Martian, but apparently it caught on in the pulp magazines and stayed that way ever after. And that was the way I designed them for Jim's picture.

— Paul Blaisdell

Blaisdell often worked on short-term projects like *Cat Girl* in between major assignments such as *The She-Creature, It Conquered the World,* and *The Amazing Colossal Man.* When notorious zero-budget producer Al Zimbalist, Jr., approached Blaisdell to ask if he was interested in designing the title creature for a film called *Monster from Green Hell,* he naturally asked for more information. Zimbalist showed him a story outline which described an experimental rocketship and a payload of insects that return to earth greatly enlarged. It was pretty straightforward stuff, another of the "big bug" pictures that clambered out of Hollywood in the wake of Warner Bros. 1954 smash, *Them!* Blaisdell agreed to work up a series of production illustrations depicting the kind of monster he envisioned from reading the outline.

When Blaisdell delivered his sketches to Zimbalist's office, he appended a note indicating that he would be available to build the title creatures for *Monster from Green Hell*, conditional upon the negotiation of an acceptable fee. Days passed with no word from Zimbalist. Blaisdell got suspicious. The producer was never in, according to the secretary who answered his phone, and Zimbalist never returned any of Paul's calls. After several weeks went by with still no word, Blaisdell gave up trying to contact Zimbalist himself and turned for help to his agent, Forry Ackerman. Blaisdell was eager to rescue his production illustrations, but Ackerman also was unable to get through to the producer. The *Monster from Green Hell* sketches were never seen again.

The creatures Blaisdell had designed for Zimbalist resembled "a cross between an insect and an insect larvae," according to Bob Burns. Blaisdell himself claimed that Zimbalist only asked for "a giant," never specifying what kind of giant he wanted for the film, but this is a curious remark to make considering that he examined the script and it is unmistakably about giant wasps.* The production illustrations were only pen and ink sketches, but Blaisdell forever regretted their loss, as he later noted:

> I designed a 30-foot giant for the producer of *Monster from Green Hell*, but the film company decided that giant wasps would be cheaper to make than what I came up with. They also kept my production illustrations and never paid me for them. In fact, Al Zimbalist, Jr., the producer, was such a nice guy when it came to taking off with things to make his pictures that I believe the studio finally fired him. I never heard from him after that. Knowing that he got his butt kicked out of Columbia gave me a great deal of satisfaction!

Zimbalist finally made *Monster from Green Hell* with a cast toplining Jim Davis, Barbara Turner, Joel Fluellen, and Robert E. Griffin. Of the four, only Davis achieved any degree of stardom. He appeared in the horribly inept *Jesse James Meets Frankenstein's Daughter* (1965) and *Dracula vs. Frankenstein* (1971), but was most often seen in middle-of-the-road Westerns. He achieved his greatest fame in American television during the 1980s on the long-running "Dallas" series.

The screenplay, which was written by Louis Vittes and Endre Boehm, fell back on that old standby—radiation—to account for its title creatures. The insects are exposed to radiation during a space test flight and crash-land in Africa (the "green hell" of the film's title). Actually, the rocket contained monkeys, guinea pigs, and spider crabs, as well as wasps, but there is never any mention of what happened to the other animals. (Maybe they were stung to death by the wasps.) Zimbalist inserted plenty of stock footage of rampaging elephants and other African wildlife from the 1939 movie *Stanley and Livingstone*, overlaying superimpositions of the monsterish wasps in the finest

---

Blaisdell made the comment in a 1979 letter to the author. Possibly the intervening years had clouded his memory.

Bert I. Gordon tradition. Most of the effects work was handled by Gene Warren, although Jess Davison, Jack Rabin, and Louis DeWitt are also credited. Warren built the wasps, which were stupendously cheap, having wire skeletons as opposed to the standard ball-and-socket armatures used by animators like Ray Harryhausen and Willis O'Brien. This made them very delicate and difficult to pose, which may explain why the creatures' movements are so stilted. The crew also designed an enormous monster-wasp head (which looked nothing like a wasp, of course) and two pincer-claws that menaced members of the cast during live action setups. The story that Paul Blaisdell built or "operated" the giant wasp head (à la Beulah in *It Conquered the World*) is untrue. The rumor probably stemmed from his peripheral involvement with the film during its preproduction phase.

After the *Monster from Green Hell* fiasco, Blaisdell decided to think twice before agreeing to do any more work for producers or outfits with which he was unfamiliar. Just before signing up to work on *The Amazing Colossal Man* for AIP, he was approached by Dan and Jack Milner and asked to design a creature for their new monster melodrama, *From Hell It Came*. The Milner brothers had produced Lou Rusoff's very first sci-fi screenplay, *The Phantom from 10,000 Leagues*, which was paired with *Day the World Ended* for release through American-International when it was still known as the American Releasing Corporation. The Milners had tried to interest Blaisdell in designing their Phantom but Paul, who was busy working on his first full-size monster costume for Roger Corman, had to turn them down. Now they wanted him to design the "Tabanga," a walking tree-creature, and once again Blaisdell was unavailable—this time because he was occupied with preparations for *The Amazing Colossal Man*. But he did design the Tabanga on paper and show the Milners how to make realistic-looking tree bark out of nothing more than foam rubber and latex.

Paul eventually provided two full-length, black-and-white drawings of the Tabanga: a close-up of the head, a reverse view, and sketches of the hands and feet. Anchoring his design on the brief descriptions given in the film's script by Richard Bernstein, Paul gave the far-out concept an unexpected, nightmarish quality. According to Bob Burns, one of the few people who ever saw the sketches, Paul's Tabanga turned out to be one of his best designs.

The story told of a Pacific island native wrongfully executed for the murder of a fellow tribesman. His spirit survives in a weird-looking tree that begins growing out of the grave. A team of American scientists conducting research into localized effects of atomic testing by the U.S. government pry up the thing by its roots and take it back to their laboratory, where they discover it has developed a heart and circulatory system. Later, the creature escapes from the lab and begins a systematic search for the culprits who were really responsible for the native's death. The monster is finally stopped when it falls into a pool of quicksand.

After reading through the script, Blaisdell decided the Tabanga monster should have a rough, hard-edged, spidery appearance. It had to look like a tree, but an intelligent tree. It also had to look as if it could really hurt somebody. Paul envisioned the limbs as elongated branches tapering to twiglike "fingers" and "toes." After completing front and back sketches of the design, he showed them to Bob Burns, who figured that the tree-creature would have to be brought to cinematic life as a marionette. "Either that, or it would have to be played by the world's skinniest human being inside a suit," Burns quipped.

Blaisdell wasn't concerned with how to bring the sketches to life; he was only being paid to provide a design on paper. Since the surface of the monster was supposed to resemble tree bark, Blaisdell prepared a 3-D sample fashioned from a thin sheet of block foam coated with latex. Using standard sculpting tools, he was able to "trench" the foam rubber and paint it in such a way that it looked remarkably like actual bark.

The Milner brothers became concerned about the cost of reproducing Blaisdell's two-dimensional design in three dimensions. Had the Tabanga been constructed using the sketches as exact blueprints, it would have had to be made as a stop-motion model, rod puppet, or marionette. There was clearly no way it would have been able to interact with the cast to the extent required by the script—at least not in 1957 and not without a more substantial special effects budget—so the Milners took Blaisdell's illustrations to Hollywood's Don Post Studios and had a standard rubber and latex monster costume made. Since Paul's original design was so thin and spidery, the basic visual concept needed to be altered. The dimensions were enlarged so that a normal actor or stunt specialist could play the part as Paul had played the monsters in his own pictures. The end result was nowhere near as nightmarish as Blaisdell's original concept, but there was no mistaking it for anything that might have wandered over from the Disney studios either.

Although the acting is substandard and the production exudes an air of artificiality, *From Hell It Came* turned out to be nowhere near as ridiculous as it might have sounded. The Tabanga monster was effective, although it was shown a little too often to seem properly intimidating. Still, it looked like what it was supposed to look like: an ambulatory tree sporting the famous "Blaisdell scowl." Michael Weldon, reviewing the film in his landmark *Psychotronic Encyclopedia of Film*, summed it up nicely when he called the Tabanga monster "the star of a six-year-old's bad dream."

Blaisdell never got a chance to see his tree-creature go through its paces, at least not until the picture was finished and in the can. While the costume was under construction at Don Post Studios, Blaisdell and the Milner brothers suffered a falling out, so Paul wasn't invited to the film set. When he caught up with *From Hell It Came* years later, he didn't disparage the film too much: "I designed the Tabanga the way I thought it should look in terms of the script, and the people that built it did a damn good job of reproducing a prop that was a nice concept and certainly an original one, but one that was very awkward. My hat goes off to the guy who had to act the part of the walking tree [Chester Hayes]. I think he did a helluva good job under the circumstances."

Allied Artists brought out *From Hell It Came* a few weeks prior to AIP's double-feature release of *The Amazing Colossal Man* and *Cat Girl*. They were up against *The Unearthly*, *Enemy from Space*, *The Cyclops*, *Beginning of the End*, *X the Unknown*, and *The Unknown Terror*, all released during the summer of 1957. None of the films lost money because monsters were bigger than ever.

Blaisdell barely had time to catch his breath before American International was ringing his doorbell again, this time with an offer to work on a new science-fiction picture which happened to be a pet project of Jim Nicholson's. For years, Nicholson had wanted to bring the classic concept of the Martian monster to the movie screen—"the little green guys with the big brainy heads," as he put it.

Blaisdell knew immediately what Nicholson was talking about. Over the years the concept of the little green man from Mars who was super-intelligent had cropped up repeatedly, usually in science-fiction and fantasy pulps of the 1920s, 1930s and 1940s. The pulp illustrators often depicted Martians as diminutive creatures with scrawny bodies and bulbous, oversized craniums. They almost always gripped a ray gun in one hand and held a screaming damsel-in-distress in the other.

Nicholson had come up with another slam-bang film title: *Invasion of the Saucer Men*. As soon as he uttered those five little words, the AIP elite grew excited. Arkoff thought it was the best title Jim had come up with since *I Was a Teenage Werewolf*, and everyone was eager to get moving on the picture that would bring the classic Martian monster to cinematic life at long last. Even Blaisdell got caught up in the excitement. Holed up in Nicholson's office, he and Nick began going over the fine points of the project's special effects, deciding how many Martians constituted an invasion and whether Paul would play one of the Saucer Men himself (he did).

The longer Blaisdell and Nicholson talked, the bigger the assignment seemed to get. Blaisdell promised he would have no problem manufacturing an entire army of little green men to take part in the film's interstellar invasion, but Nicholson reminded him that the low-budget nature of the production precluded anything more than a scaled-down version of an interplanetary attack. They still called it an "invasion," even though it was really more of a brief visit. (Somehow *Visitation of the Saucer Men* or *Stopover of the Saucer Men* or *The Saucer Men Drop By Unexpectedly* just didn't carry the same impact.) By the time they finished talking, Blaisdell had agreed to provide a total of four Martian costumes (including a mechanized head and claw which would be used for most of the close-up action) and two miniature flying saucers.

AIP had purchased the rights to a short story by Paul Fairman called "The Cosmic Frame" which became the basis for the new picture. The fiction piece was a light-hearted spoof, but AIP's vision was that *Invasion of the Saucer Men* would be a straightforward monster movie just like its other genre productions, full of creeping shadows, thunder and lightning, screaming teenage girls, and bug-eyed monsters. This was the formula that had been so successful over the years, and no one saw any reason to change it. Accordingly, cowriters Robert J. Gurney, Jr., and Al Martin ignored the light-hearted tone of the Fairman story and fashioned a screenplay around the central idea of an alien race that frames an innocent Earthman for the murder of another human being.

Teenagers became the heroes in this cinematic take on "The Cosmic Frame" because teenagers had become the focal point of all the latest AIP fantasy films. Most of the company's earlier genre outings, like *Day the World Ended* and *It Conquered the World,* were for the most part populated by young adults (Marla English in *The She-Creature*) and middle-aged heroic types (Paul Birch in *The Beast with a Million Eyes*). *I Was a Teenage Werewolf* (1956) changed all that. Most of the new sci-fi and horror pictures were overwhelmingly teen-oriented. To capitalize on the success of the new image, AIP began adding youth-oriented catchlines to its advertising. ("See! Teenagers vs. the Saucer-Men!") If a picture didn't have many teen elements, AIP simply retitled it to convince audiences otherwise, as happened with Roger Corman's 1958 film *Prehistoric World*, which saw release as *Teenage Caveman.*

Most of the teenagers in *Invasion of the Saucer Men* were rebels, not polite, law-abiding, sickly sweet "boys and girls next door." They drank beer and partied all night in souped-up jalopies, drank beer and made out at Lovers' Point, drank beer and razzed the resident backwoods farmer. (Doesn't every American town have at least one?) For the first time, there were blatant sexual references on screen ("Hey, baby, can you tell me how to get to first base with you tonight?") and characters whose sole occupation seemed to be infiltrating small country towns to "score." Compared to previous AIP productions, *Invasion of the Saucer Men* was downright rowdy and randy.

Eager to oversee production of his brain-child, Jim Nicholson decided to coproduce the film himself. Following Herman Cohen's lead with *Teenage Werewolf,* Nicholson populated the cast with fresh, young faces, including Steve Terrell and Gloria Castillo, graduates of a series of juvenile delinquent films with titles like *Dragstrip Girl* (which featured a Paul Blaisdell cameo) and *Runaway Daughters.* In *Saucer Men,* both Terrell and Castillo would portray the boy and girl next door, virginal victims of the ogres from outer space.

Although the film had been conceived as a straightforward science-fiction-monster movie, according to Paul Blaisdell, "it just sort of collapsed into a comedy" once filming got underway. Ideas central to the plot, such as the monsters' ability to inject alcohol into their victims' bodies via hypodermic-like fingers, as well as their physical appearance, seemed more funny than scary, and eventually a decision was made by Nicholson and director Edward L. Cahn to soften the tone of the film. Blaisdell later described the transition:

> We were watching the rushes day by day, and it seemed the further we went, the further the picture was getting fouled up in terms of the original story. Teenagers necking in a cow pasture? The whole thing was just so ludicrous it was natural to change it into a spoof or comedy. When Nick and Eddie made that decision, everybody picked up on it immediately, including our little Saucer Men buddies. We knew it was the right thing to do because it "felt" right. It involved a lot of extra work, especially as we were approaching the end of the filming, and during postproduction Lyn Osborne had to do a lot of extra narration. I also designed the opening titles which gave the film a comedic flavor from the very outset. But despite the turmoil, it turned into a very entertaining picture. And it made money from the first day it hit the box office. How many other films can you think of that changed direction 180 degrees halfway through production without becoming an artistic and financial mess?

Invasion of the Saucer Men opens with a night shot of a creepy-looking country shack illuminated by flashes of thunder and lightning. Before we get a chance to settle into the macabre mood, a narrator's voice intrudes, remarking sarcastically, "Spooky, huh?" This sets the tone for the rest of the film, which alternates between light-hearted comedy and dark-hearted grisliness. The narrator is Art Burns (Lyn Osbourne, who died shortly after the film was completed), who confesses to the viewer: "I gotta play it square with ya. Actually a plain old farmer lives in this house, but I learned a long time ago you gotta start your pitch with a bang." Words of wisdom from the gods of grue at AIP.

Art's partner, a hellraising con-artist named Joe Gruen (Frank Gorshin), is convinced that Hicksburg, the town they've drifted into, is "a cinch for a quick buck" and intends to hang out for a few days to follow up the action. Art is fed up, though, and wants to return to their boardinghouse, get a good night's sleep, and pull out of town in the morning. Their disagreement leads indirectly to Joe's discovery of the film's title creatures. Cruising alone through the countryside, Joe hears a high-pitched whine and sees a blinding light in the sky. A moment later a strange, manta-shaped UFO descends behind a group of trees. Joe follows the pulsating glow and locates the alien spacecraft parked smack in the middle of a cow pasture in Pelham Woods. He turns on his heel to rush back to the boardinghouse and tell Art all about what he's discovered.

A group of teenagers hanging out in front of the local soda shop are discussing the flying saucer phenomenon when they're confronted by Lt. Wilkins (Douglas Henderson), an army specialist whose silent treatment gives the guys goose pimples. One of the teenagers is Johnny Carter (Steve Terrell), waiting here to meet his girl, Joan Hayden (Gloria Castillo). They plan on eloping that night because Joan's father, town attorney Mr. Hayden (Don Shelton), won't consent to their marriage. Hayden believes Johnny is a "rough-neck," but nothing could be further from the truth. He might dig making out with Joan at Lovers' Point, but he has yet to shotgun his first beer, as we learn later in the picture. (Funny how "juvenile delinquency" and beer-drinking go hand-in-hand in this picture.)

Joe makes his way back to the boardinghouse and wakes Art to tell him about the UFO. Art thinks Joe is drunk (he is, but that's beside the point) and blows him off, so Joe takes off again on his own.

Lt. Wilkins and his army superiors have been tracking the saucer's move-ments on their radar. It seems the disk touched down in Pelham Woods, a lonely stretch of land that borders Old Man Larkin's farm property. The can-tankerous Larkin (Raymond Hatton, last seen in Roger Corman's *Day the World Ended*) is completely unaware of the weird goings-on; what concerns him is the constant sneaking back and forth of carloads of teenagers who cut across his property to get to Lovers' Point. He shakes his fist at the latest vehicle that cruises by, promising, "I'll get the law after 'em!"

Johnny and Joan, driving without lights so as not to disturb Larkin, nearly plow straight into the army jeep transporting Lt. Wilkins and his crew to the saucer's landing site. As the jeep disappears around a thicket of trees, Johnny eases past Larkin's house, reassuring his fiancée, "I could drive this road blindfolded." Suddenly, out of the darkness scurries a fleeting shape. Johnny slams on the brakes but can't avoid hitting the thing, whatever it is. There is a sickening crunch as metal and flesh are twisted together by the impact. Joan thinks they've run down a child, but a flash of lightning illu-minates something utterly inhuman jammed under the car's fender: a diminu-tive creature with a glistening, exposed brain. The car's bumper is smeared with alien ichor. "What is it?" Joan asks, volunteering the obvious: "It's dis-gusting!" Hidden from view underneath the bumper, the thing's gnarled hand detaches itself from its crippled arm and creeps away with a life of its own. Needlelike projections slide out from its fingernails and puncture the car's tire.

When he hears the hiss of escaping air, Johnny figures the impact of the collision shoved the car's fender into the tire. Without a spare, the couple have no recourse but to walk to the closest refuge from the storm, and that happens to be Larkin's house. When they arrive, Larkin is nowhere to be found, so Johnny uses his telephone to call the police. Naturally, the cops think Johnny is playing a practical joke when he describes running over "a little green man." As one cop remarks to his partner, "It's Saturday night, that's official."

A crack of thunder interrupts power to the house just as Larkin returns home. He notices a strong odor of alcohol and figures the youngsters have been drinking. "That's funny," says Joan, "I smell it too," but neither of them has touched a drop. Larkin runs them off and warns them, "You tell your young friends to stay off of my property unless they want a backside full of rock salt."

By now Joe Gruen has made it back to Pelham Woods and is searching for something—anything—that will make him and Art a fortune. He pulls over when he sees Johnny's abandoned car. Spying the crumpled form beneath the fender, Joe puts two and two together and figures this is the body of one of the spaceship's extraterrestrial occupants. As much dough as he might have made showcasing a flying saucer, it's a cinch people would pay even more to see an honest-to-goodness space man, but before he can pry the body away from the fender, he's attacked by a gang of three more aliens—live ones—who repeatedly inject him with doses of pure alcohol from their deadly hypodermic fingers. Normally these Martians merely incapacitate their prey by stunning them senseless, but for someone who is soused to begin with, the hypodermic highballs prove to be fatal.

Johnny and Joan, who have decided to go back to fix the flat, are puzzled when they spot one of the Martians hammering away at the fender of the car with some kind of weird mechanical device. "It's one of those little things, a live one," Johnny tells her. He thinks the creature is "punishing" the car for killing its friend, the way native savages might blame one of their rain gods for a thunderstorm, but actually this is all part of the Cosmic Frame.

The kids decide to hike into town, but it's not long before they hear the wail of a siren and see the flashing lights of a police car slicing through the trees. Joan figures that means the police decided to believe Johnny after all. Thinking the cops will be able to take care of any ornery alien critters hanging about, Johnny and Joan turn around and head back to the car. When they get there, the place is crawling with cops, but there's not an alien in sight—including the one that was wedged beneath the fender of Johnny's car.

Having discovered Joe Gruen's lifeless body in the bushes nearby, the cops decide to charge Johnny with manslaughter. At the police station, Joan demands they send for her father, who happens to be the town attorney. When he arrives, Mr. Hayden pooh-poohs the kids' story about invaders from space but promises to try and contact Gruen's roommate to talk him out of pressing charges against either of them. Suddenly the sound of an explosion rocks the air and while police attention is diverted, Johnny and Joan escape through an open window. Johnny steals an idling cruiser and heads back to Pelham Woods with Joan. "We've got to get some proof, something they'll believe" Johnny tells her. "If we don't, I'm going to jail."

The explosion was the result of the army's attempt to penetrate the metal of the Martian spaceship. When the soldiers accidentally ignite a hidden fuse with their blowtorches, they activate a self-destruct mechanism, blowing the ship to pieces. All that remains are shards of the strange, silvery metal. The army congratulates itself on a job well done.

When the police discover that Johnny and Joan have fled, Hayden takes charge, promising to get everything straightened out. Meanwhile, the kids begin snooping around for evidence of the Martians' existence. After an exhaustive search, they return to the stolen police cruiser empty-handed. As they head up a lonely stretch of back road, neither of them notices the disembodied Martian claw that has crawled into the car through an open back window until Joan senses it next to her shoulder. She lets out a terrified shriek; Johnny swerves and the claw tumbles to the floorboards. Before it can scramble back up the seat, the kids jump out of the car and lock the doors. "At last we've got some evidence!" Johnny cries.

With no immediate way to transport the evidence to the police station, Johnny and Joan are forced to hike back to the soda shop to retrieve Joan's car. From there they drive to the boardinghouse to tell Joe Gruen's roommate, Art Burns, their story. "Joe kept trying to tell me something about it," Art remembers, realizing there may be something to this story about invaders from another world after all. He grabs a pistol and a camera, and the three of them head back to Pelham Woods. The police cruiser is still there, now surrounded by Saucer Men who are desperately trying to get what's left of their buddy out of the locked vehicle. When they hear Joan's car approaching, the creatures scatter into the woods. Johnny aims the car's spotlight at the cruiser, allowing Art to catch a glimpse of the disembodied claw. He tries to take a snapshot of it, but when the flashgun ignites, the claw vanishes in a blast of smoke and flame. The only evidence that could have proven Johnny's innocence is now gone for good.

Art promises to back up Johnny's story of the little green men from space. But as they get ready to leave, the car's battery gives out, stranding them. Art swivels the spotlight around, illuminating a bevy of advancing Martians who unexpectedly let out an unearthly shriek. "It's the light that hurts them!" Joan cries, suddenly understanding why the claw was destroyed by Art's flash camera. Unfortunately, with a dead battery the spotlight soon gives out, and the three of them are forced to make a run for it. Art uses his pistol on a couple of the saucer men, but bullets don't seem to hurt them. He is attacked by three of the creatures, who stab him repeatedly with their hypo-nails. While the saucer men are occupied with Art, Johnny and Joan manage to get away.

One of the aliens is killed by Larkin's bull, who gores the creature's eyeball out. That still leaves three of them alive, and they carry Art's body to a clearing in the woods. Johnny and Joan make it on foot to Larkin's farmhouse and use his phone to call the police. Johnny offers to give himself up for Gruen's murder, hoping to lure the cops to the woods so they can see the alien menace for themselves. To his surprise, they blow him off. The detective (Jason Johnson) tells Johnny that an autopsy revealed that Gruen died from alcohol poisoning. Technically, that lets Johnny off the hook. When Joan complains that they should still be on the wanted list for car theft, the detective tells them not to worry. "Your father took care of everything."

A bevy of big-headed, bug-eyed monsters prepare to set up the Cosmic Frame in *Invasion of the Saucer Men* (courtesy of Bob Burns). This promotional photo shows the original martian heads, before undergoing "lobotomies" at the Blaisdell workshop.

On their own once more, Joan suggests that they go to Lovers' Point and try to convince their friends what's happening. In no time Johnny and Joan have half a dozen couples on their side. The kids form a car caravan and drive up to the clearing where the aliens are guarding Art's body. When Johnny gives the signal, everyone switches on their hi-beam headlights. The blinding lights sizzle the Saucer Men's flesh and within moments the invaders vanish in a gigantic ball of smoke.

When Johnny and Joan rush to Art's side, they find him disheveled and disorderly. In fact, he's downright drunk. But at least he's alive. That's when they realize that the aliens subdued their victims by injecting them with pure alcohol. Now it becomes clear why Joe Gruen died from a Martian attack while Art Burns did not.

Art's voice-over narration reminds us we've been watching a flashback: "So that's my story. Johnny and Joan helped me remember a little of it, but I wrote it, y'understand. A true story? That's the nice thing about this book-writin' business: you pay before you read." Ditto for motion pictures: you pay before you see.

The late Lyn Osborne gets attacked by a bug-eyed monster in this specially posed promotional photo for Edward L. Cahn's *Invasion of the Saucer Men*.

The story line of *Invasion of the Saucer Men* takes place in "real time"; everything happens in a single night. There are no time contractions. In spite of (or perhaps because of) this element, the picture turned out to be one of the best in American-International's long line of sci-fi thrillers. Ramping up the comic overtones during post production helped give the film a fresh edge.

Instead of being just another space-monster picture, *Invasion of the Saucer Men* became a glib, even hip, encounter with the unknown that managed to thumb its nose at adult conventions without once losing sight of its primary responsibility to entertain.

As often happens in low-budget movie-making, some changes were made to the Gurney-Martin script to restrict the shooting schedule and reduce production expenditures. Several noncritical scenes, such as military vehicles driving down a highway, were omitted in the interests of time and budget. For the most part, character dialogue remained the same, although in one curious instance a Saucer Man is described as "all black, except his head." In the film this line was changed to "He was all green, except his head," which was more in line with Jim Nicholson's original vision of the monsters as "little green men from Mars." (Since there is another reference to "green men" later on in the script, the original description may have been merely a mistake.)

Several lines of dialogue between Johnny and Joan (Steve Terrell and Gloria Castillo) were switched as the film approached its conclusion. Lines intended for Gloria Castillo were spoken by costar Steve Terrell, and vice versa. This was probably done to maintain proper character perspective. Throughout the picture Johnny takes the initiative in almost every instance. He is the one who decides when they should return to the stranded car; he notices the open window in the police station; he leads Joan through the woods. Except for Joan's single critical revelation—"It's the light that hurts them!"—she is a follower who trusts in Johnny's judgment and sense of righteousness.

The most interesting departures from the script are those involving Paul Blaisdell's effects work. Although Gurney and Martin described the aliens in only the vaguest terms, there is a script notation that each claw should possess a total of "ten snakelike fingers" with inbuilt "stingers." According to Blaisdell, he never seriously considered giving the Saucer Men more than five fingers per claw because the effect would have been too difficult to pull off. Of course, the "stingers," or hypodermic-fingernails, were central to the story and were retained. The idea of the monsters' eyes closing (cited twice in the script in two different scenes) was eliminated also, as it would have involved adding cumbersome mechanics to one of the Saucer Men heads.

In the single major effects sequence that was excised from the script, Johnny and Joan make a detour to his apartment after their first encounter with the seeing-eye claw. The scene as written is mostly dialogue, but there was to have been a brief interlude with a single crawling alien finger which Joan discovers clinging to Johnny's shirt. In the original script, the finger evaporates in a flash of smoke when it crawls too close to a floor heater. As Bob Burns has pointed out, animating a single alien digit would have involved building a mechanized finger, a project Blaisdell was not all that keen to tackle. Thus the apartment scene, which really didn't do anything to further the narrative, was eliminated from the script entirely.

Measured by today's critical yardsticks, *Invasion of the Saucer Men* seems a rather remarkable 1950s feature. The story line may have been routine, but the execution was not, at least when compared to most other independent productions of the time. *Invasion of the Saucer Men* could have been just a lucky shot in the dark—merely a truistic AIP title that had little going for it besides Paul Blaisdell's brain-busting monsters—but it seems more probable that, as Blaisdell has himself suggested, spirits soared once the pressure was off to produce just one more routine monster movie.

Freshening up a standard story line by peppering it with humorous touches and bits of spoof and sarcasm went a long way toward making the new film a winner. But *Saucer Men* also boasted some of the best photographic work ever to come out of the AIP school of filmmaking. Fred West's camera captured the best studio-generated night-time photography ever seen in an American International production, bar none. Movies that relied on day-for-night location photography, like *I Was a Teenage Werewolf* and *The She-Creature*, invariably suffered from inadequate filtering techniques. Lowering the camera's f-stop had the effect of darkening a shot, but day-for-night invariably appeared murky on-screen, with telltale giveaways every time the camera tilted upward to reveal a sky that was too bright to look like anything except mid-afternoon. Night-for-night photography was too expensive. *Saucer Men* benefitted tremendously from its dark, studio-bound sets and proved that not every low-budget monster movie needed to rely on location shooting just to achieve a respectable degree of realism.

The acting wasn't too bad either. Steve Terrell was a realistic enough teen who responded to events in the Gurney-Martin screenplay in convincing fashion. Gloria Castillo, too, did well with her material; she turned out to be one of AIP's best screamers. Frank Gorshin displayed an early feel for comedy, and Lyn Osborne, who had appeared in a small role in *The Amazing Colossal Man* but achieved his greatest fame as Cadet Happy on TV's *Space Patrol* (1950-55), had one of the those rubbery, expressionistic faces that could register interest, disdain, fear, or whichever emotion the story might require at the drop of a hat. It's too bad he died before getting a better chance to show Hollywood what he was capable of. (Osborne also appeared in *The Cosmic Man*, released about a year after his death.)

The film's secondary characters were pretty spunky, too. Jason Johnson (the detective), Sam Buffington (the Colonel), and Douglas Henderson (Lt. Wilkins) were the kinds of stock characters who turned up in numerous '50s genre films, but here the actors' portrayals were spot-on. Ray Hatton, one of Alex Gordon's old-time favorites, didn't fare quite as well as Old Man Larkin, but the character was too one-dimensional to begin with to offer any actor much beyond what Hatton managed to do with it.

Probably the weakest link in the *Saucer Man* formula was the direction by Eddie Cahn. Many of the film's comedic touches were added only in the later stages of filming and during postproduction, including Ronald Stein's silly-symphonic musical score, which had as much to do with establishing the light-hearted mood as anything else. It's doubtful Cahn interjected much of his own brand of humor into the mix (assuming he had any), preferring to let the actors work out their own interpretations of the script. His pedestrian direction, combined with a tendency to rush through as many camera setups in a single day as possible, only managed to obscure much of the action, with the result that some scenes became downright confusing. The geometry of Pelham Woods, for example, with its broken-down cars, idling police cruisers, cow pasture, Lovers' Point, and alien landing sight, is especially muddled. And once again some of Paul Blaisdell's handiwork got pushed aside during the scurry of budgetary corner-cutting.

Cahn had already proven his ability to get a story told reasonably well and with as few frills as possible on pictures like *Voodoo Woman*. With financing set at about $70,000 and only a seven-day shooting schedule, Cahn couldn't have done much more even if he had wanted to. Obviously, with that kind of budget nobody at AIP was expecting anything more than standard drive-in fodder. (The picture was being made to fill the bottom half of a double bill with *I Was a Teenage Werewolf*.) In spite of this, *Invasion of the Saucer Men* remains one of the best examples of cost-conscious filmmaking at AIP during the 1950s.

According to Bob Burns, who worked uncredited as Blaisdell's assistant on this film, 98 percent of *Saucer Men* was shot on a studio soundstage. AIP constructed a marvelous set that outclassed anything built previously for *It Conquered the World*, *The Undead*, *The She-Creature*, or any of a dozen other films which relied heavily on studio photography. "It was a very large stage, with the police station and the cafe situated in one corner and the farmer's house in the middle," Burns described. "The wooded area was also part of the same stage, and it was designed so realistically, with shrubs and broken fences and muddy tracks and all, you had to look up at the roof to remind yourself that you weren't really outside in the woods."

Although *Saucer Men* began life as a serious take on a light-hearted short story, once the focus of the film shifted from gasps to giggles, "Everything just sort of fell into place," remarked Blaisdell. "In the end, *Invasion of the Saucer Men* turned out to be a much more enjoyable film than anyone had envisioned. It certainly became more than the sum of its original parts." Bob Burns added, "It played better as a comedy than it ever would have as a straight science-fiction story because it still retained a share of horrific elements, like the creeping hand. The mix of comedy and horror is what helped endear this picture to a generation of film fans, and they've made it into a cult favorite." There is another reason why the film became so popular with fantasy fans, however: it has adorable little monsters who are as lovable as they are lethal.

For Paul, taking on the *Saucer Men* assignment meant taking on one heck of a lot of work. He would have to build not just one monster costume, but four. After all, a single alien being would hardly constitute an invasion. (For that matter, even four amounted to no more than a little overcrowding.) In addition to those costumes, one of which would be worn by Blaisdell himself and one by Bob Burns, the others worn by dwarf actors Angelo Rossito (whose Hollywood connection dated back to 1932 when he worked for director Tod Browning in the controversial MGM film *Freaks*), Eddie Gibbons, Dean Neville, and Lloyd Dixon, it would be necessary to construct a separate, partially mechanized Martian head as well as a disembodied claw. There was also the spaceship as well as a couple of otherworldly props. All things considered, *Invasion of the Saucer Men* turned out to be one of Blaisdell's toughest but most rewarding projects.

To relieve some of the burden, it was decided early on that the Martian monster costumes would not be full-figured monster suits. Blaisdell would make only the heads and hands. The bodies would be covered by fabric provided by the wardrobe department. Since the Martians were supposed to be spacemen, it made sense that they would be wearing some type of clothing or an astronomical suit. AIP's wardrobe specialist came up with black body costumes, each outfitted with a scalloped pattern of sequined material around the neck and wrists. Ballet shoes covered the actors' feet. In the film's low-level lighting, these appeared at least a little unusual, although any ballet fans in the audience probably had to laugh at such cheesy shenanigans.

Even with the aid of these time-savers the amount of work involved with the project had Paul and Jackie toiling six days a week for six weeks to get things ready for the first day of filming. Since Paul needed to produce a total of five headpieces (four for the actors and a separate "hero head"), he created a compound plaster-and-rubber mold which was used to generate fiberglass copies. (The old method of building a latex mask over a blank would have been too cumbersome and time-consuming because the process would have had to be repeated for each separate mask.) He started out much as he had several years earlier when he was designing his very first movie monster, the Beast with a Million Eyes. A large egg-shaped plaster mold was constructed, which served as a three-dimensional base. This was divided into two sections, the right and left brain hemispheres. Using his favorite water-based clay, Blaisdell sculpted the design of the brain tissue directly over the plaster casts. (The plaster was employed merely to define the dimensions of each headpiece.) When the clay hardened, Blaisdell moved on to the next step in the process: making fiberglass copies of the finished sculpture. The two separate hemispheres could be used to produce as many three-dimensional fiberglass "brains" as necessary.

Working with fiberglass proved to be not much more difficult than working with ordinary liquid latex. In fact, in some respects it was easier because the material seeped deep into the crevices of the sculpture, which helped make the final product more detailed.

After the fiberglass was heated, cured, and carefully separated from the mold, the two hemispheres were joined together to produce one gigantic brain. To create a network of topical "blood vessels," Blaisdell experimented with a special mixture of liquid latex and talcum powder, which when added together gave the latex a thicker consistency. The mix was then loaded into, of all things, a cake decorator. With the decorator it was easy to produce ribbons of latex of any length or thickness by firing the mixture onto a plane of glass. This insured that the ribbons remained flat on the bottom so they could be bonded to the fiberglass and latex heads and hands. A little appropriate coloring made these latex ribbons look just like a network of pulsing blood vessels.

Like the outer brain hemispheres, the vile visage of the Saucer Man was first rendered in water-based clay over a plaster base. Drops of water were periodically added to the clay to keep it soft and pliable, allowing Blaisdell to tweak the design until it satisfied him completely. He began by shaping the brow, the main portion of the skull that would later be attached to the brain. Oversized eye sockets and a unique, triple-lipped mouth were added, as well as the suggestion of a nose cavity. The ears and eyes were fashioned separately.

Blaisdell made a total of five latex faces from a positive mold. Each was texturized with special tools to give the skin a porous appearance. Veins made out of latex ribbons were added around the mouth and along the cheekbones. Each face was later joined to a fiberglass shell and painted.

Elongated ears, resembling a cross between those created for the three-eyed Atomic Mutant of *Day the World Ended* and the amphibious She-Creature, were fashioned separately from latex brushed over a positive mold. When dry, the rubber was removed and stuffed with cotton to preserve the original shape, then resealed with an additional layer of latex.

Instead of plastic, Blaisdell made eyes out of Styrofoam for *Invasion of the Saucer Men*. There were two reasons for choosing Styrofoam over plastic. Most importantly, for a scene in which one of the Martians has its eyeball gored by an irate bull, Styrofoam would make the effect much easier to pull off. Secondly, for the climax of the film, there was going to be a scene in which the Martians' eyes suddenly constrict as the creatures are surrounded by blinding car headlights. Although this effect was never filmed, Blaisdell made the necessary preparations for it by creating a series of slitted, snake-like pupils, each set smaller than the one before it, that could be made to stick to the Styrofoam. The plan was to film the effect in a series of stop-motion sequences. With the camera locked into position, one frame of film would be exposed of the normal eyes. Blaisdell would then remove the pupils and replace them with the next set, another frame of film would be exposed, and so on.

This process would continue until the pupils disappeared completely from the white of the eye, and the film would return to live action as the Martians exploded in a puff of smoke. The interchangeable pupils were made out of bits of black, self-sticking "blooping tape" (used during the 1950s to produce "wipes" and similar effects on previously exposed film). This method would have allowed for quick changes between exposures of the film, but the idea was nixed during preproduction.

Special Styrofoam eyeballs that had been hollowed out on the inside were made separately for the hero head. This consisted of just the face and part of the exterior brain. It was left open in the back so that Blaisdell could operate the mouth and eyes from inside. By pressing his fingers against the hollowed-out Styrofoam spheres, Blaisdell could make the eyes shift slightly, even getting them to look cross-eyed if he wanted. He was also able to wrinkle the rubber material between the eyes and the top of the "nose," making it appear as if the creature was snarling like a werewolf. (Actually the Martians had no noses, merely triangular nostrils.) The lips could also be made to move by manipulating a wire attached to them from inside the head. Twisting the wire would pull the rubber to either side or push it outward, giving a little bit of animation to otherwise immobile features. Unfortunately, like many of the attributes found in other Blaisdell creations, these effects were never really utilized. (Blaisdell did manage to pull off some of his Saucer Man tricks in a couple of self-produced featurettes he offered for sale to readers of his own magazine, *Fantastic Monsters of the Films*. More about that later.)

The hero head was rigged with an inexpensive system of pumps and tubes which allowed Blaisdell to squirt "venom" (actually ordinary tap water) through the open mouth. Although the effect was seen only very briefly on screen, it was effective for its time. The venom effect was not something which had been written into the film script; it was an effect Paul originated. The idea was that the Saucer Man would "spit" at an approaching enemy as a sort of warning to keep away. The effect was achieved by filling a rubber ear syringe with tap water and squirting it through a tube fitted to the syringe that ran to the mouth of the head. When the film began rolling, Blaisdell pumped the "venom" up the tube so that it shot straight toward the camera lens in a thin stream. The same equipment was used to film a similar scene in which a Saucer Man begins drooling, but that shot did not make it into the final cut of the film.

While Blaisdell and Burns were filming these insert effects (which were, incidentally, directed by Blaisdell himself), an effects artist named Wah Chang was working in the same studio on a picture called *The Black Scorpion*, which was master animator Willis O'Brien's swan song. Chang was involved in setting up *The Black Scorpion*'s single live-action effect, an oversized, drooling head of the title monster. On this particular day, he had forgotten to bring an ear syringe, which he was using to make the scorpion drool. When he noticed that Blaisdell was using the same device for *Saucer Men*, he wandered over and asked if he might borrow it. "Paul did better than that," Burns noted. "We had two ear syringes, so Paul just gave him one."

Paul had planned on using the second ear syringe to create a "tearing effect" for the climax of *Saucer Men*. He had drilled "tear ducts" into the inside corners of the eyes of the Martian hero head, where he could insert plastic tubing that would carry water forward from the ear syringes. The idea was that the bright lights that doomed the aliens to extinction would first cause the monsters' eyes to tear up. Paul and Bob rehearsed the effect and it worked perfectly, but it was just one more thing that got discarded along the way.

These minor effects—the shifting eyeballs, the constricting pupils, the spitting venom, the wrinkling of the "nose"—were a testament to Blaisdell's ingenuity and ability to solve problems on a nearly nonexistent budget. But inventive as his handiwork was, these were merely minor appurtenances when compared to the film's major effects set pieces: the flying saucer, the disembodied walking claw, the battle of the beasts (Martian and bull), and the "hypo-nails."

Blaisdell later spoke about the disembodied hand:

> The "seeing-eye hand" was one of the funniest elements of the story, and one that was going to be used extensively throughout the filming. The way I designed the eyeball on the Martian hand, it could look all around, back and forth, and signal the hand that everything was okay by nodding it up and down, and just tell the hand to go on about its business. If somebody had sneezed, for example, the eye on the hand would whip right around and look at him. But, except for one or two brief shots, they never used it in the film. "No time, no money, no film. Blah, blah, blah!"

Blaisdell made just a single fully functioning "seeing-eye claw" for *Saucer Men*. Each of the claws worn by the actors playing the aliens had its own eyeball, but it wasn't necessary (nor would it have been practical) to make them all operational. The claws were built directly over store-bought vinyl gloves. Almost every inch of the gloves was covered with rubber latex veins which were air-brushed the same desert-brown color as the headpieces. A sub-assembly consisting of a raised cavity outfitted with a plastic eyeball was later glued to the top of each hand to complete the design. (Blaisdell opted to use plastic spheres instead of Styrofoam for the hand-mounted eyeballs because plastic was easier to paint.)

The disembodied Martian claw was fashioned out of a glove and latex in much the same way as the standard claws. But whereas the eyes on the claws designed for the actors were stationary, the "hero claw" possessed a fully rotating orb. Its degree of rotation as well as its speed could be controlled by a removable crank mechanism which Blaisdell made out of coat hanger wire. Although Paul later modified the gimmick so that it would work with his

The disembodied claw that menaces the teenagers in *Invasion of the Saucer Men* contained a crank mechanism Blaisdell could use to turn the eyeball on the back of the hand. Push-rods attached to a small length of wood on the underside of the claw were used to extend the "hypodermic fingernails" for close-ups.

hand inside the claw-glove, at the time *Saucer Men* was made he couldn't wear the claw at the same time he wanted to use the revolving eye effect.

To make the eye move back and forth, Paul inserted one end of the wire through an opening in the rubber latex palm and threaded the other end into a small hole that had been drilled into the bottom of the plastic eye. The wire protruded from the latex about an inch from the palm, and this end was bent into an L-shape. Twisting the wire caused the plastic eyeball to turn. Because Blaisdell had to use his free hand to turn the crank on the underside, scenes of the rotating eyeball had to be filmed in extreme close-up.

(By the time Blaisdell's *Filmland Monsters* was produced in the early 1960s,* Paul had altered the mechanics of the device so that it was possible to rotate the seeing-eye while wearing the claw. In this instance a much longer wire was used. It ran from the bottom of the plastic eye down the interior of the claw and out of the wrist. Blaisdell would wear the claw just like a glove, with the wire resting on top of his hand. He could then wiggle his fingers to

*Filmland Monsters *was an 8mm collection of "coming attraction" trailers from AIP films of the 1950s, interspersed with new footage of Blaisdell's monsters, which was offered for sale to fans and collectors through* Fantastic Monsters. *Details appear in Chapter 14.*

give the claw a semblance of life while twisting the wire protruding from the wrist with his free hand.)

Quite a bit of footage was shot of the seeing-eye claw, but not much made it into the final cut of the film. A single close-up of the eyeball looking from right to left was edited into the scene in which a Saucer Man's hand detaches itself from the arm, just to introduce the idea to the viewer that this five-fingered beast knew exactly where it was going and what it was doing. Eddie Cahn eliminated almost all the other shots of the rotating eye, however, probably because he thought additional close-ups were superfluous.

In addition to its articulated eyeball, the disembodied claw was also empowered with comprehensive autonomous locomotion, at least in a sense. The script required the hand to crawl across a country road under its own power, scurry up the back seat of a moving automobile, and perform several other sleight-of-hand movements. Given the technological limits of 1957, it would have been difficult, if not impossible, to manufacture an automatized, self-propelled claw without access to significant chunks of time and money.* That meant Blaisdell was forced once again to rely on his own ingenuity to pull off the relatively complicated effects.

The seeing-eye claw effect turned out to be easier to perfect than Blaisdell had originally believed possible. His first thought was to make a multi-jointed marionette claw that could be manipulated off-camera with a set of wires, but he eventually dismissed this idea as clumsy and inflexible. "Sometimes the simplest answer is the best answer, depending on circumstances," Blaisdell said. He ended up cutting a slit large enough to accommodate his hand in the underside of the wrist section and extended the length of the wrist by building up additional layers of latex rubber which were sculpted to look like ragged, torn flesh. The wrist extension was filled with foam rubber to maintain its shape, and the foam was covered with latex and painted. A wedge of plastic with a jagged end was inserted into the open end of the wrist and bonded into position with spirit gum. After it had been painted, the plastic looked just like a broken wrist bone protruding from a dismembered claw. For a final gruesome effect, Blaisdell added dangling veins and ganglia—lengths of thin plastic tubing coated with painted latex.

Besides adding a touch of the grisly, the protruding wristbone and shredded flesh served as a kind of camouflage. Instead of wearing the claw in the ordinary (glovelike) fashion, Blaisdell pushed his hand through the wrist slit and let the extended bone section rest on top of his own forearm. When it was time to shoot the scenes featuring the crawling hand, Blaisdell wore a long-sleeved, black pullover shirt which further served to camouflage his arm. For the effect to work, it was necessary to photograph the claw against dark

---

*In fact, Blaisdell created just such a device several years later when he produced a homemade horror movie called The Cliff Monster. See Chapter 14.

backgrounds. Fortunately, since *Invasion of the Saucer Men* took place entirely at night, this didn't present much of a problem.

The final addition to the lineup of Martian materials was Blaisdell's hypodermic-fingernail rig. For this effect he did not make a complete working claw, but relied on a four-finger version made out of a vinyl glove which had been cut in half above the third knuckle. Since the camera would be photographing the effect in extreme close-up, a full-figured claw was not only unnecessary, it would have made the effect more difficult to pull off.

The hypo-nails consisted of four tiny, hollow aluminum rods attached to a block of wood which fit inside the open end of the glove. When Blaisdell slid the block forward, it pushed the rods out through small holes in the latex fingertips. Each rod was attached to a tube which hooked into an ear syringe pump. Pressure on the pump bulb caused tap water to squirt through the tubes and out the fingertips. The mechanism was concealed by the material of the glove which was painted with liquid latex and covered with dozens of latex veins to match the appearance of the other claws.

After finishing up work on the Martian heads and hands Blaisdell turned his attention to designing an otherworldly "hammer" for a scene in which one of the Saucer Men pounds an incriminating dent into the fender of Johnny's car. Paul opted to make the hammer out of plywood because the thinness of the material made it easy to work with. The design he wanted to use consisted entirely of curves, arcs, and round holes; there wasn't a single straight line or hard edge anywhere in sight.

The extraterrestrial hammer never appeared in the film because it was broken in two just moments after Paul handed it to Angelo Rossito, one of the actors playing a Saucer Man. "Be careful with this, Angie, it's delicate," Paul warned. "You'll have to fake the scene." Rossito decided to test the hammer by smacking it against the nearest table. Sure enough, the plywood splintered on impact. Angelo turned around and dropped the pieces in Blaisdell's lap. "Now I really will have to fake it," he muttered. Blaisdell was able to patch the prop back together but Eddie Cahn decided not to use it after all, opting instead for a mechanical drill that one of the prop men happened to find lying around the studio. (Paul's Martian hammer did turn up in a couple of AIP promotional photos. If you look closely, you can see a line near the top of the prop where it was glued back together.)

The broken hammer was actually the least of Paul's worries. When he arrived at the AIP offices to show Jim Nicholson the finished alien outfits, coproducer Robert J. Gurney, Jr., took one look and said, "Oh, no! Those heads are way too big." Dumbfounded, Blaisdell turned to Nicholson and reminded him, "But that's what we all agreed on. Little green guys with big brainy heads and bulging eyes. Remember, Nick?"

"I don't care," Gurney interrupted, "we can't use those heads. They're just too damn big." The soft-spoken Nicholson could barely get a word in during

Gurney's oral onslaught. Bob Burns later recalled how annoyed his friend was about making a last-minute change:

> Paul had built the Saucer Men heads bigger than he normally would have because that's what AIP told him they wanted. "Real big brain heads, that's what we want. Make 'em as big as you can." Those were the instructions they gave Paul. Then, when he saw them, the coproducer said, "Oh, we don't want them that big. You'll have to make them smaller." Make them smaller? How do you make them smaller without starting over? They've been made out of fiberglass, they're completely molded and painted and ready to go. It really pissed Paul off.

Since there wasn't time to construct new heads from scratch, Blaisdell did the only thing he could do under the circumstances: he lobotomized his Martian monsters. Making a fiberglass and rubber monster mask smaller was, naturally, a bit more complicated than making it larger. Blaisdell already knew that film producers could sometimes be shortsighted with their eleventh hour demands for cosmetic changes to costumes and props, having been through some nerve-wracking situations with the folks at American International on previous occasions. Whipping up a monster mask and pair of paws as part of *Cat Girl*'s 48-hour rescue mission and redesigning Harry Thomas's dreadful *Voodoo Woman* mask were just a couple of instances. The producers' decision to pull an about-face so late in the game when it came to the cranial measurements of the Saucer Men infuriated Blaisdell, who thought that Gurney was making unnecessary waves in what had so far been a relatively calm sea. But Gurney had Nicholson's ear, and the order had been given. Now the ball was in Blaisdell's court.

The only practical way to "shrink" the Saucer Men heads was to literally attack them with knives and scissors. By cutting a pie-shaped wedge out of the back of each fiberglass unit, Paul could reduce the overall volume by nearly a third. After the material had been cut away, the exposed edges were pushed together and fastened in place with bonding cement. Because the Saucer Men heads had been constructed out of two sections to start with (the fiberglass brain and the rubber face), altering the measurements of the brain had a negligible impact on the existing facial structure. (Some twisting or wrinkling of the rubber features was easily fixed with patches of latex and coloring.) When Paul and Jackie finished lobotomizing the Saucer Men, they no longer resembled the big-brained beings of Nicholson's original vision; instead, as Bob Burns was fond of pointing out: "They became cabbage heads. They were more rounded and looked just like heads of cabbage. Promotional photos survive of the original design, however."

Once the reconstructed masks were delivered to the cast and crew, *Invasion of the Saucer Men* began its short seven-day shooting schedule, which included three days of monster footage with the dwarf actors and a day of special effects utilizing the Martian hero head and other props.

All of the shots of the creatures' extended hypo-nails were filmed on the final day of shooting. Only minimal participation was required from the cast and crew, so nearly everything during this stage was done by Blaisdell and Bob Burns. Burns stood in for Steve Terrell in several scenes, most notably during the crawling hand sequence in the police cruiser, and also doubled Lyn Osborne, who had a problem working with some of the effects.

Most of Osborne's scenes involved straightforward interaction with Terrell and Gloria Castillo, although in the climax of the picture the script called for him to be subdued by alcohol injections from the aliens. But like some of Hollywood's greatest stars and starlets, Lyn Osborne believed that "his face was his fortune," and he did not want to risk getting it damaged by being poked with any "hypodermic-fingernails." Paul demonstrated how harmless the rig was, emphasizing that no one could possibly get hurt because the hypo-nails retracted into the interior of the claw as soon as they touched a solid surface. "Your fortune will remain secure," Blaisdell promised.

But Osborne wasn't having any. "I don't care, you're not coming near me with that thing." He walked off stage and refused to come back. Blaisdell grabbed the hypo-nail rig and chased Osborne down. "Lyn, look how easily this works," he said, turning around and pushing the retractable claw into Burns's face. "Doesn't hurt a bit, does it, Bob?" The surprised Burns shook his head.

"Okay, fine," Osborne said, looking at Burns. "You do it." And he walked away.

Eddie Cahn, who had been standing by watching, threw up his hands in exasperation. "Fellas, you'll have to find some way to cover Lyn during the insert shooting." That was the extent of Cahn's input into the problem.

Close-ups of the hypo-nails penetrating Osborne's flesh weren't 100 percent crucial to the completion of the scenes they were shooting that day, but Blaisdell wanted to get the effect on film. Rather than cheat the audience by using a cut-around, Blaisdell suggested that Burns stand in for the actor during the insert stage. With the proper camera angle, some dramatic low-key lighting and a little quick cutting, no one would be able to tell it wasn't Lyn Osborne. Burns agreed to do it.

Several shots of Martian claws slashing through the air were intercut with close-ups of Burns, his head cocked away from the camera, while the alcohol-engorged fingernails of the Martian claws "penetrated" his cheekbone, neck, and chest. When it was pieced together during the editing stage, the sequence turned out to be very effective. And Blaisdell was right: nobody ever noticed that Lyn Osborne was MIA.

Burns also doubled Steve Terrell for scenes with the disembodied hand inside the police cruiser. Gloria Castillo was also doubled by a stand-in during most of the effects shooting. Since all of the insert footage was shot at the Howard Anderson studios, AIP did not consider it necessary to award their two young stars an extra day's pay. Both characters would only be seen from the back while the camera was trained mainly on Blaisdell's rubber latex handiwork, so any reasonable-looking stand-ins could do the job.

Working side by side, Blaisdell and Burns managed to pull off most of the seeing-eye claw shots without a hitch. To this day the scene remains effectively creepy—one more tribute to Blaisdell's talent for devising innovative yet inexpensive movie effects. "Paul Blaisdell was just brilliant when it came to doing special effects, special makeups and costumes for these pictures," noted producer Alex Gordon, who first worked with Blaisdell on *Day the World Ended*. "It's too bad he was so vastly underrated for so long." Bob Burns agreed:

> To be absolutely realistic about it, Paul did most of these things for very little money and with very little time. AIP and other independent film companies were never able to give him the kind of luxuries other artists routinely got at Universal or Warner Brothers or the other major studios. Under those kinds of conditions, the work that he turned out was just amazing. To this day I still marvel at some of the things he was able to accomplish almost single-handedly.

In its original cut, the film contained significantly more group footage of the Saucer Men. Many of these shots were eliminated before the film went into general release. Because Angelo Rossito was the shortest of the four actors who played the aliens in long shots, Blaisdell and Burns thought it would be funny to designate him the Martian leader. Thereafter, whenever there was group activity among the monsters, little Angie led his bodacious brethren on their nefarious rounds. He actually scored a round of applause from the crew after one performance because they thought he made a marvelous Martian. The distinctive, warbly sounding Martian tongue heard sporadically throughout the film was actually the voice of Lyn Osborne. "Osborne was a real character, and he was actually a lot funnier than Frank Gorshin, who was kind of quiet and kind of moody," Bob Burns observed. "Occasionally we'd hear laughter coming from a corner of the set, and invariably it was Lyn, drawing a crowd with one of his funny stories. He was good at ad-libbing, so he did the voices of the aliens." During the recording, Osborne spoke as quickly as he could with a nasally whine, and the sound was speeded up and further distorted in the studio.

Eddie Cahn wanted to add an extra gruesome touch to the scene in which Frank Gorshin touches the dead body of the alien stuck underneath Johnny's car. He asked Blaisdell to devise some "alien ichor" which would be used to coat Gorshin's hand. Blaisdell came up with the idea of using "Wild Root Cream Oil," a supergreasy hair preparation for men, mixed together with chocolate syrup, lime jello, and a little bit of glitter. Having already completed his scenes, Gorshin had departed the production, so Cahn's camera photographed Blaisdell's hand reaching out to touch the slimy concoction. Thanks to the wonders of modern movie magic, not a soul was able to tell this wasn't really Gorshin's hand.

The first major order of on-screen business for Blaisdell's disembodied Martian mitt was a sanguine scene in which the claw detaches itself from the still-quivering arm of a dead Saucer Man, crawls across the pavement, and punctures the tire of Johnny's car. The effect required a five-stage setup. Following an establishing shot of a "dead" Saucer Man lying beneath the framework of the car, Cahn cut to a close-up of the mutilated arm to show the claw working itself free of the wristbone. The claw was loosely attached to a specially prepared latex and foam rubber wrist outfitted with the same material that made up the aliens' bodywear. To give the scene an even gristlier slant, Blaisdell attached a mass of latex ganglia and an exposed "bone" (actually a length of painted plastic) to the end of the wrist. Since the camera was tightly focused on that section of the wrist which was constructed to separate into two pieces, Blaisdell was able to hide below the frame line and operate the claw with his own hand. With the cameras rolling, Blaisdell wiggled the claw until it separated and dropped to the ground. Appropriate sound effects added in postproduction made it seem as if the claw was noisily tearing away from the tendons and tissues of the arm. (It's interesting to note that this sequence was filmed by the same director who had objected to the idea of the "lunch hooks" in *The She-Creature* just one year earlier.)

A quick close-up of the rotary eye was used to establish that this claw was not merely alive, but sentient. For the following low-angle shot showing the fully functioning appendage approaching the car tire of its own accord, a small trough was built to accommodate Blaisdell's arm as he stretched out on the floor of the set. With his hand inserted into the claw-glove, Blaisdell "walked" the alien claw toward the tire. Since the unit fit over his own hand by means of a slit in the latex rubber near the bottom of the palm, the apparent severed wrist actually rested on top of his own forearm. Careful camera panning followed the movement of the claw and helped to insure that the viewer's attention was directed toward the wriggling fingers and away from the wrist. Another close-up—this time of the engorged, dripping hypo-nails striking the tire—segued into a final shot of the disembodied hand as it scurried past the camera.

Although Cahn utilized numerous close-ups of the working hypo-nails throughout *Saucer Men*, the crawling hand was featured in only one other important sequence. Just before Johnny and Joan steal the police cruiser, there is a brief shot of the claw climbing through an open side window. This setup involved the use of the film's single optical effect, a simple superimposition accomplished by filming a black-garbed Blaisdell operating the claw against a solid black background. Although the juxtaposition of elements is good, the shot is not perfect. Close inspection of the scene reveals a vague outline of Paul's forearm on the underside of the claw, caused by a reflection of light off the material during the shooting.

The budget of *Invasion of the Saucer Men* didn't allow for use of a break-away car, a routine Hollywood prop used in just about every picture that ever required filming the interior of an automobile. When it was time to shoot footage of the claw attacking Johnny and Joan inside the police car, the crew had to thread cables and lights through the windows of a real auto in order to light the scene, while Fred West aimed his Mitchell camera straight through the back window, which had been removed. Steve Terrell's and Gloria Castillo's stand-ins were seated up front, and Paul Blaisdell was hiding on the floorboards between the front and back seats. "That was the only way they could get the scene filmed," explained Bob Burns, "because AIP was too cheap to spend the money on a breakaway car."

Blaisdell, once again dressed in black and now wearing a black hood, remained in the shadows while "walking" the disembodied claw up the back-seat cushion. Altogether the crew spent some 3½ hours setting up and shooting the scene. "Poor Paul was twisted up like a pretzel in the backseat the entire time," recalled Burns. "With the cameraman shooting through the windows, and all the criss-crossed cables running through the car, it was almost impossible for Paul to squeeze himself between the front and back-seats. And the lights were so hot, I think we both lost several pounds that day." There was one minor snafu: part of Blaisdell's black-clothed forearm became visible midway through the first shot. It was included in the final cut of the film anyway because AIP thought no one would notice.

Blaisdell also performed as the seeing-eye claw in a minor scene with Lyn Osborne. When Osborne's character spots the claw on the floorboard of the police cruiser, he attempts to photograph it with a flash camera, and it goes up in a blast of smoke. To give the appearance of the claw evaporating, a standard Fourth-of-July smoke-bomb hidden underneath one of the latex rubber gloves was ignited. The heat scorched the hell out of the rubber claw (Paul, recalling his *Voodoo Woman* experience, did have the foresight to remove his hand from it first), but the sacrifice of one Martian claw wasn't too high a price to pay to capture the effect on film. (At least that's what Eddie Cahn told him.)

Once Art has seen incontrovertible proof of the existence of the Martians, he, Johnny, and Joan try to escape Pelham Wood in Joan's car, but with its dead battery they can't get very far. Art whips out a pistol and begins shooting at the advancing aliens, but the creatures aren't fazed in the least. "Bullets don't hurt 'em!" Art mutters incredulously.

Bullets might not penetrate alien flesh, but they have a decidedly different impact on mere humans. A standard moviemaking item called a squib, used to simulate the impact of a bullet, was attached to one of the Saucer Man heads so that Eddie Cahn could show the bullet's impact on the enlarged brain. Generally, squibs are attached to pieces of background scenery, trees, clothing, etc., and are set off by a remote-controlled electric charge. Nobody had tried setting one off on a monster mask before.

Once the headpiece was rigged, Blaisdell strapped it on and filming recommenced. At a prearranged signal, the charge was set off by one of the film's two designated special effects technicians. The squib exploded on cue, leaving behind a blackened hole, a wispy trail of smoke, and one rather shaken up monster-maker. While things looked pretty good from Cahn's perspective, inside the fiberglass alien head Blaisdell could hear bells ringing. "He didn't know the blast of the squib would reverberate inside the fiberglass head," said Bob Burns. "None of us did. Paul couldn't hear anything for the rest of that day."

Fortunately, there were no such mishaps during the staging of the fight between a Saucer Man and "Old Walt," Larkin's pet Brahma bull. A little more than half the shots that make up this sequence were photographed on indoor sets at the Howard Anderson studio, using the Martian hero head and accessories as well as a phony bull's head mounted on a metal rod. The rest was filmed on the Lionel Comport Movie Ranch with a real bull and a prop body. (Comport had previously assisted in the making of *The Beast with a Million Eyes* with the loan of numerous farm animals for scenes in that film.) The dummy Martian was wired to the real bull, and footage was shot as the animal tried to shake it loose. These scenes were later intercut with close-ups of the Saucer Man hero head and the hypodermic fingernails penetrating the bull's hide (actually a piece of cowhide provided by studio property master Karl Brainard).

In the middle of the bullfight, the Martian's eyeball is gouged by the bull's horn. To pull off this illusion, Blaisdell and Burns took on the roles of the Saucer Man and steer, respectively, using the Martian hero head and the studio's rod-mounted bull head. For this scene Blaisdell prepared a special alien eyeball which had a cone-shaped wedge of material cut out to accommodate the tip of the bull horn. A small hole was drilled through the center of the Styrofoam sphere so that the nozzle of a grease gun could be inserted into the back. The grease gun was loaded with chocolate syrup, which was being used to simulate blood. The front hole in the eyeball was filled in with wax, and the finished orb was painted and popped back into the eye socket, ready to be blinded on camera without a cutaway.

When the film began rolling, Burns rammed the horn of the prop bull into the wax center of the Styrofoam eye. At the same time, Blaisdell, hidden from view on the other side of the hero head, squeezed the grease gun trigger, letting fly a stream of chocolate syrup which gushed gorily out the front of the eyeball. Burns began rocking the bull head from side to side to make it seem as if the animal was trying like mad to gouge out what was left of the eye. The juxtaposition of live elements, combined with judicious navigation of the camera, made for a convincing effect which was magnified by the inter-cutting of location footage with the actual Brahma bull. (Incidentally, the prop was not a Brahma bull head, but no one ever seemed to notice.)*

After the shot was spliced together, Eddie Cahn made a comment which had a very familiar ring: "Uhm, we can't use this, Paul. It's too horrible." He eventually decided to include a trimmed-down version in the final cut of the film, as Blaisdell later noted:

> We went through a lot of preparation just to get that scene set up, and then it got cut. The actual shot of the blood gurgling out of the eyeball was removed because Eddie thought it was too gory. He told Ron Sinclair [the editor] they were going to have to do a cut away. So when it comes back, you can see the blood all over the eye, but that's all. There was so much more originally. The blood really shot out! For its time it was a really wild scene. Frankly, I don't know which one of us was the bigger dummy—me or Bob Burns, the guy who played the bull. Sometimes I wonder if we didn't have better days fighting the bull in the producer's office!"

Burns also helped Paul with the close-up of the Saucer Man who is blinded at the end of the picture. The constricting pupil effect had already been dropped because it was too costly and time-consuming, so all that needed to be captured on film was a close shot of the hero head with a pair of claws attempting to shield its eyes, as if the monster was trying to shut out the light. The choreography of the scene was simplicity itself: Blaisdell would stand behind the head and work the mouth and eye controls to give the features a little bit of animation; Burns would sit in front of Blaisdell wearing a pair of claws. On cue, he would bring the claws up and back, covering the huge orbs in the hero head.

The only problem was, with Burns facing the same direction as Blais-dell, he had to guess where the eyes were. (Burns couldn't sit the other way around because the right and left claws would be reversed.) Every time the camera was fired up, Burns missed his mark. Sometimes he knocked the lens shield askew (the camera was very close to him); other times he had the claws covering the Saucer Man's chin, or nose, or cheeks—anything but the eyes. The harder he tried to get it right, the worse it turned out, and the funnier it seemed to get. Burns was single-handedly burning up the film stock, and no one was able to stop him.

Burns eventually got the claws lined up correctly, but by that time he and Blaisdell were laughing so hard their stomachs hurt. "It's a good thing

---

*Animal lovers, take cover: to induce the real bull to buck as if it were trying to dislodge the body of the Saucer Man, a "bucking spur" was attached to the animal's abdomen. The burr irritated the bull's flesh, which is what made it buck. (The device is routinely used in rodeo shows for "bucking bronco" stunts.) When the bull dropped to the ground as if stunned by juice from the Saucer Man's needle-tipped fingers, it had been drugged. (Look closely and you can see its eyes roll back in its head.) These kinds of tricks could not be employed by today's filmmakers, of course, but in 1957 the SPCA did not closely supervise the use of animals in independent films such as those made by AIP.

we didn't do that scene on a day when Sam Arkoff visited the set," Burns said, "because he definitely would've pulled the plug after a couple of takes. It took me at least five tries to get it right."

Along with the Saucer Man costumes, the hero head, the hypo-nails, and the articulated claw, Blaisdell designed and built the aliens' interstellar hot rod. He produced two different model saucers, one rigged to hover over a miniature set and one made specifically to be blown to bits.

The flying version of the saucer—model 1—was made out of solid white pine. While Paul gained most of his monster costuming experience during the years he worked for American International, learning as he went along and pulling rabbits out of hats on the fly, he had many more years of experience building detailed model airplanes. His devotion to the hobby was repaid on film projects that required specialized props such as the teleportation device seen in *Not of This Earth* and the Las Vegas miniatures of *The Amazing Colossal Man*.

Blaisdell's wood-carving expertise allowed him to manufacture easily a sleek, manta-shaped flying saucer that looked appropriately otherworldly, while at the same time recalling the minimalist design elements of modern art. The ship's gently sloping, parabolic perspective was offset by twin exhaust fins and a central dome made of transparent plastic. The finished model measured about 36 inches in diameter. The exterior finish consisted of over one hundred coats of silver paint.

The Martian saucer would be filmed against a miniature background as it descended from the sky to land on Larkin's farm. The model was rigged with wires, and Blaisdell operated it with the fishpole device he previously used on *It Conquered the World* to put the Flying Fingers through their aerial paces.

Paul thought it would be neat to add some life to the inanimate saucer in some fashion, so he inserted a tiny rotor under the plastic dome and wired it to spin a rod attached to two small circular mirrors. (The rotor was a commercially available novelty item advertised in youth-oriented publications of the time such as *Boy's Life* and the Marvel and DC comic lines.) The spinning mirrors were designed to reflect the studio lights, giving off a stroboscopic effect.

A duplicate spaceship was to be substituted for the pine model in a scene in which the craft self-destructs. This model was actually made out of painted cardboard and was scored to come apart in sections. Blaisdell planted a handful of cardboard "computer consoles" and bits of "machinery" inside, so that when the model was destroyed, there would be a scattering of debris to give the scene a greater sense of realism.

Prior to the scheduled shooting of the saucer effects, Paul practiced maneuvering the pine model until he could get it to arc and glide gracefully using the fishpole and wire rig. With materials acquired from a model railroading hobby shop, he put together a miniature cow pasture, complete with

The manta-shaped spaceship that helped launch the *Invasion of the Saucer Men* was carved from pine and coated with over 100 layers of paint. The jeep parked in front of the saucer was added to this specially posed photograph (taken by Blaisdell) to give the craft a sense of dimension.

orchard, trees, shrubbery, and a surrounding wooden fence. This was to become the saucer's landing site.

But the day the scenes were scheduled to be shot, the designated special effects man decided he was the person who should handle the effects. This fellow insisted that while it was okay for Blaisdell to make monster costumes and spaceships, it wasn't okay for him to do anything else. Naturally, Blaisdell objected—how was this guy going to learn to fly the saucer in a matter of minutes when it had taken its creator days to perfect the effect?—but the protest fell on deaf ears. It didn't matter how much personal time Blaisdell had spent practicing, the bottom line was that the special effects person on this production was going to play pilot.

Blaisdell threw up his hands and walked away, leaving "Mr. FX" to his own devices. Paul's meticulously crafted farmland set was set aside because FX decided he had to build his own miniature. He yanked up fistfuls of ferns from the studio grounds, glued them to a piece of plywood, and covered it with a layer of dirt. "See how easy that was?" Mr. FX remarked proudly.

There was virtually no time left to practice using the saucer's wiring rig, but the effects specialist figured, *How difficult can this be anyway?* As the

Blaisdell (right) and Bob Burns with props from American International's *Invasion of the Saucer Men*. Burns is holding the dismembered "seeing-eye hand" which had working hypodermic-fingernails and rotating eyeball. The Martian spaceship appears in the foreground (courtesy of Bob Burns).

shot was being set up, the cameraman, Howard Anderson, noticed how uncoordinated Mr. FX appeared to be at handling the saucer. Anderson decided he had better overcrank the film to slow the image down; that would help eliminate some of FX's more spastic movements. Unfortunately, while the high-speed filming smoothed out the saucer's flight pattern, it also severely diluted the strobing effect caused by the rotating mirrors Paul had inserted in the plastic dome.

The final insult came when FX set the charges to blow up the cardboard saucer. There was no backup model, so the shot had to be done right the first time.

"He was loading it with way too much explosive powder," Bob Burns recalled, "and Paul told him so." But FX refused to listen. While the effects coordinator was busy priming the model saucer for the explosion, Burns and Blaisdell decided they had better take cover. "With the amount of powder this guy was using, there was no telling how big that blast was going to be,"

Bob Burns parties with one of the alien survivors of *Invasion of the Saucer Men* in this gag photo taken by Jackie Blaisdell at the Topanga Canyon home that served as Paul's workshop for so many years. That's Paul inside the creature costume, of course.

Burns said. They found some plywood containers in a corner of the studio and pushed them together to form a kind of fort in which they could hide.

When the film began rolling, Mr. FX set off the charges. The saucer was obliterated. It was blown apart along all the right seams, but the force was so powerful that all of the little "extras" Paul had tucked away inside blew past the camera much too quickly to be seen.* Blaisdell later recalled that moment: "The special effects person planted the bombs and pulled the switch, and I can still remember the canopy going sky-high and landing on the other side of the room. I thought we'd never find it, and as a matter of fact I never did locate all the miniature consoles and electrical equipment I had put inside that thing." Ruefully, Blaisdell remarked: "Everybody makes mistakes. Some people just seem to make more of them. Then again, there are some people who just don't care."

After it was decided to turn *Saucer Men* into a comedy, AIP asked Blaisdell to design some light-hearted, cartoon-type illustrations that could be used as background for the main titles. Paul went a step further and made up an entire book that opened to reveal the film's title, with the stars' names and the names and titles of the crew on subsequent pages. When the book is closed at the end of the film, the audience sees for the first time that the seeing-eye claw has been turning the pages all along.

Perhaps because of the dubious way it portrayed American teens of the 1950s, with beer bottles and tongues alternately shoved between parted lips in parked cars, mainstream critics panned *Invasion of the Saucer Men*, sometimes vehemently. Some found the combination of twisted humor and horror bewildering. Were monsters that pumped their victims full of alcohol supposed to be scary? Were teenagers necking in the woods supposed to be funny? Even *Variety* cited the film's "poor use of attempted comedy." (How could anyone outside AIP's inner circle know that the picture had not originally been intended as a spoof?)

But the proof was in the pudding. Paired with AIP's *I Was a Teenage Werewolf*, the film was a box-office winner from day one.

Although the critics were not enthusiastic, the film remained one of Blaisdell's favorite projects:

> I really liked *Invasion of the Saucer Men*. It was funny and goofy and it really took off once we stopped taking it so seriously. Years later I was able to use the Saucer Man head and the hand with the eyeball on it in a featurette I made called *Filmland Monsters*. When we did that, I was finally able to show off the seeing-eye claw and I was also able to add a little more "life" to the face of the Saucer Man. I just wish I'd been allowed a little more time to work with these things in the original picture because it would have made it that much better.

Interested viewers will be able to spot a glimpse of these miniature "computer consoles" by frame-advancing a video copy of Invasion of the Saucer Men.

9

Bert Gordon Strikes Back

Attack of the Puppet People—man oh man, what a nightmare that was, in its own lovely way!

— *Paul Blaisdell*

Bert I. Gordon never seemed to tire of making movies about macroscopic monsters. Whether they were enlarged insects, overgrown arachnids, or plain ol' pumped-up people, Bert's big guys continued trampling drive-ins from coast to coast. And as long as the formula worked, why fiddle with it?

When Gordon decided to produce a picture called *The Fantastic Puppet People*, the prescription wasn't really being changed, it was just being inverted. Look through the wrong end of a pair of binoculars and the *Colossal Man* would become the *Puppet People*.

AIP liked Gordon's latest brainstorm. It was simple, it was formulaic, it was easy for Sam Arkoff to comprehend. With the company's backing, Gordon hired George Worthing Yates to write a screenplay based on Gordon's original outline. Yates had built a respectable track record in the sci-fi and horror film field, developing the story line for Warner Bros.' 1953 gi-ant picture *Them!* and writing screenplays for producer George Pal (*The Conquest of Space*), Ray Harryhausen, and Charles H. Schneer (*It Came from Beneath the Sea, Earth vs. the Flying Saucers*). Gordon liked Yates's work so much he would reemploy the writer to work on his next creature-feature, *The Spider*, as well as an off-the-wall ghost story called *Tormented*.

The Fantastic Puppet People, retitled *Attack of the Puppet People* by Jim Nicholson prior to its release as part of a standard double-feature package from AIP, eschewed the traditional etiologic "presto change-o" culprit, atomic radiation, in favor of something new—a shrinking ray developed by a doll manufacturer whose products are incredibly lifelike.

Mr. Franz (John Hoyt) runs a one-man business called "Dolls Inc." He hires Sally Reynolds (doll-like June Kenny) to replace his departed secretary Janet (Jean Moorehead), who is actually one of a half-dozen real human beings who have been shrunk down by Franz's incredible invention. Sally befriends Bob Westley (John Agar), a St. Louis–based distributor of doll

For *Attack of the Puppet People*, Paul and Jackie were asked to provide numerous realistic props that were either six times larger or six times smaller than life-size in order to maintain the miniature illusion as the camera's point-of-view switched between normal-size humans and the Puppet People. Here members of the cast (left to right, Hal Bogart, Laurie Mitchell, Jean Moorehead, Ken Miller, June Kenny, John Agar) are surrounded by a number of oversized Blaisdell props. (The telephone was not created by the Blaisdells but was provided by the phone company.)

equipment. He takes Sally on a date (they go to a drive-in theater to see *The Amazing Colossal Man*), and before long they're discussing marriage. The morning they plan to leave for St. Louis, Bob tells Franz that he and Sally are getting hitched; she won't be returning to work. When Bob fails to turn up at Sally's apartment, she stops by Dolls Inc., where Franz sadly informs her that Bob has already left for St. Louis by himself. Later Sally discovers a ten-inch replica of Bob, perfect to the last detail, encased in a plastic preservation tube. She becomes convinced that this is the real Bob, and that Mr. Franz has somehow made him into a real living doll.

She visits the police station and tells Sgt. Peterson (Jack Kosslyn) about Dolls Inc., Franz, the Bob-doll, and a host of similar dolls kept in a locked case; but when Peterson checks out her story, Franz obligingly displays a container chock-full of plastic Bob-dolls. "I make all my dolls in the likeness of people I know," Franz explains. Convinced that Bob has simply run out on Sally, Peterson drops the inquiry and leaves. Franz wastes little time in aiming his shrinking ray at the disobedient Sally. Such a disappointment as a personal secretary.

Sally regains consciousness next to a telephone of gigantic proportions. After Franz explains how he has miniaturized her with some special equipment of his own design, he wakes Bob and a host of other puppet people, all of whom he keeps in a state of suspended animation inside airtight plastic tubes. Stan, Georgia, Mac, and Janet have become used to their plight and accept it as a condition of their new life, but Bob is determined to return them all to normal size. When Emil (Michael Mark), an old vaudeville performer, stops by to see Franz, Bob grabs the opportunity to mastermind an escape plan. But there's not enough time, and Franz returns to the workshop before they can make any real progress.

Later Sgt. Peterson turns up at Dolls Inc. to ask Franz about the missing Sally Reynolds. That night Franz determines it's time to get rid of his puppet people, as well as himself, before the police can figure out what's really going on. He takes his miniature captives to a theater for a special "going away party," but they manage to escape when Franz is distracted by a night watchman (Hank Patterson, Mr. Ziffell of TV's mid-1960s no-brainer, "Green Acres"). Bob and Sally escape and make their way to Dolls Inc., where they use Franz's miniaturizing equipment to reenlarge themselves to normal size. As they leave to tell the police what's been happening, Franz pleads, "Please don't leave me ... I'll be alone."

While producer-director Bert Gordon handled all the photographic effects and matte exposures which married a normal-sized John Hoyt with miniature versions of John Agar and the supporting cast, Paul and Jackie Blaisdell assumed the responsibility for building most of the oversized props that were needed to make the puppet people appear comparatively tiny. Most of these props were single items, but there were a few that had to be reproduced twice, once for scenes with the puppet people using oversized props and a second time for scenes with John Hoyt, which required miniature versions. Maintaining the proper ratio between the two sets of props caused more than a few problems for Blaisdell. "We either had to make props that were six times larger than life-size, or six times smaller, or both," Blaisdell observed, "because there were these scenes where John Hoyt took the props back from the puppet people. It was all a bit confusing, believe me."

Props that were built in large and small versions included a bottle of champagne, an accompanying champagne glass, a napkin, serving tray, briefcase, and the plastic tubes in which the puppet people slept. The "people" inside the tubes handled by John Hoyt were actually photographs. During the filming Hoyt had to make sure he kept the tubes properly aimed at the camera lens, otherwise the illusion would be spoiled.

All the other props were oversized versions used in scenes with the actors playing the puppet people. These included scissors, typing paper (complete

John Agar (right) and Hal Bogart prepare to write a message to signal for help in this scene from Bert I. Gordon's 1958 film, *Attack of the Puppet People*. All the oversized props seen here were created by Paul and Jackie Blaisdell. The giant sheet of stationery reads: DOLLS INCORPORATED, 502 Tilford Building, Los Angeles 36, California.

with a "Dolls, Inc." letterhead) that was turned into a paper airplane glider, ball of string, ruler, knife, paper clip, cup and saucer, cans of "paint" and "glue," matchbox, bar of "Dove" soap, coffee can, oily rag, chocolate candy box top with the legend "Miniature Chocolates by Larry," paintbrush, lipstick, razor, pencil, several nails, and a cardboard box with a mailing label. There was also a giant version of the shrinking machine's control box, used for a single scene in which John Agar attempts to reenlarge one of the puppet people.

Jackie designed the bar of Dove soap, which was authentic down to the trademark. She also made the cup and saucer. Paul designed the other props, except the giant telephone, which was supplied by the local AT&T exchange.

In addition to these props, it was necessary to construct two versions of the Jekyll-Hyde marionette which turned up in John Hoyt's hands near the film's climax. Hoyt actually operated the small string marionette himself. A full-size model, used for shots featuring John Agar and June Kenny, was operated by an assistant stationed up in the rafters. Blaisdell made the regular marionette out of wood; the life-size model was primarily a wire frame outfitted with appropriate garb. Both sizes included a Dr. Jekyll face which

A composite shot from *Attack of the Puppet People*. Blaisdell created the giant mailing carton, complete with mailing label and handwritten address.

just happened to resemble Blaisdell himself, not too surprising considering that the visage was created from one of Paul's latex "blanks." For the large model, Blaisdell built a fiberglass Dr. Jekyll head. He also designed the Mr. Hyde mask, which can only be glimpsed fleetingly in the finished film. (A better shot of it turns up in *How to Make a Monster*, covered later in this chapter.)

There had been other movies about miniaturized people, notably *Dr. Cyclops* (1939) with Albert Dekker, Tod Browning's *Devil Doll* (1936), and Universal's *The Incredible Shrinking Man*. Even so, AIP thought the film was fresh and exciting. Bert Gordon's effects worked better here than they had in *The Amazing Colossal Man*, and with the giant props provided by the Blaisdells, the film ended up looking better than many 1950s science-fiction programmers. Even *Variety* gave a nod toward the filmmakers when their reviewer "Powe" admitted that the effects in *Puppet People*—"basically a reworking of the Pygmalion legend"—were both "ingenious and intriguing."

For the first time, Jackie Blaisdell received screen credit alongside her husband as one-half of the team providing "special designs" for the film. Indicative of the status of the majority of effects artists working for AIP and

Several of the small scale props Paul and Jackie created for Bert I. Gordon's 1958 film, *Attack of the Puppet People*. The Dr. Jekyll marionette appears in top hat and cloak, while the companion Mr. Hyde mask rests on top of the tape measure. The partially obscured, globelike object on the far left is Paul's original concept of the Flying Fingers that soared through Roger Corman's *It Conquered the World* (courtesy of Bob Burns).

other independent film companies in the 1950s, the Blaisdells' credit came *under* that of key grip Buzz Gloson. Interestingly, Bert Gordon took bows for "special technical effects" in addition to his standard writing-producing-directing, and his wife Flora grabbed an "assistant technical effects" credit.

Paul himself gave special credit to Jackie for her work on this film:

> Besides the trouble we had trying to figure out how to bend a giant paper clip or fold a gigantic sheet of paper into a giant glider, there was the difficulty of reproducing these props six times smaller as well as six times larger than life size, so that when John Hoyt took them back from the puppet people they approximated the correct measurements. But how do you make these things six times normal size and six times miniature size? Well, you could get a slide rule and go crazy. Actually, much of the credit has to go to Jackie, who helped me keep my head on straight while we were working on this film.

Bert Gordon wasted little time in developing his next sci-fi extravaganza for AIP. In fact, less than two months separated *Attack of the Puppet People* and *The Spider* (aka *Earth vs. the Spider*), which opened nationally in September and November 1958, respectively.

As he had done with his last picture, Gordon developed a story outline rather than a full screenplay for *The Spider*, turning the actual scripting chores over to George Worthing Yates and Laszlo Gorog, a new name in the AIP camp. Together they fleshed out Gordon's story idea about a mammoth tarantula that invades a small California town (it's always a small town that comes under attack in these pictures) and chows down on a diet of obnoxious highschoolers. Despite the rather ordinary premise, *The Spider* became one of American International's most entertaining drive-in classics, making up in spunk what it lacked in finesse.

Compared to Universal's similarly themed *Tarantula* of 1955, *The Spider* could not pretend to be other than what it really was: a low-budget takeoff of a low-budget Universal movie. But *Tarantula*, despite its bigger budget, generally superior effects, and its legion of Hollywood stalwarts, was too stuffy, at times even boring. In contrast, *The Spider* offered a few real chills and even some pretty decent photographic tricks.

Surprisingly, no explanation was given for the existence of the title monster. Perhaps Gordon felt the genre was becoming inundated with behemoths spawned from atomic mushroom clouds. He may have been right about that, but any explanation is usually better than no explanation at all.

The Spider opens with one of the creepiest sequences of any AIP film from the 1950s. Cruising down a lonely stretch of road at night, truck driver Jack Flynn runs headlong into a weird ropey substance stretched across the roadway. Glass shatters; the truck overturns, and the driver's face turns black with spraying blood.

At school the following day, Carol Flynn (June Kenny) complains to her boyfriend Mike Simpson (Gene Persson) that Daddy never made it home last night—pretty strange considering that today is her birthday. Mike shrugs it off with the telling remark, "This isn't the first time," but the Gorog/Yates screenplay shies away from exploring the subject of parents in absentia further, letting the adults in the audience draw their own conclusions. This is, after all, a monster movie and not a melodrama about family strife. Or perhaps this is the writers' justification for allowing the teenage leads to conduct their own investigation into Flynn's disappearance. (Why bother alerting the cops that Daddy has disappeared when the guy routinely pulls these kinds of shenanigans?)

Mike borrows a car from his buddy Joe (Troy Patterson, who looks less like a teenager and more like a flunky who has had to repeat his senior year at least ten times) so he and Carol can retrace Flynn's trail. Sure enough, Daddy's overturned pickup is found abandoned in a ditch, along with the birthday present he had bought for Carol, but of Flynn himself there is no sign.

The pair decide to investigate a nearby cave on the theory that Flynn might have sought shelter sometime during the night. There is some knuckleheaded dialogue here from Mike which tends to short-circuit the believability of the scene, but the action kicks in before the viewer has much time to complain. The kids stumble blindly into an enormous web inside the cave, almost becoming the giant tarantula's next meal before they manage to swing free and locate an escape route through the labyrinthine caverns.

Sympathetic Prof. Kingman (Ed Kemmer), local high school science teacher and all-around good Joe, convinces Sheriff Cagle (Gene Roth) to take the kids' story seriously. He doesn't, but just to humor the tendentious Kingman, Cagle outfits a search party with enough DDT to kill a spider 50 times larger than life-size and sets off to locate the missing Flynn. With Mike and Carol as its guides, the search party manages to locate the giant web and the spider, as well as Flynn's hideously shriveled corpse, which has been sucked dry of fluids by the eight-legged horror. At Cagle's signal, Deputy Sanders (Bill Giorgio) unloads every ounce of chemical DDT available, bringing the hairy behemoth to a dead halt at last.

Kingman hires a house mover to transport the spider's carcass from the cave to River Falls High School, where it is temporarily stored in the gymnasium. Like everyone else, Kingman believes the spider to be dead, but in fact it has only been stunned. During the school band's rehearsal, the spider regains its senses and immediately makes a meal out of Hugo the janitor (Hank Patterson). It stalks its way through town, snacking on the occasional resident now and again before snuggling up to Kingman's house and menacing the professor's wife (AIP regular Sally Fraser). Kingman manages to divert the monster's attention by ramming his car into its rear end and leads it on a chase out of town.

When the deputy's body turns up in the same pruny condition as the monster's first victim, Cagle and Kingman begin brainstorming ways to kill the spider. Elder reactionary Jake (Howard Wright) reports seeing the creature heading back to its cavernous home, so Kingman asks road foreman Sam Haskell (Skip Young) to dynamite the cave's entrance, sealing the spider inside for good.

No one knows that Carol and Mike have returned to the cave to try and find Carol's birthday necklace, dropped during their first encounter with the beast. Mike locates the necklace, but they take a wrong turn somewhere in the cavern's arterial channels and are soon hopelessly lost. Hours later, when Haskell dynamites the cave entrance, a chain reaction drops a mountain of debris on the young couple, knocking them—and the spider, which was a lot closer than either of them realized—out cold.

When Cagle finds out that the kids are trapped inside the cave, he orders Haskell to initiate excavation procedures, digging from the top of the mountain down through the center. Shortly after regaining consciousness, the couple hear the excited voices of the rescue team, but the spider is alive, alert, and after them again. Recalling his classroom demonstration of positive and negative electrical current, Kingman diverts power from a nearby cable line into a set of hand-held dipoles and descends into the cave to electrocute the creature.

Like many of the photographic effects that dominated Gordon's other films, *The Spider* was loaded with process shots. Although there were occasional problems with mismatched matte lines that resulted in scenes, for example, in which the tarantula's eight legs disappeared one by one into the ground, on the whole the effects were remarkably well done. (There was nothing as blatantly obvious as the spider's legs that vanished into the sky as the monster crept over a hill in Universal's *Tarantula.*) In fact, much of Gordon's matte work in *The Spider* was surprisingly convincing. The scenes which married footage of the tarantula with live actors benefited from Gordon's growing expertise in trick photographic effects. Gone were the telltale matte lines that had plagued *The Cyclops* and *Beginning of the End. The Spider* was a mammoth step forward for Gordon and AIP.

Since the film was so reliant on process shots to create the illusion of a giant tarantula stalking the city streets, cameraman Jack Marta employed macro-photography to shoot footage of the tarantula scurrying up, over, and around enlarged photographs of the cityscape, a technique Gordon had used on *Beginning of the End* to show giant locusts overrunning Chicago. Three-dimensional scale miniatures would have looked better, but they would have been too expensive and time-consuming to use. For Gordon's purposes the photo method worked fine, and as far as audiences were concerned, everything looked reasonably authentic. Gordon also used photographic enlargements of New Mexico's Carlsbad Caverns to create the illusion that his cast was wandering through a real cave full of dripping stalactites and stalagmites.

Paul Blaisdell's contributions to *The Spider* included a giant spider leg, rigged for use in close-up shots, and a dried-up husk of a corpse that was used in two different scenes. (It was supposed to be a different corpse each time.) Blaisdell also devised a tiny rubber appliance for the real tarantula that could be used to give it a monsterishly unique appearance. He later recalled how well this appliance worked:

> AIP wanted to make a kind of spinoff of *Tarantula,* and that's how *The Spider* came into being. Unbelievable as it may sound, I did create a makeup for the tarantula, as well as some of his buddies, all of which were supplied by Jim Daniels. It was designed to go on the carapace, the bony plate that the tarantula has in back of his eight compound eyes, and it made the tarantula look as if he had just two slitted, catlike, ghostly eyes. When he started crawling toward you ... *yipe!* You wanted to go right up the chimney. The appliance didn't weigh as much as a postage stamp, and it in no way interfered with the tarantula's ability to see or maneuver; he accepted the mini-minuscule load with no problem at all. Jim Nicholson and I got down on the floor and watched while the spider trotted back and forth between the two of us, and whenever we could get to its eye-level and see it coming straight toward us, we agreed that it would scare the hell out of the audience. That's not my own conceited opinion, by the way; that was the general opinion all around.

Unfortunately, Paul's tarantula makeup, which took two days to design, never got past the testing stage. It was the same old story. "The producer took one look and said, 'Nope, we can't use it, it's too horrible,'" Blaisdell recalled. "Of course, this particular producer had always been scared of bugs anyway, so it didn't much surprise me."

Several scenes in the film required the use of a "life-size" tarantula leg. The expense that would have been involved in creating a complex traveling photographic matte to show a tarantula swiping at a live actor was outside Gordon's budget (it was also outside his expertise), so the director opted to go with a mechanical mockup of the real thing.

Blaisdell figured that a mechanical leg that could interact with members of the cast in the manner which Gordon envisioned would be prohibitively expensive as well as too time-consuming to build. He convinced Gordon to use a much simpler hinged mockup, which could be wired to work off-camera. Using the wire to lift the leg up or down or left or right would allow the force of gravity to bend it in all the anatomically correct spots. It was the kind of solution Blaisdell had become famous for working out: simple, expedient, and cost-effective.

Paul and Jackie built the spider leg out of separate lengths of balsa wood that were hinged so that it would fold realistically. The balsa skeleton was covered with broom straws which were painted to simulate the hair on a spider's leg. A single wire was fitted around the lower portion of the leg, which measured nearly 9 feet in length.

Bringing the giant spider leg to life turned out to be one of the easiest jobs Paul ever had. The scenes requiring the actors' interaction with the leg were short and sweet. There were no complicated camera angles or long-running shots that took time to plan and choreograph as there had been with the Flying Fingers in *It Conquered the World*. In fact, only three scenes in the film used the prop, and one of those was a static shot of the leg jutting up from beneath a pile of rubble (when the giant spider had been buried by an avalanche). In the other scenes, Blaisdell's hirsute horror was manipulated with the wire, and everything worked without a hitch.

Two of the cast die at the fangs of *The Spider*—Carol Flynn's father and Deputy Sanders. (Presumably there were others, but these are the only two victims the story specifies.) Gordon asked Blaisdell to provide the requisite corpses. Because a tarantula attacks its food by first paralyzing it and then sucking out the fluids, the bodies needed to appear properly exsanguinated. Luckily for Paul, the script specified that each corpse would appear in a separate scene, so only a single desiccated carcass needed to be produced. Wardrobe changes would indicate the victim's identity.

Blaisdell had a free hand in deciding the wizened appearance of the spider's victims. After some experimentation with pen and paper, he settled on a design that combined elements of extreme old age with the look of the ancient Egyptian mummies seen in many museums. "Everyone knows what an old person looks like," Blaisdell pointed out, "so by extending that look, accentuating it, I was able to give the victim a solid base in reality. By adding elements of the Egyptian mummies, that look was further amplified, but whereas the skin of an old person simply sags, the skin of a mummy is tight and withdrawn."

Creating the skeletonesque body started with the use of a rubber latex blank generated by applying liquid latex to Jackie's sculpture of Paul. Once the latex was dry, the features were built up using the same methods Paul had employed on his *Cat Girl* mask. Of course, creating a human head—even one that had been squeezed like a pimple—was a bit different from creating a monster mask, but according to Bob Burns, Blaisdell had no need for anatomical reference texts or visual aids. "Paul knew anatomy so well, it was natural for him to know which features needed to be aged to make the face of this thing look like a corpse," Burns said. "He didn't rely on technical illustrations or anything like that; everything just flowed naturally from his own imagination."

Liquid latex and foam rubber—the main ingredients of any Blaisdell mask—gave definition to the corpse's face. By adding multiple layers of foam rubber to areas such as the cheekbones, temples, eye sockets, and portions of the throat, Blaisdell was able to magnify certain facial features to create the illusion that the flesh was severely sunken. A gray-streaked wig was attached to the finished mask, plastic eyes were inserted, and the head was attached to a "corpse"—a mannequin outfitted with the proper character wardrobe.

Paul was pleased with his handiwork. He thought the effect was just what Gordon was looking for—something gruesomely realistic and visually unnerving. He liked it so much he decided to call it "Uncle Elmo." Before delivering Elmo to the film set, he and Bob Burns decided to have a little fun with it, propping it up inside closets or on the other side of office doorways that some poor AIP secretary was bound to open sooner or later. They were like a couple of kids, hiding close by to watch the fun and laughing at their victims' gasps of fright. "We hadn't had so much fun since Paul scared the bejeezus out of that guy in the car with his She-Creature costume," Burns recalled.

Taking the credit of "Special Designs," Paul and Jackie (it was her second screen credit) provided props not only for *The Spider*, but for some of the theaters that booked the picture as well. Three-dimensional lobby displays depicting a giant tarantula straddling its web were made out of fiberglass and painted with acrylics using a red-and-black color scheme. The finished placards measured about five feet square. Paul added slitted eyes to the spiders on the displays, but they were a poor substitute for the real thing. In later years he often cited the never-used tarantula makeup as his least favorite creation.

Arachnid mealtime. This early victim in *The Spider* (aka *Earth vs. the Spider*) turned up later in the film outfitted in a policeman's uniform, posing as a different victim. Blaisdell dubbed the dummy "Uncle Elmo" (courtesy of Bob Burns).

Compared to some of the other American International releases that had failed to win accolades from the industry press, *The Spider* was more warmly received. Those who cited it as a low-budget turn on Universal's *Tarantula* weren't really off the mark, but even they had to admit that *The Spider* offered a lot of bite for the buck. Even *Variety* declared, "It is characterized by well done special effects, a reasonably credible plot, and will be a good feature for the exploitation market." Reviewer "Powe" marveled at Bert Gordon's photographic contributions. "Gordon uses Carlsbad Caverns background by means of split screen and traveling matte photography, and gets some eerie sequences. These technical aspects are particularly interesting and well done."

The critics returned to standard AIP-bashing with the release of Herman Cohen's follow-up to *I Was a Teenage Werewolf* and *Teenage Frankenstein*. The teenage monster movies had been so successful it was a natural to combine them in a single feature. *How to Make a Monster* took a fictitious behind-the-scenes look at monster movie-making and threw in a pinch of the old *Mystery of the Wax Museum/House of Wax* shtick as well. Cohen and Aben Kandel (writing as Kenneth Langtry) wrote the story, which offered multitudinous opportunities for self-aggrandizement by image-conscious AIP. Not only were there constant verbal and pictorial references to American International as a legitimate motion picture outfit, the behind-the-scenes locale pretended to let the audience in on movie-making "secrets." Many of the visual asides referenced purely fictitious films, but Cohen took the opportunity to publicize one of his own upcoming productions. "Our first stop will be Stage Number Three, where they're making *Horrors of the Black Museum*," a studio guide advises a busload of AIP tourists. "And folks, I think you're in luck. The big scene of the picture shoots today." Never mind that *Horrors of the Black Museum* was a British pickup made by Anglo-Amalgamated for AIP; in truth the company would have had a rather hard time entertaining the masses who wanted to see the making of any American International film, because the company had no sound stages. AIP films were shot in rented studios and on location.

How to Make a Monster was like a 75-minute-long advertisement for AIP movies. The story made extensive use of the Teenage Frankenstein and Teenage Werewolf makeups designed by Philip Scheer, threw in a new split-face monstrosity (also by Scheer), and stirred the ingredients into an entertaining, offbeat thriller. Paul Blaisdell did not work on any of the primary monster makeups, but several of his earlier creations were on display during the film's fiery finale, peripheral calling cards for other AIP pictures as he later recalled: "Some of the props hanging on the wall were oldies, very delicately put back together for the climax of the picture. They didn't last very long, especially *Cat Girl*, but at least they lasted long enough for *How to Make a Monster*."

The story line, self-serving as it was, at least offered something new. The film opens on a close-up of a snarling Teenage Werewolf. The actor under the makeup is Larry Drake (Gary Clarke), who plays an up-and-coming star at American International Pictures. Larry's costar, Tony Mantell (Gary Conway, who played the role of the monster in *I Was a Teenage Frankenstein*), is another young actor who once had a bright future. Unfortunately, the boys' starring roles in the new "Werewolf meets Frankenstein" movie will probably be their last, because this picture will be the studio's final foray into fantasy. A new regime has taken over AIP, and the newcomers have decided the public wants musicals, not monsters. Before long, the new studio owners are stalked and murdered one by one.

The Cohen/Langtry screenplay makes no bones about keeping secrets: the audience is informed right away that AIP makeup maestro Pete Drummond (Robert H. Harris) and his assistant Rivero (Paul Brinegar) are the culprits behind the killings. Drummond has discovered a means of bending any person to his will with the use of a new makeup foundation cream containing a chemical compound that temporarily destroys the victim's moral code by blocking the firing of the brain's synapses. Drummond uses his concoction on the actors playing the Werewolf and Frankenstein, secretly instructing them to kill off the new studio bosses. When an aggressive night watchman named Monahan (Dennis Cross) gets close to uncovering the truth, Drummond uses the makeup compound on himself. (But why? As the mastermind behind the murders, he obviously has no morals to be destroyed.) Hiding behind a weird split-face makeup, Drummond clubs Monahan straight into the next life.

Spineless Rivero almost crumbles under the strain of a police investigation. Drummond decides that his assistant has just about outlived his usefulness. He invites Rivero, Larry, and Tony to a special get-together at his home. Here, Drummond maintains a virtual shrine to the most monstrous movie creations of his career. Larry and Tony compare notes and decide that Drummond has gotten a little too weird for their liking, but the door is bolted and now they're trapped inside. Drummond knifes Rivero in a back room, then turns his attention to the other guests. Tony accidentally turns over a burning candle, catching the drapes afire, and Drummond suddenly descends into total psychosis. "What have you done to my children?" he gasps as the flames begin eating away at the plastic and rubber masks adorning the walls. In a frenzied effort to save his creations, Drummond becomes trapped by the blaze while the youngsters make it to safety, thanks to the timely arrival of the police.

In a repeat of a promotional gimmick used in *I Was a Teenage Frankenstein* and *War of the Colossal Beast*, the fiery climax of *How to Make a Monster* was filmed in color. Paul Blaisdell provided several props to the filmmakers for use as background decor, including the original headpieces he built for *The She-Creature* and *Invasion of the Saucermen*, and the Mr. Hyde mask from *Attack of the Puppet People.* Also included was all that was left of *It Conquered the World's* stalactite monster, Beulah. Much of it had rotted away by the time *How to Make a Monster* went into production, so only the face showed up in the new film. The "savior" mask made for AIP's British import *Cat Girl* was also loaned to the production. Unfortunately, that was the last Paul saw of that particular creation. He had designed two disposable masks to be used for "throwaway effects" during the climactic scene, but the Cat Girl was never meant to be one of them. Things got a little hectic during the filming of the fire effects, and a confused stage hand set Paul's Cat Girl mask ablaze by mistake. That was bad enough in itself, but to add insult to injury, nobody photographed it while it was burning. Perhaps worst of all was the fact that the cat-mask was never even seen in the film: it had been hung on a backdrop that faced away from the camera during the entire production.

The masks that were created specifically to go out in a blaze of glory were sculpted out of wax. The heat generated by the gas burners that were being used to create the film's fire effects slowly melted the wax, which dripped off its wooden supports in gruesome fashion. One of the masks, which Blaisdell nicknamed "Aunt Esmerelda," got the lion's share of the fiery footage.

As the image melted and the wax fell away, a plastic skull underneath was revealed. Although it was never so stated in the movie, the effect suggested that at least some of Drummond's monsterrific "children" were made out of a lot more than latex rubber.

Blaisdell later recalled the scene:

> "Aunt Esmerelda" was created entirely out of wax from scratch specifically to go up in smoke. At the appropriate time when the gas burners were turned on by the prop men, the wax began to melt, and she went up in flames rather beautifully, I thought. The fellow who played Pete the makeup artist was an actor named Robert H. Harris, but I was calling him "Pete" through the entire production. I didn't learn his real name until 1979. I guess he was either too shy to correct me, or he figured I was too ignorant to learn.

As could be expected, the loss of an irreplaceable movie prop such as the Cat Girl mask left a bad taste in Paul's mouth. Storage problems had already decimated the bulk of the mushroom monster from *It Conquered the World*, the carelessness of others had resulted in the near-total collapse of Marty the Mutant from *Day the World Ended*; and Forry Ackerman, who had been presented with Little Hercules from *The Beast with a Million Eyes*, kept it in a sun-bathed display case until it eventually fell apart, a victim of "heatstroke." Of Paul's earliest creations, only the She-Creature had survived intact. And when the folks at American International learned she was still "alive and kicking," they decided to bring Blaisdell's demonic debutante out of retirement for one final fling.

10

Missing Monsters

There's a term, "Runaway Production," which basically refers to escalating film production costs. The kind of picture Roger Corman might have been able to make for $60,000 or $70,000 in 1955 began to cost upwards of $100,000 just a couple of years later. I guess I can't blame Rog for trying to cut his costs any way he could, and that included finding even less expensive ways to come up with the real "stars" of the monster pictures. Of course, it wasn't only Roger Corman; everyone was trying to find cheaper ways of doing things. That's why the folks at American International began doing coproductions with England, like *Cat Girl* and *The Headless Ghost* and *Horrors of the Black Museum*. If they'd been made here, sure, I might've been involved with some of them. But to be perfectly honest, I was beginning to get a little tired of the whole game. AIP had made a lot of promises over the years, and I think they forgot most of what they said almost as soon as they said it.
—*Paul Blaisdell*

The decade of the 1950s would soon be drawing to a close, and with it would go the kind of monster movie that had been feeding the public's hunger for horror for the last ten years. Big changes were in store for Hollywood and for the nation as well. Although he couldn't have known it at the time, Paul Blaisdell would complete just two more major film assignments before the changing face of Monsterdom snuffed out his motion picture career forever. Bob Burns later spoke about Paul's relationship with AIP:

In the early years AIP kept telling Paul, "You're part of the AIP family, you'll grow as the company grows, and by this time next year you'll be earning twice as much money." Sam was always saying things like that, but his sentiments sure didn't last very long. Paul got upset because they never increased his salary or gave him a bonus. It wasn't Jim Nicholson's fault. If anything, it was because Arkoff was always so very businesslike. He didn't leave room for personal feelings or well-wishes or that sort of thing. Sam controlled the purse-strings, and if that meant hiring cheaper monster-makers, then so be it.

Blaisdell also commented on the range of film budgets:

> Some of the pictures I worked on in the '50s could only be termed "stingy,"
> but the same kind of picture is still being made today. *Star Wars* is basically
> the same kind of picture, it's just that the budget, comparatively, is tremen-
> dous. With larger budgets you get more time, and with more time there are
> larger and larger crews, and when you have a lot of people together working
> on them, you have more and better special effects. Actually, some of the crews
> have become as tremendous as the budgets. It's totally unlike anything I was
> involved with, where you were sometimes asked to reuse the same monster
> suit in a second movie, or where you were asked to come up with something
> new in two days for two dollars!

In 1959, Roger Corman started up his own film production company
called "Filmgroup." It was a move that would allow him to make inexpensive
pictures that could be sold outright to AIP or other interested distributors.
By using his own money and funds from investors, Corman was able to distance himself from people like Sam Arkoff and make movies without their
comments, requests, restrictions, or influence.* It was a good idea that promised filmmaking autonomy, but now Corman had to work without AIP's
backing, which meant the budgetary belt had to be pulled even tighter.

Corman called Blaisdell to tell him about a new picture his brother Gene
was preparing to make called *The Beast from Haunted Cave*. Corman's favorite
screenwriter, Chuck Griffith, had come up with a script that was basically a
mystery-thriller about a gang of thieves who encounter a mythical monster
after they become snowbound on a remote mountainside. Griffith purposely
designed the script so that the title Beast could be kept off-camera as long as
possible. The majority of the film's 75 minute running time would be spent
with various story characters as they threatened to talk themselves (and the
audience) to death. All that was needed was a pretty straightforward monster that could perform one or two actions before being toasted by the film's
hero. The creature didn't even need to be mobile because it remained in the
cave through the entire picture.

Paul couldn't believe what he was hearing. It all sounded suspiciously
familiar. A monster that was required only to do one or two things? That's
what Corman had told him about *The Beast with a Million Eyes*. A creature
that remained hidden inside a cave? He'd heard that when Corman was ready-
ing *It Conquered the World*. "Are you sure about all this?" Blaisdell asked.

"Absolutely!"

---

*Corman tried the same tactic in the early 1970s when he set up New World Pictures, the most success-
ful and influential independent production company to enter the market since the halcyon days of American International. He captained New World throughout the '70s and '80s, providing filmmaking opportunities for fledgling directors with names like Ron Howard, Joe Dante, and George Lucas. Corman
eventually sold New World and used the profits to start up another independent film company, Millen-
nium/New Horizons, which specializes in producing exploitation fare for the home video market.*

As was customary, Corman sent Blaisdell a copy of the film script. Sure enough, according to Griffith's story, the monster wouldn't be seen until almost the end of the picture. It didn't move around much, and it never came out of the cave. In fact, it didn't do much of anything, except die. The victims were going to be discovered wrapped in silk cocoons, with the Beast hovering over them like some kind of mammoth spider-fly hybrid. (In fact, the creature's appearance was inspired by an insect called the Wingless Hanging Fly.) Blaisdell figured that Corman would expect him to build the cocoons as well as the title monster, but that was okay; he and Jackie should be able to handle it. Paul phoned Corman to tell him he would be available to do the picture.

"Oh! Okay, good," Corman said, sounding a little surprised. "You've talked with Gene about the budget?"

No, Paul hadn't talked with Gene about the budget or anything else, for that matter. "What about the budget?" he asked.

"Well ..." Corman sounded funny, as if he was trying to skirt the issue of salaries. Finally Paul asked him straight out how much his company intended to pay for its title beast.

Roger quoted him a figure.

"You're kidding, I hope," he told Corman. It was less than what he had been offered the last time he got involved with a Corman production.

"That's all I can afford, Paul." As Corman explained, the fledgling Filmgroup company just couldn't afford to pay the kind of salary Blaisdell was accustomed to getting from AIP.

"Roger, I can't do it for that amount," said Blaisdell. "I'd like to help you out, but what you're offering me would barely cover the cost of the materials. You'll have to get somebody else."

That was the end of that.

Filmgroup eventually got their beast from a fellow named Chris Robinson, who agreed to make the monster in return for just a screen credit. Robinson's creature was made mainly out of chicken coop wire wrapped around a plywood base, with putty and crepe hair pasted to the exterior. The final touch was something called "Angel Hair," an item usually marketed during the Christmas season as a tree decoration. Corman knew that Robinson's monster failed to approach the standards set by Blaisdell, but he figured he had gotten too good a deal to pass up.

Blaisdell never worked for Corman again.

One rather cheesy science-fiction film that has managed to cultivate a minor degree of notoriety—for all the wrong reasons—is *Teenagers from Outer Space*, another picture that Hollywood wanted Blaisdell to work on for peanuts. Distributed by Warner Bros. as the bottom half of a double bill with *Gigantis, the Fire Monster*, this was an independent production masterminded by one-man-wonder Tom Graeff. Graeff was the film's producer, director, screenwriter, editor, cameraman, sound editor, music composer, and special effects creator. He was also one of its costars.

The title teens are an alien race who have been hot-rodding around the universe in search of a suitable spawning ground for their homegrown monsters, the Gargons. It turns out that Earth would make an excellent habitat because the Gargons would have a nutritious food supply at the ready (human beings, that is). Soon, the first Gargon is unleashed upon terra firma to graze among the human cattle.

Graeff wanted Blaisdell to design the Gargon but couldn't afford his fee, so the filmmaker ended up using silhouettes of lobsters to represent the alien species. Blaisdell routinely neglected to mention *Teenagers from Outer Space* during discussions of his Hollywood years, even though he did get involved peripherally by customizing a prop ray-gun and designing the film's one-sheet poster. The ray-gun was a commercially available toy called the Atomic Disintegrator Cap Gun. Graeff bought a quantity of the guns to provide to the cast to use on camera. Blaisdell modified the firing mechanisms by inserting tiny pieces of mirrors inside. When the sun's rays or the studio lights struck the mirror at the right angle, the reflection made it look as if the gun were actually firing. (The original Atomic Disintegrator Cap Guns are now highly priced collectibles, worth a lot more than the check Blaisdell received for his contribution to the film.)

Teenagers from Outer Space was so cheap to make that it couldn't help making a profit, but the same couldn't be said for American International's latest combination, *A Bucket of Blood* and *The Giant Leeches* (later retitled *Attack of the Giant Leeches*). AIP wanted Blaisdell to design the overgrown bloodsuckers for its leech movie, which was being produced by Gene Corman. Roger Corman had just wrapped *A Bucket of Blood*, which was the first in his black comedy film trilogy. (The other two were *The Little Shoppe of Horrors* and *Creature from the Haunted Sea*.) *The Giant Leeches* was being shot to fill the bottom half of the double bill. But once again the money just wasn't there; neither was the time. "Gene needed several costumes, but it was one of those rush-rush jobs and it was just impossible. Besides, I couldn't have made even one suit for what they were offering," Blaisdell explained. Although he would never have admitted it in print, Paul felt insulted by the meager salaries he was being offered to work on the latest monster movies. Because he didn't believe in airing "dirty laundry," only those closest to him knew how he really felt.

"AIP very much wanted Paul to make the monster suits for *The Giant Leeches*," revealed Bob Burns, "but he declined, based on the amount of work involved versus the amount of money he would be paid. They were not offering much at all. I know Paul felt taken advantage of, because he had been giving them more than their money's worth for years, but he was not one to complain, at least not publicly. But honestly, by this time he was so fed up, he'd just about had it." Despite his affection for American International's president, Jim Nicholson, Blaisdell wasn't about to set a new precedent by accepting work at a lower wage. He told them to find another body to build their bloodsuckers.

Finding a suitable replacement for Blaisdell turned out to be more difficult than anyone had imagined. No one knew how to build giant leeches. Finally Gene Corman went to Blaisdell and admitted, "Look, we don't know what to do. How do you build these things?" Suppressing a self-indulgent chuckle, Blaisdell advised the producer to go to a surplus store and buy a bunch of black raincoats. "Get some block foam and make yourself some foam rubber 'doughnuts' and glue them to the raincoats, and those will be your leech suckers," Blaisdell instructed, tongue shoved firmly in cheek. Corman thanked him and left.

"Paul was really being facetious when he told them how to make the leech costumes, but that's what they ended up doing," recalled Bob Burns. "No one involved with the film had the technical know-how to pull off these cheap outfits the way Paul could, or with his type of ingenuity. Paul was just joking about the raincoats, but AIP didn't know that. The funny thing is, although he would have used different materials, Paul probably could have made it work using raincoats."

The monster suits for *The Giant Leeches* finally were supposed to be made by Ed Nelson, who had starred in American International's *The Brain Eaters*. Nelson had the responsibility for coming up with the leechlike parasites for that film, but in the finest Harry Thomas tradition, all Nelson did was buy some wind-up toy bugs he had seen at a novelty shop and cover them with scraps of fur to make them appear more menacing. The effect on-screen was embarrassingly laughable.

According to Bruno VeSota, who costarred with Yvette Vickers in *The Giant Leeches*, Nelson was forced to turn over the making of the leeches to someone else when he was signed to play in another picture. Rumor has it that it was the producer's wife who volunteered to make the costumes. Whether it was she or someone else entirely, the fact remains that Blaisdell's expertise is sorely missed in *The Giant Leeches*.

Only two costumes were made for the movie, and if they weren't customized raincoats they obviously weren't much better. (There was even a rumor that the outfits were made from plastic garbage bags.) Whoever designed them forgot to leave room for the airtanks that would be required for the actors to film the underwater scenes, and the suits kept tearing. "Whenever you get someone who doesn't have a track record of making monster suits, you're taking an awful chance," VeSota cautioned. "Those leech suits were splitting all over the place, and they ended up pinning them together with paper clips, needle and thread, anything that was available. They looked so phony that in the final cutting the director only left in six- or twelve-frame takes. If you got any better a look, you'd laugh your head off."

The combination of *A Bucket of Blood* and *The Giant Leeches* failed to capture the hearts and wallets of the nation's youthful moviegoers, but if nothing else it provided some serious food for thought for Arkoff and Nicholson. Recently, Britain's Hammer Film Company had inaugurated a series of gothic horror pictures—remakes of the old Universal classics—photographed in flamboyant Eastman color and starring credible actors like Peter Cushing and Christopher Lee. The company was reaping fantastic financial rewards and had already started making sequels and spinoffs. Warner Bros. and Universal were backing all the company's latest products in exchange for exclusive distribution rights, so certain were they that Hammer had its finger on the pulse of future fantasy filmmaking.

Arkoff and Nicholson realized that something had to change at AIP. Perhaps it was time to do something besides low-budget science-fiction and horror. Maybe—just maybe—audiences had grown tired of the black-and-white movie monsters that had buttered AIP's bread for so many years. Perhaps they ought to follow Hammer's lead, shifting to color film stock and making their own classics. Roger Corman began thinking along similar lines around the same time and would eventually convince AIP to produce a single higher-quality fright flick for the amount of money they usually spent on two black-and-white cheapies. Roger also had an idea where they could get original material for next to nothing. The works of Edgar Allan Poe were in the public domain. And since Poe's material already enjoyed classic status among the literary elite, an adaptation would automatically generate an air of respectability for the filmmakers and distributor. If they could only hire an actor with the talents of a Lee or Cushing ...

Between film assignments Blaisdell experimented with makeup coloring techniques and used a variety of home implements to produce different kinds of textures in latex rubber. He often would turn these experiments into one-of-a-kind gifts that he presented to his friends and business associates during the holidays. He created two different versions of a monster ashtray—a traditional version that was colored "Frankenstein green," with two open eyes and a snarling mouth, and an executive version that mixed together shades of browns, yellows, and various earth tones and had one open eye and one squinted eye. He also made claw paper-weights. Jim Nicholson kept a display of Paul's unique handiwork in his office at AIP.

Paul also experimented with 35mm still photography and 16mm movie-making. In his home-made horror spoof *The Cat Man*, he had gotten a chance to reuse his *Cat Girl* mask before it ended up going down in flames during the filming of *How to Make a Monster*. In other homegrown projects, he took on the persona of a Lugosi-ish vampire, a menacing tiny-eyed Saucer Man, or a space-helmeted rocket ranger brandishing a toy ray-gun. Eventually Blaisdell would spend his leisure time developing a much more serious amateur film production using a wholly original monster never before seen on the screen, but this was still a few years away.

Paul spent a lot of his free time putting together intricate model aircrafts from high-end hobby kits. He was especially fond of replicas of aircraft from the WWI era and often spent weeks working on a single kit. Before Bob Burns was drafted into the army in 1958, he spent almost every weekend at Paul's hideaway in Topanga Canyon. Paul and Jackie were always involved in some kind of fun and games. Bob got a kick out of watching Paul put together the intricate models that could, and often did, frustrate many younger model enthusiasts.

Blaisdell was also a fan of Errol Flynn's movies. He loved to watch Flynn in action and even took special classes to learn "movie-fencing." He owned a large collection of knives and fencing equipment and sometimes invited Burns to square off with him. Burns knew nothing about fencing, so Paul would try to teach him some of the simpler moves. "But usually I ended up tripping over my own feet," Burns laughed. "I never made a good fencing partner. Paul 'killed' me every time."

Paul liked old radio shows like "The Shadow" and "Inner Sanctum" and he also enjoyed a good comedy now and again. He and Bob used to work out spoofs of some of the old shows. Together they would work out a series of gags and situations and build them up into regular routines. When they were satisfied with their "scripts," Paul would hook up his reel-to-reel tape recorder and the two would perform in front of the microphone. Jackie and Kathy Burns laughed at the gags along with the men, but the recordings were mainly "boys' toys."

Blaisdell was surprisingly good at mimicking voices and inventing wild characters for their radio spoofs. "There was just no end to his talents," Burns remembers enthusiastically. Bob held onto copies of the tapes that had been made during those long-ago weekend fiestas and continues to enjoy them to this day. "Some of the stuff we came up with was pretty silly," he admitted, "but there's no doubt that they show off some of Paul's other talents. There were things he could do that would surprise you, unless you really got to know him. The voice he used for his cameo at the end of *The Ghost of Dragstrip Hollow* is just one example."

Whenever Paul wasn't busy working on a film assignment, there was ample time to make funny recordings and photographs. "We'd do just whatever popped into our heads," Burns explained. One time Bob decided he wanted to try making his own monster mask, so Paul gave him a rubber latex blank and a few good tips, and before long Burns had conjured up a pretty decent werewolf mask. The girls took photos of Werewolf-Bob attacking Paul; then Paul would grab one of his monster masks and menace Burns. They were the kind of youthful antics that could virtually define the expression "goofing around."

"Whenever Paul got an idea, he would start whistling," Burns recalled. "He didn't whistle a tune or anything, he just whistled. For example, one time he got the idea to create a 'crowd' effect by playing a tape back and forth between two recorders, each time adding more voices to the background, so by the time it was finished it sounded like there was a whole theater full of people clapping and yelling. This was back when there wasn't such a thing as overdubbing on a portable recorder." Obviously Blaisdell used his "low-budget ingenuity" at home as well as on the job.

Few tapes survive from the Blaisdell/Burns recording sessions, but copies of the stills, some of which were photographed in 3-D, are extant in the hands of a few lucky collectors. Some of the 3-D pictures were printed in *Fantastic Monsters of the Films* magazine in the early 1960s, and color slide sets were offered for sale to the readers. Undoubtedly, many of these products were either lost or tossed out with the garbage as the young readers grew out of their monster-collecting phase, making them all the rarer in today's inflated collector's market.

Although Blaisdell never imagined that his leisure-time activities might be offered for public consumption, there is little harm in revealing a down-to-earth side of the artist that most fans never got to see or even knew existed. For those interested, and with Bob Burns's blessing, an appendix has been added at the back of the book which includes transcriptions of some of Paul's radio and movie serial spoofs.

11

Mars Needs Hemoglobin

> Early on in the shoot I tried to check in with the assistant direc-
> tor [Ralph E. Black] to see if he had gotten the extra monster arm
> that I had built for Ray Corrigan, so Ray wouldn't have to put on
> the whole suit just to push his claw through a hatch. The A.D.
> came crawling down out of the spaceship and barked, "Yeah, I got
> the extra arm, and who the hell are you?" There wasn't any of the
> sort of "M*A*S*H"-like comradery there had been on the AIP
> films, I can tell you that!
>
> —*Paul Blaisdell*

Although the majority of the decade's budget-conscious boogeymen were promulgated under the auspices of American International, Allied Artists, and other independent film companies, there were occasional freelance producers, like Ed Wood (*Plan 9 from Outer Space*) and Al Zimbalist (*Monster from Green Hell*), who made pictures on their own time and with their own (mostly meager) resources, only later ferreting out the all-important distribution deal. Another producer was Robert E. Kent, who convinced Ed Small at United Artists that making a typical AIP-style monster movie would be a sure box-office bet. Monsters were "in." *Life* magazine had devoted a cover story to the genre, and *Famous Monsters* hadn't even reached its third issue before it had to face down at least a half-dozen imitators, all encroaching on *FM*'s "terror-tory." Why should AIP, Allied Artists, and Universal be the only film companies mining gold from the fantasy film field? Kids and teens were dying to toss fistfuls of dollar bills at Hollywood to be shocked senseless. It was time for UA to grab a piece of the pulse-pounding pie.

Small took the bait and green-lighted Kent's monster project. The first thing Kent did was look up a couple of AIP alumni—director Eddie Cahn and monster-maker Paul Blaisdell. Kent figured that with their participation, his picture would almost surely be a guaranteed winner. Cahn's reputation for getting film in the can as quickly as Roger Corman—who was already on the brink of legendry as the fastest camera in the West—meant that Kent's movie would come in at or even under budget. And Blaisdell's ability to create imaginative and original monsters on a shoestring meant that Kent wouldn't have to worry whether his movie would be able to deliver the ghoulish goods.

But Blaisdell's participation hinged on the screenplay. He wanted to see it, hold it in his hands, read it. And he wanted to get Jackie's opinion. As the years had gone by, he had become more and more cautious about accepting jobs that required a major commitment of time and resources. Recent events at American International had forced Blaisdell to reconsider some assignments and bow out of others altogether. He was determined not to be exploited by AIP or anyone. The only way he could successfully avoid being taken advantage of, he decided, was to read a finished film script to see exactly what would be expected of him and not just assume that what the producer or director said was gospel.

Kent agreed to show Blaisdell the screenplay, but it was a long time coming—mainly because Kent's writer, Jerome Bixby, hadn't finished it yet. Bixby was a writer of numerous sci-fi stories and in fact had worked with H. L. Gold on *Galaxy*. He also edited *Planet Stories* (1950–51). But in actual fact, even with over 300 sci-fi stories to his credit, the majority of Bixby's work was done outside the sci-fi and fantasy field. Probably his best-remembered genre offering was "It's a Good Life," written in 1953, which was later turned into one of the most memorable episodes of television's original "Twilight Zone." (The same story was updated by director Joe Dante for the "Twilight Zone" anthology film produced by Steven Spielberg in 1983.)

When Bixby's finished script was finally delivered to him, Blaisdell looked through it, liked what he saw, and decided the job shouldn't be too much of a headache. There were none of the multiple monsters that had bogged down his work on *Invasion of the Saucer Men*; there were no outlandish props to be made, as there had been for *Attack of the Puppet People* and *The Amazing Colossal Man*; and no one expected him to redress the She-Creature and cheat paying audiences by pretending to be something else. Best of all, United Artists had no problems meeting Blaisdell's salary requirements. In fact, UA paid him more money for *It! the Terror from Beyond Space* than AIP had ever offered for any of its projects, even after five years of dedicated service.

Blaisdell told Kent he would accept the job and settled down to work on a series of production illustrations depicting the Martian monstrosity. Although Martians were getting to be just a wee bit hackneyed by this time (George Pal's trilobed invaders that started *The War of the Worlds* in 1953 had already been followed by the disembodied voice from the *Red Planet Mars* and Blaisdell's own Saucer Men), Mars still exuded an air of mystery and menace with its strange geographical features and angry, red hue. If there were any other life forms patrolling our solar system, most people thought they would probably hail from the red planet.

So Mars it was.

The story begins with the rescue of a stranded astronaut on the surface of Mars. The commander of the rescue ship, Van Heusen (Kim Spalding), believes that Lt. Eric Carruthers (Marshall Thompson), the only survivor of an earlier exploratory voyage to Mars, murdered his crew in order to hoard food supplies to keep alive until help arrived. Despite Carruthers's warnings that some hideous form of Martian life was responsible for the deaths of his crewmates, Van Heusen wants to see the lieutenant court martialed and shot. Van shows him a human skull that was found half-buried in the Martian soil. It has been fractured by a bullet. "This was one of your crew, Carruthers. What kind of a monster uses a gun?" Van Heusen scoffs.

Unbeknownst to Van or the other members of the rescue team, the Martian monster that Carruthers spoke about has climbed aboard the ship and is hiding in the compartment below. When the rocket blasts off to return to Earth, with it goes a hostile and nearly indestructible form of alien life that has acquired a taste for human flesh.

Carruthers is exonerated by a cruel twist of fate when Keinholz (Thom Carney), one of the rescue crew, turns up missing and a search of the ship uncovers the monster Carruthers has been talking about. Keinholz's ravaged body is transported to the sick bay for an autopsy by Dr. Royce (Ann Doran). Meanwhile, a second crew member disappears without a trace. Major Perdue (Robert Bice) locates Gino's (Richard Hervey) bruised and battered body stuffed inside a claustrophobic air duct. Perdue tries to reach him, but the monster appears and forces him back. Carruthers, Van Heusen, and Lt. Calder (Paul Langlon) rig up a booby trap using a string of hand grenades, then rush topside and listen on the ship's open intercom as the beast triggers the explosives.

Van Heusen and the others cautiously descend to the lower level to see if the creature is alive or dead. As Van opens the compartment door, the hulking form of the beast rises up before them. It grabs Calder's rifle and bends it as if it were the rubber it was. The crew retreats to the upper level as the seemingly unstoppable monster rips through a steel door. Van secures the hatch lock that seals the only passageway between It and them. Carruthers suggests trying to choke the thing with gas grenades, but when Calder opens the hatch door, It reaches up through the opening and claws Van Heusen's boot to shreds, drawing his blood in the process. Carruthers tosses several of the gas grenades through the opening before the hatch is relocked, but the fumes merely irritate the creature.

The autopsy on Keinholz reveals that he died from acute dehydration. Every bit of moisture in his body and every molecule of oxygen have been sucked out. Even the bone marrow and glandular secretions are gone. Since there are no puncture wounds anywhere on his body, Dr. Royce surmises that the creature derives nourishment from its victims through some weird kind of osmosis process.

While Ann Anderson (Shawn Smith) attempts to control an infection that has started to spread through Van's body, the others track the creature's movements on the ship's open intercom. Royce has an idea: if they can get to the deck immediately below the monster, they can set a trap for it. Carruthers suggests using the ship's airlocks as a way around the thing, and he and Royce suit up to make a space-walk.

When they get to the lower level, Royce and Carruthers set about wiring the ladder that runs between the floors of the ship. The plan is to make enough noise to arouse the monster's curiosity, and when it comes down the steps to investigate, switch on the current and electrocute it. "There's enough voltage in these lines to kill thirty human beings," Carruthers mentions. "The only drawback is, the thing isn't human."

Carruthers's fears are well founded. The barrel-chested beast has such a thick hide that the shock merely stings it. It lunges at Calder, who falls backward between two induction pumps, breaking his ankle in the process. He is able to keep the creature at bay with a blowtorch, but the torch has just three hours worth of fuel. With his broken leg, there is no way he can get back to the upper deck, so Carruthers promises to send help as soon as they can figure out a way to get him out of there.

Dr. Royce warns the crew that Van's infection will eventually kill him. "I'll need more plasma if we're going to try to keep him alive," she says, pointing to the empty containers of blood that have already been used. Carruthers, Royce, and Finelli (Richard Benedict) team up to collect emergency plasma from the lower deck. With Calder directing them via the intercom system (he can see the creature's movements from his position between the induction pumps), they should be able to make the trip down and back safely.

Just as they are about to start out, the intercom sputters to life and Calder announces that the monster has just wandered into the atomic reactor room. The quick-thinking Carruthers closes the door behind it via remote control and hollers to Royce and Finelli, "Now's our chance!" The three of them descend through the central hatch to the ship's storage compartment to gather the vials of plasma.

Meanwhile, the alien infection in Van's bloodstream reaches his brain, causing him to become hostile and unpredictable. He throws the switch that unshields the nuclear reactor core. The intense heat and light of the atomic pile drive the monster wild. It batters its way through the locked door and spots the crewmen trying to rescue Calder. The creature lashes out at Finelli, killing him instantly, then turns toward Carruthers and Royce. "There's nothing we can do!" Royce shouts. "Get that blood upstairs, fast!" They make a dash for the ladder leading to the next level, while Calder limps back to the safety of the induction pumps.

After Dr. Royce stabilizes Van Heusen's condition with the plasma, the crew moves up another level to put more distance between themselves and

It. Carruthers explains, "There's nothing to do now but wait; wait and see if the beast will reach us through the center hatch. We can go no higher. We are in the top level of the ship. This is where either we die, or It dies."

A sudden communication from Calder warns them that the creature is on the move. It makes its way up the ladder and tears through the hatch leading to the upper levels. With nowhere left to run, the crew prepare for certain death. But Carruthers happens to notice a gauge that indicates the ship's oxygen consumption is abnormally high. Surmising that the alien creature is rapidly using up the oxygen because of its enormous lung capacity, Carruthers gets the idea to suffocate the monster by creating an internal vacuum in the ship. "Get your spacesuits on quick!" Carruthers directs the others.

As It crashes through the last hatch, Van Heusen throws the switch that opens the airlock door. Every loose object in the ship is kicked into a frenzied whirlwind dance as the air is sucked into space. As the oxygen level is reduced to zero, It begins gasping for breath, then slowly lowers its head and dies.

Back on Earth, a tele-radio message is received from Royce: "Of the 19 men and woman who have set foot on the planet Mars, 6 will return. There's no longer a question of murder, but of an alien and elemental life force—a planet so cruel, so hostile, that Man may find it necessary to bypass it in his endeavor to explore and understand the Universe. Another name for Mars is 'Death.'"

Fade to black.

Paul Blaisdell particularly enjoyed working with the script writer: "Jerry Bixby wrote a helluva script in my opinion, and we had no problems figuring out what a Martian lizard-man should look like. Jerry likes my planetary astronomy, and I always liked his writing, so we worked pretty well together. He's great to have around because when he gets bored on a soundstage he gets so damned funny he cracks us all up. I think he must have taught Rich Little."

Blaisdell wanted to give the lizard-man an expanded, barrel-like chest to suggest the enormous lung capacity a living being would need to survive in the thin atmosphere on Mars, along with a large, upturned nose with flaring nostrils. He decided that since It was supposed to be a carnivore, it would need to have a row of needlelike fangs like those of history's most infamous killer, the tyrannosaur. And because it was more reptilian than mammalian, it should have scales and prodigious strength. It would be a massive creature, much larger than the Atomic Mutant, more bulky than the She-Creature. Everything about It was going to be big—big eyes, big teeth, big neck, big claws, big feet.

In early sketches It had facial features that were scaly but sleek, less boxlike than the final product. The changes that were made to the costume were the result of the producers opting to give the role of the monster to someone other than Blaisdell. When he was first approached to work on the picture, Paul naturally assumed he would play the part of the monster just as he had in the movies he had worked on up to this point. But the film's executive producer, Ed Small, figured to add some extra umph to the marquee value by hiring a down-and-out actor by the name of Ray "Crash" Corrigan to play the part of the monster.

Corrigan had been a popular Saturday matinee hero at the height of his career in the 1930s and 1940s. He appeared in cliff-hangers like *Undersea Kingdom* but most often played the hulking apes that stalked through films such as *Dr. Renault's Secret, Captive Wild Woman, White Gorilla*, and a slew of other adventure and horror films. By the 1950s, Corrigan was having difficulty keeping his alcoholic intake in check—that was part of the reason his Hollywood career was on the skids—and he often was disagreeable and uncooperative. He interfered with the production of *It!* by refusing to make a trip to Blaisdell's workshop in Topanga to get measured for the costume. Therefore, when Paul began work on the first part of the costume to be made—the headpiece— he was forced to build it over his own bust, just as he normally did when designing masks for other pictures. It wasn't too surprising to discover later on that the completed headpiece failed to fit Corrigan very well, as Blaisdell later noted:

> The only real headache I had on *It! The Terror* was with the headpiece, which had to be altered before it would fit Ray Corrigan. Fortunately, Ray was able to give me a pair of his long underwear so I could make the rest of the costume to fit him. And it's a good thing he did, because if I'd had to guess at his measurements I doubt we could've ever gotten him into that suit, even if the whole crew was squeezing him from every side.

For years Blaisdell had been making movie monsters in his own unique way, employing positive molds to create the haunting images that nightmare-seekers paid to see over and over again. Now he tried experimenting with more sophisticated mask-making techniques, for the first time using a negative mold to create the three-dimensional visage of *It! the Terror from Beyond Space.*

The positive molds Blaisdell had been using ever since he got into the monster business were possible only because in effect a negative mold had been created years earlier. When Jackie sculpted a life-size bust of her husband, it took the place of a life-mask that Blaisdell should have made when he designed his very first full-body monster suit in 1955. To make certain that a rubber latex appliance will fit the person who is supposed to wear it, it needs to be developed from a mold of the wearer's real-life dimensions. The process usually begins with the making of a plaster cast of the actor's face. When the plaster hardens and is removed, the inside of the cast is a negative replica of the model's likeness. Obviously a mask cannot be made from a negative mold, so the plaster mold is filled with latex which is allowed to harden and then removed. The dried latex now forms a perfect *positive* mold of the person's face. Designing makeup appliances over this latex mold guarantees that the finished product will precisely fit the actor who is supposed to wear it.

Blaisdell was able to skip most of these preliminaries by creating masks over a latex blank. Jackie's life-size sculpture took the place of the standard plaster mold that is generally the first step of any mask-making process. If she had made the sculpture too large or too small, Blaisdell would never have been able to take the short-cuts he did over the years.

Obviously, with Ray Corrigan playing the part of the monster, Paul should not have used one of his blanks to build the headpiece because Corrigan's measurements were quite different from his own, but in fact that is what he ended up doing. Producer Bob Kent and director Eddie Cahn had already looked at Paul's preliminary sketches of *It!* and given their blessings, so Paul was free to proceed with the actual headpiece. With a deadline staring him in the face, it was impossible to delay work on the mask for long, hoping that Corrigan would eventually get off his high horse and make the drive up to Topanga Canyon for a fitting. A few days later, when Corrigan's long johns arrived on the doorstep without Ray inside them, Paul figured he was going to have to use one of his blanks or the mask would never be finished in time.

Hoping that the latex rubber would stretch enough to accommodate Corrigan's hat size, Blaisdell began the monster-making process by modeling a three-dimensional version of the creature's face using water-based clay over a latex blank. He kept the design relatively straightforward, without all the hooks, horns, antennae, and other protuberances that had graced many of his other creations. The mouth was made extremely wide and fishlike, complimenting the creature's bulbous ears and enormous, upturned nostrils. Above the brow were added several bony ridges that curved downward from the temples to the eyelids, creating a perpetually scowling countenance that also gave the face a certain degree of varicosity. A larger vertical ridge ran between the eyes and up the forehead to the top of the head, where it gradually receded into the scalp. A row of aluminum plates were pushed into the clay on either side of the head to create metallic scales. These plates were about the size of playing cards and ran from the neck over the top of the head and down the other side, effectively dividing the headpiece into two parts.

Leaving the eyes, ears, and fangs for last, Blaisdell mixed up a quantity of casting plaster which would be used to create a negative mold of the finished sculpture. Water was stirred into the plaster until the mixture reached the consistency of heavy whipped cream, and it was then brushed onto the front half of the clay figure. Wet burlap strips were added to the plaster before it hardened to give the mold extra strength. Additional alternating layers of plaster and burlap were continually applied until Blaisdell had built up the mixture to a little more than an inch thick. This was allowed to dry

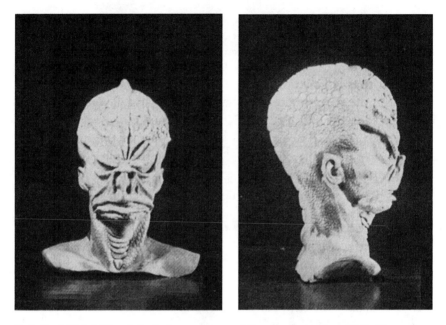

Left: Paul Blaisdell's original clay sculpture of the alien known as *It! the Terror from Beyond Space.* The dimensions of the completed latex headpiece were stretched out of all proportion by Ray Corrigan's own massive, angular head. On film the monster looked like a deformed cousin to Blaisdell's original concept. *Right:* This side view of the *It! the Terror from Beyond Space* sculpture plainly shows the original design's enormous, elongated brow and egg-shaped head, which became much more boxlike on film. The very human ear was destined to be replaced by something a little more unusual, of course.

thoroughly, and the process was then repeated for the back of the head. When this had also dried, Blaisdell pried apart the two halves of the mold with a screwdriver.

The plaster, which had been absorbed into the many nooks and crannies of the original clay sculpture, now provided detailed front and back negative molds of the *It!* headpiece. After the molds were cleaned (some of the clay invariably stuck to the plaster), Blaisdell painted each with liquid latex. He added a bit of brown poster paint to the latex mix so that the finished product would have an appropriate desert-beige hue. This would eliminate the need to paint every inch of the costume, allowing Paul to spend more time on just the highlights.

When the latex had dried, it was carefully peeled away from the plaster, and the front and back were sealed together with additional applications of latex. At this point positive molds for the ears and teeth were fashioned out of clay and pine, respectively, and used to generate rubber latex pieces that were glued to the headpiece with contact bond cement. Canine teeth were fashioned from a pine wood mold. To avoid having to glue each fang into the

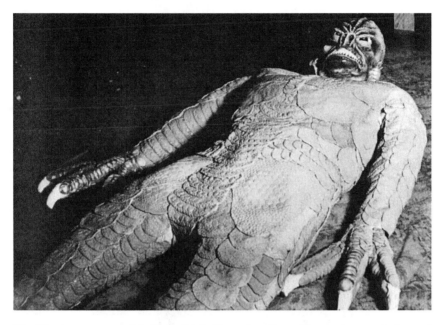

The Martian monster suit built for *It! the Terror from Beyond Space* prior to painting and detailing. The lethal-looking gauntlets were built over a heavy-duty pair of workmen's gloves. The talons are white pine (courtesy of Bob Burns).

headpiece separately, a sawtooth pattern was made from a single length of pine. Liquid latex was applied to the pine mold, then dried, removed, and stuffed with cotton. What Paul ended up with was a single horizontal strip of pointed fangs which he glued to the inside of the mask's upper lip.

The body of the Martian monstrosity was put together in a manner similar to that used for the She-Creature. Since Corrigan had provided Paul with a pair of long johns, the guesswork involved in correctly sizing the costume was eliminated. Because It was supposed to be a lizardlike being, Blaisdell elected to create separate reptilian "scales" that could be attached to the outfit in various configurations. Different size scales were sculpted with modeling clay and were then used to produce latex appliances. Altogether Paul made up a half-dozen different models, and used these to cast over two hundred separate latex scales. The scales were bonded to the long johns in overlapping patterns, which gave the costume a great deal of flexibility, allowing the actor inside to bend, stretch, and move quickly without having to worry whether the latex material was going to tear or be crushed. (Compare the She-Creature's lumbering motions to the much freer movements Ray Corrigan was able to use in *It! the Terror from Beyond Space*.) The back of the costume supported a slightly protruding, humplike spinal column that served to conceal a heavy-duty zipper sewn into the lining of the material, which allowed Corrigan easy access to the suit.

Blaisdell's completed latex rubber headpiece for *It! the Terror from Beyond Space*, outfitted with a pair of shifty eyes and newly designed, obviously inhuman ears. This close-up shows the startling amount of detail that went into one of Blaisdell's projects. Unfortunately, most of the detail was lost amid the low lighting, black-and-white photography, and rushed nature of low-budget filmmaking. Compare this photo to the monster as it appeared in the finished film to note the alterations made to the facial features and the shape of the head. Years later Blaisdell published a color photograph of the original headpiece on the cover of *Fantastic Monsters* #3.

No monster would be complete without hands and feet, of course, and in this instance Blaisdell returned to the tried and true formula of past glories, utilizing pine and latex over workgloves and sneakers to form the basis of It's triple-taloned appendages. It had the distinction of sporting the largest claws of any Blaisdell creation outside of Paul's other "It" (the one that almost conquered the world), and Ray Corrigan put them to good use doing bad things to the supporting cast.

Blaisdell worked hard to give the costume an incredible amount of detailing. The creature's face is covered with literally hundreds of minute "age lines," painstakingly etched into the latex rubber around the eyes and lips with a variety of brushes (as well as a nail file and playing card). Only a close inspection of the original mask can reveal the care Blaisdell took in the construction of his Martian lizard-man, as the detailing is difficult to notice in the finished film. Obviously, Paul's handiwork was at its peak during the making of *It! the Terror from Beyond Space*. It's really too bad this was his last 100 percent original creation for Hollywood.

From start to finish, the lizard-man costume took nearly six weeks to develop. Before it was delivered to the set, Paul got a telephone call from Bob Kent at the production office. "Is this monster of yours going to have eyes?" Kent asked.

What kind of question was that? "Of course it's going to have eyes." Blaisdell said. "How is it supposed to see unless it has eyes?"

"No, what I mean is, are you going to make eyes for it? Because we don't want to use Ray Corrigan's eyes. This thing should have really big eyes."

"Well, I can give it big eyes, but they're not going to move," Blaisdell warned.

"Oh, I don't care about that. Just so long as it has big eyes."

"Okay."

Blaisdell hung up the phone and made the trip to Frye Plastics Company, where he scored a new set of plastic orbs. Back at his workshop, he painted emerald green irises on the plastic and popped them into the mask. He decided to add an extra layer of rubber latex beneath each eye socket and glue the top edge of the latex directly to the plastic. When the latex was painted, it looked for all the world as if It had genuine, wrinkly eyelids. With the way the latex lids hugged the plastic, these turned out to be the most realistic eyes Paul had ever designed. So naturally, they were never used in the finished film.

When Blaisdell delivered the finished costume to the production office, Bob Kent was nowhere to be found; executive producer Ed Small was there instead. He took one look at the Martian headpiece and barked, "Who told you to put eyes in this thing? Those are the worst goddamn eyes I've ever seen!"

Blaisdell started to protest. "But Bob said—"

"I don't care what anybody said. Get those eyes outta there!" Paul was so steamed that Jackie could have fried an egg on his head for breakfast. He took the mask back home, yanked out the plastic orbs and latex eyelids, and put them safely away. (And it's a good thing he did. Those eyeballs came in handy a few years later when he decided to feature the original It face on the cover of an early issue of *Fantastic Monsters*.)

When the headpiece was returned to the production office, Ed Small was gone, and Bob Kent was back. Kent wanted to know why It still didn't have any eyeballs. An exasperated Blaisdell said, "Ask your boss." Bob Burns remembers how frustrated his friend was. "That was such a prime example of studio indecision. 'It's gotta have eyes!' 'We don't want those eyes!' 'Where are the eyes?' Paul had to add some more latex to the mask after the eyes came out, and then of course Ray Corrigan couldn't see anything half of the time. There's actually a scene in the film where Corrigan readjusts the eyeholes in the mask so he can see. They never bothered to cut it out."

While he was reading over the script, Paul noticed that there were one or two scenes with the monster reaching up through a floor hatch to grab at one of the astronauts. Knowing what a hassle it would be for Ray Corrigan to don the entire lizard-man outfit just to shoot a couple of scenes of the monster's arm poking through an opening, Blaisdell decided to build an extra appendage that Corrigan could slip on just for those scenes. It was constructed like the full-length suit, with rubber latex scales stretching from wrist to shoulder. It took an extra two days to put together the armpiece, without a claw. When it was finished, Paul sent it over to the studio and kicked back, figuring now was the time for a little rest and relaxation.

Wrong. The day the costume was delivered to Vogel Pictures, Bob Kent got on the horn to Blaisdell and asked him to drive down to the production office.

"Why? Is something the matter?" Paul wanted to know.

"You'll see when you get here." Click.

Forty-five minutes later Paul and Jackie arrived at the Vogel office. Ray Corrigan was standing in the center of the room wearing the It costume, holding the headpiece under one arm while the film's makeup artist, Lane "Shotgun" Britton (who later became head of the Hollywood makeup union), dusted his eyes with a mixture of powder and greasepaint. "What's going on?" Paul asked.

By way of explanation, Corrigan pulled the mask down over his head. It was a tight squeeze—the headpiece was much too small for Corrigan's considerable countenance—but with a little stretching and tugging he was able to wrestle it on. The only problem was that Ray's bulbous chin stuck out of the mouth like a half-swallowed softball. "It doesn't fit," Corrigan offered lamely.

"That doesn't surprise me," Blaisdell scolded, trying hard to hold his tongue. He wanted to say a lot more—why let Kent think that the ill-fitting mask was his own fault?—but it just wasn't in Paul's nature to take a contemporary to task, especially in front of his own boss. It probably wouldn't have mattered if Kent had found out that Corrigan had never bothered to show up for a life-mask fitting because Ed Small had been so insistent on hiring the actor to begin with. If word had got back to the front office, however, it might have cost Ray his job. Paul let the matter drop.

"You know, I've got an idea what you could do," Bob Kent interjected.

Oh God, here it comes, thought Blaisdell. *He's going to ask me to redo the whole damned thing. 'Could you make this mask a little bit bigger?' Yeah right, buddy.*

"You could paint his chin, or something," Kent suggested. "Maybe that would make it blend in better."

One of the most popular portraits of *It! the Terror from Beyond Space* clearly shows Ray "Crash" Corrigan's bulbous chin jutting out from the alien mouthpiece. Before Corrigan was pressed into service for the role of the Martian vampire, the alien visage possessed large eyes and only one row of upper fangs. The bottom dentures were added by Blaisdell to help conceal Corrigan's chin.

Paul's eyes lit up—not because he thought the idea was any good but because he was so happy that Kent hadn't just dumped the problem in his lap.

Lane Britton had a better idea. "What about this—we'll put some make-up on his chin and make it look like a tongue." Before anyone had a chance to respond, Britton pulled out his greasepaints and went to work on Corrigan's jutting jowl. A few minutes later he stopped to inspect his handiwork. "What do you think, Paul?" asked Lane.

Britton had pulled off the subterfuge remarkably well. Corrigan's chin really did look like a tongue; a big tongue, but then who was to say how overgrown a Martian's tongue would be anyway? "Not bad," Paul admitted. "But there's one small problem." He urged Lane to take a few steps back to get a better look at the overall effect. "You see what I see?"

With its "tongue" constantly protruding from its mouth, the monster seemed terribly unintelligent. "Yeah, I think I see what you mean," said Britton. "Kinda looks like he's saying 'D-uh.'" Everyone who saw the costume thought the same thing.

Luckily, Blaisdell was able to come up with a quick fix. He made up a second set of choppers and glued them into the mask, giving It a bottom row of fangs in addition to the top row. The effect was instantaneous. This second set of teeth not only helped to conceal Corrigan's masquerading chin, it screened out the shadows between his chin and neck. Now the monster looked even meaner than before. And instead of saying "D-uh," it looked like it was saying "Hisss-s-s!"

There was one other small problem left to resolve. Since the original plastic eyes had been removed from the mask at Ed Small's request, the holes left in the rubber latex tended to reveal too much of Corrigan's actual face. Paul decided to whip up a couple of specially colored latex pieces that could be applied to the skin around Corrigan's eyes with spirit gum. These doughnut-shaped appliances blended with the texture of the mask and obscured the eyeholes well enough so that only those standing close to Corrigan could tell the difference.

At last, It was ready to rock, or so Blaisdell believed: "I really thought I was finished with It when I turned everything over to the production department, but after just a few days of shooting I got a desperate call from the studio. They needed me to come down and patch things up, because 'Crash' Corrigan had crashed right through the scales on his lizard hide, and nobody at the studio knew how to fix it."

When Paul turned up at the film set with his "rescue kit" in response to Bob Kent's phone call, he walked into a situation he had never before encountered. With Eddie Cahn at the helm of *It!*, he expected that the shooting would be progressing relatively smoothly. But in fact the atmosphere on the set was unfriendly and disjunctive. Tempers flared constantly. Ray Corrigan, Paul learned, had shown up on the set three sheets to the wind on more than one occasion and was becoming decidedly uncooperative. Cahn had set up a shot using shadows that would appear early in the picture to introduce the monster to the audience, but Corrigan refused to play the scene in the It head-piece. "I'm not gonna wear that blasted mask when I don't have to," Corrigan complained. If Cahn was going to photograph only his shadow, why should he be bothered? The audience wasn't going to see the monster's face, anyway.

"You don't understand, Ray," Cahn argued. "The shape of the monster's head is completely different from your own. The audience isn't stupid. They're going to be able to see your profile, even if it is only a shadow."

"I don't care, I ain't wearin' that mask," Corrigan insisted.

Time was wasting while they argued back and forth, so eventually Cahn gave up and they photographed the scene with Corrigan in Blaisdell's monster suit, minus the head. Sure enough, in the finished film Corrigan's obviously human profile stood out in sharp contrast to the bulky monster suit he was wearing as the creature's silhouette was thrown on the spaceship's interior wall. It was easy to spot not only Corrigan's nose and chin, but even his hairline.

Cahn related to Paul the difficulty they were having with Corrigan. "He's been drinking, and he's creating some real problems for us. I don't know whether it's that, or if he's just being overzealous with his role, but he has torn the hell out of that costume of yours. 'Shotgun' [Britton] has been following him around all day with a bucket of glue, picking up the pieces that've been knocked loose and putting them back on." Sure enough, when Paul checked, he found dozens of scales missing from the costume. The zipper was stuck, too, and nobody seemed able to get Ray resealed inside the suit. "I never understood why the guy in charge of the costume department couldn't get Ray sealed into that suit," Blaisdell said, "but I figured once I got him patched up, I'd better stick around in case anything else happened."

Paul and Jackie always kept supplies of latex, glue, paint, and similar materials at the ready in their portable repair kit. It took less than an hour to replace the scales that had gotten knocked loose from the It! costume, so the production didn't suffer much downtime. Once Corrigan was good to go, Blaisdell stepped back to the sidelines and kept to himself. He was really hanging out more for Corrigan's benefit than anyone else's. "Frankly, I think Ray appreciated the company," said Blaisdell. "Everybody had their nose in the script, and it was really just a tight fit. It wasn't the kind of 'loose' situation we'd had at American International, where we'd all learned to work together. I never heard anybody kidding anybody, or anybody laughing. It was really a stuffy, sad sort of set."

Marshall Thompson seemed to be the only one enjoying himself on the picture. His costar, Shawn Smith, who played the love interest, turned out to be almost as much of a problem as Corrigan. No one seemed to be able to figure out whether she was angry at Ray for his inebriated misbehavior, angry at Eddie Cahn for putting up with Corrigan's shenanigans, or angry with her agent for signing her to the picture. "All we knew was that she was a real snit," said a source close to the production. "Everybody stayed as far away from her as possible."

Although Blaisdell never said much about it, Ray Corrigan continued to be a source of headaches for the producers of It! Often he failed to pay attention to Cahn's direction or misconstrued a set of instructions. In one particular scene that was never excised from the final print, the monster was supposed to search for its prey in a cramped, tubelike corridor that snaked through the spaceship. While Corrigan was playing the scene, the mask worked itself loose from the latex around his eyes, obscuring his vision. Cahn yelled from his director's chair, "Lift your head! Lift your head! We can't see your damn face!" Corrigan, not quite understanding that Cahn wanted him to look up at the camera, reached out with one of his huge three-fingered monster gauntlets and literally pushed the mask back on his forehead, realigning the eyeholes. It was definitely not one of It's better moments.

Cahn had never intended for his Martian lizard-man to ape the antics of a gorilla, but as Bob Burns often pointed out, Corrigan essentially played the role of the monster as if he were playing a simian in one of the old movies he had made years earlier. But the critics apparently never noticed. *It! the Terror from Beyond Space* received better notices than most other grade-B sci-fi films of the day, and paying audiences seemed to love it. Buoyed by a better-than-average budget, the film looked good and played better. Jerry Bixby's timeless tale generated a fair amount of suspense as well. Topped off by Blaisdell's nightmarish vision of a Martian vampire, the United Artists release became one of the most popular of the late 1950s monster movies.

The costume Paul built ended up being used in another low-budget movie called *Invisible Invaders*, released about a year after *It! the Terror from Beyond Space*. This disjointed quickie, which has almost been forgotten, has the single distinction of picturing armies of the walking dead menacing remote pockets of human beings almost ten years before George A. Romero popularized the concept in his nightmarish *Night of the Living Dead* (itself inspired by Richard Matheson's classic sci-fi novel, *I Am Legend*). But there the similarities end. The basic concept of *Invisible Invaders*, that the aliens are invisible and ride around in invisible spaceships, allowed the film to be made as cheaply and effortlessly as possible. It was produced by Bob Kent and directed by Eddie Cahn, the same team that had given us *It! the Terror from Beyond Space*, so it is not all that surprising that Paul's monster outfit turned up at the conclusion of *Invisible Invaders*.

The story begins with the death of Dr. Karol Noyman (John Carradine), who accidentally blows himself to smithereens in his own laboratory. An invisible presence shuffles toward his graveside at the funeral, and later that night Noyman's reanimated corpse (Carradine again, now sporting hollow-eyed greasepaint makeup) visits level-headed Dr. Penner (Philip Tonge), an outspoken opponent of nuclear testing. The corpse begins a dialogue with Penner, revealing its alien origin and demanding that Penner deliver a message to his people (presumably associates at the Atomic Energy Commission). The message, not surprisingly, is that since human beings are now capable of space travel, we must stop fooling around with nuclear toys or risk the threat of extinction. If the leaders of Earth fail to capitulate to the invaders' demands, this extraterrestrial race will take over the bodies of our dear departed loved ones and wage an all-out war against humanity.

Twenty-four hours later the aliens make good their threat, and lots of dead guys get up and stagger around. (There are no dead girls, interestingly enough.) Lots of stock footage of natural disasters such as earthquakes, floods, and the like is inserted here just to show us the aliens mean business.

Meanwhile, a crack team of scientists headed up by a no-nonsense military type, Major Bruce Jay (John Agar), works feverishly to devise a means to combat the invaders. They manage to trap one of the creatures by luring an ambulatory corpse into a pool of liquid acrylic. This has the effect of sealing the body's pores, thus trapping the alien inside. (Previously it was learned that the aliens enter the flesh through the pores.) Jay and the others transport the body back to their lab for testing. Later a fistfight breaks out between Major Jay and Dr. LaMont (Robert Hutton), and a bottle of acid strikes an air conditioner during the scuffle. The air conditioner emits a loud screeching sound, which sends the imprisoned invisible invader into paroxysms of pain, eventually killing it. A chance accident has inadvertently led to the discovery of the key to the mystery (this happens all the time in these 1950s films): amplified sound waves will destroy the menaces from outer space. Incidentally, the sound waves also turn the invaders visible for a short time just before they die.

With time running out, the scientists in the bunker devise high-powered "sound rifles" to be used against the invaders. It's just a matter of time before hundreds of the units are manufactured and shipped all over the world to combat the menace, returning ownership of terra firma to the living once more.

Paul's *It!* costume was worn briefly by those actors in the film who portrayed the dying invaders, who for some odd reason become visible just as their vital signs shut down. To help camouflage the costume, optical effects were added to lighten the image and give it a distinct blur, so that it's very difficult to tell that the invaders' true form matches that of Paul's Martian lizard-man. (If this had been an American International release, the dying invaders would probably have been seen very clearly, most likely as a bunch of She-Creatures.)

Invisible Invaders garnered absolutely terrible reviews, and deservedly so. Even children, who by 1959 made up the bulk of the sci-fi movie audience, seemed to hate it. (I know I did.)

No filmmaker ever looked to *Invisible Invaders* for inspiration, but the same is just not true of *It! the Terror from Beyond Space*, despite its B-budget origin. Jerome Bixby's story of a stowaway monster knocking off the crew of an earthbound spaceship one by one was so popular it was repeated twenty years later in 20th Century Fox's blockbuster hit of 1979, *Alien*. That film, written by Dan O'Bannon, suffered critical barbs fired by fans who remembered *It! the Terror from Beyond Space* and believed it to be the uncredited inspiration for Fox's multimillion-dollar extravaganza. Genre magazine *Cinéfantastique* ran an article comparing the plotlines of the two films, and examined another motion picture called *Planet of the Vampires* (retitled *The Demon Planet* for American television) that seemed to have suggested a major subplot of *Alien*. Blaisdell acknowledged the connections between all three films but didn't think there was any intentional plagiarism on the part of any of the writers. "Lots of movies tell the same stories," he pointed out. "I've seen

Alien, and I'm not surprised it has become the success it has with the kind of budget and manpower involved. Remind me never to be a one-man band again."

Typically, Paul had nothing but kind words for the creative team behind the picture. "Personally, I thought the creature itself was great. It kind of suggested the head of a moray eel attached to the body of a sea horse, with a lizard's tail and human legs," he said. "My hat's off to the guy that played the monster. What a great job he did."

After the release of *It! the Terror from Beyond Space* Blaisdell set aside his latex and foam rubber for a while and concentrated on painting while waiting for another film assignment to turn up. A very minor project presented itself when James Warren and Forrest Ackerman were working out the contents of the premiere issue of *Famous Monsters of Filmland* magazine. Warren wanted to have a "behind-the-scenes" story about the creation of a movie monster, so Forry asked Paul to contribute some photographs of himself working on one of his AIP monsters. Paul sent Ackerman some material on *Invasion of the Saucer Men*, but none of the photos demonstrated the step-by-step process of monster-making that Warren and Ackerman had in mind. Paul turned for help to Bob Burns, who agreed to photograph Blaisdell at work creating a "giant brain." For the photo session, Paul whipped up an enormous plaster brain—nearly three times the size of a Saucer Man cranium—and highlighted it with airbrushed folds of "tissue." The magazine ended up using several of these photographs in a pictorial entitled "How Hollywood Creates a Monster," the implication being that the plaster brain seen in the pictures was built for an actual Hollywood production. (It wasn't, of course. It was created specifically for the article and was never used in a movie. It did provide raw material for the Blaisdell/Burns gag-photo sessions, however.)

As 1958 segued into 1959, those days of fun-filled photo sessions, 16mm home horror movies, and radio spoofs were drawing to a close. For the last few years, Bob and Kathy Burns had visited with the Blaisdells nearly every single weekend, and Paul and Bob had become the best of friends. Traditionally the Blaisdells shied away from big Hollywood brouhahas, preferring each other's company over that of Hollywood bigshots, stars, and showpeople. Now that Paul had gotten to know someone on his own wavelength he truly enjoyed Bob's and Kathy's company.

Unfortunately, things would be a heck of a lot different very soon. Bob Burns was leaving town to stay with a relative, and the relative's name was Uncle Sam.

12

The Last Her-rah

I've played some oddball roles in my career, I guess. I've been a three-eyed atomic mutant, I've been a perambulating plant from the planet Venus, I've been a bug-eyed Martian with alcohol for blood; I've even played a prehistoric female with a big tail, big teeth, and big boobs. But who could ever forget *The Ghost of Drag-strip Hollow*, where I had to come on like a real dingbat?
— *Paul Blaisdell*

The plotline of Herman Cohen's *How to Make a Monster* had turned out, in a way, to be a bit prophetic for Paul Blaisdell. Paul even considered the film "somewhat autobiographical"—not in terms of the characters (he obviously wouldn't have described himself as a maniacal makeup artist), but in terms of the story. Motion picture themes really were changing. The science-fiction and monster cycles were winding down, gothic horror was winding up, and AIP was preparing to diversify. Already the company was bringing home new coproductions with Britain's Anglo-Amalgamated Films such as *Horrors of the Black Museum* (1959) and *Circus of Horrors* (1960). These pictures, filmed in color and CinemaScope, heralded the new face of AIP circa 1960.

Goosed by the profits Hammer Films was generating with its new color renditions of the Frankenstein and Dracula mythos, Roger Corman shifted into overdrive and went to work convincing Sam Arkoff and Jim Nicholson that the time was ripe for a new line of bigger-budget, higher-class motion pictures. As it happened, neither Arkoff nor Nicholson required much convincing. Returns on recent double feature programs were anemic. It was obvious to them that something new was needed to buck up the box office. Despite healthy sales of *Famous Monsters* magazine and its black-and-white pulp-paper brethren, moviegoers seemed to be growing weary of 1950s-style fears like *The Giant Leeches* and *The Brain Eaters*.

At the same time that Corman was betting audiences would queue up to see well-made adaptations of the classic horror tales of Edgar Allan Poe, screenwriter Lou Rusoff was also making changes in the way he approached the genre. Straightforward thrillers like *Day the World Ended* had become passé. The youth audience that had buttered AIP's bread for so long had become more sophisticated, and they were demanding that Hollywood keep up with them.

While AIP steeled itself for the plunge into color, widescreen, and name-brand actors such as Vincent Price, Boris Karloff, Peter Lorre, and Basil Rathbone, it green-lighted a few final projects that seemed to offer new twists on tried and true themes. One was a new Lou Rusoff script called *The Haunted Hot Rod*. Rusoff was hoping to appeal directly to the contemporary teenager's preoccupation with fast cars, fast chicks, fast music, and juvenile delinquency by stirring all those ingredients into a monstrous mix frosted with touches of comedy, suspense, and fantasy. The story did have a haunted hot rod, but it didn't show up until the end, so Jim Nicholson decided to change the title to *The Ghost of Dragstrip Hollow*. The problem with that title was that there really wasn't a ghost. But that didn't matter to AIP. It had fibbed before on more than one occasion, and it was still around making pictures.

Fibbing was becoming more and more prevalent in the late 1950s, especially in 1958 and 1959, as the standard kind of "B" picture AIP specialized in began to dwindle in popularity. Low-budget productions were becoming even lower-budget. A movie called *Tank Battalion* was made with only one tank; *The Brain Eaters* were wind-up toy bugs; *The Astounding She Monster* was partially filmed without synch-sound, and when the zipper broke on the she-thing's slinky, silver, skin-tight costume, the director decided to have her enter and exit each scene facing the camera so no one would notice. *The Giant Leeches* had various problems discussed earlier.

Not surprisingly, *The Ghost of Dragstrip Hollow* was going to be another super-low-budget affair. Rusoff's story contained enough comedic/horrific elements that the film had a chance of repeating the success of *Invasion of the Saucer Men*. But the budget dictated a rushed and sloppy execution, and the result was an uneven and terribly unfunny "horror-comedy" that proved an embarrassment to almost everyone connected with it.

Hot rods and dragsters were big news among the teen set in the late 1950s, so Rusoff had filled his screenplay with lots of tough jargon about race cars, hot rods, drag clubs, and the embryonic generation gap. These elements combined to make up most of the story's suspense, while the comedy was generated almost entirely by the characters and a few mildly horrific situations. It was a far cry from the bleak vision of *Day the World Ended* or the time-tunneling *The She-Creature*, but AIP was convinced that contemporary audiences were weary of shivering at their budgetary boogeymen.

After Rusoff submitted his script to AIP for approval, Nicholson and Arkoff assigned a director. They hired William J. Hole, Jr., on the strength of a picture he had directed for Crown International called *The Devil's Hand*, about a black magic cult that worships the blood god, Damba. The film's only distinction is that it marked the last appearance of Robert Alda (Alan Alda's father) in an American-made film.

While Hole was familiarizing himself with Rusoff's script, Nicholson called Blaisdell to tell him about the new project. "This isn't just another monster movie," Nicholson promised. "It's more like *Saucer Men*. It's a comedy, so you'll be able to do something a little different than usual."

Blaisdell's ears perked right up. Something different? That sounded good. He would definitely enjoy being involved in a comedy, even a horror-comedy. "I'm going to send over the script right away so you can check it out," Nicholson promised. Then he held out the carrot. "And you'll actually have some dialogue to speak in this one, Paul."

That was even better. Paul couldn't wait to see the script.

When it arrived by carrier the next day, Blaisdell eagerly scanned the script, looking for telltale signs that might indicate which part Nick had in mind for him. It took less than ten minutes to figure out that he would just be playing the monster role again. He called Nicholson at the AIP office.

"Look, Nick, I read Lou's script, and it looks to me like it's just another monster part."

"Well, it is, but the monster's not really a monster. It's you, Paul."

"Yeah, I figured that out."

"Isn't that something?"

"Yeah."

Blaisdell couldn't hide his disappointment, but as Jackie pointed out, monsters were Paul's business. It made sense to play the Dragstrip Hollow Ghost—except that he wasn't going to be a "real" ghost. He was going to play himself, Paul Blaisdell, resident AIP monster-maker, pretending to be a ghost. Rusoff's script was very specific in that regard. The character wasn't just some old geezer hanging around a haunted house and scoring his jollies by scaring young kids. He wasn't some evildoer trying to con a rich widow out of her inheritance. He was just a helium-headed Halloween prankster trying to have a little fun. "Maybe it won't be so bad," Paul decided.

Naturally, once Blaisdell had gotten over his initial reluctance to play a parody of himself, Arkoff called up with the bad news.

"Hello, Paul?"

"Yeah?"

"This is Sam Arkoff."

Oh, great, thought Paul. *He's calling to tell me they can't afford me. They're going to get somebody else to do the costume.* "What is it, Sam?" Paul asked.

"Just wanted to let you know that everything's 'Go' on *Dragstrip Hollow.*"

Well, that was good news. "Okay, good. How long are you able to give me to work up the design of the Ghost?"

"Uhh ... didn't Lou tell you?"

"Tell me what?"

Arkoff hesitated, then stormed ahead: "Well, you know, Paul, that you're basically playing yourself in this picture. You're not a real ghost, you're a guy wearing a mask. So, ah, we thought we could save a little time and money if we just used your She-Creature outfit. See, it makes perfect sense because at the end of the picture you take off your mask and you even mention the other monsters you've played for us."

"But Sam, that costume has already been seen in three different movies," Blaisdell protested. "You can't be serious!"

But, of course, he was. "We don't have enough money in the budget for anything new, Paul. Look, just take your She-Creature costume and change it around a little bit."

"We already did that," Blaisdell reminded him, "in *Voodoo Woman*."

Arkoff put his foot down. "Paul, that's the way it's gotta be."

And so it was.

The Ghost of Dragstrip Hollow can only be defined as a slight comedy with horrific overtones. It isn't a horror-comedy, like *Invasion of the Saucer Men*, and it's clearly not a black comedy in the vein of Roger Corman's *A Bucket of Blood* or *The Little Shop of Horrors*. Scriptwriter Lou Rusoff apparently was more concerned with the ridiculous than the sublime because the humor in *Ghost* is immature, condescending, and not very funny. In fact, *The Ghost of Dragstrip Hollow* could almost be a blueprint for AIP's series of beach party movies made in the early 1960s. That's not too surprising, considering that the first beach-bum film, which set the style for all the rest to follow, was written by Lou Rusoff. All the elements of the surf-'n'-sand pictures were present in *Ghost*: the "good" kids, the "bad" kids, the asinine jokes, an adolescent preoccupation with sex, an adult figure who established what few plot elements there were, and a surprise cameo by a horror film "star." (Recall that Vincent Price, Boris Karloff, and Peter Lorre all turned up in climactic cameos in the beach party pictures.) In a way, *The Ghost of Dragstrip Hollow* could almost be the first beach party picture, except that it was filmed in black-and-white rather than color and featured hot-rodders on asphalt instead of surfers on sand. Other than that, it was really the same movie.

Also as in the AIP beach films, a lot was going on in *Ghost*, and yet nothing much ever really happened. The opening sequence is a hot-rod race through the streets of Los Angeles. The opponents are Lois Cavendish (Jody Fair) and Nita (Nancy Anderson). Nita cracks up her crate as she's trying to escape a pursuing motorcycle cop, but Lois gets away.

Stan (Martin Braddock), the leader of a local hot-rod organization called the Zenith Club, is working with a magazine writer named Tom Hendry (Russ Bender). Hendry plans to write a series of articles about the dragster clubs and their connection to juvenile delinquency, but he has latched onto the worst club in the city to pursue that particular angle. The Zenith members are juvenile, but they aren't delinquents. They take their hot-roddin' hobby seriously. So seriously, in fact, that local genius Dave (Henry McCann) has invented a new type of car that can think and act on its own.

The Zenith Club has lost its lease and is about to close up shop, scattering the members back to the streets, but Lois's aunt, loopy Anastasia Abernathy (Dorothy Neumann, the hook-nosed witch in Roger Corman's *The Undead*), inadvertently comes to the rescue when she mentions a creepy old house she owns in Flint Canyon—an area the kids call Dragstrip Hollow. Anastasia's pet parrot, the wise-cracking Alfonso, clucks in terror at the mention of the place. According to Anastasia, the house is haunted by her departed husband, Old John Abernathy the First. "The last woman who lived there was actually scared to death by a monster." Anastasia cautions. The members of the Zenith Club volunteer to "de-spirit" the place if she will rent it to them as their new club headquarters.

That evening, when the kids check out the house, horrible moans, high-pitched shrieks, and weird noises can be heard all around, but Hendry feels sure that someone is playing games with them. After one particularly intense bansheelike howl, he says, "I have a feeling I've heard that scream before." (Actually, this is a clue to the picture's surprise ending. It is also one of the very few plot points that makes any sense at all.)

Hendry and Stan takes turns keeping watch on the house that night, but neither of them notices the weird, glowing eyes staring out of the darkness at them. Lois, sitting in front of the fireplace, is spun around like a carousel when the Dragstrip Hollow Ghost presses a secret panel which causes the hearth to swivel in a circle on a hidden axis. Dave is visited by a strange apparition, and one of the girls is pinched by the Ghost itself. Moving candles, spinning portraits, and collapsing tables are some of the other unexplainable events these hard-headed kids keep on snoozing through.

In the morning, Hendry forms a plan. To expose the real culprit behind the weird goings-on, they will throw a "spook ball" that night and award prizes for the best costume. He drives into town to buy a bunch of cheap Halloween outfits while the kids start decorating the house. By nightfall the party is going strong, with everyone wearing a different costume. The Ghost ventures out and meanders through the crowd. Meanwhile, Nita and her gang of delinquents shows up. Nita challenges Lois to another drag race to try to even the score. Even though Lois risks suspension from the club, she won't back off from Nita's challenge. The gals hop into their crates and take off for a wild late-night ride.

By the time Lois returns—triumphant—it's close to midnight. Hendry and Stan slip away from the festivities and comb the house from top to bottom, looking for what Hendry calls "the Ghost's sanctuary." They can't find it, so they appeal to Dave's wondrous, all-knowing, all-seeing auto, which he has dubbed Amelia. "Is the house haunted?" Stan wants to know.

"Y-e-s-s-s," croaks the car engine. (We assume it's the engine. What other part of a car could possibly talk?)

"Will you show us the Ghost's hideout?" Hendry asks.

"N-n-n-o-o-o-o!" (This car is a chicken!)

From the sidelines, Dave gives Amelia a direct order. It shimmies into action, unveils a telescoping rod, and drives straight into the hearth. The rod touches a concealed switch, and the fireplace spins open to reveal a control booth—just what Hendry has been looking for. He and Stan check it out and find it loaded down with gadgets, microphones, and electrical apparatus. To Hendry, this proves that the Dragstrip Hollow Ghost is not a real spook, but an ordinary human being playing tricks on visitors for his own purposes.

Hendry turns to the party-goers and announces, "Now for the best costume award. Everybody take your masks off."

There's one costumed creep who seems to be slinking away, so Hendry rushes over and lifts up the mask. Inside is Paul Blaisdell.

The crowd gasps. Who is this man? He looks familiar, somehow.

Blaisdell whimpers, "Y-you spoiled everything, you monster."

"I knew I had seen you before," gloats Hendry, recalling the sound of the scream he heard last night.

"Of course you've seen me before," cries the monster-maker. "I scared you to death—to death—in *Day the World Ended*. You shivered when you saw me in *The She-Creature*. (Sniffle.) Oh, the shame of it, the indignity, they didn't use me in *Horrors of the Black Museum* after my years of faithful service. (Sob.) They just discarded me." Blaisdell notices a girl dressed in a Halloween costume that almost matches his Dragstrip Hollow getup scale-for-scale. "What picture did you work in?" he asks innocently.

As the band cranks up another tune, she chases Paul away from the house. All seems well, until the real Ghost of Old John Abernathy the First walks through the crowd and out the front door. "The rock 'n' roll got rid of him!" chirps Alfonso.

With the house finally exorcised of haunts, the party rages on. As the closing credits assure us, it's *The Endest, Man*.

Audiences were probably glad it was "The Endest" because *The Ghost of Dragstrip Hollow* was not only the worst of Paul Blaisdell's monster movies, it was very nearly the worst picture American International ever released. Sloppily staged and executed, the film has stood the test of time extraordinarily poorly. Rusoff's plotline wandered all over the place without really going anywhere, the jokes were lame, the acting was horrid, the photography was flat, and the rock 'n' roll was, well, at least most of it was in tune. (All of the recording artists featured in the picture were signed to AIP's own record label, American International Records. As far as can be determined, a sound-track album was never released.)

The last time Blaisdell's She-Creature costume had been seen on the screen—in the 1957 *Voodoo Woman*—it had been partially concealed by a burlap dress and most of the accouterments had been removed. For *The Ghost of Dragstrip Hollow* Blaisdell performed a mastectomy on the creature-costume, in effect changing its sex. (Without those double-barreled knock-ers, "Cuddles" definitely looked more male than female.) The wings, fins, horns, dorsal fins, and tail had already been removed, and now Paul took out the lunch-hooks from the abdominal cavity as well. Newly cut pieces of block foam were used to fill in the gaps to maintain the jigsaw pattern of the mon-ster's skin. The hands Paul had created for *Voodoo Woman* were reused for *Dragstrip Hollow*, but the monster feet were changed to sneakers. Although the Ghost's feet were seen only fleetingly in the film, neither Blaisdell nor the filmmakers tried to hide the sneakers from the audience because this mon-ster, after all, was merely a human being in disguise.

The original headpiece of the She-Creature, last seen hanging on a wall in *How to Make a Monster*, was changed radically for *The Ghost of Dragstrip Hollow*. Most of the plastic tubing that made up the hair was removed, and a new rubber latex appliance resembling a cross between a bat's wing and a fish fin was bonded to the center of the forehead, where it tapered back to the crown of the head. The bottom two antennae were removed, and the top antennae were bent backwards so that they touched the ears, which remained the same. The fangs were taken out and replaced by two single protruding canine teeth, the decorative "circular-saw neckpiece" was removed; and the black, shiny eyes were repainted stark white.

It took about ten days to patch up the suit and get it into shape for filming. After all the changes were made, the suit was repainted. But instead of carefully airbrushing the latex, adding highlights here and there to bring out the detail, Paul literally "slopped the paint on" with a brush, according to Bob Burns. This tended to fill in the creases and crevices of the foam padding that made up the jigsaw pattern, so that the costume took on more of a stiff, "hardened" appearance, giving the scales a shell-like texture. The repainted costume had a blue-green hue, whereas the original She-Creature was more of a sea-green color. When Paul was finished altering the creature's appear-ance, it looked more like a cousin to the She-Creature than anything else. "He really hated to make the changes to the She-Creature head, because it was one of his favorites," revealed Burns. "I think that's why Paul didn't take the same care with *The Ghost of Dragstrip Hollow* that he did on the other films, in terms of making the suit look as good as possible."

Making the eyes "blink" on camera involved the use of tiny lights attached to the headpiece at the corner of each eye. Connecting wires ran around the head and down the back of the costume to a portable battery. At the director's cue Blaisdell switched the battery on and off, causing the lights to flash. The low-wattage bulbs provided just enough light to reflect off the white paint of the Ghost's plastic eyeballs. With Blaisdell stationed in a darkened hallway or closetlike secret entrance of the mansion, the flashing lights made it appear that the creature was opening and closing its eyes. The effect worked remarkably well.

The blinking eyes were the only special effect Blaisdell built into the Dragstrip Hollow Ghost, but director William Hole was much more open to suggestions for trick shots such as the blinking eyes. Had he been at the helm of *The She-Creature* or *Invasion of the Saucer Men*, there is little doubt that the attributes Blaisdell had built into those costumes, such as the lunch hooks, the slapping tail, and the seeing-eye hand, would have been featured more in the final cut of the film.

The filming of *The Ghost of Dragstrip Hollow* turned out to be much less arduous than was the case for most of AIP's other films. It was made in seven days. The director didn't want Paul to swim out in the ocean or have the monster do things it wasn't capable of, no one came down with the flu, no one asked just who the hell Blaisdell was, and no one asked him to change the size of the creature's cranium. The only objection Paul had to the picture came during the showdown, when the Ghost's identity was revealed. Hole wanted Blaisdell to act just the opposite of his movie monsters. Instead of coming on strong with a big, booming voice, he wanted Paul shrunk down inside the costume, speaking like a browbeaten worm in a whiny voice that sounded as if it had "loser" written all over it.

Bob Burns still finds the film disturbing:

> I can't stand to watch the end of that picture because it really was prophetic. The lines they gave Paul hit too close to home. It wasn't ad-libbed; that's exactly how it was written in Lou Rusoff's script. While they were making it, I don't think anyone was really conscious that an era was ending. And I don't think Paul realized at the time he made the film just how true those lines he recited would turn out to be. In a way, AIP really did discard him. *The Ghost of Dragstrip Hollow* was his last movie, and it saddens me to watch him reciting those lines of dialogue, all in the spirit of good fun, in the spirit of just making one more monster movie, and never knowing that they were really through with him. I think later on Paul realized what had happened, and probably felt that, in a way, they were making fun of him. I mean, what Lou Rusoff wrote in that script was just too true to life. He had made all these pictures for AIP, and they didn't use him in *Horrors of the Black Museum* or anything else that came out after that. It's really terrible to watch.

By the time Paul went to work on *The Ghost of Dragstrip Hollow* Bob Burns had been drafted into the army. He was stationed in San Antonio, Texas, where he did some television appearances at the local CBS affiliate. Having picked up the rudiments of monster-making from Blaisdell over the years, Burns was able to construct his own budget monster costumes and props, which he put to good use at CBS. Like most other big-city stations across the U.S., Channel 9 in San Antonio was running Universal's syndicated "Shock Theatre" package of fright films, and Burns would turn up during *Shock*'s commercial breaks, taunting the viewers with wisecracks about the movies while wearing one of his newly made costumes. "If they were running *Werewolf of London* or one of Lon Chaney, Jr.'s Wolfman pictures, then I'd come out dressed as a werewolf," Burns explained. "If they ran a mummy movie, I'd come out wearing a mummy costume. It was pretty straightforward stuff, but it went a long way toward keeping me sane while I was in the army."

It was while Burns was in San Antonio that he heard about Paul's latest film project. Blaisdell often sent his friend "care" packages of monster-related goodies, including photos from the latest films being made at AIP. Burns opened a package from "Cuddles" and, seeing the 8x10 glossy photo of Paul in his Dragstrip Hollow Ghost garb, figured that AIP was making a sequel to *The She-Creature*. Paul's accompanying letter disabused him of that notion pretty quickly, however. "If you get a chance to see this stinker on base, don't tell anybody you know me," Blaisdell pleaded. Burns could only shake his head when he found out Paul had pulled Cuddles's costume out of mothballs once more at Sam Arkoff's request.

The Ghost of Dragstrip Hollow was panned by both the critics and the public. The fans thought they deserved better. Within a year AIP would reply by giving them better movies, but audiences wouldn't be seeing Paul Blaisdell any more. At least not for a long while, and never again on the silver screen.

Blaisdell at least had some kind words for Jim Nicholson:

> I never thought *The Ghost of Dragstrip Hollow* was as bad as most people seemed to think. Hell, there were lots worse pictures made, but some of the critics sounded like Judith Crist, that snotty critic who reviewed films for *TV Guide*. If the critics could have seen some of the budgets we had to work with, they would've flipped. And if they had been film producers trying to work with those kinds of budgets ... forget it.
>
> One thing that Jim Nicholson tried to do at AIP was keep in mind Shakespeare's axiom of "a simple story, simply told." That was a general kind of motto, if you will, for all of the AIP films, and Jim tried to make sure that his producers and directors and, really, just about everybody involved with motion pictures at AIP in those days kept that motto in mind day by day. If you think back on it and look at some of the pictures that were made at American International, you've got to admit that they tried. And in spite of all the work I did myself on the monster designs for those pictures, I wouldn't have looked half as interesting if I hadn't had the help of a helluva lot of good teammates, both on stage and off.

13

Beyond the B's

Young people didn't want monster movies anymore. They wanted movies that they were more oriented to—beaching, surfing, stuff like that. The whole style changed. And styles do change. They change in the motion picture industry just like they do anywhere else. You went from something like *Day the World Ended* to something like *The Ghost of Dragstrip Hollow*. It became a comedy, a semimusical, it started featuring young people more and more, and finally you went to movies like *Beach Party* and stuff like that. Little by little, the monster movie was phased out.

—Paul Blaisdell

American International didn't stop making scary movies as society entered the turbulent new times of the 1960s; it just started making them differently. The new science-fiction and horror productions were more colorful and enjoyed healthier budgets. Pictures like *The Angry Red Planet* and *House of Usher* took the place of *It Conquered the World* and *How to Make a Monster*. The days of the humanoid monsters at which Blaisdell excelled were dying. They wouldn't return for almost twenty years, until 1979, when *Alien* single-handedly resurrected the entire monster movie genre.

But AIP expected to keep Blaisdell employed. It had a number of exciting projects on the drawing board—bigger-budgeted, full-color productions that held the promise of new work, new horizons. George Worthing Yates, who had worked with Bert I. Gordon and wrote *The Spider, Attack of the Puppet People*, and *War of the Colossal Beast*, was now a head producer at AIP. Yates had been playing around with a story idea that combined space travel and time travel with early American colonialists who are discovered living in the future on Mars. These "Martians" decide it's high-time to return to Earth and take possession of the motherland. A futuristic war breaks out between two peoples descended from the same stock, each battling it out for interplanetary supremacy.

Jim Nicholson asked Paul to do a series of concept sketches for the film. "I consulted with George, I consulted with Nick, and I went to work on the production illustrations," Blaisdell recalled. "Everyone was happy with them because I had designed things in such a way that nobody in the prop department or the costume department would have any trouble reproducing them down to the last detail." Some of the sketches were done in full color because AIP's new sci-fi extravaganza was going to be filmed in color and wide-screen. Many of Paul's illustrations depicted futuristic kinds of fighting equipment such as atomic-powered guns, nuclear tanks, and enormous machines that would be used to take over the world.

AIP had been doing coproductions with England for several years now, releasing pictures like *Cat Girl*, *The Headless Ghost*, and *Circus of Horrors*, and before long it would import Mario Bava's directorial debut, *Black Sunday*, as well as a host of Italian-made, sword-and-sandal fantasy epics, including a series of Goliath films. There was even a Danish deal for a picture called *Reptilicus*. Japanese coproductions were just around the corner, with pictures like *Godzilla vs. the Thing* (*Godzilla vs. Mothra*) and *Destroy All Monsters* from Toho studios. The film written by Yates was to be the first such Japanese coproduction. "Contracts were drawn up, and everybody seemed happy with the arrangements," said Blaisdell. But the picture was never made, and Paul never found out why. He later commented:

> The way George wrote it, and the way I discussed it with him, this wasn't going to be just a science-fiction "slam-banger" with ray guns; it involved the psychology of a people that had remained in the same environment versus people who had learned to live with a harsh environment. It was more like a Ray Bradbury story, in spite of all the things that I designed for it. George really wrote a little feeling into it, and of course I did the Buck Rogers bit, but that was just the trimming. Although, frankly—I'm not going to put myself down—I thought the trimmings looked pretty darned good. Unfortunately, no one ever got to see them.

AIP had already registered the projected film's title as *In the Year 2889*. Rather than discard that title after the production was canceled (Arkoff couldn't stand the thought of paying for something and not using it), AIP slapped it on a completely different picture made a few years later by hack director Larry Buchanan. (Buchanan's tenuous connection to Paul Blaisdell is discussed in Chapter 15.)

Another picture American International had on the production slate was *Strato-Fin*. By this time AIP had already released Roger Corman's *House of Usher* and *The Pit and the Pendulum*, as well as a bigger-budgeted picture called *Master of the World*, which was actually a combined adaptation of Jules Verne's "Robur the Conqueror" and "Master of the World." The returns on these new productions were better than Arkoff and Nicholson could have imagined, and now they were thinking big. *Strato-Fin* was going to expand on the central idea of *Master of the World* by turning its flying airship into a submersible as well. According to Blaisdell, the concept of the film was supplied by two young men who were trying to break into the film business.

A cutaway view of Paul Blaisdell's model for AIP's unmade fantasy film, *Strato-Fin*. Interestingly enough, a few years after AIP scuttled the project, the Toho Company of Japan produced a picture using a very similar concept called *Atragon* (courtesy of Bob Burns).

"They had the help of an artist friend of theirs, and they commissioned Jackie and I to make a three-dimensional model of the Strato-Fin," said Blaisdell. "It was really a kind of rocket-submarine that was capable of going underwater, sailing on the surface, or soaring clear into outer space." In fact, Jackie did most of the work on the model, which was sculpted out of pine and balsa wood. Blaisdell thought the finished product resembled nothing so much as an enormous shark. "It was sleek and gray, complete with a gray topside and white underbelly," he described, "and when it 'came to life' it released rockets and guided missiles."

Paul also designed a second version of the Strato-Fin model which could be photographed underwater. "It was done with a light box and a smaller model of the ship. It was very detailed and looked really nice," he said, "but the whole time we were designing it I kept thinking to myself, this just ain't gonna fly. Let's face it, undersea submarines that turn into rocketships are as old as *Flash Gordon* and Big-Little Books. There was really nothing new about it, except the concept that it would look like a shark." In fact, AIP pulled the plug on *Strato-Fin* before it got off the launching pad, but at least Paul and Jackie got paid for the work they put into the project. They even got to keep the finished models for their own collection after AIP decided to abandon the film.

A few years later, AIP did in fact coproduce a film with Toho that was strikingly similar in concept to *Strato-Fin*. Entitled *Atragon*, this 1965 release concerned an ancient underwater civilization that wages war with modern man. Japanese scientists develop a super rocket-submarine that can fly, float, dive, and burrow underground, and it becomes the "nuclear weapon" that ends the amphibious assault once and for all. All the trademarks of *Strato-Fin* were there. Blaisdell never saw the Japanese film but admitted the concept sounded suspiciously similar to the picture he was supposed to work on.

On the Italian front, AIP began importing a series of sword-and-sandal fantasies to cash in on the strong-man phenomenon that had sprung up with the U.S. release of *Hercules* and *Hercules Unchained*, starring Steve Reeves. AIP named their muscle man Goliath, and he appeared in the guises of Mark Forest and Gordon Scott in pictures like *Goliath and the Vampires* and *Goliath and the Sins of Babylon*. Jim Nicholson asked Blaisdell to produce a concept painting for the first in the series, *Goliath and the Dragon* (1960). Paul, not knowing that the title character would be played by Mark Forest, based the look of his barbarian on the face of Steve Reeves. His green-scaled behemoth, with its razor-edged fins, fangs, snakelike eyes, and horned "sideburns," combined elements of traditional dragon designs with typical "Blaisdellian" features that made the creature uniquely his own.

Goliath and the Dragon proved popular enough to generate two sequels, but Blaisdell was involved with neither. He did do a production illustration for another straightforward fantasy film, this one inspired by the success of Ray Harryhausen's 1958 classic, *The Seventh Voyage of Sinbad*. While Harryhausen was busy working on a follow-up (*Jason and the Argonauts*), the young Jim Danforth, a very talented stop-motion animator in his own right who suffered through years of perpetual obscurity in Harryhausen's shadow, brought to life the fantasy figures of *Jack the Giant Killer* (1962). Although it was condemned by many as a blatant rip-off of the earlier Harryhausen film (Kerwin Matthews and Torin Thatcher appeared in both pictures as the hero and villain respectively, and Nathan Juran directed the films), no one could argue the fact that *Jack the Giant Killer* held its own when it came to stop-motion effects. Blaisdell was brought on board to deliver several concept sketches for the film's fantasy figures, such as the double-headed giant, but the studio had also commissioned artwork from Marcel Delgado and Wah Chang. Delgado, of course, was most famous as the designer of *King Kong*. Chang had cut his teeth on low-budget pictures like *The Black Scorpion* and would eventually create some of television's most memorable monsters in episodes of *The Outer Limits* and the original *Star Trek*. In the end, Delgado's and Chang's designs for *Jack the Giant Killer* won out over Blaisdell's.

At least Blaisdell was well paid for his work:

> Speaking of the production stuff I did for *Jack the Giant Killer* and *Goliath and the Dragon* and one or two other pictures in the 1960s, those paychecks ended up being bigger than I ever thought they were supposed to. Did someone fall asleep in the bookkeeping department? Did somebody fail to communicate with somebody else? I dunno, all I can tell you is what I was advised in my early movie days—"Don't ask questions, Paul, just grab your money and run like hell."

Blaisdell did a number of production sketches for motion pictures in the early 1960s, including this concept painting for the Italian-made *Goliath and the Dragon* (courtesy of Bob Burns).

During the early 1960s, Paul had maintained an ongoing correspondence with Bob Burns, who was still stationed in Texas and nearing the end of his tenure with the army. In several letters Paul mysteriously referred to a "Project X," which was actually the aborted original version of *In the Year 2889*. There was another "special" project that Blaisdell was about to get involved in, however, a little something called *Out of This World*, which would have the distinction of marking American International's debut in television. The concept, as Jim Nicholson explained it to Blaisdell, was that *Out of This World* would be much like an hour-long mini-movie shown once a week in syndication. There would be no continuing characters; the tales would be totally unconnected except for their preoccupation with the unnatural, like ABC's *The Outer Limits*. Nor would there be a host in the tradition of Rod Serling's *The Twilight Zone* or Boris Karloff's *Thriller*, each episode of *Out of This World* would stand or fall on its own merits.

Nicholson wanted Blaisdell involved with *Out of This World* from the beginning. Paul was to be responsible for all sorts of effects, from miniature work to full-bodied monster outfits. It sounded like an exciting project. AIP was expanding its production schedule and beginning to make different types of movies for a broader range of audiences. It was only natural that it should expand into television as well.

But *Out of This World* never got past the conceptual stage. It was talked about a great deal, and everyone was geared up to do it, but somewhere along the line someone (probably Sam Arkoff) decided it was too risky a venture. The projected series was quietly killed, and with it went the promise of solid, long-term employment for Blaisdell. Instead of making a TV series, AIP's new television subsidiary decided to finance a series of ultracheap independent films, produced solely to inflate the "Chiller" and "The World Beyond" creature-feature packages. Blaisdell was never involved in an AIT (American International Television) production.*

There was another TV series AIP wanted to do that was called *Beyond the Barriers of Space*. This was to have been a more traditional sci-fi show, with continuing characters and interconnected storylines à la *Star Trek* or *The X-Files*. The science-fiction theme of the show would encompass faster-than-light time travel, alien civilizations, and mutiny in outer space. AIP paid Blaisdell to do a full-color painting for its *Beyond the Barriers of Space* promotional brochure, which was used to help sell the idea for the series to prospective backers and commercial time buyers.

Although *Beyond the Barriers of Space* was one more project that never got beyond the preproduction stage, a couple of the series' basic ideas turned up in a low-budget feature released by AIP called *Beyond the Time Barrier*. Directed by Edgar G. Ulmer, the man responsible for the 1935 version of *The Black Cat* starring Boris Karloff and Bela Lugosi, the film circumvented its low-budget heritage with brisk pacing and an interesting story line. But how many of the film's plot threads were unraveled from projected synopses of *Beyond the Barriers of Space*? At this point there is no way of knowing, but since AIP would never abandon an idea it had paid for, it clearly seems possible that *Beyond the Time Barrier* was cobbled together from discarded drafts of the projected TV series.

Blaisdell later commented on some of the changes taking place at AIP:

> Jim Nicholson was the artistic half of American International Pictures, and Arkoff was the business half. Jim had teenaged children of his own, and he liked to get together with them and pal around with them and talk to them about movies because Jim was a movie buff himself. He would always ask them what they would most want to see in movies. And he really listened to them. He did not go on down the same old tired line, making detective movies that would bore you to death and stuff like that. Nick was very astute and very responsive to what the kids wanted to see, and he acted accordingly. And me being half-juvenile myself, I kinda liked the idea too, so I went along with it.
>
> Now then, when it came time for a change, which happened around 1960 or 1961 for AIP, that was because Jim was still listening to his kids. They were still telling him what they wanted to see, but their tastes were changing, as was most of society's at that time. I really think we all were getting fed up

---

Blaisdell did have a kind of peripheral connection to some of the pictures produced by American International's television subsidiary, however. Details appear in Chapter 15.

with the cold war type of movie and thinking about building bomb shelters in the backyard and wondering how soon the world was going to come to an end. And I honestly believe that's one reason why AIP began making different kinds of pictures. The Poe movies, for example, were so gothic and so far removed from the average person's experiences, they were more fantasies than horrors. So it was all right to move in that direction because the audience didn't have to think about what was going on in the Soviet Union or China or even in the U.S. They [AIP] didn't abandon science-fiction altogether— they still made the occasional thriller like *Panic in Year Zero*—but those pictures were few and far between anymore. It was nothing like when they first started out, making pictures like *Day the World Ended*.

With the continued diversification of its film product, AIP offered less and less work to Paul Blaisdell. Although the dialogue of his cameo in *The Ghost of Dragstrip Hollow* probably didn't seem particularly prophetic just yet, by 1962 Paul couldn't help but notice that the types of movies he had been making for American International and other film companies were fast disappearing. Only five years earlier he had segued from one picture to another with barely a break in between. With *Voodoo Woman*, *The Amazing Colossal Man*, *Invasion of the Saucer Men*, and *Attack of the Puppet People* all produced in 1957 alone, Paul and Jackie had their hands more than full. Now there were only minor assignments and periodic requests for production illustrations. Neither of them could know that the future held more spare time than anything else, but as the months crept by with less and less work coming their way, at some point the Blaisdells must have realized that the glory days were already behind them.

But Paul still happily involved himself in his own personal projects. With more free time on his hands than ever before, he began work on a brand-new type of monster of his own invention. It wasn't a foam rubber or latex costume, it wasn't a hand-puppet, it wasn't a stop-motion model, and it wasn't a figure controlled by wires. Yet it could "act" in front of a camera in 15- and 20-second takes. Perfecting this creature was taking a long time, longer than Paul had anticipated, but in the end it would be worth it. Bob Burns had finally come home from the army, and Paul was eager to introduce him to the newest fiend of the family.

14

Black and White
and Bled All Over

I never thought horror movies or monster movies could be harmful to the younger members of our society as long as the parents of the youngsters had the intelligence to teach them the difference between enjoying fantasy and living in reality. If I had, believe me, I would never have gotten involved with producing a magazine like *Fantastic Monsters*, which we knew from the beginning was going to be read mostly by kids.

—*Paul Blaisdell*

As soon as Bob Burns got back to California, he got in touch with his old friend and made a date to drop by Blaisdell's reclusive Topanga Canyon homestead. The first night they got together, time seemed to contract; the years between visits melted away like the wax skin of Aunt Esmerelda in *How to Make a Monster*. There was a lot to catch up on, and the four of them— Paul, Bob, Jackie, and Kathy—stayed up almost until dawn shooting the breeze.

Burns had brought with him several of the latest monster movie magazines. That field was expanding almost exponentially. After *Famous Monsters* made its debut in February 1958, the first wave of would-be usurpers appeared: *World Famous Creatures, Monster Parade, Monsters & Things*. Now there was a second wave of monsterzines edging into *FM*'s terror-tory: *Horror Monsters, Mad Monsters, Thriller, Monster Madness, Modern Monsters, Monster Party, Shriek!*, and the only worthwhile competitor, *Castle of Frankenstein*. Blaisdell thumbed through the lot of them. "Hell, we could do better than these guys," he snorted.

Burns had to agree. Most of the new monster film magazines were poorly researched, lazily written periodicals barely worth their 35¢ or 50¢ cover prices. "We could do one so much better. Give the fans real information about movie making," Burns suggested. Neither of them pursued the idea further just then, but that night Burns kept mulling over the idea of starting their own publication. Was it possible? The following day he called Paul to ask,

"Were you serious last night when you said we should publish our own magazine?"

Blaisdell admitted he had made the statement half in jest. True, he thought the field was overrun by mediocrity, but he had never given much thought to actually trying to publish something of his own.

Burns had. "Let's think about this some more, Paul."

In fact, they both thought about it a lot more, and finally they decided to do something about it, as Burns later explained:

> What we wanted to do with *Fantastic Monsters* was to give the readers the "inside dope" on movie-making. We wanted it to be a "behind-the-scenes" kind of thing, and that of course was what Paul was good at, and what he was going to write about. But the printer [who helped finance the magazine and thus was able to call at least some of the shots] wanted a more traditional kind of magazine. We weren't going to call it *Fantastic Monsters*; our title was *Fantastic Films*. But it had to have the word *monster* in the title or it wouldn't get distributed, so that's how it became *Fantastic Monsters of the Films*.

Once Burns and Blaisdell decided they were going to tackle the magazine project for real, they started getting themselves psyched up for it. There were dozens of meetings at Paul's house that lasted late into the night—sometimes all night—with Jackie serving round-the-clock doses of coffee to keep the guys on their toes. Both of them were determined to avoid the pitfalls that plagued most of the other monster fan magazines. One thing they decided early on was not to use too many puns or funny captions underneath the photos. Both Paul and Bob felt that the genre deserved a modicum of respect, and up to now it hadn't been getting any. Why publish a magazine that was going to make fun of its own subject matter?

But in fact, humor became an integral part of the magazine's prescription for success. By confining the humor to specific pages or articles, they could continue to talk about the films they were going to cover thoughtfully and respectfully. The magazine would end up with single- and double-page humor pieces with titles like "Dead Time Tales" and "How to Become a Vampire Victim in One Easy Lesson." "Dead Time Tales" were the ever-popular photos with funny captions (the Marvel Comics Group had begun publishing a magazine called *Monsters to Laff With* that was nothing but captioned photos), but "Vampire Victim" was a refreshingly perverse twist on the usual puns and gags. With obvious faith in the intelligence of their audience, the authors invited their readers to push two straight pins through the life-size fangs of a vampire's portrait ("make sure the sharp points are facing you") and slowly bring the magazine toward their necks ("all the while moaning and groaning softly, for effect").* Then, "quick like a bunny, jab the page into your neck."

*The vampire was Baron Meinster (David Peel) in Hammer Films' 1960 classic, Brides of Dracula.

"Wasn't that fun?" the editors snickered. "Try it on the members of your family. They'll die laughing." Obviously, this magazine was going to offer something a wee bit different.

Most of the editorial content was of a serious nature. Blaisdell didn't want to be an editor, but he knew what the magazine should look like, and he knew what he wanted to see in it. He and Burns were determined to give their readers more than mere fantasy fluff; they were going to provide facts and behind-the-scenes information for the serious film student, while making sure to provide plenty of pictures for the small fry who thrived on portraits of messed-up faces and bogeymen.

Still, there was more to it than facts, figures, faces, and funny stuff. To give their magazine an edge of sophistication over the competition, Paul and Bob outlined a plan to acquire material from respected writers in the fantasy fiction field like the late Robert Bloch, who had begun writing stories of suspense and horror in the 1920s and 1930s under the epistolary tutelage of the twentieth century's foremost master of the macabre, H. P. Lovecraft (1890–1937).

Short stories by established genre authors would go a long way toward beefing up the magazine's text, but Blaisdell and Burns wanted to do something similar for the pictorials. The obvious thing to have done with pictures would have been to print them in color, but a full-color layout would have been prohibitively expensive. As it was, the magazine was going to carry a premium cover price of 50¢, and the only other publications that cost that much were special hundred-page editions of *Famous Monsters*. Eventually it was decided to tint some of the photos, which would at least give the magazine a unique look and sense of novelty. Lastly, they decided to make the first issue of the magazine a little extra-special by including a "giant full-color pinup." If *Playboy* could have girlie foldouts, why couldn't they have ghoulie foldouts?

Blaisdell wanted the first monster pinup to be the Karloff monster from James Whale's 1931 *Frankenstein*. But no matter how hard they searched, a color photo just didn't seem to exist. Finally it was decided to make the She-Creature the pinup because Paul had several outstanding color transparencies of the costume on hand.

Once the direction and overall content of the magazine had been decided, Bob hired two writers named Ron Haydock and Jim Harmon to do most of the article writing. Blaisdell was going to write a how-to piece on making a film monster; Burns would write and help with layout. By the time everyone had finished their assignments, the name of the magazine had been changed—not once, but twice, as Bob Burns later noted:

> The very first idea Paul had was to do a magazine called *The Devil's Work-shop*. He was going to exploit his own talents and techniques, and basically it was going to be a magazine about how to create your own monsters and

props and things like that. Eventually we realized this was too narrow a focus, so we changed the name to *Fantastic Films* and made "The Devil's Work-shop" a column in the magazine. Then the printer came in and said, "well, you have to put 'monster' in the title; otherwise it won't sell." So that's how it became *Fantastic Monsters of the Films.*

Most of the monster magazines of the 1960s featured artwork by staff artists—some good, some not so good—on the cover. Blaisdell obviously could have provided *Fantastic Monsters* (or *FanMo*, as the readers soon nicknamed it) with original cover art, but he and Burns both preferred to use photographs of the real thing. Sitting side-by-side with the competition, *FanMo* theoretically would "jump out" at the newsstand browser—provided, of course, that Paul and Bob were able to get hold of some pretty nifty color photographs.

As it happened, Burns had in his possession a clear, sharp color slide of Christopher Lee in all his sanguinary fury from Hammer Films' *Horror of Dracula.* Surprisingly, an actual publicity photo of the snarling, crimson-eyed, bloody-lipped countenance of the Count didn't exist. Burns had lucked into the shot when a 35mm print of the movie being shown on his army base broke at a crucial point in the film. Burns extracted a frame from the film's famous library scene and kept it in his collection for several years until it ended up being used as the cover of the first issue of *Fantastic Monsters.*

No matter how much time and sweat was put into it, the magazine couldn't have existed without the financial support of the printer. Getting a national magazine written, laid out, typeset, printed, and distributed cost big bucks. Without outside advertising to subsidize the expenses involved, such a magazine could have easily cost as much to produce as an early AIP film. (For comparison, it cost approximately $45,000 to produce an issue of *Famous Monsters* in the early 1980s. *FanMo* was printed on better paper than *FM*, had tinted photographs, and a full-color pinup.) To get *Fantastic Monsters* off the drawing board and onto newsstands across the country, Bob Burns anted up $6,000 of his own savings; Blaisdell sunk in more than double that amount. The rest of the bill was absorbed by the printer, an unnamed individual who operated out of Iowa. *FanMo* was the printer's only national publication; all the other titles published by his outfit were regional and local titles—an important point to keep in mind as the *Fantastic Monsters* drama unfolds.

With editorial assistance from Jim Harmon and Ron Haydock, Burns and Blaisdell finally got the premiere issue of their fantasy film magazine completed. One of the last things to be readied for the printer was the She-Creature poster. For this, they used a color photo taken of the costume outside of Blaisdell's home before the film went into production. For some reason the laboratory that made the transparency for the printer could never seem to deliver a sharply focused image. When Blaisdell saw the lab work, he exploded. The content of the first issue was due to be shipped to the printer in just a few days, and they had no satisfactory color shot of the She-Creature.

With a deadline staring them in the face, Blaisdell decided to touch up the photo with an airbrush to get rid of the unfocused edges. All the detailing in the costume, especially in the face, had been lost. Painting in the minutia would be too troublesome, and besides, anyone who saw the photo would realize they weren't looking at the real thing. In exasperation he decided to accentuate the individual features. This is how the She-Creature ended up with pouting, full-bodied, blood-red lips in her *FanMo* debut. Blaisdell later described the incident:

> The foldout photo of the She-Creature was from a photo Bob Burns took of me on the Alpine suspension bridge in front of [my home] studio, right after *The She-Creature* was finished. He did it with a flash gun and how in the hell both of us managed to stand still on that crazy bridge, I'll never know. Considering the circumstances, it wasn't bad at all. Unfortunately, the guy in the agency didn't seem to know how to enlarge a 35mm to an 11"×14" print. His developing technique made it look like a bleached bedsheet. That's when I had to snatch the proof and lay on the airbrush, like I was painting a billboard. No time to be artistic—the printer was snapping at my heels with a deadline. (P.S.—We made it.)

The first issue of *Fantastic Monsters of the Films* hit newsstands early in 1962. The startling *Horror of Dracula* cover wrapped around to a full-color, photo-montage back cover, which included a rare color shot of Blaisdell's original sculpture of Little Hercules from *The Beast with a Million Eyes*. There were also color stills from a recent Bert I. Gordon fantasy called *The Magic Sword* (another film with giant monsters) and a duo-tone photo of Blaisdell himself as Count Downe, a character created as a kind of mascot for the "Tombstone Times," a hodgepodge of information, pictures, artwork, and humor set up in a newspaper format.

Behind the cover were the first "colorized" (tinted) interior pages ever seen in an American horror movie magazine. Hot pink, lemon yellow, aquamarine, and sky blue hues hit the reader full in the face as the pages were turned. Articles on vampire movies, the "Eye of the Beholder" episode of *The Twilight Zone*, the Wolfman of Lon Chaney, Jr., prehistoric monster movies, and Bob Burns's look at two science-fiction classics, *The Day the Earth Stood Still* and *Destination Moon*, rounded out a diverse and impressive first issue. In terms of fiction, Jim Harmon contributed a short shocker called "The Two-Tale Heart," and Robert Bloch was represented by "Black Lotus."

Blaisdell's contributions to the first issue of the magazine were inspired. He wrote an article called "Dawn Age Beasts," which was an overview of prehistoric monster movies, and he captioned the photos and wrote text for "Horrors of Hollywood," which focused on Glenn Strange's portrayal of the Frankenstein Monster in Universal's *Abbott & Costello Meet Frankenstein*. But Blaisdell's best feature was "The Devil's Workshop." Here he outlined the process by which he had created *The Beast with a Million Eyes*, writing earnestly and straightforwardly and illustrating his text with never-before-seen photos of Little Hercules in various stages of completion. Blaisdell even took the opportunity to explain why his monster seemed to be missing 999,998 orbs. It was the first time the mystery of the "slave monster" had been explained in print.

Blaisdell also had some good moments in both the "Tombstone Times" and "Monster of the Month" featurettes. The latter, with its luscious, rainbow-color rendition of the She-Creature, was like nothing that had ever appeared before in a monster magazine. Included with the foldout poster was a bit of behind-the-scenes information about the making of the film—the kind of article, however brief, that would endear this publication to a generation of fantasy fans.

Count Downe (Paul in high-collared cape and stenciled-in widow's peak), the "epitaph editor," was a character cooked up by Blaisdell and Bob Burns for the magazine's newspaper spoof. It was in this section that readers' questions were answered (in the initial installment, questions were selected from personal correspondence or filtered through the fan grapevine). Other departments included "Slaymate of the Month" and "Haunt Ads," no-cost classified ads for fans who were looking for posters, comics, books, and film-related items. (*Famous Monsters* also ran a "Haunt Ads" section which fulfilled the same function.) Above the legend "Slaymate of the Month" was a photograph of none other than "monster makeup fan" Lionel Comport of Burbank, California. Lionel, of course, was the poor devil who had lost his eyelashes to the evil Count Downe some years earlier. Blaisdell also included a "Ghoulden Opportunity" announcement in the "Tombstone Times," inviting readers to become a "noose reporter" by sending in articles, artwork, and photographs concerning their own monster fan activities.

Like *Famous Monsters*, outside advertising in *FanMo* was virtually nil. Items advertised for sale in the magazine were sold through a company called "Castle Dracula" in Topanga, California. Of course, Paul and Jackie were the proprietors of this particular castle. Paul and Bob Burns rounded up a number of items they thought would appeal to the readership of the magazine, including the Mad Lab Radio. ("It appears to be one of those little imported transistor radios, but just turn it 'on.' Wow! The dummy speaker flips to one side and a 'killer shrew' jumps out with a wild squeal!"). Other items offered were the Mad Lab Hypo ("Life size! 8 inches fully extended!") and Mr. Bones, the Pocket Skeleton ("Even *feels* creepy!"). In each of these cases, Blaisdell set the 'scene' and Jackie took the photograph. Typically, Blaisdell opted to create elaborate backgrounds for photos of some of the mail-order items, which usually sold for a dollar or two. The Mad Lab Camera rested on a table with a background of test tubes and coiled wires, and Mr. Bones sat on a miniature coffin next to a realistically detailed tree with a gothic castle in the background. Such novelty-store staples as the Devil Spider and Unlucky 13

Rattlesnake were rigged with wires to menace a familiar female figure; the damsel in distress was actually a miniature Paul had made for *Attack of the Puppet People*.

One particularly noteworthy ad was labeled "Monster Feet": "Horribly distorted monster feet, with twisted toes and gnarled claws! Slip over your shoes, and go shuffling after friends! Feet cover entire foot and ankle! Heavy duty latex, in realistic flesh color, with black toenails and claws! Great fun for parties, or to complete your monster outfit! Wear them down the street at night, if you like screaming neighbors! Only $3.00, postpaid." A photograph depicted two different monster feet. One had big, gnarled, goofy-looking toes. The other had three toes with enormous, hooked, black nails. In fact, this triple-toed foot was the very same commercially produced monster foot that Blaisdell used in *Day the World Ended* for his Atomic Mutant. Although he customized the monster feet extensively, the origin of Marty the Mutant's footwear is at long last revealed. (But wouldn't *FanMo* have racked up better sales if they had advertised the monster foot as "the very same foot that tramped through the radioactive valley in *Day the World Ended*"?)

To break up the monotony of the ads, *FanMo* occasionally ran advertising spoofs. Underneath a picture of a menacing-looking Karloff holding a syringe (the photo was from *Black Friday*) ran the copy: "9 out of 10 doctors agree … SLAYER brings faster pain! Contented Normalcy is often caused by complete freedom from strain, minor aches, tenseness and other comforts. When you take SLAYER aspirin at bedtime, you increase your sensitivity to these sensations. Thus, SLAYER doesn't *make* you ache, it *lets* pain come *naturally*. And when you wake up you feel wonderfully miserable, with a heavy trace of the 'sedative hangover' always following a good drugged sleep. So when no discomforts are bothering you, feel pain *better* with SLAYER." This from the same minds that concocted "How to Become a Vampire Victim in One Easy Lesson" It's no wonder some parents didn't want their kids reading that "monster trash."

The masthead in the first issue of *Fantastic Monsters* listed Ron Haydock as editor; Paul Blaisdell as editorial director; Bob Burns as research editor; and Jim Harmon as associate editor. In time those credits would change significantly. Although a publishing credit was not given, Blaisdell was more or less the 'head honcho,' given that he had sunk more money into the venture than anyone. Jackie eventually gained a credit as the magazine's circulation manager, and Paul kicked himself upstairs from editorial director to managing editor to—finally—publisher. Burns retained his title of research editor throughout the life of the publication.

Most of the stills seen in *FanMo* came from Bob Burns's collection, but Blaisdell contributed some materials of his own. For the cover of the second issue, they used a superb color shot of Paul's Aunt Esmerelda mask (which burned in a flash in *How to Make a Monster*). Inside, a special article on 3-D movies included shots of Blaisdell holding the giant syringe from *The Amazing Colossal Man* along with a chess-playing Saucer Man. Both photos were double-printed in "stereo" so that readers could see the images in real 3-D using a pocket mirror. It was a complicated process, but for those who were able to follow the magazine's instructions closely, the trick worked.

Blaisdell didn't write "The Devil's Workshop" column in *FanMo* #2, but he did contribute the 3-D article and a piece on movie robots called "Diary of a Tin Can Terror." There was also the conclusion of his Glenn Strange feature from the first issue and a new Count Downe picture in the "Tombstone Times."

Reader response to the first issue's Monster of the Month foldout poster was so overwhelmingly positive that the staff decided to make it a regular feature. This month the magazine offered a color portrait of the Metaluna Mutant from *This Island Earth*. Not that Burns and Blaisdell didn't have plenty of color material on Paul's monsters, but Blaisdell was reluctant to load the magazine down with his own work for fear that readers might accuse him of using the magazine as a kind of pictorial soapbox. To their everlasting credit, neither Blaisdell nor anyone else connected with *Fantastic Monsters* trumpeted the professional credentials of its editorial director.

Paul and Bob couldn't believe the number of letters that were pouring in from all over the country. Just about everyone loved the foldout posters and interior color tints. As they had suspected, "The Devil's Workshop" became one of the magazine's most popular features, and the staff decided to accent the technical aspects of Hollywood movie-making in as many future articles as possible. Although Paul and Bob didn't learn about it until many years later, two youngsters particularly influenced by the "Workshop" series were Bob and Dennis Skotak, who grew up to become highly paid industry professionals. Their marvelous miniatures and effects have been seen by millions of moviegoers in such pictures as *Aliens, The Abyss,* and *Terminator 2: Judgment Day.* The Skotaks were very young at the time they began reading *Fantastic Monsters,* and they studiously applied the principles outlined in "The Devil's Workshop" to a variety of home horror projects. Perseverance paid off handsomely in the long run, and today the Skotaks point to Blaisdell's series of behind-the-scenes articles as their major source of inspiration when, as young monster lovers, they first began dreaming about carving a niche in Hollywood as special effects artists.

Blaisdell created an oversized membership card for readers who sent in $3.00 to join the Fantastic Monsters Club. For their money, members got the card, an 8"×10" glossy photo from *Invasion of the Saucer Men,* a periodic club bulletin, and a year's subscription to the magazine. The membership card featured drawings of several Blaisdell horrors, including Marty the Mutant from *Day the World Ended,* the *Dragstrip Hollow* version of Cuddles, Beulah and a Flying Finger from *It Conquered the World,* several Saucer Men and their flying saucer, and a curious, never-before-seen humanoid creature with a ridged scalp and stark white eyes. Just what *was* this wicked-looking thing? Readers would have a chance to find out when *Fantastic Monsters* announced its "Name the Nameless Monster Contest" in the next issue.

Unfortunately, problems were developing with the printer, as Bob Burns recalls:

> I hate to say it, but I really think we were being set up to take a fall from the beginning. If you look at the entire run of *Fantastic Monsters*, you'll notice that the printing gets worse and worse as time goes on. Paul and I couldn't understand it. What the heck was this guy doing out in Iowa? Paul would call him up and chew him out, but there was always some excuse. "Oh, well, my printer is messed up, but don't worry, I'm going to have it fixed. The next issue will look a lot better." But it never did.

The cover of *FanMo* #3 featured a gorgeous color photo of Blaisdell's Martian menace from *It! the Terror from Beyond Space*. Here at last was the original It!, the sleeker It!, the scarier It! ... It! as It! was supposed to be seen—without Ray Corrigan's massive mug stretching the latex rubber completely out of shape. Readers could now see the monster as Paul had originally designed it, without the extra set of lower fangs and with the large emerald eyes. The remarkable detailing of the mask was evident, with minute pores and age-lines running from the lidded eyes to the protruding cheekbones, all the way down to the wide, batrachian mouth. The overall effect was so different from the movie version that some readers thought it was a different monster.

Blaisdell's contributions to the third issue of *FanMo* included another installment of "The Devil's Workshop" and a short fiction piece entitled "Specimen," which he also illustrated. For this issue's "Workshop," Paul described methods for creating a homemade giant monster movie using a live reptile and miniature sets. (Undoubtedly, this was Bert I. Gordon's favorite article in the magazine.) At the time he wrote the feature, Blaisdell was keeping a female "Alligator Lizard" in a dry-dock fish tank. He named her Lizzie (what else?) and described how he got her to pose for the pictures that accompanied the article by holding food (meal worms) and water (in an eye-dropper) just out of reach of the camera lens. With miniature foliage, jeeps, and other structures strategically placed around the set, Blaisdell could encourage Lizzie to crawl across the models to claim her reward. The photographic effects were surprisingly good, and the layout undoubtedly inspired many readers to try their own hand at creating giant monster movies.

The big news in *FanMo* #3 was the Nameless Monster Contest. When readers turned to page 33, they saw a brand new Blaisdell monster, although nowhere in the magazine was Blaisdell credited with its creation. The contest was simple: make up a name for this beast and win a prize.

In fact, Blaisdell had already named the so-called Nameless Monster when he featured it in his own 16mm movie, *The Cliff Monster*. While Bob Burns was still in the army, Paul had been playing around with the idea of creating a true automaton—something that could be programmed to move and act, hands off. He knew what he wanted to do; he just wasn't sure how to go about it. After some experimentation, he sculpted a miniature monster over the framework of a toy robot. Like Paul's other fabulous creations, "Cliff" was customized with soft pine, block foam, and rubber latex and approximated the scale and dimensions of Little Hercules from *The Beast with a Million Eyes*. The body was humanoid but squat, with long, apelike arms ending in three-fingered extensions, much like *It!* The feet also suggested It. The face was rounded, and a downward-slanting triple-ridge running from the top of the head to the bridge of the nose—again somewhat resembling feature of It— gave the creature the famous Blaisdell "scowl." The nose was full and slightly resembled the She-Creature. There were no fangs, but the creature did have bared teeth. There were several raised, veinlike lines running between the jowls and the eyes that somewhat resembled the blood-engorged brain vessels of Paul's Saucer Men. The eyes (plastic globes from the Frye company) were white and pupilless, which gave the creature a startlingly malevolent appearance.

Inside the 18-inch miniature was an assemblage of push-rods, gears, and wires. "Cliff" needed to be wound up just like an old alarm clock, but he could be programmed to perform certain movements. His acting range was limited but effective. Bob Burns has described the interior mechanics of the model as something akin to a "clockwork mechanism," but only Blaisdell knew how it actually worked.

Burns first saw the Cliff Monster upon his return from the army. While he and Paul were playing around with the model, a thought struck both of them simultaneously. Why not use Cliff in a homemade featurette? The more he thought about it, the more excited Paul got about making a new home-made horror flick. He sought out an inexpensive source of 16mm film stock and began working out the details of a simple plotline with Bob. What he ended up with was a story that incorporated elements of *Jack the Giant Killer* and, coincidentally, a Japanese production from Daiei Pictures called *Majin, the Monster of Terror* (which Paul had never seen).

Paul called his new film *The Cliff Monster*. It featured Lionel Comport (Paul's standby guinea pig) and a friend of Jackie's who lived down the street from the Blaisdells. The story opens with the young couple strolling through a park. Legend has it that eons ago a strange and terrifying monster was imprisoned in this very spot. Lionel notices a cliffside rock formation with a skull emblazoned high up on the granite. Testing the validity of the legend, he picks up a rock and throws it at the skull. Sure enough, the rocky cliffside cracks open and the monster emerges. It traps the girl and is about to do the "King Kong Meets Fay Wray" bit when Lionel produces a pocket knife and throws it at the creature, stabbing it below the shoulder. While the monster

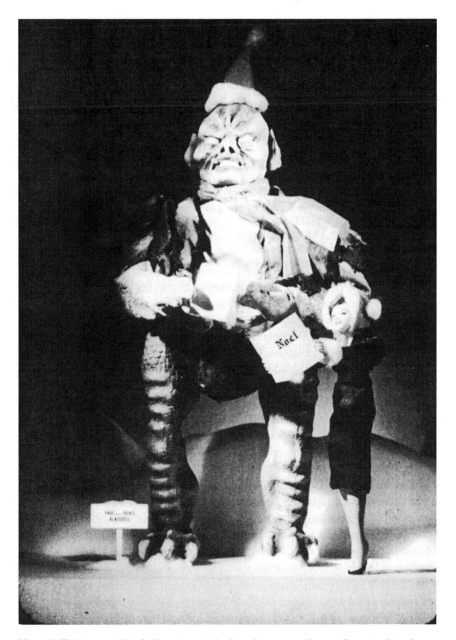

The Cliff Monster, Blaidell's unique "clockwork creature," turned up in this photograph which Paul and Jackie used as the cover of a Christmas card greeting sent to friends and relatives in the early 1960s. The girl in the photo is actually one of the miniatures designed for *Attack of the Puppet People*, outfitted with a new wardrobe. Cliff stood about 18 inches high.

works the knife out of its flesh, Lionel rushes back to his truck and grabs a few sticks of dynamite. (What self-respecting movie hero would neglect to keep a supply of dynamite on hand?) He ignites the dynamite and throws it at the creature's ponderous feet. The explosion sends the monster to its doom, sparing the young lovers from a crushing fate.

Bob Burns was especially impressed by this monster:

> "Cliff" was about a foot and a half tall, maybe a little taller. Paul had built some cams or some kind of clockwork-type mechanism into the interior— that's the only way I can think of to describe it. He was able to program moves for the creature, such as walking, lifting its arms, bending, and so forth. It could point, the mouth worked, and the head moved from side to side. Paul was able to get a couple of really neat movements out of this thing, like when the knife went into its chest. The monster reached down, plucked out the knife, and kind of cocked its head to one side while it studied the blade. It was a typical "Paulism!" This automaton, or whatever you want to call it, had to be wound up, and of course that meant it would eventually wind down and stop, but it ran long enough to get some good shots on film. It was definitely a unique invention, especially for its time.

The Cliff Monster was filmed with Burns's 16mm Bolex camera, an excellent piece of equipment that had inbuilt backwinding capabilities. This meant it was possible to perform in-camera double-exposures on the same strip of film. Blaisdell tried doing some split-screen effects to combine the miniature Cliff Monster with the live actors. Unfortunately, the film stock he had bought turned out to be outdated, and it started shrinking inside the camera. This caused most of the mattes to be misaligned, so the split-screen effects suffered tremendously. Other than that, *The Cliff Monster* turned out to be a very decent amateur production. Blaisdell thought enough of it to offer copies of the film to fans through *Fantastic Monsters*. The price was $2 for an 8mm edition, $6 for 16mm. Of all the copies sold, only two were returned by customers who were disappointed with their purchase.

A few weeks later Paul tried putting together a second automaton. Modeled after a real monster—the prehistoric tyrannosaurus-rex—this eighteen-inch model could also be programmed to perform a few independent moves, but it wasn't as versatile as Cliff. Blaisdell took some still photographs of the tyrannosaur terrorizing other miniature models amid scenery purchased from the local hobby shop, but he never shot any movie footage of the beast.

Two other "exclusives" offered for sale in the pages of *Fantastic Monsters* were *Hollywood Monsters* and *Filmland Monsters*. These were color slides and black-and-white film footage of Blaisdell's highest-profile movie monsters. *Hollywood Monsters* was a combination of slides from *The She-Creature, It Conquered the World, The Spider, Invasion of the Saucer Men, It! the Terror from Beyond Space, Voodoo Woman, The Beast with a Million Eyes*, and *How to Make a Monster*. Each 2"×2" slide was in full color, a novelty at the time because Paul's monsters had appeared only in black-and-white motion pictures.

Filmland Monsters was a blend of new and old film footage from *Day the World Ended*, *It Conquered the World*, *The She-Creature*, and *Invasion of the Saucer Men*. AIP gave Paul permission to excerpt scenes from the films' original theatrical trailers as long as he didn't use any footage of the actors, so *Filmland Monsters* contained only monsters and animated titles ("A Ghost of a Ghost ... Growing into a *Massive Murdering MONSTER!*"). Paul took the opportunity to incorporate never-before-seen footage of all the creatures except Marty the Mutant, who had perished during his *Day the World Ended* promotional tour. Unused footage of Beulah from *It Conquered the World* was included that showed off the malevolent mushroom's ability to roll its eyes and gnash its fangs, and there was a brief interlude of one of the Flying Fingers as it fluttered to life in front of Beulah's face, operated by Paul using his standard fishrod method. This was followed by scenes from *The She-Creature* trailer and a brand new close-up of Cuddles from *The Ghost of Dragstrip Hollow*, looking slightly the worse for wear but displaying some interesting dental work for the camera.

The trailer title from *Invasion of the Saucer Men* was followed by new monster footage that included close-ups of the extended hypo-nails, the seeing-eye claw, and a mug shot of a Saucer Man as it wrinkled its nose and stroked its chin thoughtfully. For the shot of the seeing-eye claw, Blaisdell devised a new crank mechanism that allowed him to manipulate the eyeball while keeping his hand inside the glove.

Both *Filmland Monsters* and *Hollywood Monsters* sold briskly and are highly prized and expensive collector's items today.

As time passed, *Fantastic Monsters* began selling better and better. Fan mail was running at a 98 percent approval rate. The readers overwhelmingly liked the interior tints and the full colors of the Monster of the Month, and almost everyone thought the staff was doing a very good job with the content as well. By the time the fourth issue rolled around, circulation had more than doubled. "It was going great guns," remembered Bob Burns. "The response was so good we all thought the magazine was going to last forever."

The fourth issue featured a cover shot of Beulah and an article on the making of *It Conquered the World*. Actor Vincent Price wrote a one-page piece entitled "In Defense of Horror Films," and Blaisdell contributed another article on prehistoric monster movies, "Dawn Age Beasts Strike Back." He also did an illustration of a gigantic spaceman rampaging through a futuristic alien city for a short story by Redd Boggs called "The Monster of Planet X." And this time around, "The Devil's Workshop" focused on the amazing talents of a young makeup artist named Bill Malone, who demonstrated the art of mask-making for the readers. Bill was only 13 years old at the time he wrote this piece for *Fantastic Monsters*. Now, like Bob and Dennis Skotak, he is an award-winning Hollywood professional.

**In the early 1960s, Blaisdell created an intricately detailed, 18-inch model of a tyran-
nosaur as a companion piece to another model he called the Cliff Monster. Both were
actually miniature automatons capable of performing a variety of movements that Blaisdell could program into them via an internal clockwork mechanism of his own design
(courtesy of Bob Burns).**

By now the masthead credits had been updated to include Contributing Editor Larry Byrd (who had been writing freelance articles for the magazine for some time), and a "crumbling" editor, the "Mad Mummy," an invention of Bob Burns. In the "Tombstone Times," Burns appeared as Major Mars,
a character he had invented during the 1950s as the host of Saturday afternoon movie matinees. There was an announcement that Paul's alter ego, the
sinister Count Downe, was down for the count after an angry mob of vil-
lagers drove a stake into his heart. Contributing Editor Larry Byrd became
Downe's successor.

To this point Blaisdell had been cautious about allowing his name to
turn up in places other than the masthead. That policy changed with the
publication of the fifth issue, which finally included a full feature on Blaisdell and his movies by Associate Editor Jim Harmon. Here at last was the
first in-depth look at "the man with no face," as Paul sometimes jokingly
referred to himself. The last time a genre publication had even mentioned
Blaisdell's name was in 1958, when *Famous Monsters* published an article on
the making of *Invasion of the Saucer Men*.

But there was still more Blaisdell in *FanMo #5*. In "The Devil's Workshop," Paul demonstrated the steps involved in creating *It! the Terror from*

Paul Blaisdell (left) offers a giant brain to the obviously famished Bob Burns in one of the pair's many gag photos, taken during a weekend get-together in 1957. The brain was a fiberglass prop created for a series of behind the scenes photographs published in the first issue of *Famous Monsters of Filmland* magazine, which appeared on newsstands in February 1958 (courtesy of Bob Burns).

Beyond Space. There was a picture of Chester Morris and Cuddles in "Dead Time Tales." The caption read, "You act like a smile would break your face!" but since Morris was frowning as hard as Cuddles, it was impossible to know to whom the caption was referring. There was another fantastic close-up of the She-Creature emerging from the ocean with sunlight glinting in her eye, and the cover featured a beautiful color close-up of the monster with a black cowl draped over her head. Unfortunately, there was a boner of a caption: "American International's *Voodoo Woman.*"

The "Tombstone Times" ran a short feature called "Meteor Monster," about a couple of fans from Rosemont, Pennsylvania, who made their own home horror film starring the illegitimate daughter of Beulah the Mushroom. Filmmakers Walter and Peggy Shank and their friend Chuck Hodgkinson built their own papier-maché version of Paul's monster from *It Conquered the World*, and it was a respectable rendition of the real thing. It must have made Paul feel good to know that there was someone out there who dug his crazy cucumber.

As *Fantastic Monsters* continued to reach new readers month after month, far away in Iowa the seeds of destruction were slowly being sown. Printing problems had begun to show up as early as issue #3, but became especially noticeable in later issues. There was half a blank page in #5 where there should have been a photograph, and some of the pages were marred by vertical lines that ran through the pictures and text. Blaisdell had become so preoccupied with ironing out problems with the printer via long-distance communications that he had no free time left to write articles for his own magazine. Both issues #6 and #7 (the final number) were written entirely by the other staff members.

Bob Burns describes the decline in the quality of printing in this way:

"We were both concerned about what was happening. The first couple of issues looked so good, but later some of the photos looked splotchy and washed out, and things just got worse and worse as time went on. I think we both felt that something was about to happen, but we had no idea what. And then—BOOM!—all of a sudden, it happened."

When copies of *Fantastic Monsters* #7 were received from the printer, there was a brand new name on the masthead—Jiro Tomiyama, who was credited with "Art and Production." The trouble was, nobody had ever heard of Jiro Tomiyama. Technically, Blaisdell was the publisher and even he didn't know who Tomiyama was. Obviously this was someone involved with the magazine at the printer's office in Iowa.

In fact, the printer admitted as much. Rather than pay an independent team of layout artists to set up each issue of the magazine, which had been the procedure until that point (in fact, *FanMo* used the same production team that *Famous Monsters* used in its early years), Tomiyama had been brought in to handle everything on his own. Coupled with the inferior printing techniques that had been employed on the later issues, *Fantastic Monsters* seemed to be taking a quality nosedive.

As much as Paul and the rest of the staff hated the look of the latest issue, there was nothing they could do. Tomiyama was now the magazine's official art director. *Maybe he'll get better in time,* thought Blaisdell.

But there *was* no time. The articles and photographs that made up the interior of *FanMo* #8—a special edition devoted to the films of Boris Karloff—were forwarded to the Iowa office. Blaisdell and the rest of the staff started working out the contents of the next bimonthly issue, expecting to receive the brown-lines for #8 any day.

But weeks passed with no word from the printer. When Paul tried to put a long-distance call through, he found out the phone had been disconnected. Stunned and not quite knowing what to think, he called in Bob, Jim, and Ron and told them what had happened. Panic set in. The printer had thousands of dollars worth of film photos, lobbycards, posters, and pressbooks that belonged to the *FanMo* staff. Rare stills from Karloff's *Frankenstein* and *The Bride of Frankenstein* were on loan from Bob Burns's collection—items that were irreplaceable.

The materials were never recovered. Everything that made up the contents of *Fantastic Monsters* #8 went up in smoke when the printer suffered a fire that destroyed the entire building. Blaisdell learned about the fire from associates in the business who heard about what happened through the grapevine. No one ever got to speak with the printer, or Jiro Tomiyama for that matter; both seemed to have vanished into Never-Never Land.

That fire sent *Fantastic Monsters* to an early grave. There was no way to recover the one-of-a-kind materials that had been entrusted to the Iowa printer, and there was no way to recover the monetary losses incurred by the magazine's destruction. Together Paul and Bob lost nearly $20,000—their combined investments in the magazine. Neither of them could afford to lose that kind of money. Burns was still working at CBS, which had secured his job when he was drafted into the army in 1958, but the *FanMo* loss wiped out his entire savings account. Paul's bank account had been bigger, but he had invested more money in the magazine—almost twice as much as Burns. With no new film work forthcoming from American International—or indeed, from anywhere in Hollywood—Blaisdell had no way to recoup his losses.

In reality the fire that destroyed *Fantastic Monsters* also destroyed Paul Blaisdell's dreams of the future. By the end of 1964, he must have realized that if AIP hadn't encouraged him to contribute to their current crop of film projects, they were hardly going to remember him even further down the road.

Years later, suspicions about the origin of the fire were confirmed, as Burns recounts:

> We were able to find out that the whole thing had been a setup. Paul and I had our suspicions, but we could never be sure until one day when we talked to somebody who knew something about it. The whole thing was a scam. This printer must have had the place torched as part of an insurance fraud. He had never made much money because he only printed local things, Iowa farm magazines or whatever. *Fantastic Monsters* was his only national publication. And evidently he needed a national publication to make this insurance scheme work. It made his operation worth a lot more, having a national magazine like ours. Maybe he had to have a national title going for a year before the insurance kicked in, who knows? We figured this guy collected his money and retired to a private island or something. Besides losing all those thousands of dollars, I lost almost my entire still collection. I'd say 80 percent of my collection was destroyed along with everything else in that fire because the printer hadn't returned many of the materials that had been used in the earlier issues. But the truly sad thing is, *Fantastic Monsters* was doing so well! The readers loved it, and the circulation kept going up and up and up. And it really hurt Paul, not just in terms of finances, but in terms of his whole life. He was so embittered by the whole experience, and coming on the heels of the way he was treated by AIP, it helped drive him into a hermit-like existence. Paul and Jackie had never gone out much to begin with, but now they hardly ever went out.

Unfortunately for the people who loved Paul and the people who loved his work, the end of *Fantastic Monsters* magazine signaled the end of Blaisdell's professional career. As the years crept relentlessly by, the name Paul Blaisdell receded farther and farther from the public consciousness. Many of the older AIP films began showing up on "Chiller" and "The World Beyond," syndicated successors to television's original spook show, "Shock Theatre." The pictures played again and again, and Blaisdell's name was listed in the credits alongside Corman, Cahn, Rusoff, Griffith, Gordon, Cohen, Arkoff, and Nicholson, but no one seemed to take much notice. Young fantasy fans weaned on *Famous Monsters* (which remained the best-selling magazine of its kind) were occasionally reminded that it was Jack Pierce at Universal who devised Boris Karloff's makeup in *Frankenstein* and *The Mummy*, or that Lon Chaney, Sr., created his own monstrous makeups, but that's about as far as it went. Shamefully, in *FM*'s short-lived series "The Men Behind the Monsters," the name Paul Blaisdell was never mentioned. A long-running but erratically published competitor, the clinical *Castle of Frankenstein*, occasionally reviewed Paul's films when they made their television debuts, but *CoF* liked to think of itself as an "intellectual" film magazine not given to feelings of nostalgia. Consequently, the editors rarely had a kind word for any of the AIP pictures.

Now, with *Fantastic Monsters* gone from the scream scene, it would be many years before the next generation of monster fans finally learned a few of the details about Hollywood's "forgotten" monster-maker. They would not read about Blaisdell in *Famous Monsters*, as he noted:

> Insult by omission doesn't bother me. But just because I was the managing editor of a rival magazine? It's a shame, because the Blaisdell name did appear in the first issue of James Warren's magazine [*Famous Monsters*]. I met him at Forrest Ackerman's house, and he begged me to do that article, complete with the original photos. I was always ready to give "King James" credit for almost anything; the trouble is, I can't think of anything to give him credit for. You may not know this, but in fact I wrote the text for that article. It was subsequently rewritten in "Ackermanese." Actually, I like your writing better. Come to think of it, I even like my writing better. Come to think about it, they have a trained chimpanzee at M.I.T. that ... aw-w-w, let's just forget it.

15

Travesties and Tributes

In the Year 2889 was a good science-fiction yarn by George Worthing Yates, but it never got made. The title had been registered by American International, and they slapped it on an unbelievably miserable remake of *Day the World Ended.* Don't get me wrong, I'm not saying that *Day the World Ended* deserved an Academy Award. Far from it. All I'm saying is that horrible remake was ten times worse!

—Paul Blaisdell

Once *Fantastic Monsters* bit the dust, there was nothing for Paul to do except retreat to the security of his secluded Topanga Canyon home and keep busy with some of his favorite hobbies. Blaisdell never lost his enthusiasm for model airplanes (his favorites were the World War I biplanes), fencing, science-fiction, art, inventions, and handicrafts. He shut himself off from the world of Hollywood make-believe, and that bothered some of his friends but they couldn't say they didn't understand. After so many years of dedicated service, giving his all to people like Jim Nicholson, Alex Gordon, Roger Corman, Eddie Cahn, Bob Kent, and others, it must have hurt to know his services were no longer needed. He might have felt otherwise if things had worked out differently, but in fact Corman et al. were as active as ever. It was difficult to understand why they couldn't make room for him on some of the movies they were making at this point.

But Paul was a proud man, and refused to let the wounds show. He kept things to himself, and if someone were to ask his opinion of Jim Nicholson or Roger Corman, Paul had nothing but nice things to say. Even Harry Thomas, who had pulled a fast one on everyone with his zero-budget *Voodoo Woman* mask, was spoken of only in the most respectful of tones.

There are some obvious questions that beg honest answers, but I don't think we will ever get them. Why couldn't American International keep Blaisdell employed during the 1960s and even the 1970s? Why didn't Jim Nicholson look out for a long-term AIP employee whose career had begun almost concurrently with his own? These questions are ones that undoubtedly Paul asked himself, and like the rest of us, he probably couldn't think of a good answer.

While Paul and Jackie remained sequestered in Topanga Canyon, AIP was throwing a little money (very little money) at a film director named Larry Buchanan, who worked out of Dallas, Texas. In the 1950s, Buchanan had worked in front of and behind the camera in several legitimate Hollywood productions, including *The Marrying Kind* (1952) and *The Gunfighter*, starring Gregory Peck. But after almost ten years kicking around tinseltown without lucking into the big time as either an actor, producer, or director (he didn't care which), Buchanan drifted back to Dallas and settled into the exploitation niche.

Buchanan made a film called *Free, White, and 21* which caught the attention of American International. AIP distributed the film, and it made enough of a profit that Arkoff and Nicholson decided to bankroll a series of super-low-budget films for their television subsidiary. By making the films in Texas, production costs could be minimized. With Larry Buchanan directing, AIP knew they wouldn't be getting any Oscar-calibre work; but at least they were assured of receiving exposed film with images on it. When it came to making film sales to television, sometimes that was all that mattered.

AIP sent Buchanan four screenplays—*Day the World Ended, It Conquered the World, The She-Creature,* and *Invasion of the Saucer Men*—with instructions to make new versions under alternate titles.* Because they would be going directly to television, Buchanan's films were made in 16mm at an average cost of $22,000 per picture. Produced under the moniker Azalea Films, the first of the four remakes was *The Eye Creatures*, sometimes known as *Attack of the Eye Creatures*, with "the" appearing by mistake twice in the title. (How shoddy can you get?) This was Buchanan's reinterpretation (as opposed to a copy) of *Invasion of the Saucer Men*. Like the original, it's an attempted mix of comedy and horror. But whereas *Saucer Men* managed to be both funny and scary, *The Eye Creatures* was neither. Instead, it was merely ridiculous. The costumes (which, as the title implies, were covered with eyes) were the work of Jack Bennett, a Dallas advertising executive who taught himself the rudiments of theatrical makeup and film technique. Bennett supplied creature costumes for all of the Azalea films. In at least one instance, a Bennett monster was used in two different pictures, recalling Blaisdell's experience with the She-Creature. The big difference, of course, was that Paul's monster costumes looked a hundred times better than the best thing Bennett ever did.

It would be redundant to capsulize the plotlines of the Buchanan remakes because they tell the same stories with almost exactly the same dialogue. In

---

Buchanan also directed three original films for AIP's television package. The first of these was It's Alive! (not to be confused with Larry Cohen's 1973 film about a mutant killer baby), a title that had already been registered by AIP for a planned horror-comedy to star Boris Karloff, Vincent Price, Basil Rathbone, and Peter Lorre. Lorre died before the film went into production, so AIP used the title on Buchanan's picture. Curse of the Swamp Creature and Mars Needs Women were the director's other two nonremake titles for AIP.

terms of differences, *The Eye Creatures* contained the largest percentage of new or rewritten material and dialogue. Buchanan added a couple of effeminate comic-relief soldiers who used some electronic eavesdropping gadgetry to spy on the teenagers necking at Lovers' Point, but this was the only real addition to the story. The cast included a single recognizable name: John Ashley, who went to work for AIP in the 1950s and achieved a kind of semistardom in the early 1960s as second banana to Frankie Avalon in the *Beach Party* series. After that, it was all downhill, as his Azalea work testifies.

When *The Eye Creatures* was completed, Buchanan began shooting *Creature of Destruction*, a flaccid recitation of *The She-Creature*. Although in almost every instance cast members were rounded up from local amateur groups, old-timer Les Tremayne, who had fought through *The War of the Worlds* and squared off against *The Monster of Piedras Blancas*, assumed the role of Dr. Lombardi (played by Chester Morris in the original). Like many actors, Tremayne had had his share of ups and downs, having appeared in a number of low-budget losers, but now he was scraping rock bottom. (Buchanan typically hired actors who found themselves no longer employable by Hollywood. John Agar and Tommy Kirk were two other actors abandoned by the industry who had to make their way to Buchanan's doorstep just to keep working.)

The monster in *Creature of Destruction* might possibly have been the worst piece of work Jack Bennett ever contrived. With eyes made from ping-pong balls and rubber-tipped claws that bent every time there was a strong breeze, it looked like nothing so much as an assembly-line Halloween costume for undiscriminating trick-or-treaters.

It Conquered the World went through the Buchanan blender and became the infamously titled *Zontar, the Thing from Venus*. This time Bennett scared up a slightly better monster suit (and slightly is definitely the operative word), an insectlike creature with bat-wings. Buchanan, unlike Roger Corman, had the good sense to keep his Venusian inside the cave, even during the climax. But the rest of the film was so awful it's difficult to imagine anyone staying awake long enough to see it.

The last of the Azalea remakes was *In the Year 2889*,* a horrendous retread of *Day the World Ended*. Jack Bennett's atomic atrocity was no Marty the Mutant, but it did look a little better than his version of Cuddles, the *Creature of Destruction*. But it didn't really matter what Bennett came up with; Larry Buchanan's pitiful direction was so awful it destroyed any part of the picture that threatened to rise above the mediocre. It's doubtful Buchanan lacked the technical know-how to make a decent film—he had, after all, been

---

Recall that In the Year 2889 *was the title of an original George Worthing Yates script for AIP about a group of American colonialists living in the future on Mars. Since AIP had paid to have the title registered, they decided to use it on Larry Buchanan's remake of* Day the World Ended. *Naturally, nowhere in Buchanan's film is there the slightest hint that the year is 2889. In fact, it looks a lot like 1966, which happens to be the year the film was made.*

involved with the industry since the early 1950s—but with budgets that were less than that of *The Beast with a Million Eyes* and shooting schedules that never exceeded seven days, it was difficult, if not impossible, to bring in a decent product. (But let's not forget that minor miracles have been worked under equally distressing circumstances. A case in point is Herk Harvey's haunting *Carnival of Souls*.)

Paul Blaisdell was caught completely off-guard when he chanced across *In the Year 2889* one Saturday afternoon in 1967:

> I was trying to dial in the news when I caught that film by accident, and I damn near fell off my dinosaur. I probably would have just skipped right by it if I hadn't recognized some of the dialogue that was coming out of the actors' mouths because it was a direct steal from *Day the World Ended*. I sat there like an idiot in front of the boob tube, staring at it, and I just couldn't believe it. I was absolutely spellbound. Believe me, the original *Year 2889*— the picture I was going to work on and had done the production illustrations for—had absolutely nothing to do with a remake of *Day the World Ended*.

When he learned about Azalea's other remakes, Blaisdell said, "It's just unbelievable that they did those. I don't want to know a damn thing about them. I hope I never see them. One was more than enough!"

The Azalea pictures could never be called "tributes" to Paul Blaisdell's work, and clearly they were never intended as such. Although Paul never lived to see it, director Jim Wynorski made a horror spoof for Roger Corman's Concorde Films that was not only entertaining, but did contain a tribute to Blaisdell. The film was called *Transylvania Twist*. Wynorski, whose professional debut in the fantasy film field was as a writer for *Fangoria*, ended up going to work for Concorde, where he made a number of forgettable quickies that forfeited good storytelling for lots of low-I.Q. violence and a dash of T and A. Wynorski's prolific but undistinguished output threatened to brand him as a "horror hack" until he got involved with *Transylvania Twist*. Inspired by a fun script written by R. J. Robertson, Wynorski grabbed the film and ran with it.

Transylvania Twist mixes good-natured, wacky humor with a campy story involving vampires, creaky castles, family curses, and even a touch of H. P. Lovecraft's Cthulhu Mythos. Robert Vaughn, who once worked for Roger Corman in *Teenage Caveman*, returned to the fold to appear as Lord Orlok, a scheming bloodsucker who is surrounded by inanity as well as insanity. Orlok intends to invoke "the Evil One" as soon as he can lay his hands on the Book of Ulthar,* a forbidden tome that contains mystic spells to summon

---

*A double reference to Lovecraft. Not only is the book obviously modeled on Lovecraft's own Necronomicon, but one of the author's earliest fantasy tales was called "The Cats of Ulthar." In addition there are references to Arkham (a fictional town Lovecraft modeled on Salem) and a character named Dexter Ward, after Lovecraft's "The Case of Charles Dexter Ward."

transdimensional demons. Most of the film is a deliciously silly romp with various characters trying to uncover the book's location before Orlok can get his greasy mitts on it. Dexter Ward (Steve Altman) tracks down Orlok's niece Merissa (Teri Copley), and together they journey to Transylvania, where Dr. Van Helsing (Ace Mask) helps them thwart the vampire's evil plans.

The tribute to Blaisdell shows up in the film's last five minutes, when Orlok reads an incantation from the Book of Ulthar. "Arrroooohhh ... pah ... pah ... papa-ooh-mow-mow ... in-a-gadda-da-veeeeeeedahhhh," Orlok crows. With a guttural rumbling the earth cracks open, and out of the boiling gases and hissing vapors rises the Evil One, a fang-for-fang copy of the mushroom monster from *It Conquered the World*.

"It's the Evil One," Van Helsing gasps, "come forth to conquer the world!" (Obviously scriptwriter Robertson knew his Corman as well as his Lovecraft.)

Waving its lobsterlike claws in the air, the cucumbersome creature is about to step out of the crater (if it could step, that is) when the Book of Ulthar is destroyed in a fire, sending the Evil One back to the hell where it was spawned. Looks like the world won't get conquered this time either.

Most viewers probably didn't get the joke, but that's okay; *Transylvania Twist* is funny enough without the inside jokes. Besides "Beulah 2," the film featured Boris Karloff in scenes lifted from Corman's 1963 quickie, *The Terror*, cleverly edited to match footage of Steve Altman as he enters a room and declares, "Boris Karloff? Gee, nobody's seen you since 1969." Karloff conveniently replies, "I've been here for 20 years," an original line from *The Terror*. Since *Transylvania Twist* was released in 1989, the references matched perfectly.

It's nice to see Paul's work lovingly venerated on the screen. The reference to *It Conquered the World* is respectful. Neither the film nor the monster is made fun of in any way, and for this we can thank Jim Wynorski as well as the executive producer, Roger Corman.

It might come as a surprise to learn that Beulah made "guest appearances" not only in *Transylvania Twist*, but in magazines and on postcards as well. In fact, several of Blaisdell's monsters have turned up in the oddest places. In the early 1960s, the Venusian mushroom was featured on a humorous postcard, and the She-Creature turned up on a plastic button labeled "Teacher." In the mid-1970s, a miniature rubber rendition of Paul's Saucer Man could be had for next to nothing if you were lucky enough to get one of them out of a 25¢ gumball machine. I chanced across the Saucer Man myself and managed to get two out of the same machine. One I kept; the other I mailed to Paul. Typically, Blaisdell turned around and sent it to Angelo Rossito, who had played one of the little green men in the film so many years before.

Not surprisingly, Paul and Jackie never received a dime from the sales of such novelties. In fact, according to Bob Burns, most of these adaptations of Paul's creations were done without the cooperation or knowledge of

American International, which held the copyrights. In that respect, the items are "bootlegs," and who's to say how rare they might be?

By the early 1970s, the old AIP films had been played and replayed so many times on television that the sprocket holes were wearing out. Eventually they were retired, one by one, to TV limbo. With the films went the royalty checks, so Paul was forced to rely on income from other sources. He was still an artist—a very good one—but the 1960s had robbed him of the drive to further his artistic career. Fortunately, Paul owned an apartment building in Santa Monica, and it became a welcome source of income throughout the 1960s, 1970s, and 1980s. Paul inherited the building when his mother died in the mid–1960s, and it was a lifesaver for him and Jackie. The wishy-washy movie business could turn anyone into a prince or a pauper, depending on the roll of the dice or the whim of a producer. Unless you were lucky enough to strike it rich—which seldom happened to anyone other than actors who graduated to full-fledged stardom—you could well end up on skid row. Independently wealthy film directors were not common. There was Alfred Hitchcock, of course, and Orson Welles, and a few others. But as for special effects and makeup technicians—forget it. In Blaisdell's day there were no makeup "stars" like there are today. If Dick Smith or Rick Baker or Rob Bottin or Stan Winston or Tom Savini or Steve Johnson had created their movie monsters and effects in the 1950s rather than the 1970s and 1980s, it's doubtful their futures would have been assured, either. Who, other than Lon Chaney, Sr., Jack Pierce, and perhaps the Westmore brothers, could make a pre–1960 claim to fame? Makeup effects really only began to be noticed in 1968, when John Chambers invented the first "million dollar makeups" for *Planet of the Apes*. By that time Paul Blaisdell had been out of the business for almost six years, and his last major assignment—*The Ghost of Dragstrip Hollow*—was already nine years old.

Paul continued to fiddle around with amateur photography in his spare time. In the early 1970s, he was experimenting with a "black box," an invention of his own that could be used to fix mistakes and add effects to previously exposed film. Paul built the device out of wood. According to Bob Burns, it functioned as a kind of super slide copier. With room to insert filters and mattes and the ability to compensate for under and over-exposure, the "black box" could significantly alter the look of the original photo. "It's capable of doing all the things you wish you had done when you clicked the [camera] shutter, but didn't," Blaisdell said. He may have been thinking about trying to get the device patented and marketed, but as far as can be determined this idea never panned out.

Paradoxically, as the 1970s wore on and his Hollywood heyday dimmed further and further into the past, Paul began receiving more and more fan mail. Some of it was from youngsters who had ferreted out his name from

An original Paul Blaisdell pen-and-ink drawing presented to the author in January 1977.

occasional television showings of the AIP films; a lot of it was from older fans who had grown up watching his movies during their first run on "Chiller" and "The World Beyond." It surprised Paul to be noticed at all; it doubly surprised him to be so fondly remembered and so well liked. "Where were you when I needed you?" he might have asked.

"We were busy growing up" was all any of us could have answered.

There was one fan, however, who was almost able to lure Blaisdell out of "retirement" for one final fling with film fantasy in the late 1970s. Fred Olen Ray, a fan-turned-professional who always had a soft spot in his heart for the kind of drive-in fare produced by AIP in the 1950s, was about to go into production on one of his early sci-fi pictures, *The Alien Dead*. Fred adored Blaisdell's movie monsters, and often sought out memorabilia on *The She-Creature*, *Voodoo Woman*, and other favorites. (Several of the photos in this book are from Fred's personal collection.) He thought it would be great to get Blaisdell involved in his picture, which at the time was shooting under the title *It Fell From the Sky*. A friend of Ray's (probably either Don Fellman or James Brummel) put him in touch with Blaisdell.

Ray introduced himself and asked if Paul might be interested in doing some effects work for *It Fell from the Sky*. As a matter of fact, he *was*. Many years had passed since Blaisdell's last film project, but he hadn't forgotten protocol. He asked Ray all about the movie and what he had in mind in terms of special effects.

The story called for an alien monster, which clearly would have been up Paul's alley, but since Ray wasn't working with much of a budget, he described instead a relatively straightforward scene in which a flaming meteorite strikes the earth. That sounded easy enough to Paul, and he offered to do the effect for a thousand dollars. Unfortunately, even this relatively minor sum was outside Ray's projected budget. Negotiations never went any further. "I was sorry I couldn't muster the money," recalls Ray, who has recently been directing pictures for Roger Corman. "I was a big fan of Paul's work and was anxious to have him associated with my film. I'd heard he was out of the business, reclusive, and not interested in the biz—but the impression I got [from talking with him] was just that maybe nobody was asking. I definitely believed that he was very interested in working [in film] again, but maybe only on small stuff. Or maybe our film was just a lark."*

Through the perseverance of a few dedicated fans, magazine articles about Paul Blaisdell and the AIP films began to turn up in film publications. *Fangoria* published a two-part interview with Blaisdell in 1979. This was followed by articles in magazines like *Filmfax* and the British publication *Halls of Horror*. There was an in-depth retrospective of Paul's work in *Cinéfantastique* in 1990. Unfortunately, except for the two-part *Fangoria* piece, Paul didn't live to see the international press coverage or experience the resurgence of interest in his career these articles precipitated.

It is hardly surprising that he remarked at one point: "I certainly can't be called 'The Man of a Thousand Faces.' I'm more like 'The Man with no Face.'"

Several years before his death, negotiations were under way with *Fangoria* to initiate a series of Blaisdell articles. Paul's friend, producer Alex Gordon, had begun writing a column for the magazine, and the editors were keen on adding Blaisdell's name to their masthead. Unfortunately for everyone concerned, Paul's health began to fail him just after he and *Fangoria* touched base on the details of the column. Blaisdell wanted to set up a question-and-answer system with the readers. He would select the most interesting questions, compose the responses, and turn over the resulting manuscript to *Fangoria*, along with a photo or two. It could have almost been "The Return of the Devil's Workshop," if Prince Sirki had not stepped in to dismantle the proceedings before they ever got started.

Fred Olen Ray to the author, personal correspondence dated March 24, 1995.

16

Sunset

When I look back on it, I guess I can't complain too much about leaving the film industry when I did. I was getting kind of tired of it anyway. Things had become so much different from when I was first starting out, and I'll give you a for instance: I flew the Venusian bats from *It Conquered the World*, although technically I wasn't supposed to because I was supposed to belong to the SAG [Screen Actors Guild], period. But union rules were getting tighter and tighter all the time, and they started sending out "watchdogs" whose job was to make sure there was no "funny business" going on on the sets. When we were shooting *Invasion of the Saucer Men*, I wasn't allowed to fly my own spaceship, and that was made less than a year after *It Conquered the World*. Technically, it got to the point where I wasn't even supposed to do makeup because I didn't belong to the Make-Up Union. So, like many other people in Hollywood, I decided to quit, and I didn't do it alone; there were a few others who jumped over the back fence with me. Everything about the industry and the entire composition of Hollywood was changing so rapidly, although to me, it seemed more like a *de*composition.

— Paul Blaisdell

As ridiculous and purposeless as it might seem now, there was a time when a kind of anti–AIP prejudice blanketed much of fantasy film fandom. It became fashionable to disdain the black-and-white "cheapies" made during the 1950s. As the fans grew older, they even shrugged off *Famous Monsters of Filmland* as "kids' stuff." The serious film student had to appear to be at least somewhat discerning. By categorizing certain films or groups of films as either "worthwhile" or "worthless," these fans believed they were legitimizing their devotion to the genre in the eyes of their compatriots. Trashing easy targets like *The Beast with a Million Eyes* seemed to prove that they were no longer indiscriminating monster lovers, but serious devotees of horror film art.

The problem, as many fans later recognized, was that in their eagerness to prove to the world that horror films should be taken seriously, they damned anything that failed to match a set of preconceived standards that purported to define what was good and what was bad. Could these elitists admit to actually liking pictures with titles like *How to Make a Monster* or *I Was a*

Teenage Werewolf? Of course not. Not if they wanted to be taken seriously. The result was that nearly every one of American International's pre–1960 productions was denigrated as substandard fare unworthy of the attention of the Horror-as-Art constituency.

It took a long while for this generation of film fans to outgrow their own self-accelerated hubris, but once they did they were better able to understand the notion of relative values, to discriminate without being discriminatory, and to salute the AIP films for what they were. True, *The She-Creature* was not in the same league with *Curse of the Demon*, but that didn't make it any less worthwhile a picture, merely a different kind of picture. Eventually a term was coined to describe certain AIP productions: *drive-in classic*. Today at last, no one shies away from admitting a certain fondness for some of the films AIP produced during the 1950s and 1960s.

Toward the end of the 1970s, Blaisdell began feeling ill. He was constantly having problems with his teeth, which required extensive dental surgery. That, of course, cost money, a lot of money. His and Jackie's savings, which had been seriously eroded by the *Fantastic Monsters* fiasco, took an even further beating.

California began experiencing a series of rainstorms and severe flooding around this same time, but Paul somehow managed to maintain a stiff upper lip through it all. Remarkably, his correspondence remained as light-hearted and cheerful as ever. Every time he and Jackie experienced a setback, they just brushed the debris from each other's shoulders and got back to work. As Paul commented at the time,

> If you've seen or heard the news, you know about the California floods. Here in the southland, Mandeville and Topanga canyons were two of the hardest places hit. We make *Robinson Crusoe on Mars* look like the Conrad Hilton. There's lots of damage to repair, and lots of pain and strain to recover from. I wonder if anyone could supply us with a surplus WW2 U-Boat? I'm not worried about raising a crew. Since the flood started, we've got 'em all the way from one foot to eight legs. I don't need spooky movies, I need a biology book.... Two flood seasons practically back to back, with tons of roaring water coming storm after storm, propelling thousands of pounds of wreckage ahead of it to smash all obstacles like giant battering rams.... Homes battered, destroyed, and obliterated, along with cars, vans, corrals, and businesses. With twelve miles of wall-to-wall wreckage in this canyon, it looks like the aftermath of a Martian invasion! Consider the creeping cold and dampness, along with the mold, mildew, and wood rot, complete with undermined collapsing foundations and breaking trees, and you can figure it takes a long time to pick up all the pieces. I could cheerfully strangle the guy that first said "sunny Southern California." People who have to live in this godforsaken state are lucky if they see the sun four months out of the year! By the way, if anyone wants to send us a "Care" package, be sure and send canned ham. It goes with my theatrical career!

Paul had held onto many of the props, masks, and costumes he and Jackie had made over the years, and some of them were irreparably damaged by the

Paul and Jackie Blaisdell's secluded Topanga Canyon, California, home, with Bob Burns peering out the back window. A suspension bridge (not visible here) led to the front of the house. Paul's workshop was in the basement (courtesy of Bob Burns).

floods. Most of his glossy stills were saved, thanks to their protective backings and glass frames, but one of the few remaining Saucer Men heads came close to being totally destroyed, and what was left of the She-Creature costume was ruined entirely. (Years earlier, a family of raccoons had crept into the Blaisdell homestead and discovered that Cuddles was very soft and warm and would make quite a nice nesting place. After that, there wasn't much left to get water-damaged.)

More trouble was the last thing in the world the Blaisdells needed at this point, but as Paul worked day-by-day to air out the house and straighten up the wreckage, he began feeling worse and worse. Dental problems were one thing, but this was something else again. He felt weak. There were intermittent pains, sometimes very bad ones, and he was losing weight. Something was seriously wrong.

But Paul was loath to schedule an appointment with a doctor. Perhaps he was afraid of finding out what was wrong, or maybe he thought it was something that would clear up in time. Then again, he might have sensed the truth, and merely dreaded hearing a doctor's confirmation.

Whatever the reason, Paul put off going to his physician for as long as possible. No matter how much Jackie pleaded with him to go, he refused, until he was too weak and exhausted to protest any longer.

The diagnosis, when it came, was exactly what Paul had feared most:

cancer. By now it was too late to do much of anything about it except treat the pain and the symptoms. Paul had let things drag on too long without getting diagnosed. He was shot through with cancer; it was everywhere. There was no hope.

Cutting out localized cancer cells was one thing. Along with radiation therapy, this was the kind of treatment that had already rescued thousands of victims from a life of intolerable pain and suffering. But treatment wasn't possible in Paul's case. The cancer was no longer localized. In fact, at this late date there was no telling exactly how, where, or when the cancer had first gotten its hold on Paul's metabolism.

They left the doctor's office and returned home, Paul clutching a prescription for painkillers. Even now he could barely move from one room to another without feeling exhausted.

Months passed, and the disease slowly ate away at Paul's physique. Each week he lost more weight. When the pain attacked, he exorcised it with a pill. One day the pills didn't work any more. His doctor wrote a new prescription for even stronger medication. The pain subsided again. For a while.

The end came relatively quickly and was a blessing. Paul's body had been ravaged by the disease, and he was down to just over 80 pounds. Cancer had robbed him of everything, even his dignity. In his final months, he couldn't walk. Jackie carried him to the bathroom, washed him, dressed him, talked to him, read to him, loved him.

It was a great relief for them both when Paul closed his eyes for the final time, on July 10, 1983, eleven days shy of his 56th birthday. Jackie later expressed her great loss by noting: "Needless to say, nothing is the same ... nor will it ever be, for me. There are cherished memories, nearly forty years of them, but they are certainly surrounded by an awful emptiness."

The loss of his friend moved Bob Burns deeply:

> Over the years Paul had become more and more secluded. Then he got cancer, but no one except Jackie knew. He was on heavy-duty cancer medication, but I didn't know that at the time. When I talked to him on the phone, he would say, "Oh, I just got back from the dentist and the novocaine hasn't worn off." He was trying to give me a reason why he sounded so weak and out of it, you see. He did not want me to know how bad off he was. I guess he wanted me to remember him as he had been, young and robust. You can't imagine how much I miss him. He and Lionel [Comport, Jr.] were my best friends.

Sadly, but perhaps not surprisingly, Blaisdell's death went unnoticed in the film industry. No obituaries appeared in either *Variety* or *The Hollywood Reporter*.

Many artists have toiled during their own lifetimes only to receive little or no recognition for their efforts. Sometimes their works have captured the fancy of later generations, belatedly catapulting them to a posthumous fame. Paul's story doesn't end much differently. Neglected for the most part during his own lifetime, long forgotten by an industry that benefitted from his love of films and fantasy during the 1950s, Blaisdell's name finally achieved a degree of prominence in the field in the late 1980s and early 1990s. A series of model kits manufactured by a company called Billiken USA brought Blaisdell's creations to the attention of a new coterie of fans. The company's U.S. president, Michael Ruffalo, was a fan of Blaisdell's work and wanted to add his creations to the Billiken lineup. Like many other youthful monster lovers, Ruffalo had put together the plastic models issued by Aurora in the early 1960s, but he wondered why the company only produced kits based on Universal characters. He had been watching "Chiller Theatre" along with millions of other youngsters, and some of his favorite film fiends had originated amid the nuclear nightmares of the 1950s.

Years dragged by without further ado until Ruffalo finally decided to take matters into his own hands and recreate his favorite 1950s monsters himself. Living in Japan at the time, he befriended gifted artist and sculptor Hama Hayao and convinced Hayao to lend his talents to the project. Ruffalo wasn't interested in mass-producing cheap plastic kits to turn a quick profit; his ambition was to create top-of-the-line, finely detailed, faithful renditions of motion picture "B-creatures" to offer to serious collectors. To realize that dream, he began amassing photos from as many different sources as he could to show Hama what he had in mind. Eventually he got in touch with Bob Burns, who loaned Ruffalo dozens of black-and-white and color shots from Blaisdell's films. Ruffalo also got hold of clippings from *Famous Monsters, Monster World, Fantastic Monsters*, and similar publications, and had literally hundreds of 35mm frame blowups made from the original theatrical prints. These were turned over to Hayao, allowing the sculptor to see in great detail every scale, antennae, fang, hair, and claw.

Ruffalo's vision finally bore fruit in 1985 when Hayao finished the first model in the Blaisdell series, the mushroom monster from *It Conquered the World*. Using frame blow-ups and 8"×10" glossy stills supplied by Bob Burns as reference materials, Hayao was able to create a perfectly detailed replica of the mushroom monster, even down to the "porthole" between its eyes (the viewing aperture that Blaisdell used when stationed inside the costume). Photographs of the work in progress were forwarded to Burns so that he could see how things were proceeding, but nothing could prepare him for the unveiling of the sculpture "in the flesh." The exactitude of the finished work was simply astounding. "They are great lovers of Paul's work in Japan," Burns pointed out, "and that is made obvious by the great amount of care and detail that Hama Hayao put into his work on this project. It's just incredible."

Before models of Hayao's sculpture could be developed and marketed to the public, it was necessary to seek permission from the one person who still owned the legal rights to Blaisdell's work—Sam Arkoff.

"Arkoff was very helpful," Michael Ruffalo noted, "and he was delighted with the idea of a series of model kits based on his company's pictures." (Why wouldn't Arkoff be delighted? This was going to mean more money in his already-bulging pockets, though it would have been nice to at least share the windfall with Jackie Blaisdell.) Ruffalo had to pay Arkoff a copyright fee for each Blaisdell monster whose likeness would be packaged and sold in kit form.*

Although Hama Hayao had completed Beulah from *It Conquered the World* first, his second work in the series was actually marketed in the U.S. first. While details of the copyright agreement were being ironed out between Ruffalo and Arkoff, Hayao had begun working on a unique sculpture of a Martian and one of the diminutive actors of AIP's 1957 production, *Invasion of the Saucer Men.* With this piece Hayao showed he could sculpt not only monsters, but human figures as well.

Once Arkoff's monetary interest in the AIP monster models had been sated, Ruffalo was free to begin selling kits under the Billiken banner. He opted to release the *Invasion of the Saucer Men* kit first because he thought (probably correctly) that fans were more familiar with the exophthalmic Saucerians than Beulah the magic mushroom. Initial sales of the Saucer Man model were brisk, so Ruffalo instructed Hayao to begin work on a third in the series, the She-Creature, while *It Conquered the World* kits were readied for release.

Blaisdell's original costume was so detailed it took Hayao over nine months to sculpt the She-Creature to his own exacting standards. But the long wait turned out to be more than worthwhile because the finished piece was a triumph, perfect in the most minute detail.

In fact, all the models released by Billiken were so finely crafted and had taken so long to produce that the company was forced to ask $48 for the She-Creature kit and $33 each for the kits of the mushroom monster from *It Conquered the World* and the Saucer Man. In terms of actual production expenses, it cost Ruffalo about $19 to produce each She-Creature unit, not including costs for advertising, packaging, and shipping.† The hand-crafted kits were being produced at the rate of twenty per day in Japan—an extremely slow rate by American manufacturing standards—in order to maintain optimum quality. "The consumer was really paying for the craftsmanship," Ruffalo pointed out. "We could have made these kits very easily and very cheaply, but that's not what I wanted to do. These are collector's items. They are limited editions." Despite strong initial sales of the Saucer Man model, profits

---

*Ruffalo never revealed how much money was involved but admitted that the fees paid to Arkoff were "substantial."
†The sale prices included a percentage of the copyright fees that were paid to Sam Arkoff.

Billiken's Saucer Man model kit came with an extra Martian head that could be placed over the actor's own (courtesy of Bob Burns).

leveled off. The mushroom monster model sold respectably well, though not as well as the Saucer Man. Surprisingly, sales of the She-Creature kit were disproportionately low.

(The AIP movie monster kits may have been ahead of—or behind—the times. A few years earlier American toy manufacturers such as Kenner had

The She-Creature model kit produced by Billiken USA. Sculptor Hama Hayao studied hundreds of photographs and frame blowups from the AIP film to make certain the model would be anatomically exact (courtesy of Bob Burns).

been producing models kits and movable "action figures" of popular movie monsters such as the *Alien*, which were generally priced between $5 and $20. Similarly, just a few years after Billiken's mid– and late–1980s releases, a new line of high-priced collectibles from Japan began enjoying a reign of success in the U.S. as fantasy fans willingly laid out $100 and more for "supermodel" imports of Godzilla, Rodan, and other Japanese film characters. Reactionary American manufacturers immediately began producing their own self-described "collectibles," including a variety of high-priced figures from the movies *Aliens* and *Alien³*. The ongoing popularity of these high-ticket items remains a mystery.)

The sparse sales of Billiken's later releases impacted on Ruffalo's plans for releasing kits of Paul's monsters from *It! the Terror from Beyond Space* and *Day the World Ended*.* The final Billiken release associated with an AIP film was the monster from *War of the Colossal Beast*.

Although the Billiken model kits appealed mostly to a specialized customer, Blaisdell's work could be judged by an entirely new audience when the original films finally began turning up on home video in the early 1990s. *Day the World Ended, The Spider, It Conquered the World, Voodoo Woman, It! the Terror from Beyond Space, Cat Girl, Invasion of the Saucer Men, How to Make a Monster, The Amazing Colossal Man*, and *War of the Colossal Beast* were all issued by Columbia-Tristar Home Video in just a little over a year. Although valued at "sell-through" prices (generally $10-20) for the home market, retail sales were spotty, and future releases were pulled from the company's schedule. (*The She-Creature*, penciled in for a May 1993 release, was canceled at the last minute.) Rights to the AIP material, of course, reverted to Sam Arkoff, who is not interested in rereleasing the films unless there is a significant buck to be made. In 1995 he was approached by a company which was interested in releasing definitive versions of a number of AIP pictures on videodisc, but negotiations were stalled by Arkoff, who was holding out for a high-dollar percentage. Unfortunately for the fans, unless Arkoff realizes that any profits to be gained on the American International movies from the 1950s are going to be marginal at best, the films may never be released.

Paul's monsters sometimes turn up in the oddest of places. Most recently, cartoon caricatures of "Cuddles" and "Beulah" appeared in a 1994 special edition of *Cracked*, a competitor of *Mad*. Typically, the drawings in *Cracked's Monster Party* credit neither Blaisdell nor AIP. They also do not mention film titles. Presumably *Cracked's* editors would like their readers to think that the

---

A stunning model of "Marty the Mutant" was more recently developed by sculptor Bruce Turner. When Billiken canceled its Day the World Ended project, Turner decided to issue his own version to the collectors' market in a limited edition.

The Billiken model kit of Beulah from *It Conquered the World* was accurate to the last detail. It even included the peephole (between and slightly above the eyes) that allowed Blaisdell to see outside the wood and foam-rubber hide of the creature costume (courtesy of Bob Burns).

magazine's own artists came up with the She-Creature and the mushroom monster concepts on their own.

With Paul's monsters still appearing in national publications 40 years after their celluloid debuts, it's certainly reasonable to think that they will continue to be resurrected from time to time both in print and on film. That in itself is a testament to Blaisdell's artistic vision and talent. Those who derided his contributions to film fantasy as too low-budget to withstand the test of time—and there have been many—have been proven wrong. Before it became fashionable to embrace the films of the 1950s, few people had a kind word to say about Paul Blaisdell, his monsters, or the movies in which they appeared. For far too long, low-budget was equated with low-value and low-talent and even low-intelligence. The true fans, those who applauded Blaisdell's visions of otherworldly nightmares, were few and far between. Today, thankfully, things are much different, and the 1950s are recognized as a legitimate source for monsters, mayhem, and most important of all, memories.

Even the most dedicated Blaisdell fan will admit that some of the pictures he worked on during his all-too-brief career were less than inspired. Nevertheless, the quality of these films is not an issue, for they cannot compromise Blaisdell's inherent artistry. He gave us a legacy of low-budget wonders that remain as endearing (if not quite as popular) as the movie monsters produced by Jack Pierce and a host of other Hollywood artists.

In an era that celebrated anonymity as opposed to the high-profile, high-priced effects experts of today, Blaisdell was a one-man wonder who was equally comfortable flying bats and spaceships or making monsters, miniatures, micro- and macroscopic props, arachnid makeups, wind-up automatons, and full-scale corpses. He could figure out how to make a disembodied hand with injectable fingernails crawl up the back of a car seat or how to get a Flying Finger to "breathe" on camera. In today's market, with not just individuals but entire organizations specializing in the production of one type of film effect, be it miniatures, masks, animatronics, props, or what-have-you, doing everything yourself might seem preposterous, improbable, or impossible. In Paul's time, it was simply a matter of logistics dictated by necessity. "Do I have any regrets?" he once said. Well, sure. "If I could go back and change anything, the first thing I would change would be my paycheck. And the second thing would be my expense account!"

Most important to remember, however, is this: whatever Paul Blaisdell's creations might have lacked in photo-realism and big budget finesse was more than compensated for by that most important, but least costly ingredient of all—imagination itself.

Appendix

In a way it's kind of fun to listen to these old things again after so many years, and in another way it's not because it makes me realize how much I miss Paul and all the fun we used to have. The stuff on these [pages] shows a side of Paul that not too many people knew about. He was really good at this type of thing, and he used to really enjoy it and have a lot of fun doing it. So many people thought he was strictly a monster-maker, and that he was pretty serious all the time. But if he knew you and liked you, it was a whole different story.

—*Bob Burns*

Paul Blaisdell and Bob Burns spent numerous hours together recording humorous skits and radio spoofs on a home tape recorder. Most of these recordings were made in the mid– and late–1950s and in the early 1960s.

Transcribing an audio recording to the printed page can be somewhat difficult, especially when working with amateur recordings made with nonprofessional equipment. The following transcriptions include as much verbatim dialogue from the tapes as it was possible to obtain. Sound effects have been rendered in typical comic-book style ("KA-BOOM!"). I found this to be the most effective shorthand way of transcribing a particular effect.

I have endeavored to be as accurate as possible in the transcriptions; the quality of some of the tapes tended to obscure certain words and phrases, however. In these cases my own personal judgment was exercised, which sometimes meant adding the word which seemed most likely to have been used by the actors in the appropriate context. I believe the transcriptions are about 98 percent accurate.

Please keep in mind that except for the titles marked with an asterisk, the following performances were made in a home setting, not a professional studio.

"The Joust"

"The Joust" was a two- or three-minute skit that was really an experiment to see if the sounds of a crowd could be created by just two

people. Sound effects generated from clapping hands, gloved hands, and different kitchen utensils were added by both Burns and Blaisdell, although it was Blaisdell who used a harmonica to simulate the sound of the trumpets.

Trumpets blare. A sepulchural voice calls out: "Let the tournament begin. The Black Shield against the Black Knight." There is the sound of horses' hooves thumping against the cracked earth. Then the impact of the steel lance as it penetrates a warrior's flesh.

"Ooooohh ... oh, oh, oh, oh ... yowwch ... ungh." A body collapses on the ground.

A voice pipes up: "Curse you, Black Shield!" The whoosh of an unsheathed sword surprises the opponent. Unexpectedly, the piercing clash of steel against steel rends the still air. The fight continued, now on foot. Before long ...

"Aarrghhhh!" Somebody collapses. Again.

"The Black Shield has won the match," intones the announcer. "And now—urgh" Someone—presumably the Black Shield—runs the announcer through as well.

The trumpets blare, the crowd cheers. Fade out.

———

"The Professor and Horace in 'Conquest of Mars'"

Some of Jackie's favorite skits involved characters Paul called "The Professor and Horace." The characters first appeared in the following skit, "Conquest of Mars." According to Bob Burns, there was no script prepared in advance. Blaisdell and Burns just sat down with the tape recorder, brainstormed a couple of ideas, then did a "take." The final product is somewhat rough, as might be expected, but it illuminates a side of Blaisdell that many did not know existed. "Paul could be very aloof, very quiet, especially on the film sets," explained Burns. "Because of that, some people thought he was just kind of stuck up. That couldn't have been farther from the truth. People would have been surprised to learn how funny and zany Paul could actually be when he wanted."

Harmonica intro.

Announcer (Bob Burns): Bagby's Bunsen Burner Company, in conjunction with the British Broadcasting Company, presents for your listening pleasure, "Conquest of Mars," starring Professor Lancelot Lushwell and his assistant, Horace Higgenbottom.

Narrator: As our story opens, we find them in their laboratory early one Monday morning ...

Prof. Lushwell (Paul Blaisdell, using an elderly British accent) : Horace, be a good fellow and light the bunsen burner for me.

Horace (Bob Burns): Right-o, professor!

B-BLAM! There is the sound of a near-nuclear explosion. A moment later, Prof. Lushwell pushes his way out of a pile of debris.

Prof. Lushwell: Horace old fellow, I believe there's a gas leak in the laboratory somewhere.

Horace: By the way, professor, you know that Comono Dragon we brought back last year that lived in the cage back there? I believe he's getting hungry.

Prof. Lushwell: Good heavens, Horace, I know what it is! He's after the bloomin' lollipops in me hip pocket!

Dragon: Aarrrrooooaaarrrrr!

Prof. Lushwell: We can't escape by the front door, Horace. All the creditors are out there waiting for us. Whatever will we do?

Horace: I say! We can get out the back door here and blast off in our rocketship!

They scurry out the back door and arrive huffing and puffing at the rocket pad.

Prof. Lushwell: Here we are, old boy. I'll open the hatch so we can climb in.

They climb inside the craft.

Horace: I say, it's awfully dark in here, professor.

Prof. Lushwell: I haven't had the batteries installed yet, Horace. But here, I brought this bunsen burner with me. Will you give us a light, old fellow?

Horace: Right-o, professor!

KA-BOOM! There is another explosion, the sound of more debris being shoved aside.

Prof. Lushwell: Oh well. Give me a hand here, Horace, and we'll try to swish some of this wreckage out of the hatch.

Horace: Right-o, professor!

The debris is swept away.

Horace: I believe that's all of it, sir.

Prof. Lushwell: Very good, Horace. Which planet shall we blast off to, old boy?

Horace: Oh, I'd like to see Mars, sir, hee-hee-hee!

Prof. Lushwell: Well, slip yourself in your seat and Mars it is. Stand by for takeoff.

Horace: Oh, jolly well!

Prof. Lushwell: Start the pumps, Horace.

Horace: Right-o, sir.

The rocket engines kick into high gear. The craft lifts off from its launching pad on a direct course for Mars.

Prof. Lushwell: I say, Horace, that's a little bit of all right, we're past the moon already, old fellow!

Horace: Hoo-hoo! By George! Sir, look out the window out there. I see a disc-shaped object coming at us. I wonder if it's hostile?

Prof. Lushwell: I don't know, Horace. Do you suppose it could be one of those confounded flying saucers?

Horace: Ooh, oh, ho-ho! Do you think so, sir? Oh, ho!

Prof. Lushwell: It seems to have some sort of a weapon on top, a projectile cannon or something.

Horace: Oh, ho-ho! I'm getting frightened, sir! It's getting too close!

Prof. Lushwell: So am I, Horace. I'm afraid we never should have left the laboratory.

Horace and Prof. Lushwell (together): Aieeeee!

KA-BAROOM! An explosion rocks the ship. After a moment, the rocketeers push their way out of yet another pile of debris.

Prof. Lushwell: Sometimes I have a horrible feeling that this has all happened before. Oh, well. It's a good thing we had our spacesuits on. No one got hurt. I'll turn up my radio a bit. Horace? Horace, can you hear me? Over!

Horace: Yes, sir, I can hear you, sir. But I—I just don't quite see this floating around like this, sir, in a spacesuit. It sort of scares me. I lose my sense of up and down, sir.

Prof. Lushwell: Don't worry, Horace, old fellow. We still have the ship's original velocity. We should reach Mars very shortly even without our rocket.

Horace: Oh, ho-ho! Jolly well once again, sir.

He looks up.

Horace: I—I say, professor, Mars is getting frightfully close, and at our present velocity I'm afraid we'll make quite an impression on it. Is there any way we can slow down, sir?

Prof. Lushwell: I have an idea, Horace, old fellow. I just happen to have a bunsen burner here in the pocket of my space suit. Would you be good enough to light it with your acetylene torch, old fellow?

Horace: Right-o, professor!

Prof. Lushwell: When you have it lit, Horace, point it in the general direction of Mars. That should slow us down sufficiently.

Horace: Oh, ho-ho! Right-o sir, right away!

KA-BLAM! There goes another explosion. And here come the bodies crawling out from under the debris. (Debris from where? Who knows?)

Prof. Lushwell: Oh dear, dear. Now my spacesuit's gone, too. Well, I shan't need it anyway. There seems to be air on the bloody planet. I still have my long johns, too. I say, Horace, this doesn't look much like Old Blitey, does it?

Horace: No, sir, it doesn't. But it does look an awful lot like the Sahara Desert, sir. I wonder if we could find one of those canals they're always talking about, sir?

Prof. Lushwell: Well, it's quite possible. Here now Horace, I'll go this way, and you go over there. Now don't forget to holler if you find water.

Horace: Oh, ho-ho! Right-o, sir, I certainly will. There must be some place around here that's got some water.

Horace looks all around. He spots something.

Horace: By George! Professor! I found some waaaaaaaaaa—

Horace steps off the edge of a cliff.

Horace: Gulp, gak! Cough-cough!

Prof. Lushwell: Hang on Horace, old fellow, I'm coming. Oh. Heh-heh. I see you found the water, didn't you, eh? Heh-heh.

Horace: Gak!

Prof. Lushwell: Here, give me your hand and I'll pull you out of the bloody mess. Ummph!

The professor strains to rescue Horace.

Horace: Whew! Why, thank you, sir! I'm afraid I ... I ... achooo!

Prof. Lushwell: Ugh! Don't catch cold now.

Horace (now speaking with stopped-up sinuses): Oh, I don't think I will, sir, but I wonder, is there any way possible we could light a fire? I'd like to dry out, sir. Eh? I'm afraid that I ... I ... achooo!

Prof. Lushwell: Well, I'll tell you, Horace old man, I believe I have here in my long johns another one of those ... ah, yes, here it is ... a bunsen burner. Now light this, old fellow. It'll warm you up in a jiffy.

Horace: Oh, jolly good! I'm bound to get some warmth pretty soon. Now, where is that match? Oh, here it is, hee-hee.

BA-BA-BOOM! Yep, there's another explosion. After a few moments, the professor and Horace pull themselves free of the debris.

Prof. Lushwell: Oh dear, oh dear....

Horace: Ummph....

Prof. Lushwell: I say, Horace, old fellow, we'd be lost if I ever ran out of bunsen burners now, wouldn't we?

Horace: He-heh. You're certainly right, sir. Uh, by the way, sir, have you noticed these thousands of little creatures standing around us? They must not be over two feet high, sir!

Prof. Lushwell: By George, you're right, Horace!

Shrill, high-pitched voices gibber noisily all around them.

<u>Horace</u>: I say, sir, can you understand what they're saying, sir?

<u>Prof. Lushwell</u>: I'll tell you, Horace, thanks to the fact that I spent long years in His Majesty's Foreign Service in India, I believe I can translate what they're saying.

<u>Horace</u>: Well, I'd suggest you start translating, sir. They look rather mean.

<u>Prof. Lushwell</u>: Oh, very well, Horace. Here, this little fellow seems to be their chief. I'll talk to him.

<u>Alien Chief (excitedly)</u>: Gobble-de-gook-de-gobble-de-gook-de....

<u>Prof. Lushwell</u>: Uh, he says, Horace, that, uh, they're going to boil us in oil because they think we've declared war on them. That last explosion, you know.

<u>Horace</u>: Oh, hoo-hoo-hoo! What are we going to do now, sir?

<u>Prof. Lushwell</u>: Well, there's only one thing to do. I'll have to show him that we come in peace and friendship. Here, I'll bring this little present I brought along with me to the chief.

The professor hands over a gift to the Martian chief.

<u>Horace</u>: By George, it looks like he sort of likes it, all right.

<u>Prof. Lushwell</u>: Quick, Horace! Run for it while he's looking at the present!

They begin running across the Martian sands.

<u>Horace</u>: B—but why are we running away, sir? He's just going to open the present. What should we run for?

<u>Prof. Lushwell</u>: I'll tell you, Horace. It just so happens that the present I gave him is one of those bloomin' bunsen burners.

<u>Horace</u>: Oh, ho-ho-ho-nooo!

<u>Prof. Lushwell</u>: Right-o!

KA-BLOOEY! And after a moment, the sound of debris being pushed aside.

<u>Prof. Lushwell</u>: Umph! Umph! Oh, lord, I say, what a bloody nuisance. You know, Horace, sometimes I have a feeling we should've never left home.

<u>Horace</u>: I believe you're right, sir.

<u>Prof. Lushwell</u>: I say, Horace, look over there. It seems to be some sort of machine that the little people left.

<u>Horace</u>: By George, it is. Why, look! It says here, "Step inside—teleportation machine. Set dial for destination. Mercury, Earth, Venus ..." Earth! Oh, let's go home, sir. I'm awfully tired of this place.

<u>Prof. Lushwell</u>: All right Horace, old fellow. I've had enough myself. Let's get inside here and close the door.

<u>Horace</u>: All right.

<u>Prof. Lushwell</u>: Are you ready now?

<u>Horace</u>: All ready, sir.

Prof. Lushwell: Okay, let's step inside.

Horace: All right.

They climb inside the machine.

Prof. Lushwell: There, the door is closed.

Horace: Sir, it's awfully dark in here. I can't see anything, sir.

Prof. Lushwell: Well, I tell you, I can just make out a button over there in the corner. Why don't you push it? It seems to be a light switch of some sort.

Horace: Right-o, sir.

KA-BLAMMEY! The two compatriots climb out of the debris.

Prof. Lushwell: Ummph.

Horace: Huff-huff-puff.

Prof. Lushwell: Lordie ... I say, that was a jolly fast way to get home! I'll have to make a note of that sometime when I have a pencil. Oh, oh dear, I seem to have lost my long johns, too, this trip.

Horace: Oh no, sir.

Prof. Lushwell: Uh-oh. I believe I'm catching your cold. Cough-cough! I—I think I'm going to sneeze,—aaaahhhhh ...

KA-CHOOO! The sneeze turns into another explosion.

Announcer: Bagby's Bunsen Burner Company has just brought you "The Conquest of Mars," starring Prof. Lancelot Lushwell and his assistant, Horace Higgenbottom. However, in future programs, these two men will no longer be with us due to circumstances beyond our control. However, next week we will have a very interesting program for you. And let me leave you with this thought. If you like bunsen burners, you'll get a bang out of Bagby's.

Harmonica outro.

———

Bob Burns recalled the making of "Conquest of Mars" with much fondness, even though he admitted, "It was rather crude. But we never thought about that. We never even thought that anybody other than ourselves would ever hear it. We were just messing around and having fun."

"The Professor and Horace in 'Submarine Attack'"

Another of the duo's skits was called, simply, "Submarine Attack." There were some surprisingly realistic sound effects used in this recording which, again, was made in Blaisdell's home without the benefit of studio resources.

The German (Paul Blaisdell, using an exaggerated German accent by way of Hollywood): Acht! Those stupid English swine would never dream that I'm sitting here in my U-boat in the middle of the English Channel. Listen! There's the ship now. Distance, about 500 meters. Load the torpedo, Hans.

Hans (Bob Burns, also using an exaggerated accent): Ya, Kapitan.

The German: Fire!

A torpedo whooshes through the sea.

Narrator (Burns): Meanwhile, back on the surface, we find a ship crossing the English Channel. On it are our two old friends, Prof. Lancelot Lushwell and his assistant, Horace Higgenbottom.

Prof. Lushwell: Oh, I say, Horace, it's a good thing to have a vacation on a lovely night like this. I was getting awfully sick of those exploding bunsen burners.

Horace: Oh-hoo-hoo-ho! I was too, sir. I didn't know if I was going to last for long. By the way, sir, look out in the water out there. There's something shiny coming through, leaving quite a wave. I wonder what that could be, sir?

Prof. Lushwell: Why, Horace, I believe it's a bloomin' torpedo!

Horace: A—a bloomin' torpedo? Oh, my!

KA-BA-BLAM! The explosion subsides into an underwater bubbling. After a moment or two ...

Prof. Lushwell: Umph, cough, hack! Horace? Horace? Are you all right?

Horace: Y—yes sir. That is, I think I'm all right, sir, I don't know. I'm frightfully wet, I'll tell you that. You know what happened the last time I got wet, you know!

Prof. Lushwell: Oh, well. Give me a hand over the side of this lifeboat, will you, old man?

Horace: All right. Here, come on, umphhh!

They struggle to climb into the lifeboat.

Prof. Lushwell: Do you see anything of the U-boat or torpedo?

Horace: No, sir, I didn't. But look over the side, sir, look underneath us. I see a long, silver object under there!

Prof. Lushwell: By jove, I'll bet that's the bloody submarine. I'll fix 'em! It just so happens I have something here in my pocket I brought along for our vacation.

Horace: Oh, no! Not another bunsen burner, sir.

Prof. Lushwell: Right! Now here, I'll drop it over the side—

Horace: Oh, hoo-hoo-hoo!

Prof. Lushwell:—and, ah! There! All right, Horace, row like the devil!

Horace: Right-o, sir.

Narrator: Meanwhile, back at the sub ...

The German: Acht! See? Good, Hans! The English boat is kaput.

Hans: Ha-ha-ha!

KA-KLANG!

The German: Acht! What's that, Hans? Did you hear something hit the hull of the submarine?

Hans: I'm not too sure. I heard something, but I'm not sure what it was. I don't think—

KA-BLOOM! The sound of the explosion eventually subsides into the bubbling gasps of the Germans.

The German: Acht! A mine! We are sinking! Glub-glub!

Narrator: And so, we leave our two friends, Prof. Lancelot Lushwell and Horace Higgenbottom, rowing on to more adventures, into the sunset.

Prof. Lushwell: Stroke ... stroke ... stroke!

Horace: Pant-pant. Y—yes, professor! Pant.

Prof. Lushwell: Stroke!

Horace: Right-o! Pant-pant.

Prof. Lushwell: Stroke ... stroke ... stroke!

———

As Bob Burns explained, most of the skits he and Paul recorded on tape were single-take episodes. None were very polished because they were meant merely as an afternoon's entertainment for two buddies who just liked to cut up and kid around with each other.

Untitled Poem

Blaisdell was a voracious reader. Although he was first and foremost an artist, he occasionally tried his hand at writing. Some of his work would eventually find its way into Fantastic Monsters *magazine during the 1960s. (His story "The Specimen" is included at the end of this Appendix.) At this late date, it is not known whether Paul actually wrote the poem that follows or if he was simply reciting a favorite piece by another author. The recording was made in the late 1950s.*

Shaped like a teardrop, pale as haze from down where the mirage
   city stands,
Here is a blue enamel vase brought overseas from the fabled land.
Studded with turquoise and trimmed 'round with golden symbols
   that curve and flow,
Like a guardian serpent, the flask is bound in some secret spell
   from long ago.
If curious fingers should break the seal, what would be found in
   its narrow hole?

Poisons to murder? Herbs to heal? Garter of roses or dust of gold?
Beware in a cloud as black as shame, these eyes might see a form
    appear
With curious wings and hair of flame, the jinni enraged is impris-
    oned here!
AHH-HA-HA-HA-HA-HA-HA-HA!

"The Strange Island of Dr. Nork"

*Fooling around with the tape recorder every weekend strength-
ened Paul's interest in writing and performing his own material. Bob
and Kathy Burns had formed a radio group known as the Burbank
Amateur Radio Group (BARG), which met regularly to perform their
own original material. Bob was eventually able to talk Paul into join-
ing the little group, and of course Paul brought along Jackie. The group
included two other local radio enthusiasts, Jim Harmon and Ron Haydock, who worked alongside Burns and Blaisdell on Fantastic Monsters magazine. A fellow named Zeke Lapein made up the seventh member of the troupe.*

*Most of BARG's material was comedic, but there was the occa-
sional drama as well as some science fiction and fantasy. A few of the
performances that were recorded still survive in the collection of Bob
Burns, who provided the tapes from which the following were tran-
scribed. With access to a library of previously recorded sound effects and
music, BARG was able to embellish its productions to such an extent
that they sounded more like authentic broadcasts than amateur skits.
One of the best things the team ever did was "The Strange Island of
Dr. Nork," a spoof of the mad-scientist thrillers that proliferated in
radio and movie serials during the 1930s and 1940s. The recording was
made at Bob Burns's home. The musical soundtrack consisted of pas-
sages from The Man with the Golden Arm and The Mister Magoo
Suite.*

Eerie musical intro.

<u>The Narrator, Dave Porter (Jim Harmon)</u>: The sign in front of me read
"Harascus Nork, M.D. The doctor is in. Please be seated." I had nothing to
sit on except my valise. It was all I had brought with me from the mono-
plane that had landed me on the sandy beach of this island, somewhere
between the Greater Antilles and the Lesser Antilles, along with the
Medium-Size Antilles. Finding the residence, its front door, and the sign on
it hadn't been hard. The whole works was on a plateau overlooking the beach,
the sea, the jungle. And of course, it's impossible to ignore anything that over-
looks you.

A Peter Lorre-ish voice emanates from a hidden speaker near the door.

Disembodied Voice (Paul Blaisdell): *Snort* ... Eh-henh-eh-henh-henh-enh, who's calling?

Porter: That was a good question. I could've asked it myself when I heard that voice coming out of thin air! Instead, I said, "Dave Porter of *Next-Week Magazine*. I'm here to interview Dr. Nork about the experiments he's doing out here. People get curious about a Nobel prize winner who drops out of sight."

Voice: Eenh! Please enter the reception chamber and wait a few moments. *Giggle-giggle*, henh-eh-henh ...

Porter: I opened the door—

C-r-e-e-e-a-a-k.

Porter:—and went inside. The hallway was spacious and white, like something out of an old Dr. Kildare movie. At the end of the corridor, a door stood half open, spilling out mixed blue and amber lights. I was looking around for a table with the latest issue of *Collier's* when I heard—

Disembodied Female Voice (Jackie Blaisdell): E-e-e-e-e-e-e-e-k-k-k!

Porter: Someone was in danger! There was only one thing for me to do: I ran! Instinct made me run towards the girl who needed help. Although it didn't seem very sensible, I dashed through the open door.

He dashes through the open door.

Porter: Huff-puff-huff ...the harsh glare of light from the domed roof illuminated a scene of horror. A huge, steel operating table occupied the center of the room. And it was in use. Strapped securely to its surface was a half-clad girl, hair streaming, mouth contorted, eyes wide with terror. Hovering above her was a tall, thin, red-bearded man with a big nose and slanted eyes. Like a surgeon, he wore a white gown. Like a surgeon, he had a glittering knife. As I watched, he raised the cruel blade, and then his arm swooped down toward the girl's bare, white bosom. S-stop!

Dr. Nork (Paul Blaisdell): Henh—what? Oh! Eh-henh-henh ... be with you in a second, Mr. Porter. I hope my knife isn't too chilly, Mabel. Henh-eh-henh, I wouldn't want you to catch a cold in your chest again, henh-henh. Y-you got it, Fred?

Fred (Ron Haydock): Uhh ... hold it a second more, Dr. Nork. Say, can ya try t'look a trifle bit, uh, madder?

Dr. Nork: Eh-henh-henh-henh-enh! *Grrrrr* ... Henh-enh, like this?

Fred: Uhhh, yell, swell. Uhhh, okay. I got you penciled on these roughs all right. Uhh, hey, Mabel, can you try to inhale a little deeper?

Mabel (Jackie Blaisdell): Not unless the doc moves that darn knife of his back a couple of inches.

Dr. Nork: Eh-henh, stop bragging.

Porter: Eh, what the devil's going on here? You mean you're just posing a scene for that artist over there in the corner?

Dr. Nork: Yehn, eh-henh-henh-enh, something like that. Henh-here, let me help you up, Mabel ...eh-henh-enh-ummph! Curse these knots! Henh-henh, I ought to use the disintegrator ray on them, henh ... henh-enh-enh-ahh! There you are, Mabel!

Mabel: Thanks.

Dr. Nork: Eh-henh, Fred, fix my bullup, hunh? Henh...

Fred: Yeah, okay.

Dr. Nork: Tomorrow, Mr. Porter, we'll have a nice talk. Henh-enh! You look tired after your trip. Eh-henh-henh. Maybe you'd prefer to lie down? Ya-ya-henh-enh-yeah, how about right over here on the operating table.

Porter: Uh, no thanks. So you're Dr. Nork?

Dr. Nork: Eh-henh-enh, of course! Eh-henh! So glad to see you. Enh-yenh-you're with *Next-Week Magazine*, you say? Eh-henh. Book reviewer, I suppose.

Porter: N-o-oo, associate science editor. I'm here to do a feature story on the experiments you're doing out here, Dr. Nork. If it isn't government security stuff—and I happen to know it isn't, or I wouldn't have gotten this far—I'd like to hear all about them.

Dr. Nork: Eh-henh-henh, you just saw one of them! Henh, I'm engaged in industrial research. Yenh-yenh-yeah, research into the comic book industry.

Porter: Comic books? A man of your reputation working for comic books?

Dr. Nork: Enh, I don't work for comic books, I work for money! Yenh, the Nobel prize plaque isn't very tasty on toast, yenh. B. J. Flushing of the Flushing chain of comics has a lot of money, eh-henh, and I'm getting as much of it as I can from him. Yenh! He endowed this laboratory, set up a fund for research to make sure that the sixty million readers of "Captain Torture, Hatchet Man" get only the finest and most realistic literature. Yeah-eh-henh-henh! W-we work out everything in advance to make sure it's true to life.

Porter: I-I-I-it did seem pretty realistic when I walked in on you.

Dr. Nork: Enh-enh-enhxactly! Ye-yeah, but before I took over, eh-henh, B. J. Flushing only published three comic books, and two of them were actually funny. *Giggle!* Ridiculous! Enh, and I told him so. Eh-henh! Everybody knows there's no point in a comic book that's funny. Hmmph. Why, people would just laugh at it. What they want is thrills, y-yeah, girls with big busts and men with big muscles.

Porter: Well, what about the muscle boys? You may be able to stage mad doctor scenes, but how can you realistically stage the exploits of super-characters for your artists to copy?

Dr. Nork: Eh-henh, I give them the powers. Why do you think Flushing hired a scientist, yenh-henh-henh. My experiments in physics, chemo-biology, and andro-conology have borne fruit ... enh-henh, yeah, eh-hmm, strange fruit! Eh-henh, speaking of fruit, it's time for lunch.

Time dissolve ...

Porter: Belch! Ahh. You set a nice table, Dr. Nork. All these unusual dishes and exotic foods.

Dr. Nork: Eh-henh, some more 7-Up?

Porter: No, no, I'm fine. Uhh, who is this girl coming our way?

Dr. Nork: You mean the blonde in the leopard-skin, enh, with the boa constrictor around her neck?

Porter: Uhh, yes-s-s.

Dr. Nork: *Giggle!* Enh, that's my daughter, Albino, White Goddess of the Jungle. Eh-henh-eh-henh, she's a sweet kid.

Porter: Your ... daughter.

Dr. Nork: Yenh-yeah! Decided to make a female Tarzan out of her at an early age. Brought her up among the animals. Henh! My daughter was just a plain, ordinary little girl until I taught her how to behave like a monkey.

Porter: Ooh, won't you have a seat, Miss Albino?

Albino (Kathy Burns): Where'd ya find this jerk, Pa? You know I don't like sissies! ... Do you want some papaya, snakey-dear? I know you like it salted. Hey! Think you could lift the salt, buster?

Porter: D-oh, yeah ... h-h-h-h-h-h-here you are.

Albino: What are you, a new character? The Human Salt-Shaker, maybe?

Porter. Hah-hah. Sorry, I'm afraid my hand is shaking just a little bit.

Albino: I know! It's shaking on my knee! Now watch it!

Porter: Q-quite an aggregation you have for lunch, doctor.

Dr. Nork: Y-enh-yeah, the result of years of experiments. Eh-henh! Take Water-Boy there. One of my most difficult cases.

Porter: Uhh, who...?

Dr. Nork: Water-Boy, the Flushing chain's answer to Aqua-Man and Sub-Mariner. Eh-henh, as a result of a unique series of experiments, he's now more frog than human. Henh, it was risky business to turn a man into a frog, eh-henh. Once I thought he'd croak.

Porter: I ... see. Now, who's the guy eating licorice?

Dr. Nork: Not licorice, coal. That's Firebug, the Human Torch. Eh-henh! Crime makes Firebug hot under the collar, and he's pretty quick to flare up. I've developed his metabolism to the point where he can actually live on fire!

Porter: And the one with the space helmet and flying belt?

Dr. Nork: Enh-enh-enh, that's our spaceman Rogers.

Porter: Oh, Buck Rogers?

<u>Dr. Nork</u>: No, Two-Dollar Rogers. Enh, he's twice as good as Buck.

<u>Porter</u>: Uhh … yes. Very interesting. Uhh, now, you mean to say that this Firebug is really eating coal?

<u>Dr. Nork</u>: Not just eating it, he's wolfing it down! Enh, if he keeps it up …

<u>Firebug (Ron Haydock)</u>: B-u-u-r-r-r-rp! Oh, pardon my heartburn. Hi-hi-wh-o-o-o-o-s-s-h-h-h!

<u>Porter</u>: Hey! H-he hiccuped fire! It singed Water-Boy's gills, and … g-great Scott! Firebug's caught himself on fire!

<u>Dr. Nork</u>: Oh, I wouldn't worry about it. Henh … I see Water-Boy opening his mouth….

<u>Water-Boy (Zeke Lapein)</u>: B-a-a-r-r-r-f-f-f!

Water-Boy discharges a stream of water.

<u>Firebug</u>: Glug, glug, glug… H-hey, stop it!

<u>Dr. Nork</u>: All right, all right, that's enough of that! You behave yourselves or I'll sic the Faceless Fiend on you.

<u>Albino (to Porter)</u>: If these characters scare you, wait until you meet the Faceless Fiend.

<u>Porter</u>: I think I can wait a long time, thanks. Who is he, Dr. Nork?

<u>Dr. Nork</u>: Eh-henh, one of my few failures. My agent spirited away a mass murderer from the penal colony in French Deanna. Yenh, that's where I get most of my subjects. Enh, you'll find that comic book characters are best when they have criminal minds, eh-henh-henh! Enhyhow, this time I intend to create a super-criminal for a new book, eh-henh! The man was frightfully disfigured, and I attempted plastic surgery, enh-henh, to give him a new face.

<u>Porter</u>: A new … face?

<u>Dr. Nork</u>: Sigh! Yenh-yenh-yeah. Naturally I had to get rid of his old face as the first step, but he escaped before I got around to the second step. Enh, when he removed the bandages and found that he no longer had any face whatsoever, eh-henh, he developed a deep resentment of me and the world in general. Mm-eh-henh-henh, as a result he became the perfect super-criminal. Yenh-yenh … the Faceless Fiend.

<u>Porter</u>: You mean he's loose on the island and just—

Cr-crash!

<u>Porter</u>: Hey! Somebody threw a rock through the window!

<u>Dr. Nork</u>: Mmm … there's a note wrapped around it. Enh-henh, let's see … henh … "Hail and fire well, Dr. Nork, and all your stooges. Enh, I have planted a time bomb under your house, eh-henh, to blow you all up at one o'clock. Signed, enh, the Faceless Fiend." Eh-eh-enhyone got the time?"

KA-B-BOOM!

An unknown amount of time passes.

Porter: When I opened my eyes, I was strapped to a table in a long, narrow, underground chamber. Blue light flickered a pathetic gloom. Crouching above me was a cloaked figure. I stared up and was rewarded only by a blank look. This creature ... this monster ... this being with an empty gap between neck and hairline, something not to be countenanced, was beyond all doubt the Faceless Fiend. His chuckle came out of the emptiness, slithering off the slimy walls.

The Faceless Fiend (Bob Burns): Don't look so unhappy, my friend. You ought to thank me for rescuing you. Here you are safe and sound in a nice, comfortable sewer, when above us the entire laboratory has collapsed. And your friends have all perished. No one is left but the two of us.

Porter: They can't all be dead! N-not the girl, not Albino!

The Fiend: Ha-ha-ha! They're destroyed. You have to face it. Speaking of facing it, I'm about to perform a small experiment of my own. Ever since I lost my face I've waited for a chance to find another. Sorry I can't offer you any anesthetic, but time is short, you know.

Porter: You mean you want to steal my face?

The Fiend: Well, I prefer to think of it as a little face lifting job. Now, now ... where did I put my meat cleaver ... oh, yes! Here we are! Now then— oof! What the—? I almost tripped over that vine. Drat it, that jungle stuff gets in everywhere.... Hey! The vine seems to be crawling up my leg! By Jove, it's a boa constrictor! Fancy that! I must say that—urph! Gasp! Ch-choke! Cough! Hack! Gasp! Unnnngh.

Albino: Good work, snakey-dear, you saved this poor helpless jerk from the Faceless Fiend. There. I'll set you free, buster.

Porter: Ahh, thanks. B-but how did you escape?

Albino: I went through the same trap door the Faceless Fiend dragged you through. Pa nor any of the others made it. Now I have nobody left but Snakey.

Porter: You-you're an orphan. I'll have to take care of you.

Albino: You couldn't—ooh! Save me, save me!

Porter: Uh, what?

Albino: That mouse, that mouse!

Porter: Hmm? Oh, oh yes. Back, you mouse! Get back there! Ah. See? He's gone. Now, back in civilization you're more likely to run into a mouse than you are a lion or tiger or boa constrictor.

Albino: I-I guess you're right. I do need you to take care of me.

Porter: Yeah, yeah, only ... I think I'm going to have to find a new job when I get back. My editor is never going to believe this story. You know, with Dr. Nork gone, P. J. Flushing is going to need a new writer for his comic books. And after all this, I think I've got just the experience for the job.

Music swells as they walk into the sunset.

———

"One Summer Night"

The BARG group performed a creepy little scenario with a punch ending entitled "One Summer Night." Jim Harmon brought it to the attention of the group members, who agreed it should be performed and recorded. Unfortunately, I have been unable to determine whether Harmon wrote "One Summer Night" or if he merely found it in a short-story collection or heard about it from someone else. The Saki-style ending doesn't come across quite as well in print as it does in the radio play, but at any rate it's an enjoyable little skit that's worth repeating here.

The Man in the Coffin (Paul Blaisdell): The fact that I was buried does not seem to me to convince me that I am dead. I've always been a hard man to convince. The rainwater dripping onto my nose is unquestionably real; I cannot deny the testimony of my senses that I am actually buried in a coffin in a grave. I am flat on my back, my hands crossed on my stomach, tied with some string that I can break easily, although it does not seem to profitably alter my situation. I'm still in strict confinement, wrapped in black darkness and profound silence, except the occasional drip of water. All in all, the situation is inescapable: I have been buried alive. I'm not dead, just ill. Very, very ill. No doubt everything will work out, if I just get some rest, gather my strength and wits. Musn't waste my time just lying here thinking idle thoughts. Must get right to sleep. Sleep, aahhh ...

Narrator (Ron Haydock): All is peace with Henry Armstrong in his grave. But something was going on overhead. It was a dark summer night, with a full wind blowing the cold rain during a lull in the thunderstorm. This distant lightning brought out the ghastly distinctness, the monuments, the headstones of the cemetery, and seemed to set them dancing. It was not a night in which any creditable witness was likely to be straying about a cemetery. So the three men who were there, digging into the grave of Henry Armstrong, felt reasonably secure. Two of them were young students from the medical college a few miles away. Talbot Lawrence is digging down into the grave. Pretty hard work, isn't it?

Talbot (Bob Burns): Y-yes, but—umph!—it's going to be worth all the work—urgh!—to get that body. Never enough of 'em to go around. I've got a theory that ... that ... no, I don't want to talk about it. I don't want to think about it. No, not until I can write up my paper for the journal.

Narrator: Mr. Lawrence doesn't want to talk. The other student, striking an orange glow to his cigarette as he leans on his shovel, is R. G. Junior Gordon. He always likes to talk.

R.G. (Ron Haydock): I've got plans, big plans. And I'm not gonna let a few crummy exam points stop me. Once I get this body I can catch up on those lectures I missed, and then ... then there are a lot of things a doctor can do that an ordinary man can't. There are all sorts of possibilities. Why, I could tell you—

Narrator: Yes, he could tell us endlessly. He has many plans. He will never realize any of them. This third man is Jess, a man of all work about the cemetery. Jess has only a few plans, but nothing will stop him from carrying them out. Jess knows people.

Jess (Zeke Lapein): I knows people. I knows ehhh-very soul in this here place. Heh-heh-heh. Ha-ha-ha-ha! AH-HA-HA-HA!

Later, after the men have uncovered the coffin …

Talbot: Take it easy with that coffin, Jess. I don't want the bones to get all broken up.

Jess: Jis stand clear. Outta my way, now! Umph! Now I'll get me to work on these here lid screws.

Squeak, Squeak!

Talbot: Did you hitch the horse up good? I don't want to be stranded out here.

Jess: Here comes dat old lid….

Cre-e-e-e-a-a-a-k-k!

Jess: Ah! Here be yer body, all laid out nice in a white shurt an' blek pants.

Talbot: Aughh! H-he's sitting up!

The Man in the Coffin: Arrrhhh … umph! Oh, hello!

Talbot: Aaaaaaaah!

R.G.: Oh my *God*!

Jess: Aieeee!

Later …

Narrator: Gray morning. Grayer faces on Lawrence and Gordon as they pass a horse and white wagon and enter the dissecting room of their college. Are you still sure you saw it, Mr. Lawrence?

Talbot: I saw it, I tell you!

R.G.: That's right, I did, too! And—oh, here comes Jess!

Jess: Howdy, Mr. Gordon, Mr. Lawrence.

Talbot: Is that your wagon out front?

Jess: Yassah.

Talbot: And that's your shovel in the corner?

Jess: Yassah.

Talbot: Well, what are you doing here?

Jess: I was waitin' for you to pay me fer th' merchandise.

R.G.: Lawrence, that shovel … look! That isn't rain, or r-rust, it's … it's … oh my God!

Jess: Heh-heh-heh.

"The Specimen"

Lastly, here is a piece of light-hearted fiction written by Paul Blaisdell. This whimsical slice of sci-fi first appeared in Fantastic Monsters #3. The BARG radio troupe changed Paul's title to "Scouting Party" and performed their own version of the story, but it was still the same tale with relatively few changes. Below is the text of the original version.

Somewhere across the city, a church bell sleepily tolled the hour of midnight as the two strangely attired figures moved silently throught the puddles of moonlight in the littered alley.

"This planet's atmosphere is choking me, Zilnik!" hissed the heavier of the two. "Let us return to the spaceship for atmosphere suits."

"There is no time, Gilno," breathed the other. "We must capture our specimen and go as quickly as possible before an alarm is given."

"Then here is our chance," whispered Gilno. "I sense an Earthman less than fifty zats away. Quietly now; and if we can't take him by force, use your weapon."

Mike crouched against the warm bricks of the factory near the mouth of the alley, and reflected bitterly on the passing thundershower that had soaked his coat, and left him shivering in the chill night air.

The soft rustle of clothing barely warned him in time as he ducked, and spun to face his shadowy assailant.

A blunt object thudded into the wall he'd been leaning against as he lashed out savagely with his hairy fist, burying it in his opponent's stomach. A chopping right cut off a groan of pain in mid-air, and the figure crashed into a pile of boxes six feet away.

Mike let out a grunt of surprise as he straightened, and a second assailant landed heavily on his back. Lunging forward, he sent the figure flying over his shoulder in the direction of the first, then turned and ran for the mouth of the alley and safety.

He never saw Zilnik rise painfully to his feet and level a flowing rod at his retreating back, but he felt the shock as the purple ray splashed over him in a shower of irridescent sparks and his brain sank slowly into oblivion....

It was sometime later, when the silver spaceship flashed past the orbit of the moon, that Zilnik limped painfully into the control room, gingerly feeling his discolored third eye with one of his intermediate tentacles. With a sigh, he eased himself onto the pneumatic cushions.

"Gilno, I had no idea that the Earthmen fought so savagely," he wheezed. "Even now, when we have him safely in a cage, it frightens me to look at him. Nevertheless, I shall attempt to communicate with him."

It was with visible effort that Zilnik forced himself to stand squarely in front of Mike's cage. Drawing himself up to his full sixteen inch height, he pointed to himself and pronounced his name slowly in his native tongue.

But the only answer he received was the cold unwinking stare of a pair of luminous eyes. Eyes that belonged to Mike, the toughest, scrappiest alley cat in Flagstaff, Arizona!

———

Memories of these creative sessions at Topanga Caynon remain strong for Bob Burns:

I remember how Paul used to come up with these crazy ideas for things to do while [Kathy and I] were up there [in Topanga]. One time I did a Frankenstein monster makeup on myself, and Paul made himself up as Dracula, and we did a thing called "The Girl Who Sold Dracula's Castle," which was a story told entirely with photographic slides. We'd do tons of stuff like that, and all sorts of funny things that Paul would come up with. When he started to whistle—not a tune, but just a kind of whistle that seemed to say "I may look innocent, but I've got a trick or two up my sleeve"— he'd give me this look, and that meant his brain was clicking away. He would walk from one side of the room to the other, and from one room to the other, opening up all these drawers and doors and cabinets, and he'd start dragging all these things out, things that he'd think how to use on the spur of the moment to create a funny gag or a story or something like that. Now when I listen to some of these tapes we used to make, it reminds me of the fun we used to have, and how much I miss it. It's very bittersweet. It's fun to hear them, yet it kind of hurts. I guess it's just something I'm never going to get over."

Filmography

The Amazing Colossal Man (1957). An American International release of a Bert I. Gordon production. Produced and directed by Bert I. Gordon; screenplay by Mark Hanna and Bert I. Gordon; director of photography—Joe Biroc; production supervisor—Jack R. Berne; film editor—Ronald Sinclair; special technical effects—Bert I. Gordon; music—Albert Glasser; assistant to the producer—Henry Schrage; assistant technical effects—Flora M. Gordon; assistant director—Jack R. Berne; second assistant director—Nate D. Slott; property master—James Harris; production designer—Bill Glasgow; sound editor—Josef von Stroheim; set decorator—Glen Daniels; makeup artist—Bob Schiffer; men's costumer—Bob Richards; sound recorder—Jack Solomon; hair stylist—Joan St. Oegger; chief set electrician—Joe Edessa; music editor—Lloyd Young. Running time: 81 minutes.

Cast: Glen Langan (Lt. Col. Glenn Manning), Cathy Downs (Carol Forrest), William Hudson (Dr. Paul Lindstrom), James Seay (Col. Hallock), Larry Thor (Dr. Eric Coulter), Russ Bender (Richard Kingman), Lyn Osborne (Sgt. Taylor), Diana Darain (Typist), William Hughes (Control Officer), Jack Kosslyn (Lt. in Briefing Room), Jean Moorehead (Girl in Bath), Jimmy Cross (Sgt. at Reception Desk), Hank Patterson (Henry), Frank Jenks (Delivery Man), Harry Raybould (Army Guard at Gate), Scott Peters (Sgt. Lee Carter), Myron Cook (Capt. Thomas), Michael Harris (Police Lt. Keller), Bill Cassady (Lt. Peterson), Dick Nelson (Sgt. Hanson), Edmund Cobb (Dr. McDermott), Judd Holdren (Robert Allen), Paul Hahn (Attendant), June Jocelyn (Nurse), Stanley Lachman (Lt. Kline), Keith Heatherington (uncredited).

Attack of the Puppet People (aka *The Fantastic Puppet People* 1958). An American International release. Produced and directed by Bert I. Gordon. Screenplay by George Worthing Yates. Story by Bert I. Gordon. Director of photography—Ernest Laszlo; editorial supervisor—Ronald Sinclair; production supervisor—Jack R. Berne; special technical effects—Bert I. Gordon; music composer and conductor—Albert Glasser; title song "You're My Living Doll," music by Albert Glasser and Don Ferris, lyrics by Henry Schrage; singer—Marlene Willis; assistant to the producer—Henry Schrage; assistant technical effects—Flora M. Gordon; assistant director—Jack R. Berdel; second assistant director—Maurice Lessay; set designer—Walter Keller; production coordinator—Jack Diamond; associate editor—Paul Wittenberg; men's costumer—Chuck Arico; ladies' costumer—Pauline Lewis; makeup artist—Phillip Scheer; hair stylist—Key Shea; chief set electrician—Roy Roberts; property master—Walter Veady; sound recorder—Frank Webster; set director—Jack Mills; special devices—Charles Duncan; key grip—Buzz Gibson; sound effects editor—Edgar Zone; special designs—Paul and Jackie Blaisdell; script supervisor—Judy Hart. Running time: 78 minutes.

Cast: John Agar (Bob Westley), John

Hoyt (Mr. Franz), June Kenney (Sally Reynolds), Michael Mark (Emil), Laurie Mitchell (Georgia), Jack Kosslyn (Sgt. Patterson), Scott Peters (Mac), Jean Moorhead (Janet), Ken Miller (Stan), Susan Gordon (Agnes), Marlene Willie (Laurie), June Jocelyn (Brownie Leader), Hank Peterson (Doorman), Hal Bogart (Mailman), Bill Giorgio (Janitor), Jaime Forster (Ernie), Troy Patterson (Elevator Operator), George Diestel (Switchboard Operator), Mark Lowell (Salesman).

The Beast with a Million Eyes (1955). An American Releasing Corp. presentation of a David Kramarsky production; produced and directed by David Kramarsky; screenplay by Tom Filer; associate producer—Charles Hanawalt; assistant director—Donald Myers; film editor—Jack Killefer; music—John Bickford; technical director—Sheldon Mitchell; art director—Albert Ruddy; special effects—Paul Blaisdell. Running time: 78 minutes.

Cast: Paul Birch (Allan Kelly), Lorna Thayer (Carol Kelly), Dona Cole (Dandy Kelly), Richard Sargeant (Larry), Leonard Tarver (Him), Chester Conklin (Old Man Webber), Bruce Whitmore (uncredited).

Cat Girl (1957). An American International Pictures release. Produced by Herbert Smith; directed by Alfred Shaughnessy; executive producer—Peter Rogers; director of photography—Peter Hennessy; production designer—Jack Stevens; art director—Eric Sawr; editor—Jocelyn Jackson; production manager—John W. Green; camera operator—Paddy A'-Hearne; assistant director—William Hill; sound recordist—Len Page; continuity—Olga Brooks; make-up—Philip Leakey; hairdressing—Nina Broe; wardrobe—Vi Murray. Running time: 79 minutes.

Cast: Barbara Shelley (Lemora), Robert Ayres (Dr. Marlowe), Kay Callard (Dorothy Marlowe), Paddy Webster (Cathy), Ernest Milton (Edmund), Jack

May (Richard), Lilly Kann (Anna), John Lee (Allan), John Watson (Roberts), Martin Body (Cafferty), Selma Vaz Dias (Nurse), John Baker (Male Nurse), Geoffrey Tyrrell (Caretaker), Frank Atkinson (Guard).

Day the World Ended (1956). An American Releasing Corp. release. A James H. Nicholson and Samuel Z. Arkoff presentation. Produced and directed by Roger Corman. Original story and screenplay by Lou Rusoff. Music—Ronald Stein; "The S.F. Blues" solo by Pete Candoli; executive producer—Alex Gordon; photography—Jock Feindel; production supervisor—Bart Carré; film editor—Ronald Sinclair; sound—Jean Speak; special effects—Paul Blaisdell; makeup—Steven Clensos; wardrobe—Gertrude Reade; set decorator—Harold Rief; property master—Karl Brainard; key grip—Charles Hanawalt; script supervisor—Barbara Bohrer. Running time: 78 minutes.

Cast: Richard Denning (Rick), Lori Nelson (Louise Maddison), Paul Birch (Captain Jim Maddison), "Touch" Connors (Tony Lamont), Adele Jergens (Ruby), Raymond Hatton (Pete), Paul Dubov (Radek), Jonathan Haze (Contaminated Man), Paul Blaisdell (the Mutant).

The Spider (aka *Earth vs. the Spider* 1958). A James H. Nicholson and Samuel Z. Arkoff Production. Produced and directed by Bert I. Gordon. Story by Bert I. Gordon. Screenplay by Laszlo Gorog and George Worthing Yates. Special technical effects—Bert I. Gordon; director of photography—Jack Marta; editorial supervisor—Ronald Sinclair; production supervisor—Marty Moss; music composer and conductor—Albert Glasser; assistant producer—Henry Schrage; assistant technical effects—Flora M. Gordon; assistant directors—Marty Moss and John W. Rogers; set designer—Walter Keller; script supervisor—Elayne Garnet; assistant editor—Paul Wittenberg;

costumer—Marge Corso; makeup artist—Allan Snyder; hair stylist—Kay Shea; chief set electrician—Cal Maehl; property master—Jim Harris; sound recorder—Al Overton; set decorator—Bill Calvert; special devices—Thol Simonson; key grip—Del Nodine; sound effects editor—Bruce Schoengarth; special designs—Paul and Jackie Blaisdell; spider handler—Jim Dannaldson. Running time: 72 minutes.

Cast: Ed Kemmer (Mr. Kingman), June Kenny (Carol Flynn), Gene Persson (Mike Simpson), Gene Roth (Sheriff Cagle), Hal Torey (Mr. Simpson), June Jocelyn (Mrs. Flynn), Jack Kosslyn (Mr. Fraser), Sally Fraser (Helen Kingman), Mickey Finn (Mr. Haskel), Hank Patterson (Janitor), Troy Patterson (Joe), Skip Young (Sam), Bill Giorgio (Sanders), Howard Wright (Jake), Bob Garnet (Pest Control Man), Shirley Falls (Switchboard Operator), Bob Tetrick (Dave), George Stanley (Man in Cavern), Merritt Stone (Mr. Flynn), Nancy Kilgas (Dancer), David Tomack (Foreman).

From Hell It Came (1957). An Allied Artists Pictures Corp. presentation of a Milner Bros. Production. Produced by Jack Milner. Directed by Dan Milner. Screenplay by Richard Bernstein. Story by Richard Bernstein and Jack Milner. Associate producers—Richard Bernstein and Byron Roberts; music composer and conductor—Darrell Calker; director of photography—Brydon Baker; art director—Rudi Feld; film editor—Jack Milner; production supervisor—Byron Roberts; assistant director—Johnny Greenwald; set decorator—Morris Hoffman; wardrobe—Frank Delmar; property—Ted Mossman; script supervisor—M.E. Gibsone; recorder—Frank Webster, Sr.; makeup artist—Harry Thomas; hair stylist—Carla Hadley; special effects—James H. Donnelly. Running time: 78 minutes.

Cast: Tod Andrews (Dr. William Arnold), Tina Carver (Dr. Terry Mason), Gregg Palmer (Kino), John McNamara (Prof. Clark), Linda Watkins (Mrs. Kilgore), Suzanne Ridgway (Korey), Baynes Barron (Maranka), Robert Swan (Tano), Mark Sheeler (Eddie), Lee Rhodes (Norgu), Grace Matthews (Orchid), Tani Marsh (Naomi), Chester Hayes (Maku), Lenmana Guerin (Dori).

The Ghost of Dragship Hollow (1959). An American International release. Produced by Lou Rusoff. Directed by William Hole, Jr. Written by Lou Rusoff. Associate producer and production manager—Bart Carré; music score and supervision—Ronald Stein; director of photography—Gil Warrenton; film editors—Frank P. Keller and Edward Sampson; art director—Dan Haller; set decoration—Harry Rief; assistant director—Lou Germonprez; properties—Karl Brainard; sound editor—Joseph Von Stroheim; music editor—Albert Shaff; music coordinator—Jimmie Maddin; wardrobe—Marjorie Corso; hair stylist—Scotty Rackin; makeup—Bob Marks; sound—Jimmy Thompson; script supervisor—Judy Hart. Special songs: "Charge," "Geronimo," "Ghost Train," by Nick Venet; "Tongue Tied" by Jimmie Maddin; "He's My Guy" by Charlotte Braser; "I Promise You" by Bruce Johnston and Judy Harriet. Running time: 75 minutes.

Cast: Jody Fair (Lois), Martin Braddock (Stan), Russ Bender (Tom), Kirby Smith (Wesley), Jack Ging (Tony), Nancy Anderson (Nita), Leon Tyler (Bonzo), Elaine Dupont (Rhonda), Sanita Pelkey (Amelia), Henry McCann (Dave), Dorothy Neumann (Anastasia), Beverly Scott (Hazel), Judy Howard (Sandra), Jean Tatum (Alice), Bill St. John (Ed), Tommy Ivo (Allen), Marvin Almars (Leon), George Dockstader (Motorcycle Cop), Paul Blaisdell (the Ghost).

Goliath and the Dragon (aka *The Revenge of Hercules* and *The Vengeance of Hercules*; original title: *La Vendetta de Ercole*; 1960).

An American International release. Produced by Achille Piazzi and Gianni Fuchs. Directed by Vittorio Cottafavi. Screenplay by Mario Piccolo and Archibald Zounds, Jr. Art director—Franco Lolli; cinematography—Mario Montuori; editor—Maurizio Lucidi; music (U.S. release only)—Les Baxter. Running time: 90 minutes.

Cast: Mark Forest (Goliath/Hercules), Broderick Crawford (Eurystheus), Eleonora Ruffo (Dejanara), Gaby Andre (Alcinoe), Sandro Maretti (Ismene), Phillipe Hersent (Illus), Frederica Ranchi (Thea).

Hot Rod Girl (1956). An American International release. Produced by Norman Herman. Directed by Leslie Martinson. Screenplay by John McGreevey. Running time: 75 minutes.

Cast: Lori Nelson, John Smith, Chuck Connors, Roxanne Arlen, Mark Andrews, Paul Blaisdell (uncredited, the "near-miss victim").

How to Make a Monster (1958). An American International release. Produced by Herman Cohen; directed by Herbert L. Strock; original story and screenplay by Kenneth Langtry and Herman Cohen; music—Paul Dunlap; "You've Got to Have Ee-Ooo" music by Paul Dunlap, lyrics by Skip Redwine; director of photography—Maury Gertzman; production manager—Herb Mendelson; art director—Leslie Thomas; assistant director—Herb Mendelson; script supervisor—Mary Gibsone; set decorator—Morris Hoffman; property master—Sam Gordon; wardrobe—Oscar Rodriguez; production secretary—Barbara Lee Strite; makeup—Philip Scheer; editorial supervisor—Jerry Young; dance choreographer—Lee Scott; music editor—George Branel; sound effects editor—Verna Fields; sound—Herbert Lewis. Running time: 88 minutes.

Cast: Robert H. Harris (Pete Drummond), Paul Brinegar (Rivero), Gary Conway (Tony Mantell), Gary Clarke (Larry Drake), Malcolm Atterbury (Richards), Dennis Cross (Monahan), Morris Ankrum (Capt. Hancock), Paul Maxwell (Jeff Clayton), Robert Shayne (Gary Droz), Walter Reed (Det. Thompson), Heather Ames (Arlen Dow), Thomas B. Henry (Martin Brice), Eddie Marr (John Nixon), Jacqueline Eboior (Jane), John Phillips (Det. Jones), Rod Dana (Lab Technician), Pauline Myers (Millie), Joan Chandler (Marilyn), John Ashley (as himself).

Invasion of the Saucer Men (British title: *Invasion of the Hell-Creatures*; 1957). An American International release. A James H. Nicholson and Samuel Z. Arkoff presentation of a Malibu production. Produced by James H. Nicholson and Robert J. Gurney, Jr. Directed by Edward L. Cahn. Screenplay by Robert J. Gurney, Jr., and Al Martin. Based on an original story by Paul Fairman. Executive producer—Samuel Z. Arkoff; music—Ronald Stein; photographer—Fred West; production manager—Bart Carré; editorial supervisor—Ronald Sinclair; art director—Don Ament; film editor—Charles Gross, Jr.; property master—Karl Brainard; makeup—Carlie Taylor; wardrobe—Marjory Corso; sound recorder—Phil Mitchell; technical effects—Paul Blaisdell; special effects—Howard Anderson and Alex Weldon; script supervisor—Judith Hart. Running time: 69 minutes.

Cast: Steve Terrell (Johnny Carter), Gloria Castillo (Joan Hayden), Frank Gorshin (Joe Gruen), Lyn Osborn (Art Burns), Raymond Hatton (Mr. Larkin), Douglas Henderson (Lt. Wilkins), Sam Buffington (Colonel), Russell Bender (Doctor), Bob Einer (Soda Jerk), Ed Nelson (Boy), Scott Peters (1st Soldier), Calvin Booth (Paul), Kelly Thorsden (Sgt. Bruce), Ray Darmour (Sgt. Gordon), Don Shelton (Mr. Hayden), Jan Englund (Waitress), Patti Lawler (Irene), Jim Bridges (Boy #2), Buddy Mason (Policeman), Joan Dupuis and Audrey Conti

(Girls), Jimmy Pickford and Orv Mohler (Boys in Soda Shop), Angelo Rossito, Lloyd Dixon, Edward Peter Gibbons, Dean Neville (Saucermen), Bob Burns (uncredited—Saucerman); Paul Blaisdell (uncredited—Saucerman).

It Conquered the World (1956). An American International release of a Sunset production. Produced and directed by Roger Corman. Screenplay by Lou Rusoff [and Charles B. Griffith, uncredited]. Executive producer—James H. Nicholson; music—Ronald Stein; photographer —Fred E. West; property manager—Lou Place; film editor—Charles Gross; makeup—Larry Butterworth; music editor—Jerry Irvin; sound—Jay Ashworth; property master—Karl Brainard. Running time: 68 minutes.

Cast: Peter Graves (Dr. Paul Nelson), Beverly Garland (Claire Anderson), Lee Van Cleef (Tom Anderson), Sally Fraser (Joan Nelson), Russ Bender (Gen. Pattick), Charles B. Griffith (Pete Sheldon), Richard Miller (Sgt. Neil), Jonathan Haze (Pvt. Manuel Ortiz), Karen Kadler (Ellen Peters), Taggart Casey (Police Chief N. J. Schallert), Paul Harbor (Floyd Mason), Tom Jackson (George Haskell), Marshall Bradford (Secretary Platt), David McMann (Gen. Carpenter), Jim Knight (Bazooka Man), Paul Blaisdell (Visitor from Venus).

It! The Terror from Beyond Space (1958). A United Artists release of a Vogue picture. Produced by Robert E. Kent. Directed by Edward L. Cahn. Screenplay by Jerome Bixby. Director of photography—Kenneth Peach; art director—William Glasgow; assistant director—Ralph E. Black; set director—Herman Schoenbrun; makeup—Lane Britton; sound—Al Overton; music—Paul Sawtell and Bert Shefter; supervising editor—Grant Whytock; effects editor—Robert Carlisle; script supervisor—George Rutter; property master—Arthur Wasson; wardrobe

—Jack Masters. Running time: 68 minutes.

Cast: Marshall Thompson (Col. Edward Carruthers), Shawn Smith (Ann Anderson), Kim Spalding (Col. Van Heusen), Dabbs Greer (Eric Royce), Ann Doran (Mary Royce), Paul Langton (Calder), Robert Bice (Purdue), Thom Carney (Kienholz), Richard Benedict (Bob Finelli), Richard Hervey (Gino Finelli), Ray "Crash" Corrigan ("It!").

Jack the Giant Killer (1962). A United Artists release of an Edward Small production. Produced by Edward Small. Directed by Nathan Juran. Screenplay by Orville H. Hampton and Nathan Juran. Associate producer—Robert E. Kent; art directors—Fernando Carrere and Frank McCoy; cinematography—David S. Horsley; makeup—Charles Gemora; editor—Grant Whytock; music—Paul Sawtell and Bert Shefter; special effects—Howard A. Anderson, Jim Danforth, and David Pal. Running time: 94 minutes.

Cast: Kerwin Matthews (Jack), Judi Meredith (Princess Elaine), Torin Thatcher (Pendragon), Walter Burke (Garna), Barry Kelley (Sigurd the Viking), Don Beddoe (the Imp); Roger Mobley (Peter), Dayton Lummis (King Mark), Anna Lee (Lady Constance), Tudor Owen (Chancellor), Helen Wallace (Jack's mother), Robert Gist (Capt. McFadden), Ken Mayer (Boatswain).

Monster from Green Hell (1957). A DCA release. Produced by Al Zimbalist. Directed by Kenneth G. Crane. Screenplay by Louis Vittes and Endre Bohem. Executive producers—Jack L. Gross and Philip N. Krasne; associate producer—Sol Dolgin; production manager—Byron Roberts; director of photography—Ray Flin; music—Albert Glasser; production design—Ernst Fegté; assistant director—John Greenwald; film editor—Kenneth G. Crane; script supervisor—Doris Moody; special effects—Jess Davison; sound editor—Charles Biltz; music editor—Robert Post; sound (Robert W. Roderick)—Shirley Cooley; set decorator—G. W. Bernsten; property master—Robert Benton; makeup—Louis Haszillo; wardrobe—Joe Dimmitt; special photographic effects—Jack Rabin and Louis Dewitt. Running time: 77 minutes.

Cast: Jim Davis (Quent Brady), Robert E. Griffin (Dan Morgan), Barbara Turner (Lorna Lorentz), Vladimir Sokoloff (Dr. Lorentz), Eduardo Ciannelli (Mahri), Joel Fluellen (Arobi), LaVerne Jones (Kuana), Tim Huntley (Territorial Agent), Frederic Potter (Radar Operator).

Motorcycle Gang (1957). An American International release of a Golden State production. Produced by Alex Gordon. Directed by Edward L. Cahn. Screenplay by Lou Rusoff. Running time: 78 minutes.

Cast: Anne Neyland, Steve Terrell, John Ashley, Carl Switzer, Raymond Hatton, Paul Blaisdell (uncredited bit as "a victim").

Not of This Earth (1957). An Allied Artists Pictures Corp. release of a Roger Corman production. Produced and directed by Roger Corman. Screenplay by Charles Griffith and Mark Hanna. Music—Ronald Stein; photographer—John Mescall; editor—Charles Gross, Jr.; production manager—Lou Place; sound—Philip Mitchell; key grip—Charles Hanawalt; makeup—Curly Batson; property master—Karl Brainard. Running time: 67 minutes.

Cast: Paul Birch (Mr. Johnson), Beverly Garland (Nadine Storey), Morgan Jones (Harry Sherbourne), William Roerick (Dr. Frederick W. Rochelle), Jonathan Haze (Jeremy Perrin), Richard Miller (Joe Piper), Anne Carrol (Davanna Woman), Tamar Cooper (Joanna Oxford), Roy Engel (Sgt. Walton), Pat Flynn (Simmons), Harold Fong (Specimen), Gail Ganley (Girl), Ralph Reed (Boy).

Oklahoma Woman (1955). An American Releasing Corp. presentation of a Sunset production. Produced and directed by Roger Corman. Screenplay by Lou Rusoff. Music—Ronald Stein; cinematography—Fred West; editor—Ronald Sinclair. Running time: 73 minutes.

Cast: Richard Denning (Steve Ward), Peggie Castle (Marie Saunders), Cathy Downs (Susan Grant), Tudor Owen (Ed Grant), "Touch" Connors (Tom Blake), Paul Blaisdell (Henchman), with Martin Kingsley, Bruno VeSota, Dick Miller.

The She-Creature (1956). An American International release of a Golden State production. Produced by Alex Gordon. Directed by Edward L. Cahn. Story and screenplay by Lou Rusoff. Original idea by Jerry Zigmond. Executive producer—Samuel Z. Arkoff; director of photography—Frederick E. West; production supervisor—Bart Carré; film editor—Ronald Sinclair; music—Ronald Stein; art director—Don Ament; assistant director—Bart Carré; set decorator—Harry Reif; property master—Karl Brainard; wardrobe—Marjorie Corso; makeup—Jack Dusek; sound—Ben Winkler; script supervisor—Judith Hart. Running time: 76 minutes.

Cast: Chester Morris (Dr. Lombardi), Marla English (Andrea), Tom Conway (Timothy Chappel), Cathy Downs (Dorothy Chappel), Lance Fuller (Dr. Ted Erickson), Ron Randell (Lt. Ed James), Freida Inescort (Mrs. Chappel), El Brendel (Olaf), Frank Jenks (Police Sergeant), Paul Dubov (Johnny), Flo Bert (Marta), Kenneth MacDonald (Prof. Anderson), William Hudson (Bob), Jeanne Evans (Mrs. Brown), Paul Blaisdell (the Creature).

Sorority Girl (aka *Confessions of a Sorority Girl*, 1957). An American International release of a Roger Corman production. Produced and directed by Roger Corman. Screenplay by Ed Waters and Leo Lieberman. Cinematography—Monroe

FILMOGRAPHY

289

P. Askins; editor—Charles Gross; music—Ronald Stein. Running time: 61 minutes.

Cast: Susan Cabot (Sabra Tanner), Fay Barker (Mrs. Tanner), Barbara Crane (Billie Marshall), June Kenney (Tina), Dick Miller (Mort), with Barboura O'Neill, Jeane Wood.

Teenagers from Outer Space (aka *The Gargon Terror*, 1959). A Warner Bros. release of a Tom Graeff production. Written, produced, and directed by Tom Graeff. Production associates—C. R. Kaltenthaler, Gene Sterling, and Bryan G. Pearson. Running time: 85 minutes.

Cast: David Love (Derek), Dawn Anderson (Betty Morgan), Harvey B. Dunn (Grandpa Morgan), Bryan Grant (Thor), Tom Lockyear (Joe Rogers), King Moody (Captain), Helen Sage (Miss Morse), Frederic Welch (Dr. Brandt), Sonia Torgeson (Swimmer).

The Undead (1956). An American International release. Produced and directed by Roger Corman. Screenplay by Charles Griffith and Mark Hanna. Music—Ronald Stein; photographer—William Sickner; assistant director—Lou Place; film editor—Frank Sullivan; choreographer—Chris Millner; makeup—Curly Batson; sound—Robert Post; key grip—Charles Hanawalt; property master—Karl Brainard. Running time: 77 minutes.

Cast: Richard Garland (Pendragon), Pamela Duncan (Diana Love/Helene), Richard Devon (Satan), Allison Hayes (Lydia), Bill Barty (the Imp), Mel Welles (Smoukin), Bruno VeSota (the Innkeeper), Dorothy Newman (Meg Maud), Val Dufour (Quintus), Richard Miller (uncredited), Aaron Saxon (uncredited), Paul Blaisdell (uncredited, as a corpse).

Voodoo Woman (1957). An American International release of a Carmel production. Produced by Alex Gordon. Directed by Edward L. Cahn. Story and screenplay by Russell Bender and V. I. Ross. Executive producers—Samuel Z. Arkoff and James H. Nicholson; director of photography—Frederick E. West; production supervisor—Bart Carré; film editor—Ronald Sinclair; music composer and conductor—Darrell Calker; "Black Voodoo" music by Darrell Calker, lyrics by John Blackburn; art director—Don Ament; assistant director—Bart Carré; set decorator—Harry Reif; properties—Karl Brainard and Richard M. Rubin; wardrobe—Bob Olivas; makeup—Carlie Taylor; special makeup—Harry Thomas; sound—Bob Post; script supervisor—Judith Hart. Running time: 77 minutes.

Cast: Marla English (Marilyn Blanchard), Tom Conway (Dr. Roland Gerard), "Touch" Connors (Ted Bronson), Lance Fuller (Rick), Paul Dubov (Marcel), Mary Ellen Kaye (Susan Gerard), Norman Willis (Harry West), Martin Wilkins (Chaka), Otis Greene (Bobo), Emmett E. Smith (Gandor), Jean Davis (Native Girl), Giselle D'Arc (Singer), Paul Blaisdell (the Monster; also an uncredited bit part as a drunken tavern customer).

War of the Colossal Beast (aka *The Terror Strikes*, 1958). An Amercan International release. Produced and directed by Bert I. Gordon. Screenplay by George Worthing Yates. Story by Bert I. Gordon. Director of photography—Jack Marta; production manager—Herb Mendelson; editorial supervisor—Ronald Sinclair; special technical effects—Bert I. Gordon; music composer and conductor—Albert Glasser; assistant producer—Henry Schrage; assistant technical effects—Flora M. Gordon; assistant director—H. E. Mendelson and John W. Rogers; art director—Walter Keller; set decorator—Maury Hoffman; property master—Walter Broadfoot; chief set electrician—Babe Stafford; assistant film editor—Paul Wittenberg; sound editor—Josef Von Stroheim; special makeup—Jack H. Young. Running time: 68 minutes.

Cast: Sally Fraser (Joyce Manning), Dean Parkin (Glenn), Roger Pace (Major Baird), Russ Bender (Dr. Carmichael), George Becwar (Swanson), Roy Gordon (Mayor), Robert Hernandez (Miguel), Charles Stewart (Capt. Harris), Rico Alaniz (Sgt. Luis Murillo), Jack Kosslyn (Newscaster), George Navarro (Mexican Doctor), Howard Wright (Medical Corp. Officer), George Milan (Gen. Nelson), George Alexander (Army Officer), John McNamara (Neurologist), Bill Giorgio (Bus Driver), Warren Frost (Switchboard Operator), Stan Chambers (Television Announcer), Loretta Nicholson (Joan), June Jocelyn (Mother), Bob Garnet (Correspondent Pent).

Index